IMAGES
of America

CORAOPOLIS

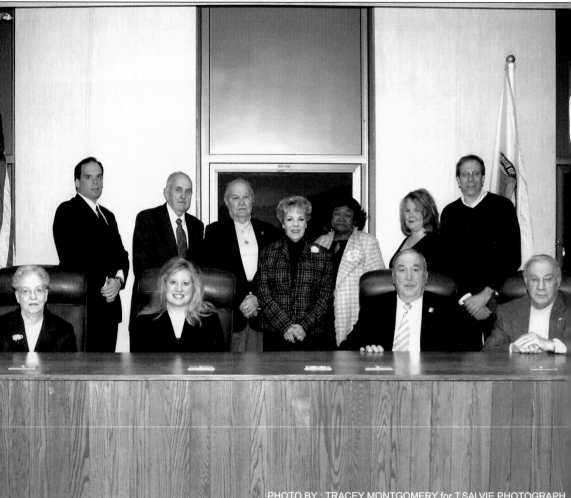

Coraopolis Historical Society members are pictured here, from left to right: (first row) secretary Edith Spatara, author/writer Gia Tatone, president Joseph V. DiVito, and vice president Robert Barone; (second row) Richard Betsch, Norman Miller, Daniel Iacobucci, treasurer Helen (Letterle) Manna, Kay Hunt, Kerri Douglas, and photographer Tom Salvie. Daniel LaRocco is not pictured.

On the cover: Taken in the 1940s, this photograph was found in the Kiwanis archives by Rick Mariano. This amazing picture depicts the town and its business thriving on Fifth Avenue and the corner of Mill Street. It was a sunny, cool day when this photograph was taken. Observe the shadows and clothing worn by the people. Also seen here are the cars going both north and south on Fifth Avenue. Today it is a one-way street that travels only south. (Courtesy of the Kiwanis Club.)

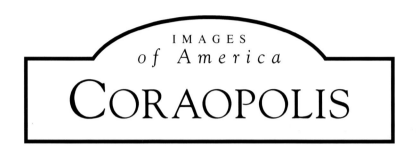

IMAGES
of America

CORAOPOLIS

Gia Tatone
with the Coraopolis Historical Society

ARCADIA
PUBLISHING

Published by Arcadia Publishing
Charleston, South Carolina

Printed in the United States of America

Library of Congress Catalog Card Number: 2007926415

For all general information contact Arcadia Publishing at:
Telephone 843-853-2070
Fax 843-853-0044
E-mail sales@arcadiapublishing.com
For customer service and orders:
Toll-Free 1-888-313-2665

Visit us on the Internet at www.arcadiapublishing.com

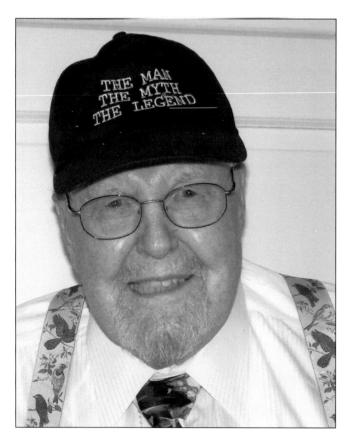

This book was written to honor Dr. Frank Braden Jr. Combined, his father and he served the Coraopolis community as physicians for a century beginning in September 1907. Thank you, Dr. Braden, for the many provisions, endless time given, and the many contributions you freely made to make this book possible. You are the true historian.

CONTENTS

ACKNOWLEDGMENTS

Twelve community members created the team to fulfill the vision of this book. I would like to offer my deepest thanks to Joe DiVito, who gifted me with mentorship and introduced me to all that was necessary for this book to become a reality. Your trust and faith in me is an invaluable blessing. I would like to acknowledge the muscle behind the operation, our photographer, Tom Salvie, whose advice and input have been invaluable. You are a shining example of a local businessman with a true sense of heart. A debt of gratitude belongs to Kerri Douglas whose café was a meetinghouse for many hours of operation. Special thanks also go to Bob Barone for his continual gift of hope. Your heartening words lifted my spirits. I also cannot offer enough thanks to Helen Manna, whose encouraging words sustained me through this project. You are an inspiration to me. It has been a pleasure to work with Edith Spatara on this journey. Thank you for the many telephone calls and your never-ending patience. Danny LaRocco, your jubilant smile and personality were incessantly refreshing. Richard Betsch, if it had not been for you and the time you made yourself willing and available to this project, many of these photographs would never be seen. To Kay Hunt, thank you for representing the African American history of Coraopolis and your enduring kindness to me. For Danny Iacobucci and Norman Miller, I want to offer special thanks for being part of this team. Your listening ears are appreciated.

On behalf of the historical society, I would like to thank Raymond Antonelli of NIRA Engineering for your generosity and investment in the town's future through the purchasing of books for the Cornell School District. May the students be inspired to carry on the legacy. We are also indebted to George Douglas, another fine example of a generous businessman. The office space you freely donated for this project demonstrates your dedication to this community. I would also like to thank Rick Mariano for generously donating many photographs and for providing the cover.

On a personal note, I would like to thank my church community of the Episcopal Diocese of Pittsburgh, Charis 247, for being a wall of prayer for me and believing in me. I love you all! I am indebted to Rev. Sam Jampetro for your benevolence in helping me obtain many hours of recorded details and facts that were desperately needed for this book. Your tutelage and guidance in my life is the very reason I am here. Finally, and most importantly, I want to thank the two who gave the sacrifice of themselves, and all their needs, as I worked on this project—my dear husband, Frank, and my beloved daughter, Amelia. Your undying love and support have kept me standing. I love you two with the deepest eternal flame of love that I could ever offer anyone.

To the town of Coraopolis, thank you for entrusting both the historical society and me with your photographs and your precious memories. I hope Coraopolis will always be seen as the hidden treasure that it truly is.

INTRODUCTION

Coraopolis is a town that is highly community oriented. Everyone knows one another and newcomers are readily welcomed. But long before that, Coraopolis stood as a place where forests and rolling hills covered the region. According to the 1937 *Semi Centennial* and the 1986 *Centennial* publications, it all began in Canada around the time of 1664. A Frenchman by the name of Montour had a daughter known as Madame Montour. Madame Montour was a pioneer to the English colonists and actively loyal to them as a peacemaker and interpreter. She came to Pennsylvania in July 1727 and continued her services to the colonists. She had four sons; one named Andrew, who also went by Henry, continued her legacy after her death in 1752. Because of their long and faithful service, a grant of land, 300 acres, was given to Andrew Montour in the name of peace and thankfulness by the English colonists. As Andrew never intended to live on the land, it was settled by Robert Vance, formerly from Virginia.

In 1759, Fort Vance, one of the most historic forts ever fashioned along the Ohio River, was assembled and Coraopolis history began. The land was then pioneered by Robert Vance, and he became the first permanent white settler in Coraopolis. He established his residence, and his mission was to bring safety and stability to the area. In 1816, the area was given the name Middletown. It was not until 70 years later, in 1886, that the town became incorporated into a borough and became known as Coraopolis.

Much debate has surfaced over the years as to how the town found its name. Popular legend is the town was named after an early resident and pioneer's daughter named Cora Watson who was born on February 2, 1870. Thus is the name *Coraopolis*. However, upon doing some research, Dr. Frank Braden Jr. of Coraopolis made a discovery when he obtained a very old newspaper. The newspaper is simply called the *News* and was published in Coraopolis, Pennsylvania, on June 5, 1897. The newspaper discusses the confusion that was occurring with the post offices in regard to the name Middletown. Several other areas in the state of Pennsylvania shared the same name. With a borough now being established, the Reverend Josiah Dillon, a pioneer clergyman, suggested the name to be changed to Coraopolis. Dillon knew Greek and was also the first burgess (mayor) at the time. So he suggested combining *Kore* meaning "maiden" and *opolis* meaning "city" (maiden city) to achieve *Koreopolis*. However, when Greek letters and pronunciation were turned to English, it is said the spelling therefore accidentally got changed.

The images featured depict a 100-year history that is based off the community that has developed from the efforts and dedication of the town's forefathers. This town has formed out of much giving, perseverance, and faith. The photographs are meant to give the reader a sense of the life and spirit in this community and to be able to get a glimpse of just how this town is like a delicate treasure box with the people as its gems.

One

LIFE IN CORAOPOLIS

The community of Coraopolis reflects over 100 years of memories. Memories throughout the decades vary from person to person, but many can reflect back to the days when a quarter was a decent allowance and there was a willingness to reach down into a gutter for a penny. Laundry detergent would commonly have free glasses and towels hidden inside the box. Many can remember when it took five minutes for the television to warm up and Mom wore nylons that came in two pieces. Metal ice cube trays had levers, and roller skates had keys. In the general store, children would buy 5¢ packs of bubble gum cards and chew the awful pink stick of bubble gum that came with it. A night out as a family or on a date would be going to the drive-in. Often newsreels were seen before the movie.

Most homes would have milk delivered in glass bottles, and soda machines would dispense glass bottles as well for a dime. Popular chewing gums people enjoyed were Blackjack, Clove, and Teaberry. When going into a local coffee shop, it was not uncommon to find table sides with jukeboxes. A favorite treat would be wax Coke-shaped bottles with colored sugar water inside.

Favorite toys of children included Tinkertoys, Lincoln Logs, Erector Sets, peashooters, and cork popguns. On television, Beanie and Cecil cartoons were hits among all ages, and Howdy Dowdy was an all-time favorite. Gone but not forgotten are reel-to-reel tape recorders and 45-rpm records. Life in Coraopolis can be reflected upon as the desire to slip back in time and savor the slower pace in a yet thriving and booming community.

CORAOPOLIS FROM MOONCREST

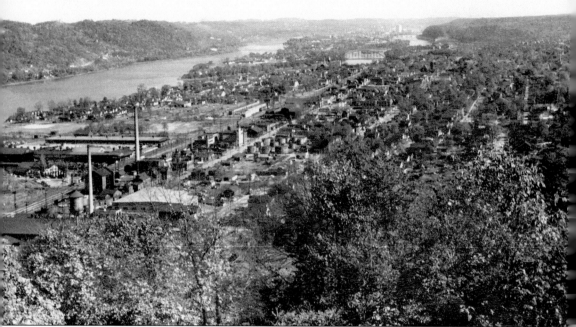

This photograph was taken from the heights of Mooncrest and displays an aerial view of the town of Coraopolis. This photograph is kept in the office of the town's current borough manager, Tom Cellente.

The year is 1949, and Diana Gail Nichay is babysitting her little brother Michael and enjoying the summer day in Coraopolis.

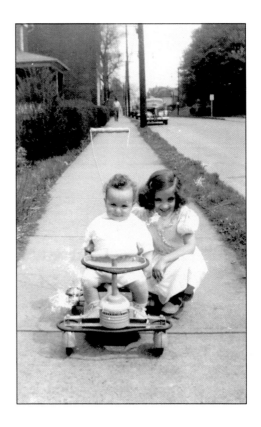

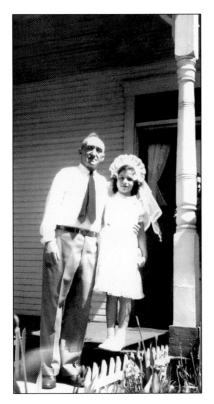

Seen on 515 Fifth Avenue are lovely Christina Piccolo and George Fussoia posing for a photograph in May 1955. It is first holy communion day for St. Joseph Church.

11

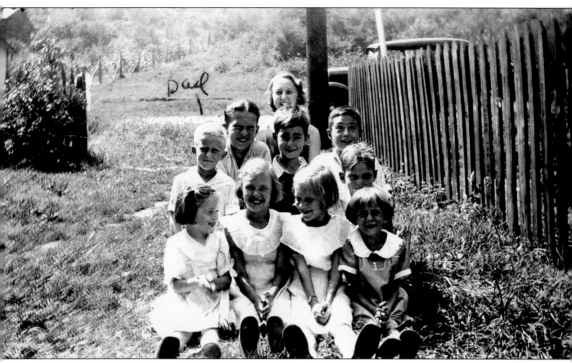

The integrity of the people in the town of Coraopolis is demonstrated in these children on August 27, 1935. The children's faces are bright and happy, seemingly unaffected by the universal anguish felt by their parents over the fact that they are losing their home. This is on the account of their father losing his job as a grinder at the Consolidated Lamp and Glass Company. All he would have needed to save their home, which he built in 1928 on St. Frances Street, was the arrears of $300. A generous neighbor, a Mr. Yeck, agreed to allow them to move into his small rental home on Vine Street.

Daniel (Danny) LaRocco (Coraopolis's councilman in the Fourth Ward) is photographed here as a two-year-old little boy with his father, Anthony, known as "Tony." His dad taught him basic lessons such as if one gives respect one will get respect, and if a person keeps smiling, others will see it.

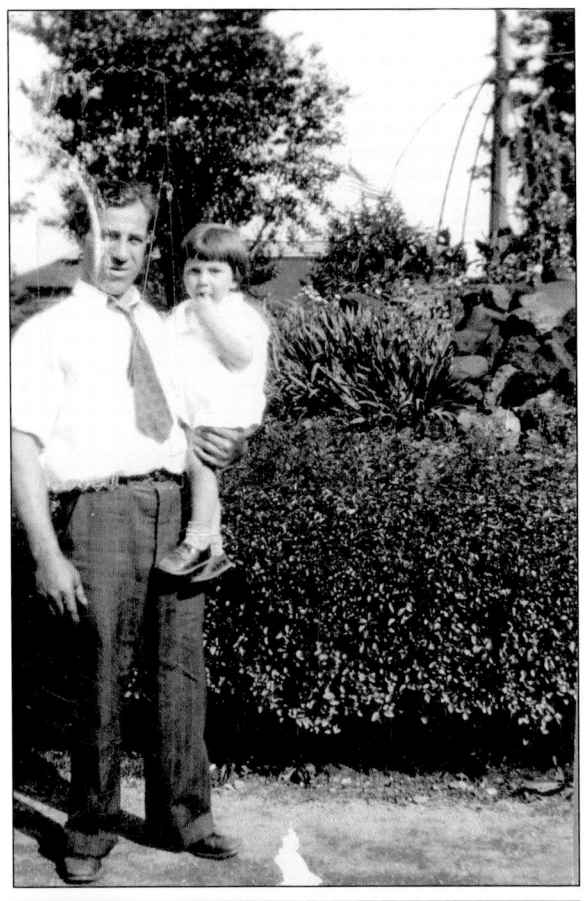

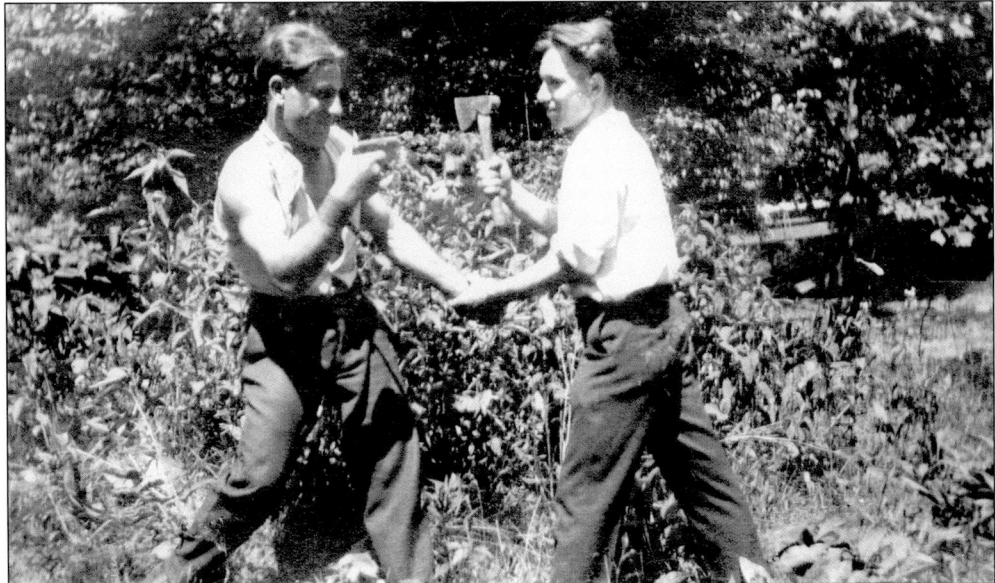

Tony LaRocco and his cousin Al DiNell are taking a few minutes to fool around behind the Glass House and show off some muscle.

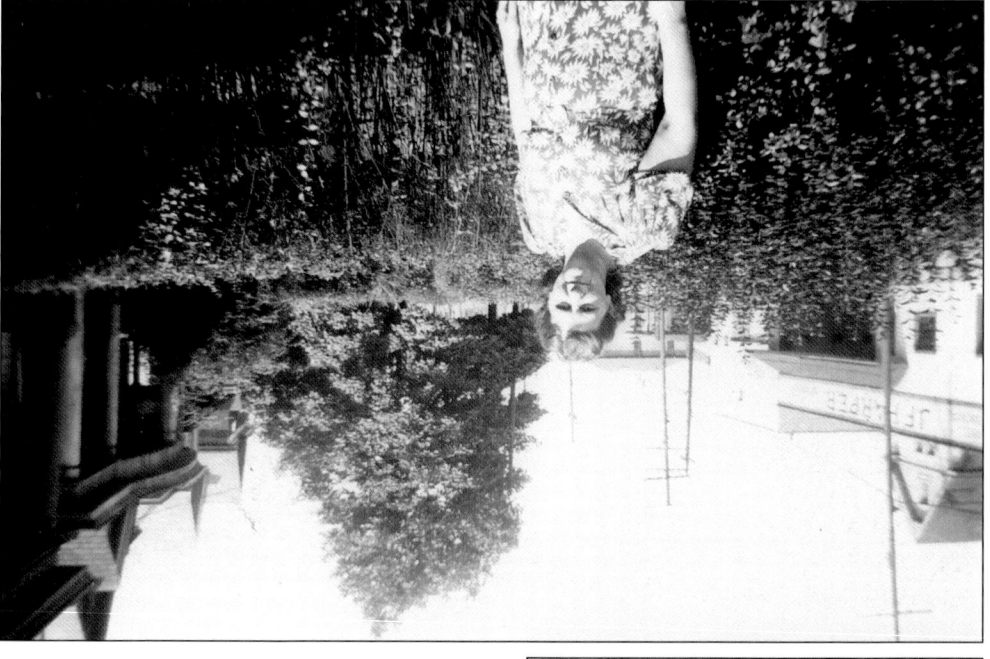

On a simple sunny day in Coraopolis, many folks enjoy being outside tending to their gardens, hanging laundry to dry, and just being out in the community.

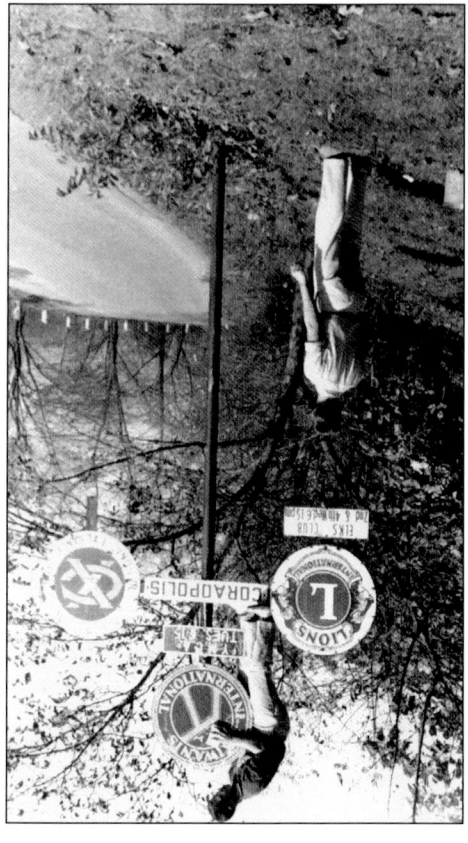

A new sign for the Kiwanis Club was put up for all to see in 1958. This sign was installed in the area of Coraopolis that was across from the Cornell school entrance.

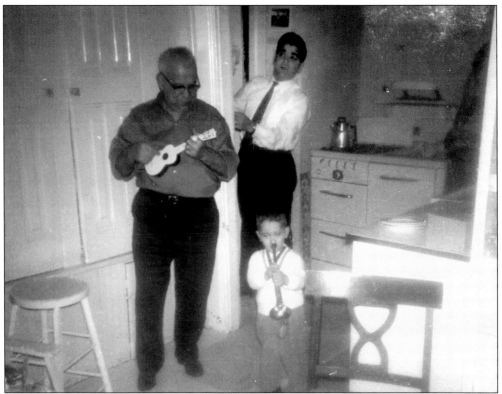

Three generations are proud musicians in this family. The time is 1961, and music was thriving in the Palaio household as Nicola, Paul, and little Nicholas enjoy the sounds of the instruments.

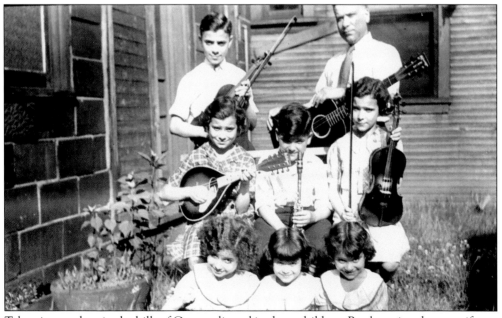

Talent is prevalent in the hills of Coraopolis and in these children. By observing the magnificent string and wind instruments, it is easy to see budding musicians on the rise.

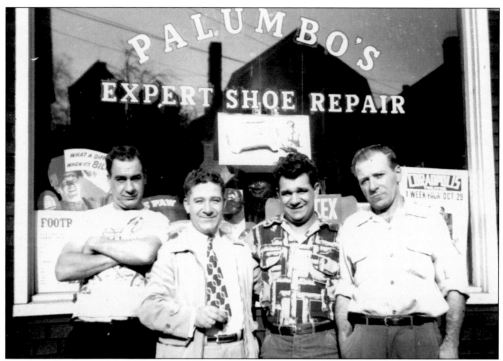

From left to right, Paul Brunette, Fred Barone, Teddy Burnette, and Virgil Palumbo proudly pose for this photograph on Fifth Avenue in front of the well-known Palumbo's Expert Shoe Repair. It is a Sunday afternoon in 1955.

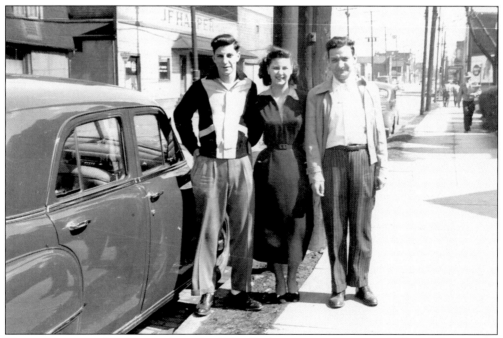

Hanging out was a fun thing to do in the 1950s. In this picture, the year is 1951, and these young folks, Sam (left), Catherine, and Serafino Murgia, are sporting the classic look of the 1950s.

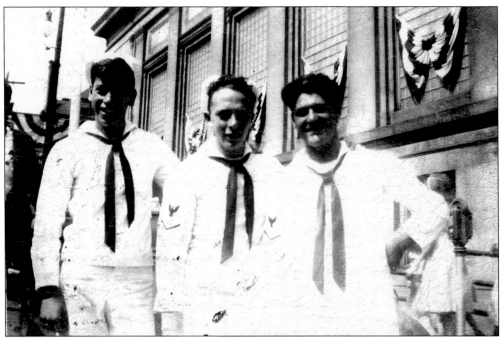

In July 1946, after World War II, Roland Casasanta, Pat LaMark, and Munda Trello (from left to right) stand in front of the First National Bank on the corner of Mill Street and Fifth Avenue celebrating the Fourth of July parade in Coraopolis. The First National Bank in Coraopolis was built in 1897.

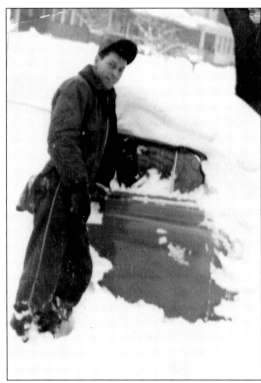

The year 1950 was known as the "Year of the Big Snow" in Coraopolis. Twenty-two-year-old Roland Casasanta stands next door to the Coraopolis Armory on Fifth Avenue digging out a brand-new 1949 Nash automobile.

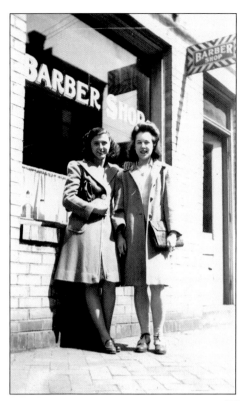

Minne Guaragno (left) and
Josephine Falcione pose for a lovely picture
in front of the community barbershop.

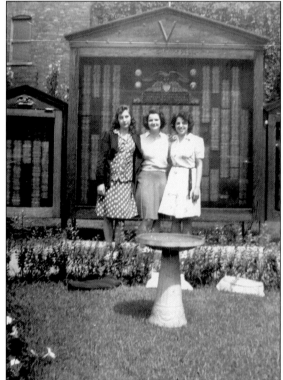

The picture of these ladies is in
front of the World War II memorial
on Fifth Avenue. Unfortunately
the memorial has been taken
down and is no longer there.

Sitting proudly on this would-be antique Nash, this gentleman is enjoying a hot 1930s summer day in Coraopolis.

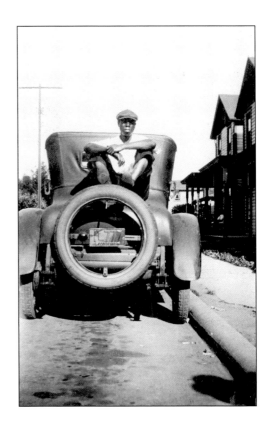

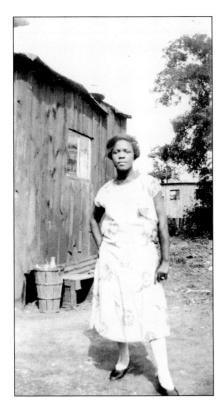

Alice Hunt stands as a radiant 24-year-old living on First Avenue.

This photograph was taken in the recreation hall on Neville Island. The woman in the middle is entertaining all by dancing the tarantella. By observing the other woman in the picture, one can see that the ladies of Coraopolis were movers and shakes no matter their age.

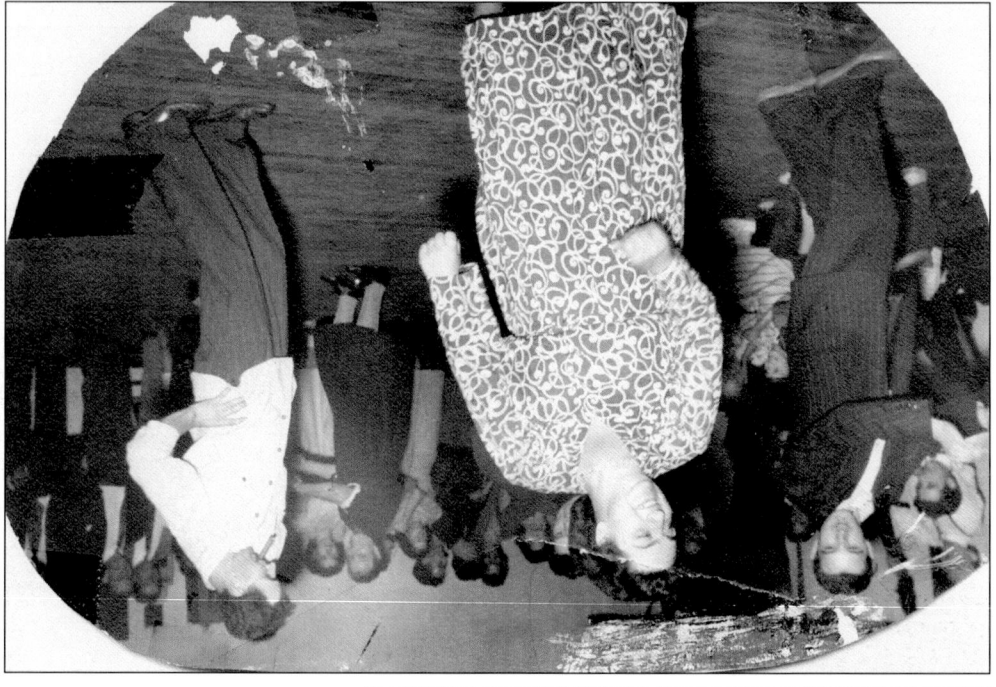

Anthony Mangine casually stands in front of his fine dairy store that was known as the local mom-and-pop store in the 1950s. It was located off Fifth Avenue and housed a yummy ice-cream bar where one could order a milk shake or coffee in addition to basic dairy products. Customers could also order a hamburger for lunch that would have been grilled to order and help themselves to the Coca-Cola machine where they could get a bottle of pop for 10¢.

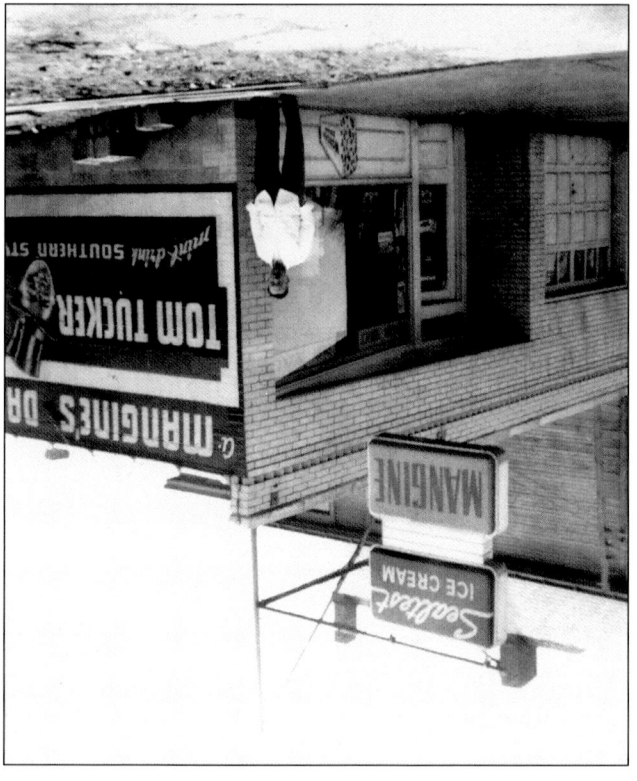

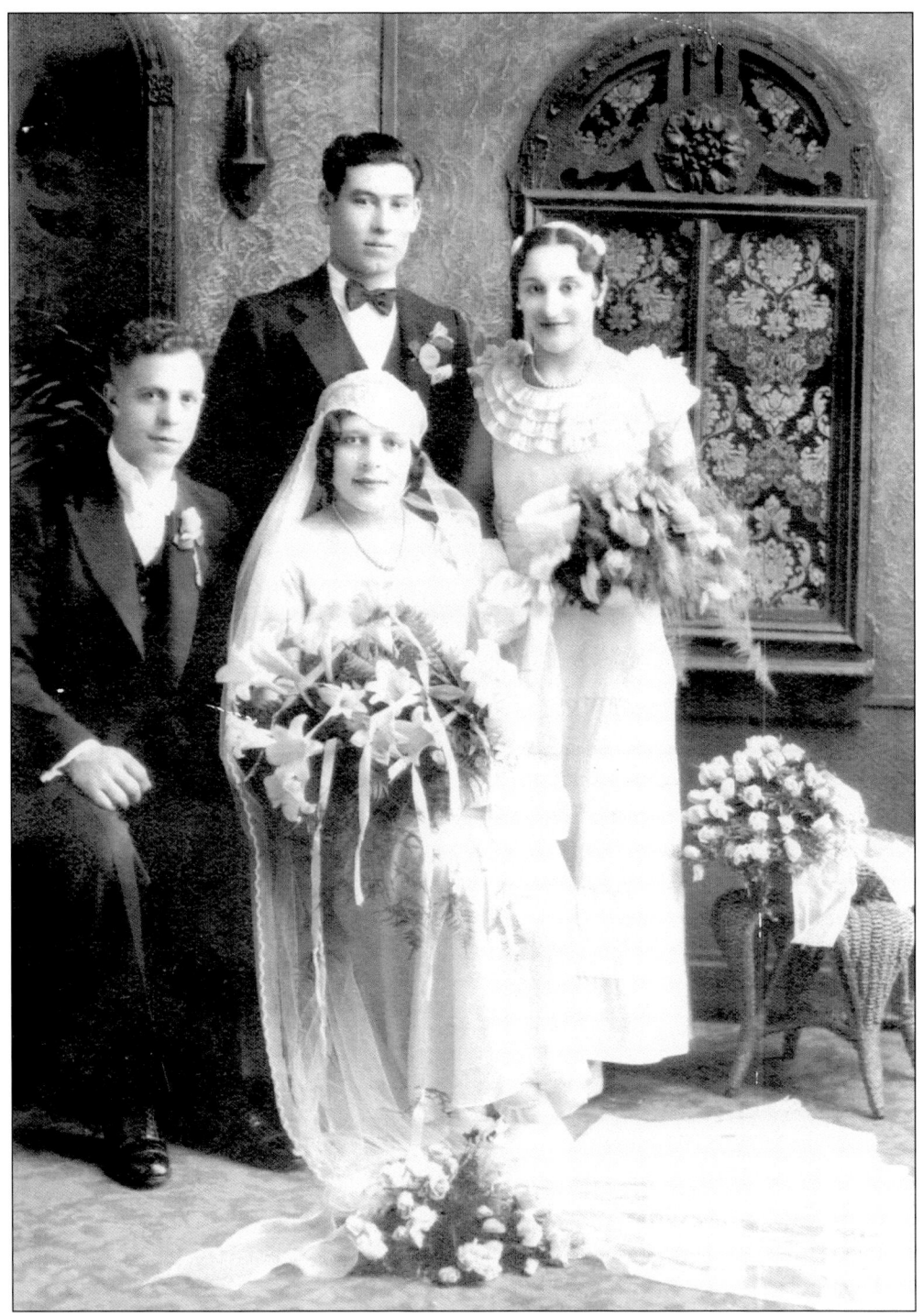

In 1927, Joseph Letterle, a German immigrant, came to Coraopolis to work as a machinist for the Lewis Foundry in Groveton. In 1934, he met and married Clara Loria, a first-generation Italian. In 1936, they had a daughter Helen, who grew up to serve the Coraopolis School District for 24 years as a teacher and then later became the community tax collector.

This photograph was taken in front of the Fourth Avenue Shoe Repair store. It is the year 1942, and Jerry Frissora (right) has been enlisted in the army and is getting ready to leave the town of Coraopolis to serve in West Africa and then on to Italy. After serving in the war, he later moved on to a job at Robert Morris University and remained employed there for 18 years.

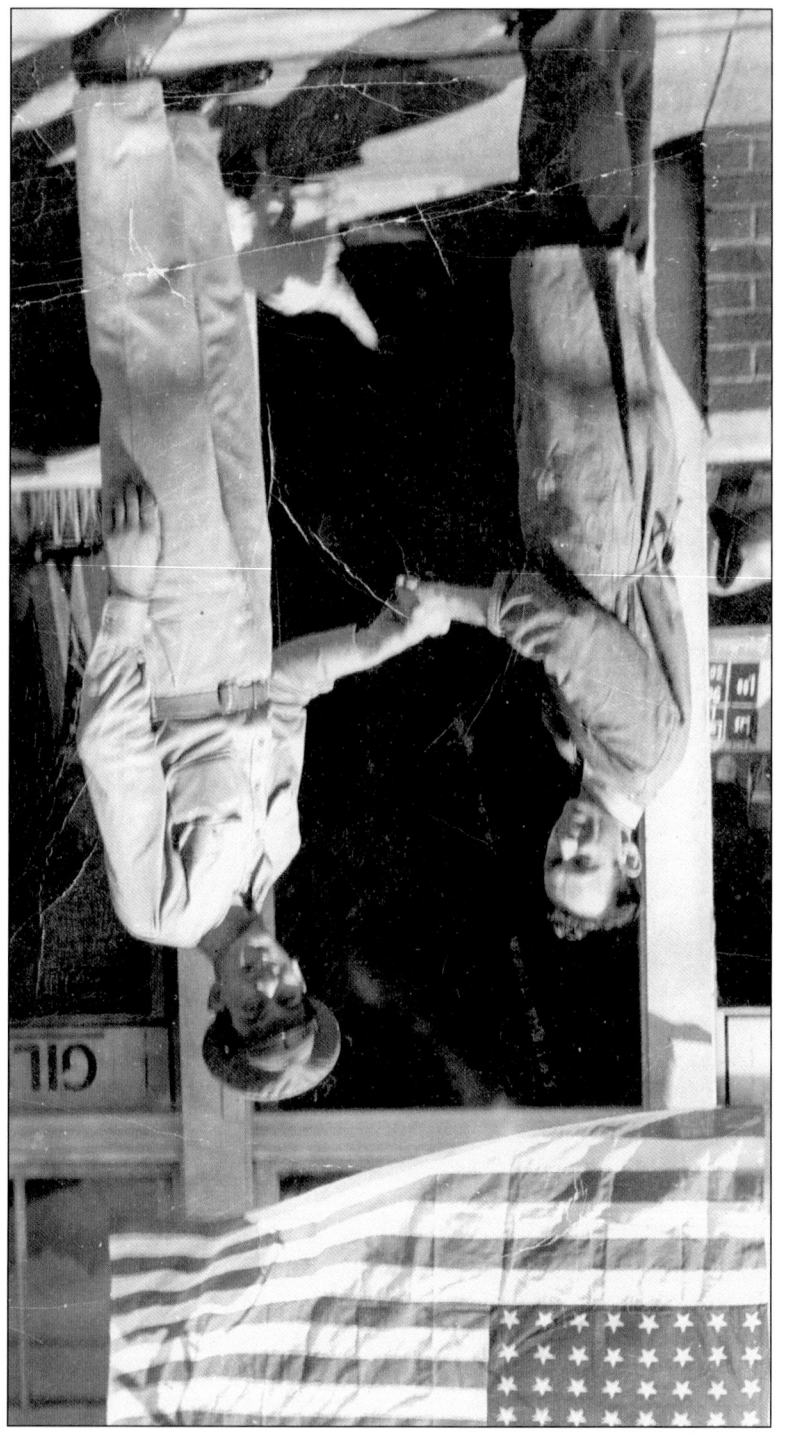

The folks of Coraopolis took their jobs seriously and worked them appreciatively. Notice the level of concentration on this gentleman's face as he is carefully hammering together a shoe that is in need of repair.

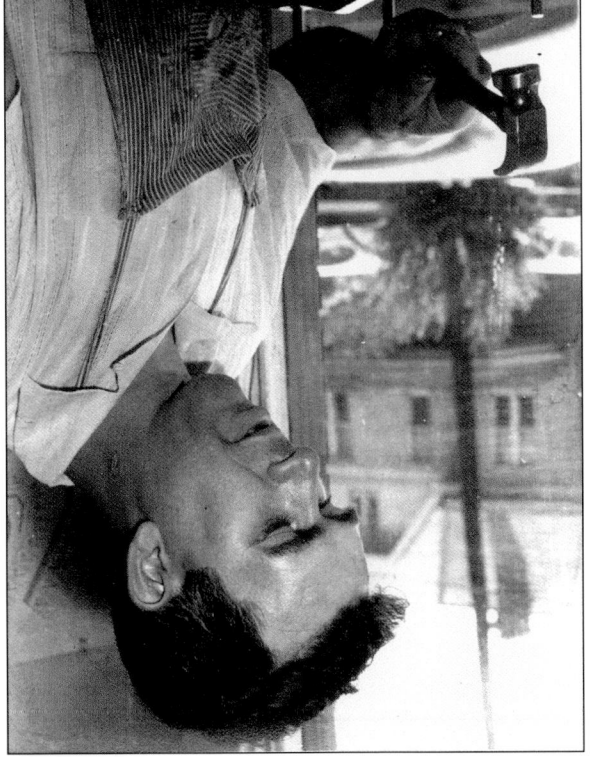

Inside this shoe repair shop many repairs were done by Jerry Frissora. Shoes were generally repaired rather than replaced during this era. Note the calendar in the background. The month is April and the year is 1958.

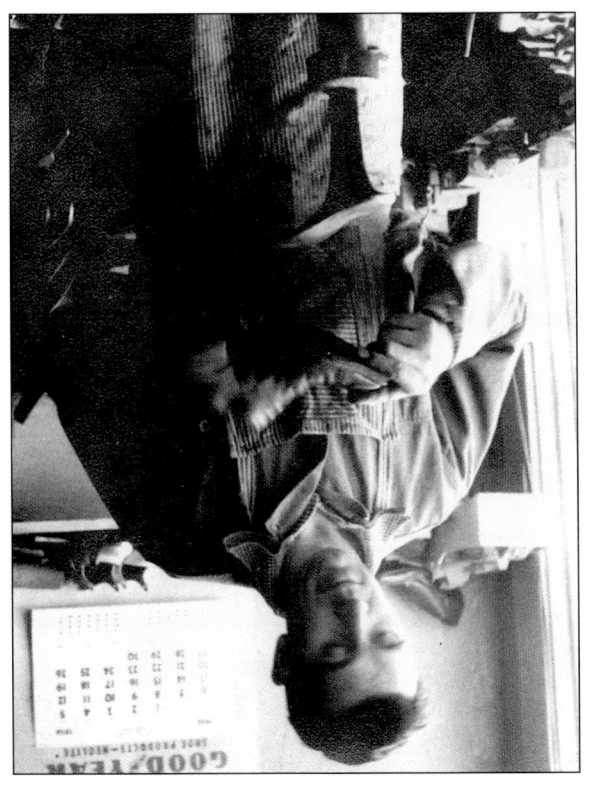

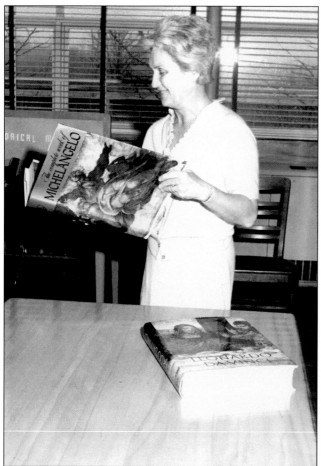

Helen Tussey is looking at a book in the brand-new Coraopolis Public Library that held its grand opening in 1955. The first public library opened in the borough building in 1937.

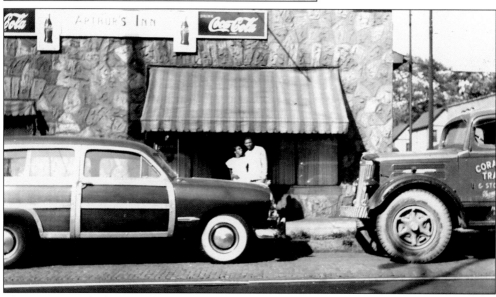

This young couple depicts a day of togetherness in the town of Coraopolis.

This dignified couple, Virginia and Mike Nichay Sr., just purchased a new home on State Avenue after living in an apartment. The flower on Virginia's jacket illustrates the time was Mother's Day, as ladies commonly wore flowers on that day.

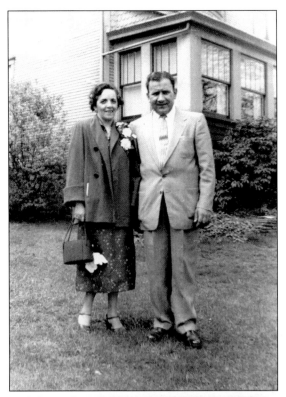

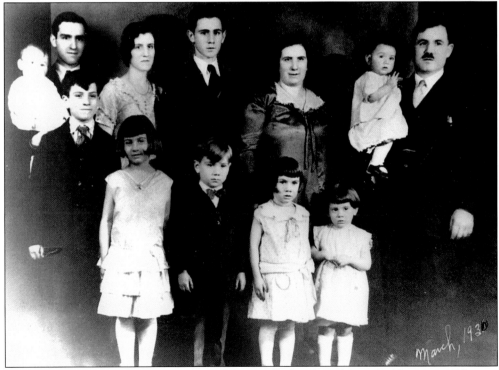

This beautiful family portrait was taken of the Tarallo family and Louis Baldassare in 1931.

This is an image that captures the Coraopolis Service Station on 914 Fifth Avenue in 1938. This station is now the location of the Coraopolis Post Office. Featured here is the Coraopolis Volunteer Fire Department truck.

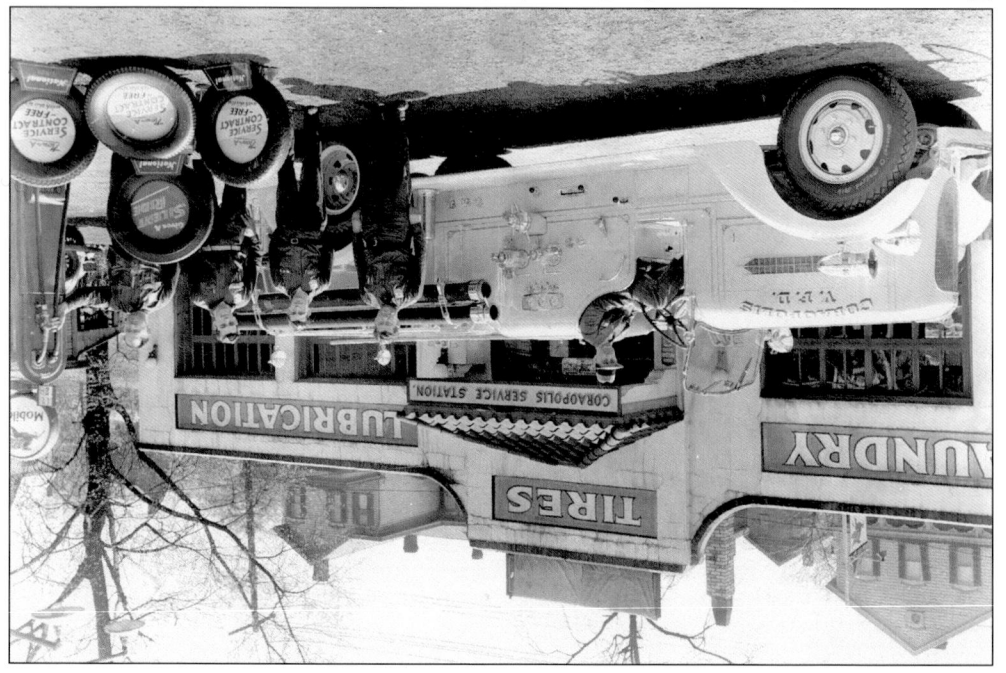

Located on Fifth Avenue and Chess Street was the Graff's first service station. It was managed by Joseph Graff and his son William J. (Bill) Graff. Pictured here is Bill in front of the service station about the year 1950. This station was sold in 1956, and Bill's next service station was the Arco unit at Fifth Avenue and Ferree Street.

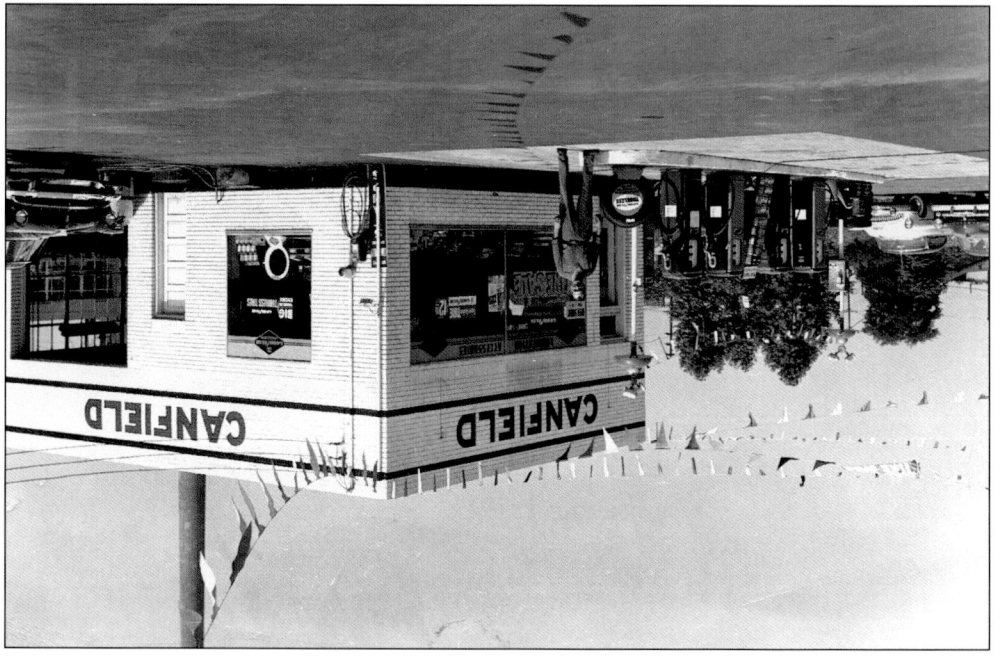

Two

HISTORY AT A GLANCE

Coraopolis demonstrates a compelling history. It carries with it the puzzle of legend and tradition. It has been said George Washington, when crossing through, spent the night of October 20, 1770, on the Ohio River bank. According to the coordinates in his diary, it describes the location of his stay based on having passed through Neville Island. Despite this occurrence, Robert Vance was officially the pioneer settler as Washington moved on and did not settle. Robert Vance devoted himself to settling the land of Coraopolis and building a community. He passed away on August 18, 1818, and is laid to rest in the cemetery at Montour's Church.

Over the past 100 years, Coraopolis has seen many historic celebrations and has conquered many challenges. It has seen its streets developed and industries created. Families have moved into this town from across the oceans to begin a new life and settle down. Generation after generation has written the history of this town. Coraopolis has seen the eyes of disaster, depression, and wars, yet still thrives today. The town takes pride in its history, which highlights the town's families and their heritage. Over the decades, this community has been observed honoring the valor of its hardworking citizens. The view of history shows how time has progressed and things have changed. But one thing is certain and that is the people of this town remain constant and steady, creating new history every day.

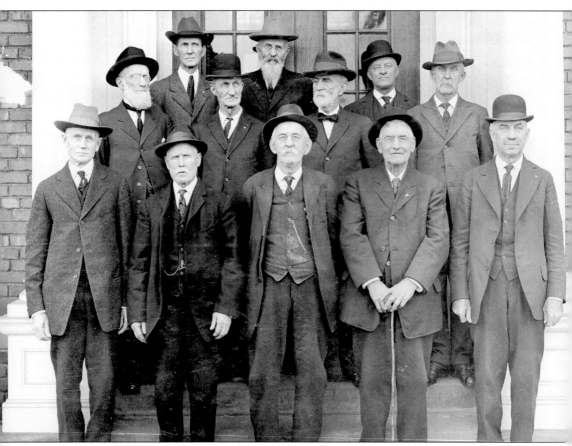

The founding fathers of Coraopolis are pictured here, from left to right, (first row) W. R. Gardner, William McKinley, Frank Kepner, James K. P. Lighthill, and A. D. Sutton; (second row) J. S. Burns, W. Reed McCabe, Frank Dillion, and G. W. Morrison; (third row) J. N. Moore, Thomas Brand, and D. K. Ewing.

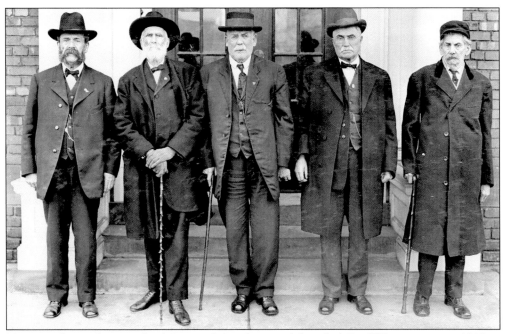

Here is a classic photograph of Coraopolis's valiant and dignified Civil War veterans in 1907.

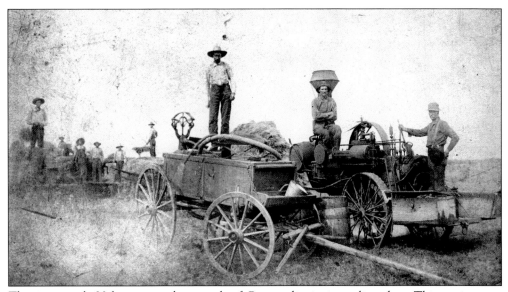

This is an early-20th-century photograph of Coraopolis, in its earliest days. This engine may have been used to thresh wheat.

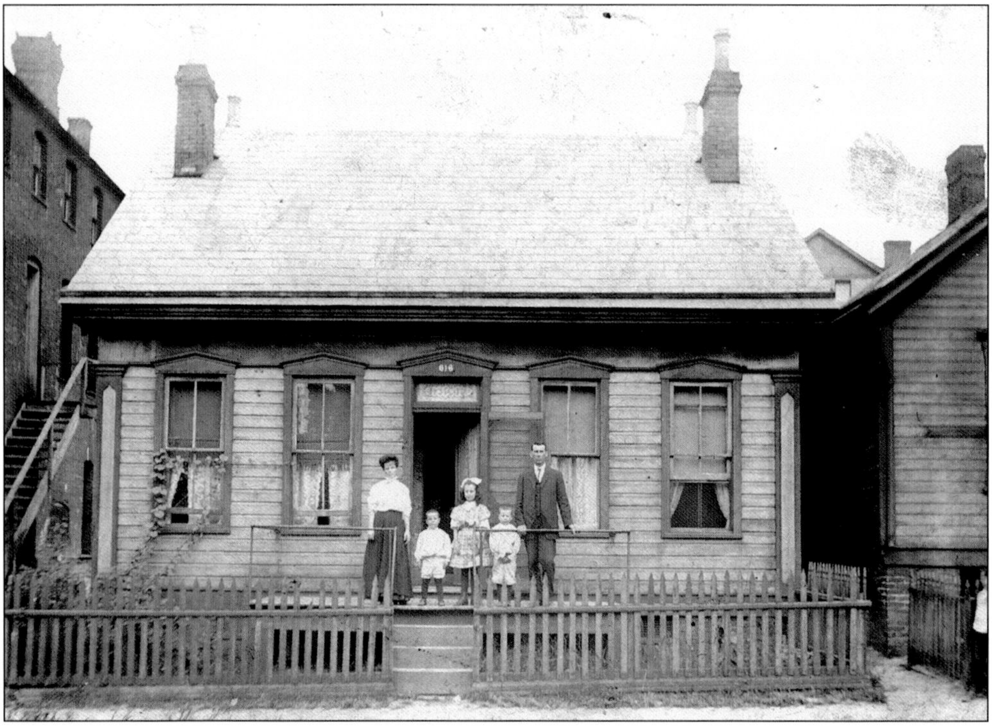

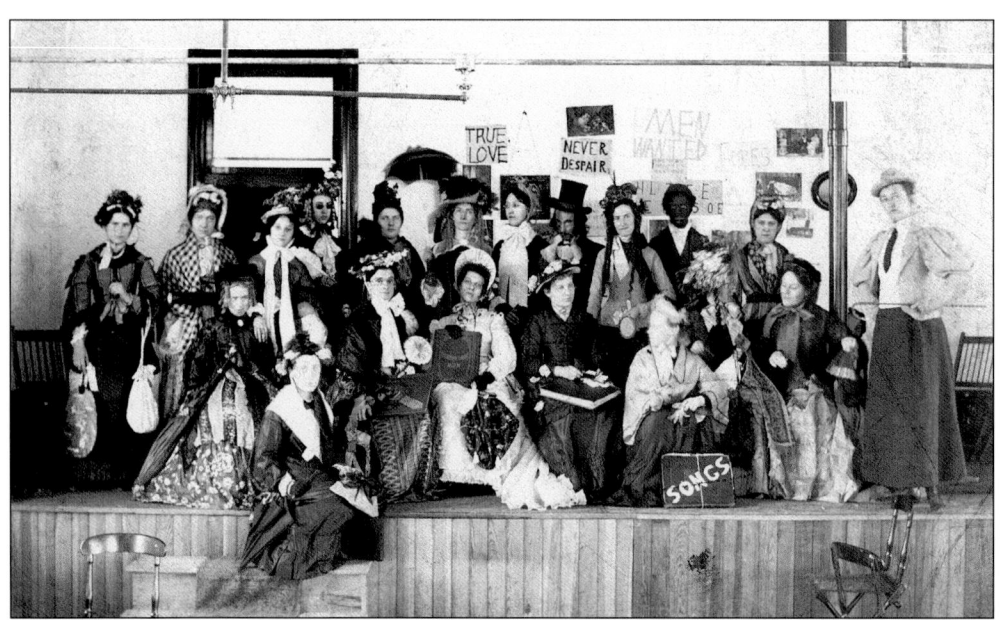

Images of early-20th-century pioneering families in Coraopolis, such as the one featured here, are rarely seen.

This photograph was taken in the bank building on the second floor. Many shows were performed, and graduation ceremonies were held here. Notice the elaborate costumes and props the actors are using. Today this would be considered the second floor of the building where Kerri's Corner Café is located.

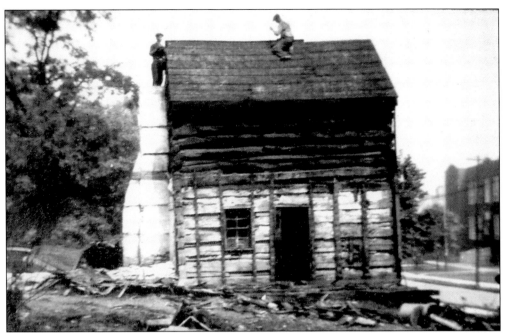

One of the first homes in Coraopolis was this log cabin built in the 1700s. James McCabe, one of Coraopolis's early settlers, married the daughter of Robert Vance. Together they bought 20 acres of land and built this home. Gentlemen are delicately doing work on the roof of this building. The geographical location of this log cabin in Coraopolis is State Avenue.

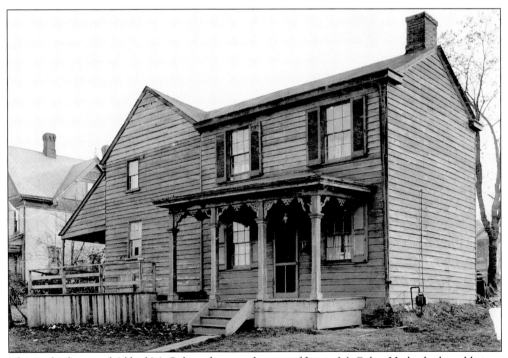

This is the home of Alfred McCabe, who was the son of James McCabe. He built the additions onto the log cabin and converted it into this beautiful home on State Avenue around 1800.

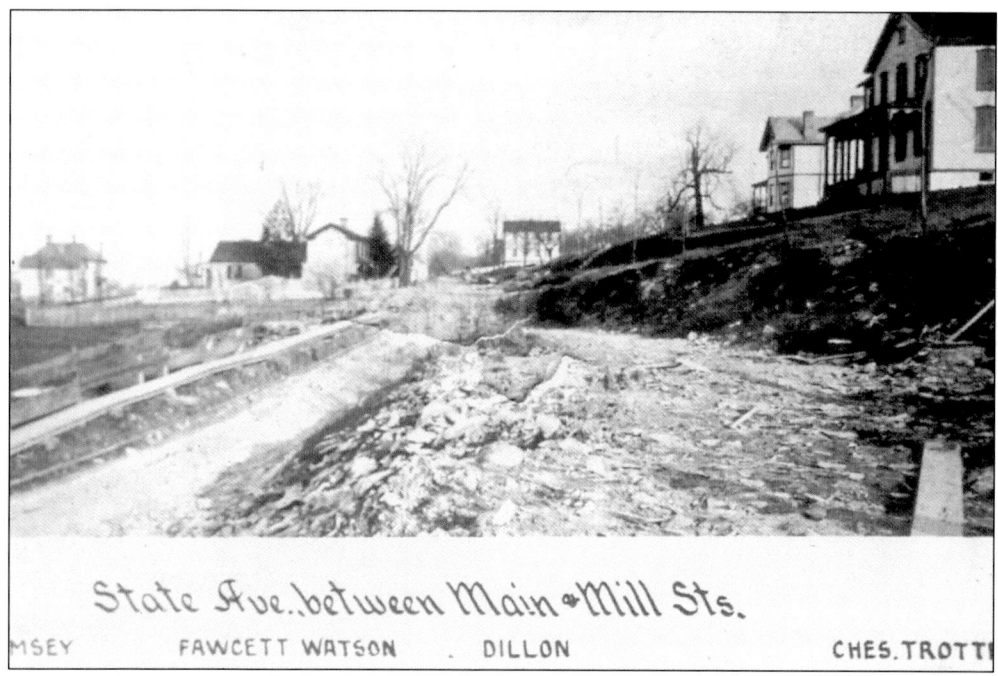

State Ave. between Main & Mill Sts.

MSEY   FAWCETT WATSON   .   DILLON   CHES.TROTT

This early-20th-century photograph shows State Avenue between Main Street and Mill Street. The homes in these pictures are some of the earliest homes in Coraopolis ever built and belonged to the town's forefathers.

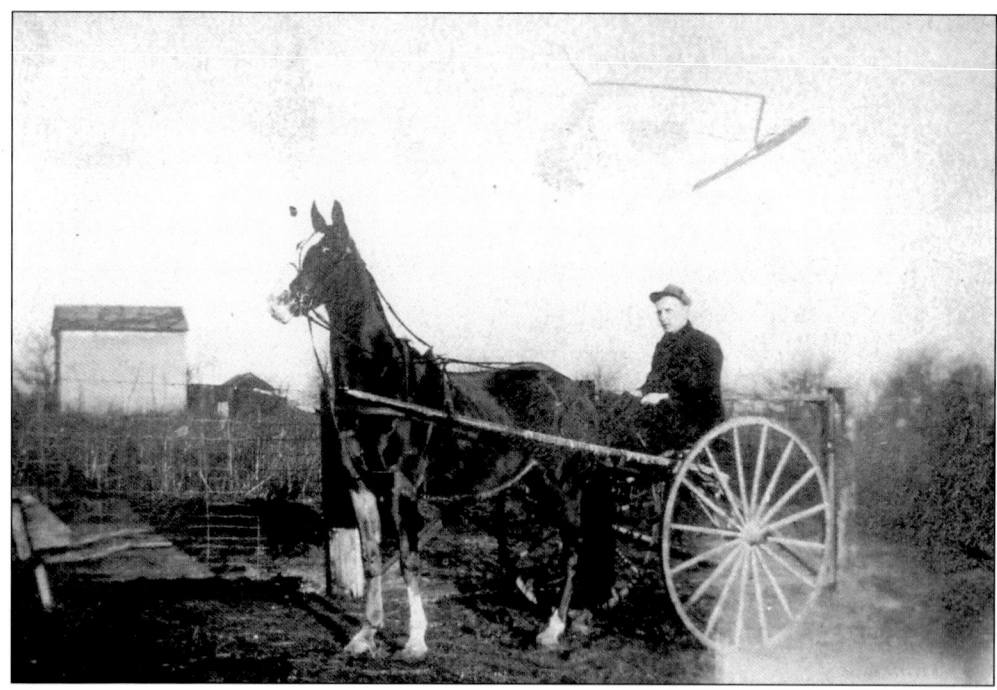

This classic photograph of Coraopolis during its horse-and-buggy days displays when the hills were still rolling over vast land.

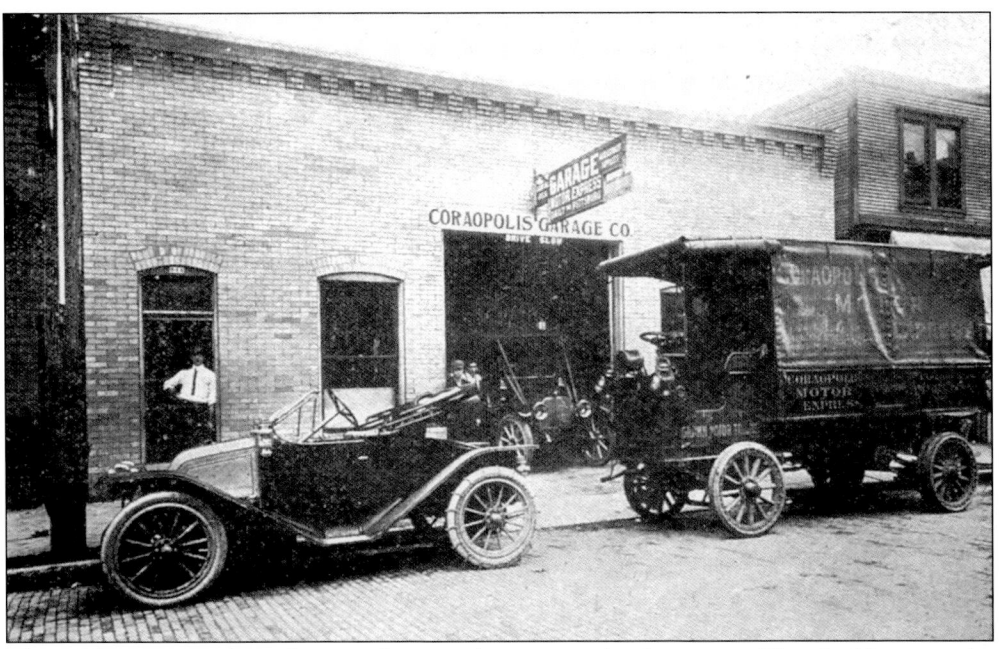

The old cars in this photograph are classics nearly forgotten. The building is the Coraopolis Garage Company.

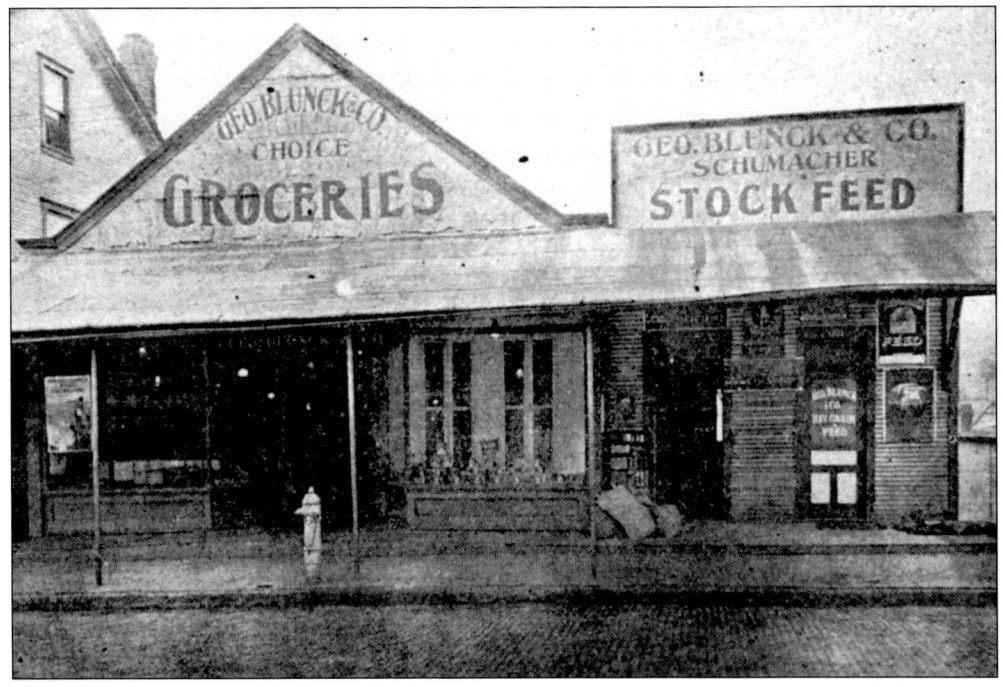

The George Blunck and Company Choice Groceries and Stock Feed store was one of the earliest stores in Coraopolis.

The early settlers of this town are seen here showing a variety of transportation methods, most including the necessity of horses.

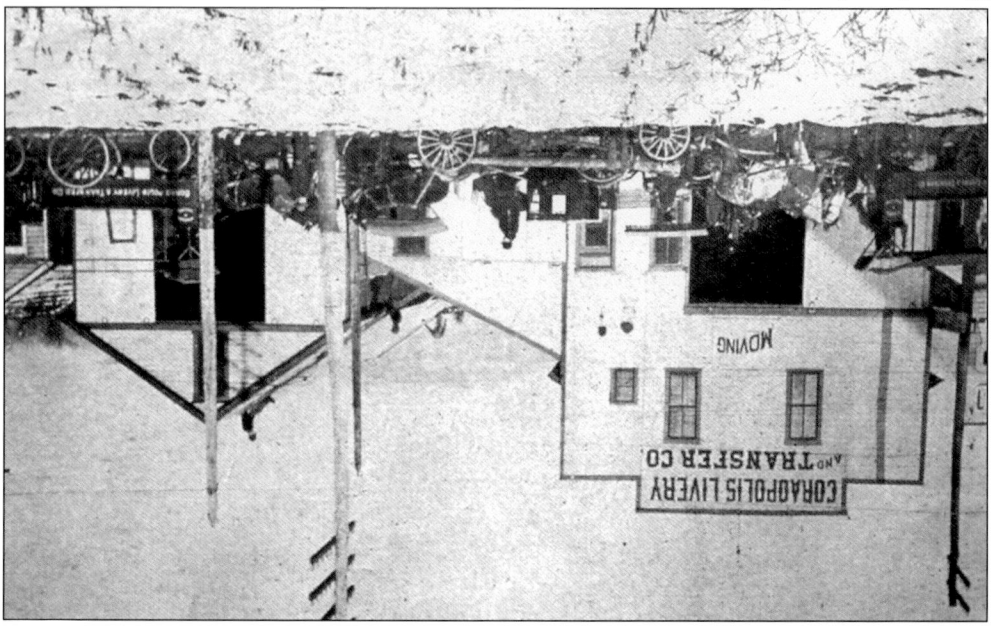

In the early years, couples would go to Scott and Ewing Livery and Feed to rent a horse and buggy for a Saturday night date. However, this company was the same company whose horse and buggy would unfortunately be seen at times acting as a hearse carrying a coffin on the way to a funeral.

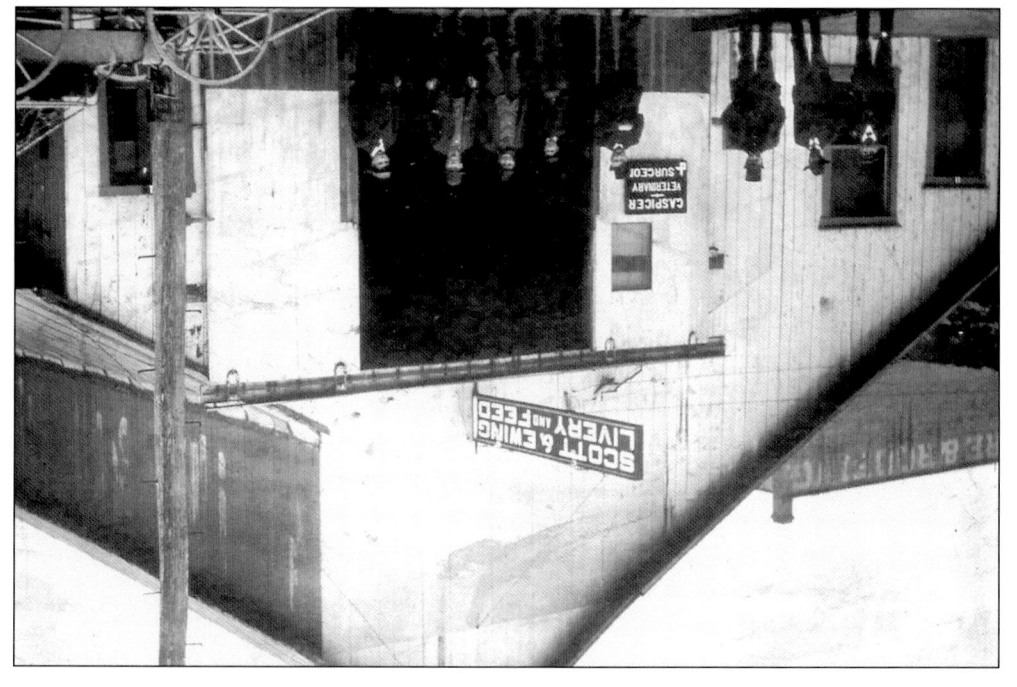

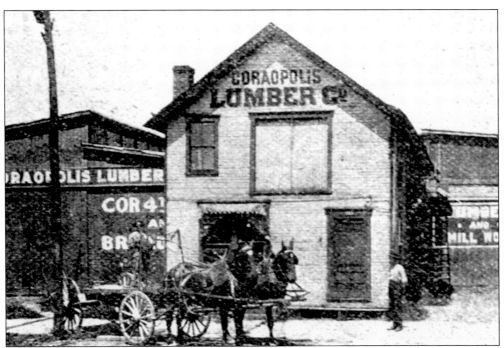

The Coraopolis Lumber Company was located on Fourth Avenue. At the beginning of the 20th century, Fourth Avenue was busy with the kind of horse and buggies seen in this picture.

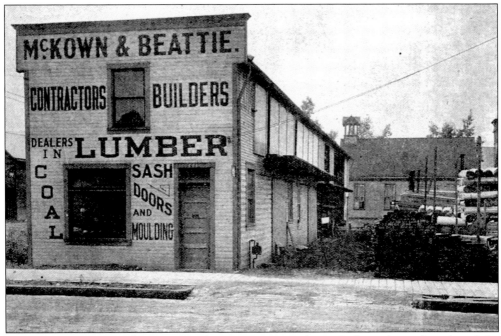

Originally McKown and Beattie Lumber Company was located where the parking lot of the Presbyterian church is today. In the background of this photograph is First Presbyterian Church. The company ended up on Fourth Avenue where the Moose Club is currently located.

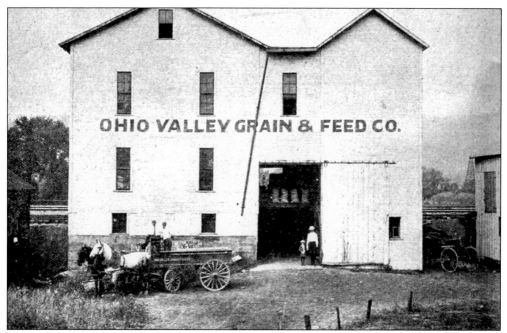

The Ohio Valley Grain and Feed Company was located on Fourth Avenue near the Montour train station. In the background the Pittsburgh and Lake Erie Railroad tracks are visible.

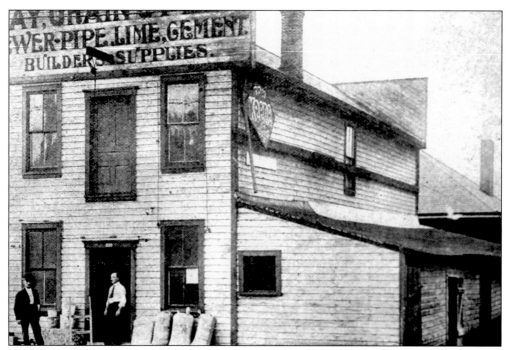

Bags of cement are seen here leaning against the front of the building. Workers and companies would come here to purchase the necessary supplies, particularly cement, for building many of the foundations for businesses and homes in the town of Coraopolis.

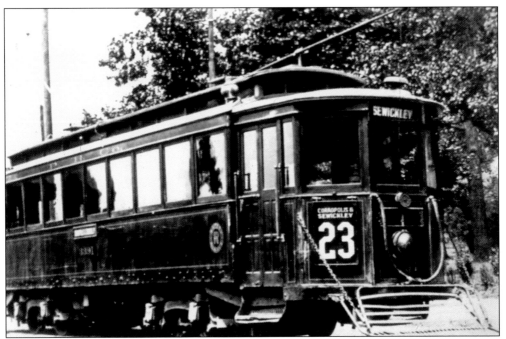

As seen in this photograph, this electric streetcar would have been going near Mill Street heading toward Sewickley. Streetcars became one of the main sources of transportation, aside from the railroad stations in the early days of Coraopolis. The first electronic street railway began operating in 1894.

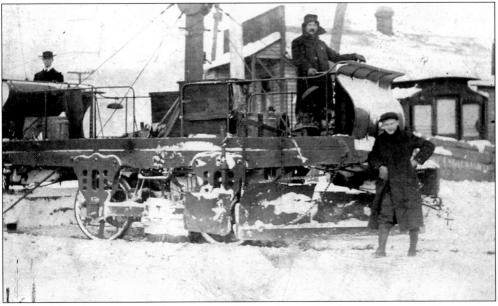

Vehicles like this were used for sweeping the tracks so that the streetcars could run more fluently after a heavy snow. They were just simply referred to as "rail sweepers" and not by a formal name.

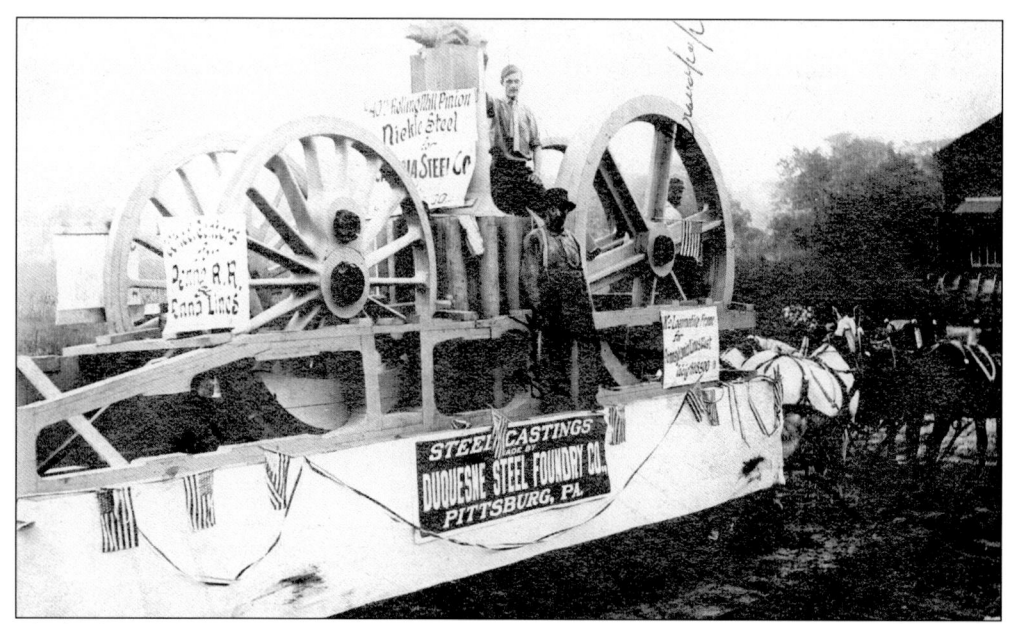

The bridge celebration for Sewickley and Coraopolis was in 1911. The front two black horses are named King and Queen, and the white horses are named Fred and Harry. In the front center of the photograph is Frank Ritchie, and off to the far right, peeking through the giant wheel, is Harold Harper. The gentleman at the top center of the photograph is unidentified.

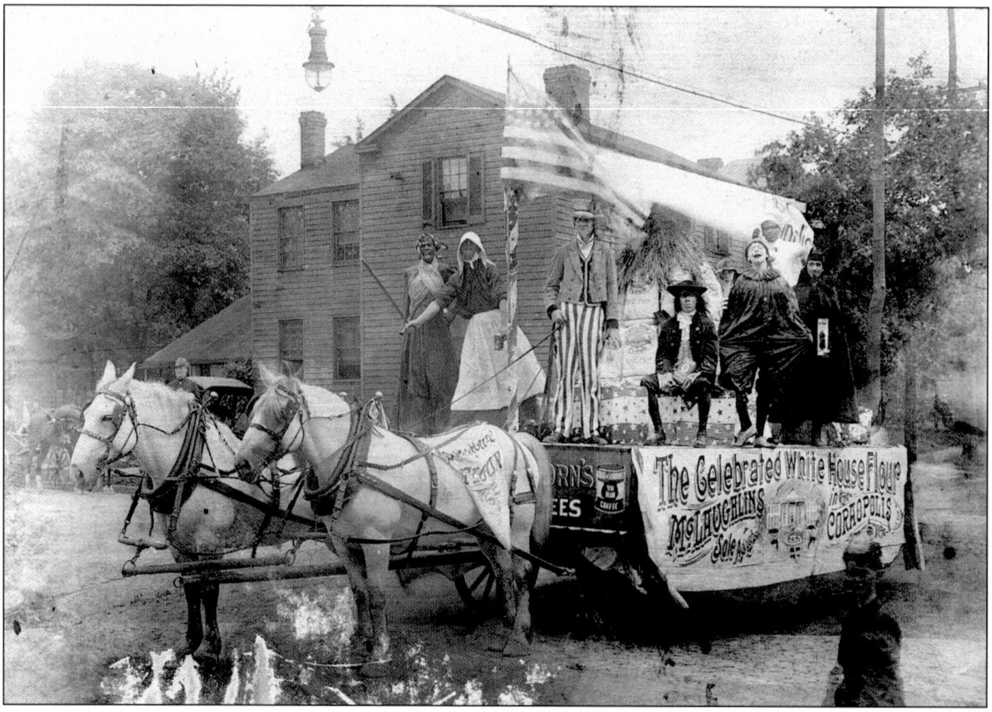

Continuing the bridge celebration is the float seen here that is being balanced with entertaining characters of all sorts. The eyes of the little boy at the bottom right corner of the photograph are following the parade.

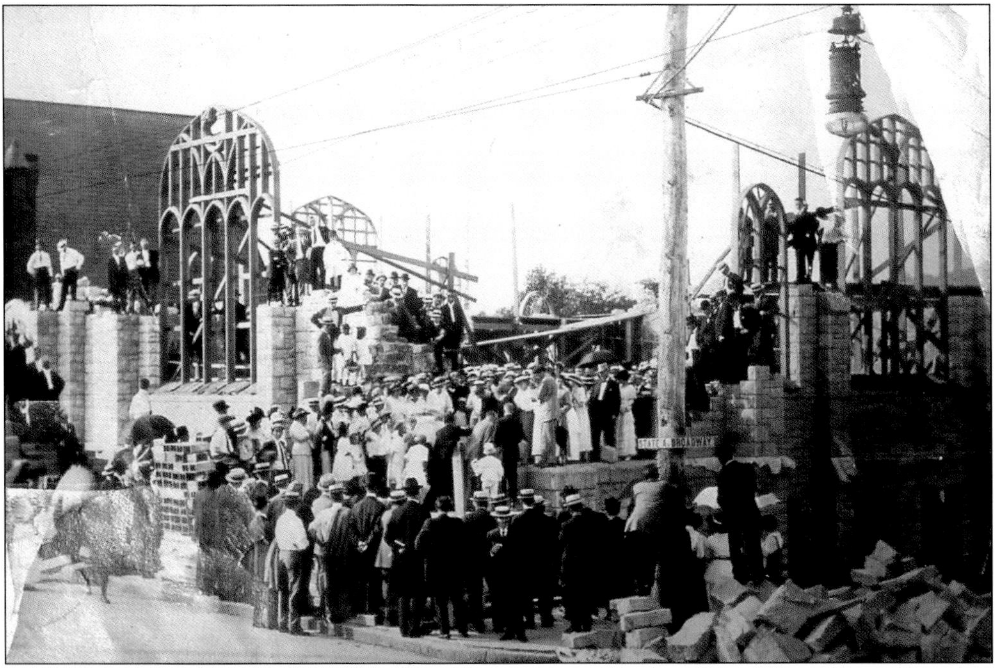

Coraopolis Church of God in Christ is now located on 1046 State Avenue. According to the church's history, the congregation began as a "house church" in 1925 with the congregation meeting as a group of people with a mission on a member's back porch. Eventually a church building was found, and the first baptism ceremonies were held in the Ohio River at the base of Main Street.

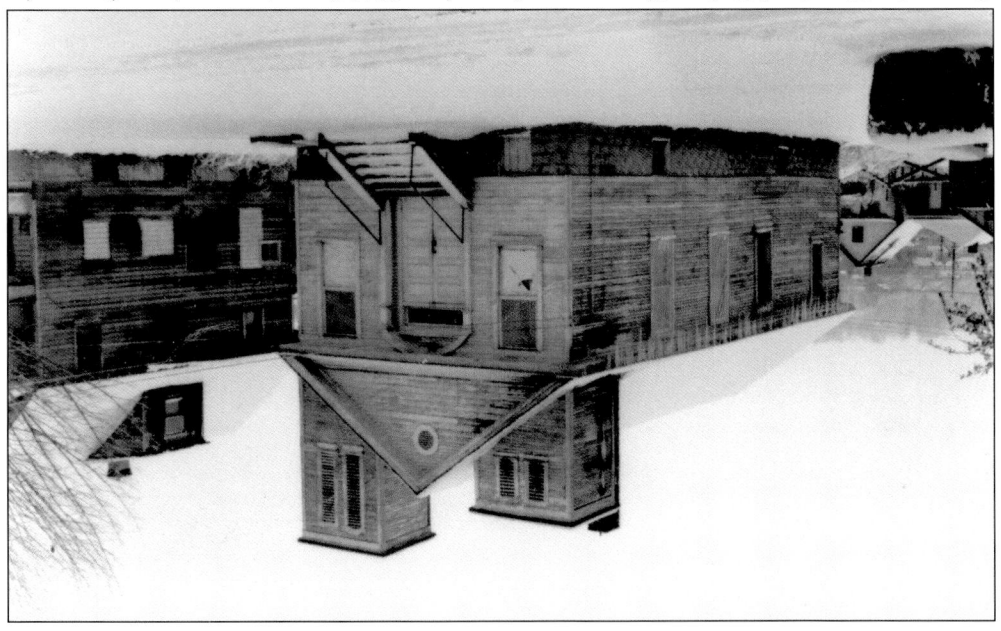

The community gathers together to observe and explore the building of the United Presbyterian Church on Broadway Street and Fifth Avenue. Folks today refer to the church as the "Gray Stone Church."

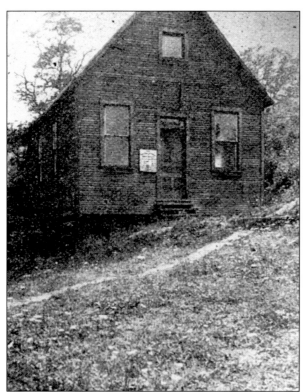

The first Mount Olive Baptist Church was a wooden church located past Maple Street on Vance Avenue. The father of the former police officer of Coraopolis Charles White, known to local residents as "Chickie," was a deacon at this church.

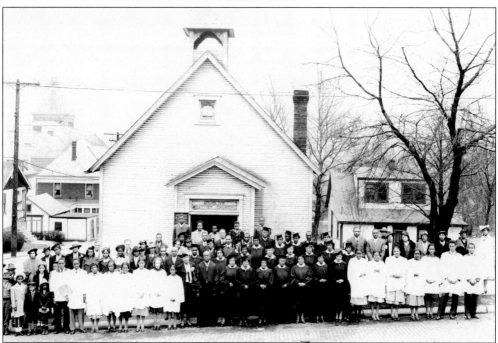

The church was later rebuilt and currently sits on School Street and Highland Avenue. The individuals seen here in the 1930s are the senior adult choir members dressed in black robes and youth choir members dressed in white robes.

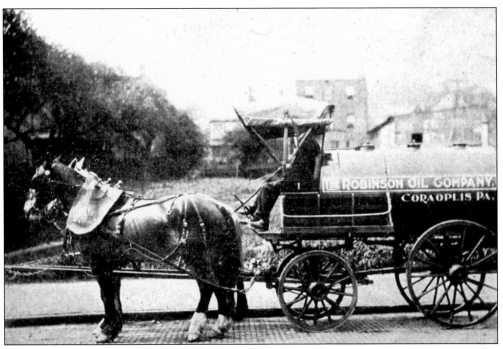

Here is a horse-drawn carriage for the Robinson Oil Company going down a street in Coraopolis.

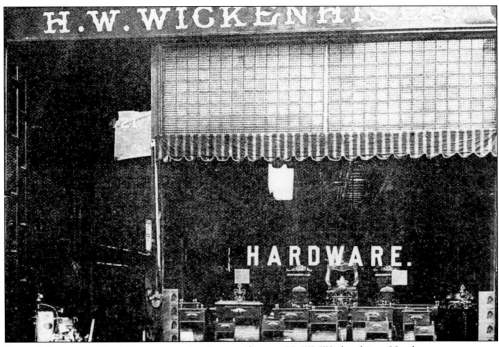

One of the earliest hardware stores in Coraopolis was H. W. Wickenhiser Hardware.

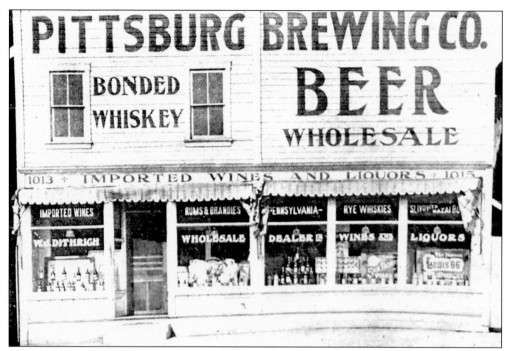

The Pittsburgh Brewing Company was located on Fourth Avenue by the Hotel Helm.

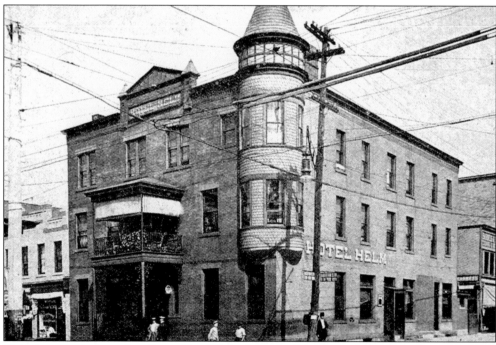

This photograph shows the vibrant Hotel Helm. Its beautiful tower and front balcony are captured here. It stood on the corner of Fourth Avenue and Mill Street and still stands tall today.

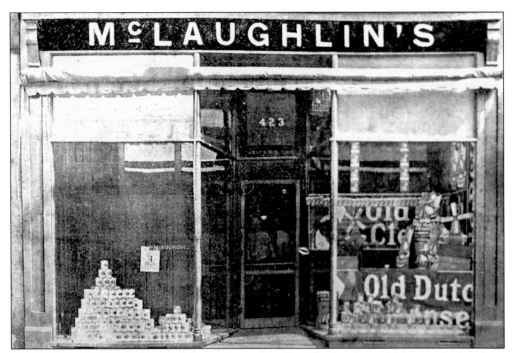

McLaughlin's was located on Mill Street above the alley. The locals would frequently shop here for meat as it was known as a meat market and grocery store.

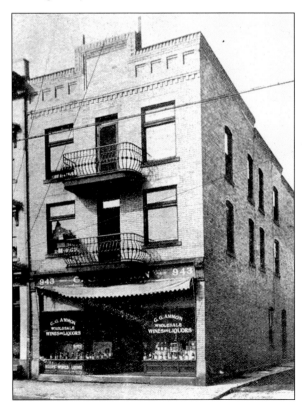

On Fifth Avenue was G. G. Ammon Wholesale Wines and Liquors store. This photograph was taken after Prohibition ended.

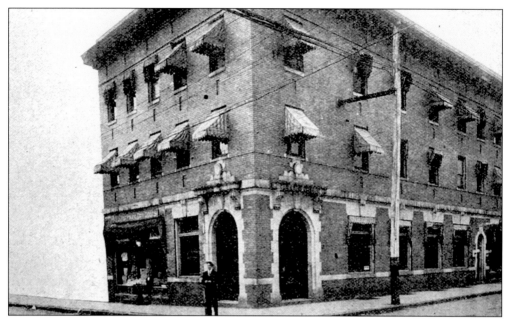

Constructed in the early 1900s, this building, which today is referred to by the elders of the community as "the old bank building" and by youth as where Kerri's Corner Café is located, was vibrantly known for housing graduation ceremonies, plays, and many social functions on the second floor. Notice in this photograph the vastness of Mill Street and how this building seems to stand alone.

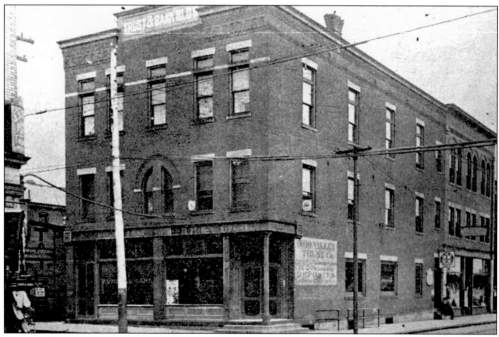

Portrayed in this photograph is the Ohio Valley Trust building located on the corner of Mill Street and Fourth Avenue. In the mid-1920s, C. B. Ferguson was president, and J. E. Thompson was secretary and treasurer.

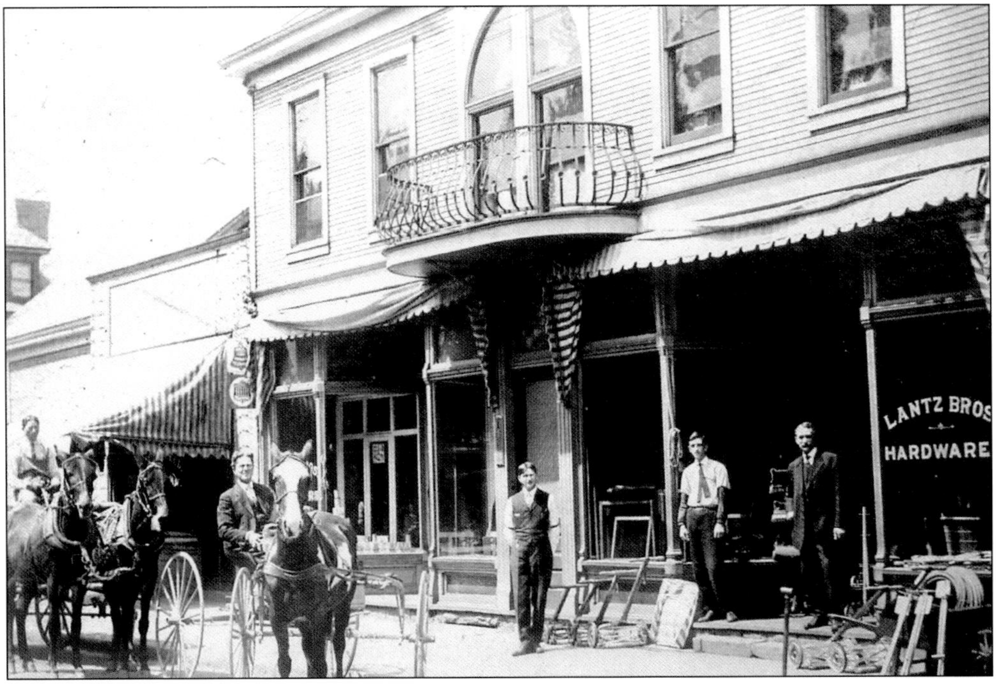

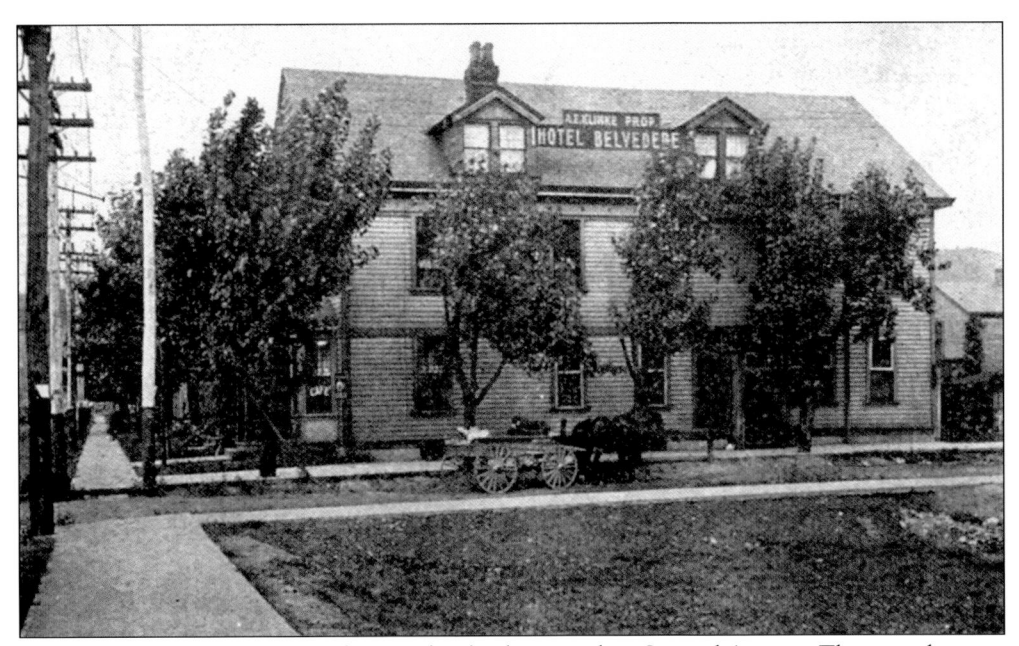

Permanently etched in time is this photograph of Mill Street taken in the very early 1900s. Mill Street became the first permanent street in 1897. Much activity is seen here as people travel down Mill Street in their buggies. To rent an apartment on Mill Street in 1913 would have cost $19 a month.

This iconic grand hotel called the Hotel Belvedere stood on Second Avenue. This snapshot was taken around 1910 and shows again how horse and buggy was the main source of local street transportation in the early days of Coraopolis. This hotel has since been torn down.

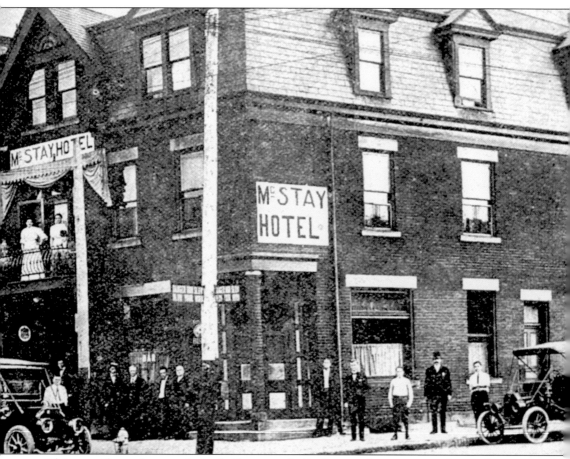

This magnificent photograph clearly illustrates the liveliness and great activity that was beginning to take place as the century was progressing. Seen here are some of the most beautifully fashioned early vehicles, and the days of horse and buggy are fading away. The people line the street, and on the balcony, ladies are looking on Fourth Avenue and all its bustling. The McStay Hotel was located on the corner of Fourth Avenue and Montour Street. The date is May 1, 1909. The hotel still stands there today, but the name has been changed to the Montour Hotel.

Three

COMMUNITY DAYS

Coraopolis also reflects 100 years of dreams and visions from its forefathers. Industry began to flow and schools and churches flourished. Families settled and thus the days of community were born.

The days in Coraopolis were filled with families venturing out together and children playing throughout the town. Social clubs and Little Leagues entertained the community, and summers were filled with bicycle rides, baseball games, hula hoops, and bowling. During this era, many can recall playing with friends and correcting mistakes by simply yelling, "Do over!" Decisions were commonly made among friends by saying "eeny-meeny-miney-moe" and by double-dog daring. Baseball cards would be used to transform any bicycle into a raging motorcycle. Water balloons were known to be the ultimate weapon for a sneak attack. Afternoons were spent laying on one's back, looking up at the sky with friends, and imagining what cloud was coming to life on clear blue days in Coraopolis.

Isaly's and the Dairy Queen were community favorites where many would go to buy yummy treats to take into the theater. To buy a gallon of gas during this era would cost a mere 35¢. People would get their windshield cleaned, oil checked, and gas pumped without having to ask and all for free. No one would ever lose their keys because they were kept in the car and the doors were never locked. The streets were crowded until well into the evening as people of all ages went about living and loving their treasured town.

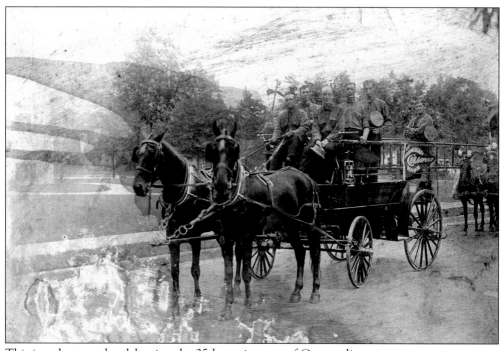

This is a photograph celebrating the 25th anniversary of Coraopolis.

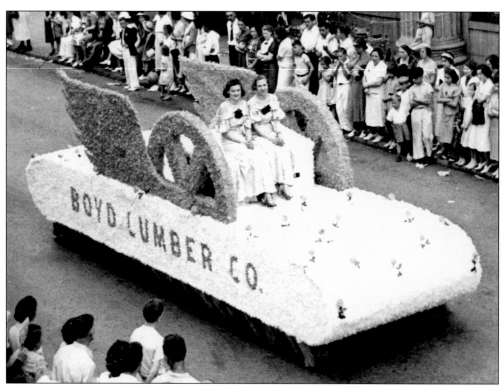

This is a photograph celebrating the 50th anniversary of Coraopolis. The date is July 5, 1937. The semicentennial was postponed one year because of the 1936 flood.

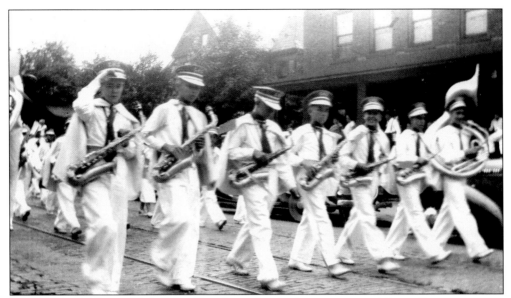

The Coraopolis Senior High School band marches in the semicentennial parade.

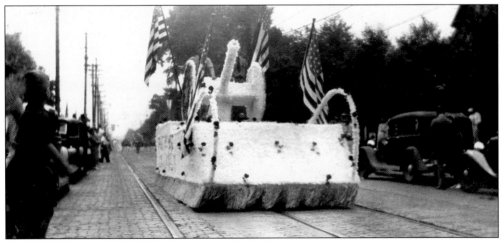

The VFW float coasts in the semicentennial parade.

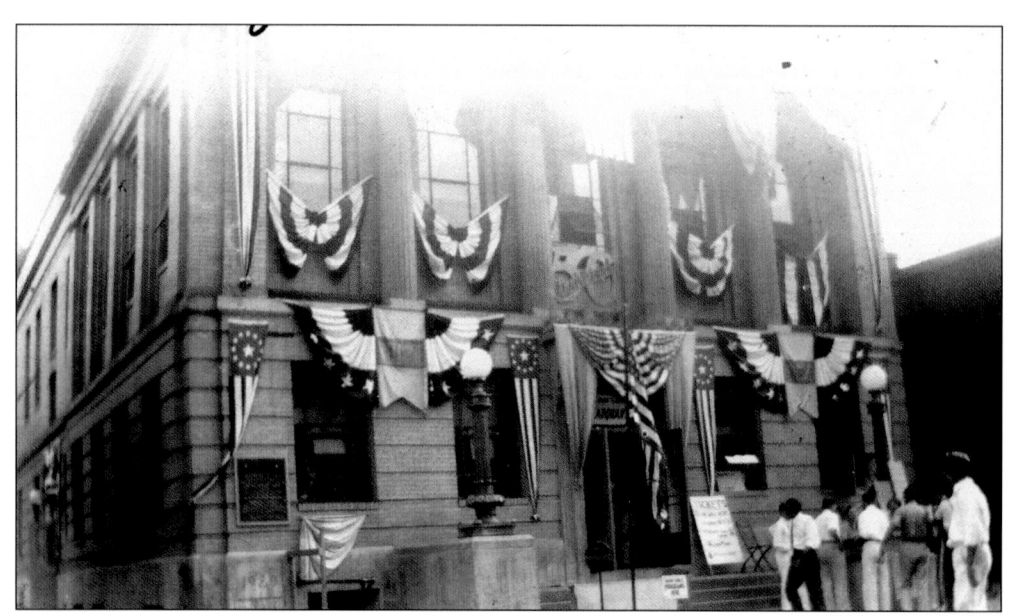

The Coraopolis Borough Building is extravagantly decorated for the semicentennial celebration.

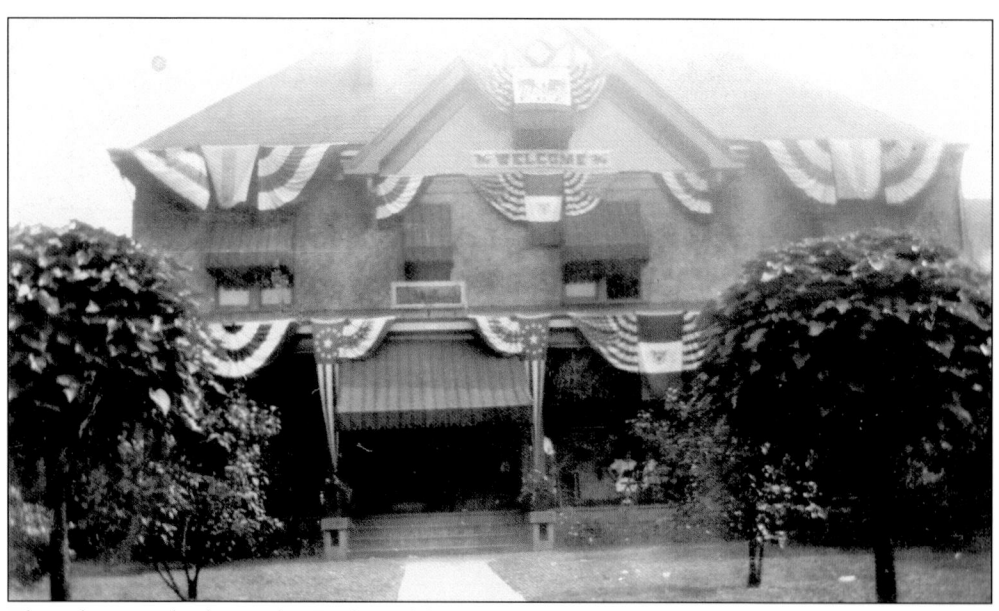

This photograph shows the Eagles Club. Many functions were held at the Eagles Club in Coraopolis. If it were still standing today, it would be visible from Segneri's Italian Restaurant on Fourth Avenue.

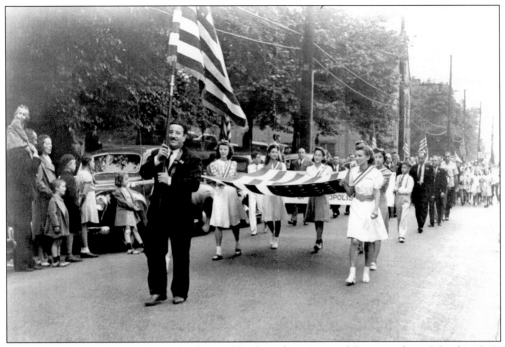

Guy Pisano is seen here holding the flag and leading the Memorial Day parade on May 31, 1942.

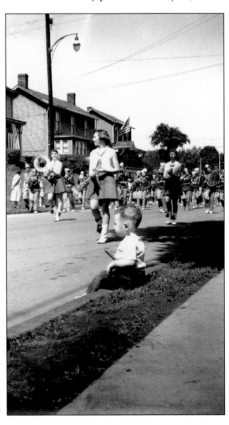

Folks march triumphantly in the 1958 Coraopolis Memorial Day parade.

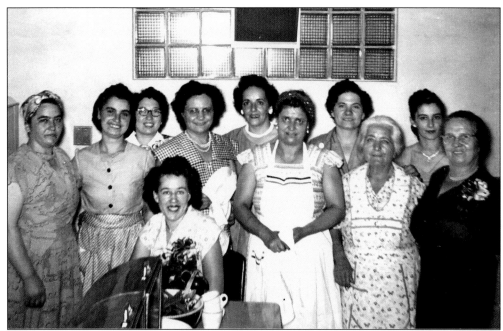

Preparing a wedding feast at the Son's of Italy Hall, these ladies take a minute to pose elegantly as they are getting ready to serve the meals. The woman on the right side of the picture with the corsage is the mother of the groom, and she is giving the meal instructions.

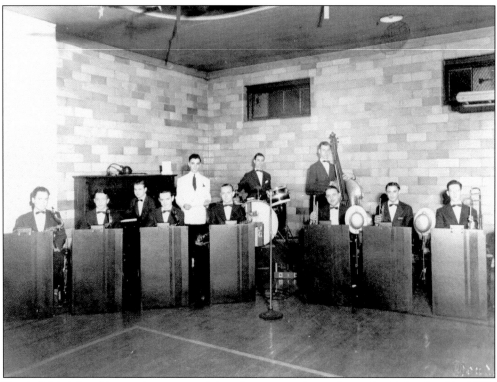

Frank Palaio's band is seen here entertaining the community at the senior high school in 1938.

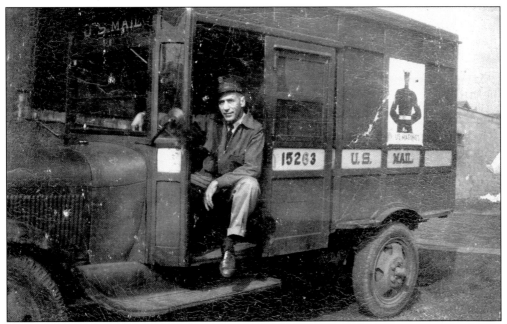

Anthony Gilberti sits and takes a break from delivering the mail in the town of Coraopolis to pose for this classic photograph in the 1930s.

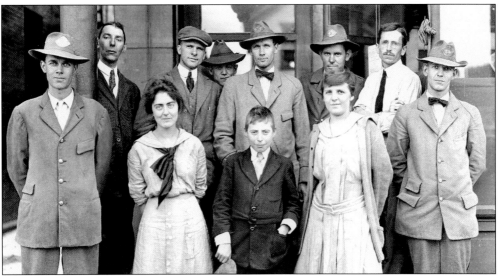

The first post office was established in 1861 under the name Vancefort. In 1907, postal workers were given a raise that took their salary from $1,200 to $2,200. This photograph is the Coraopolis Post Office force in 1917.

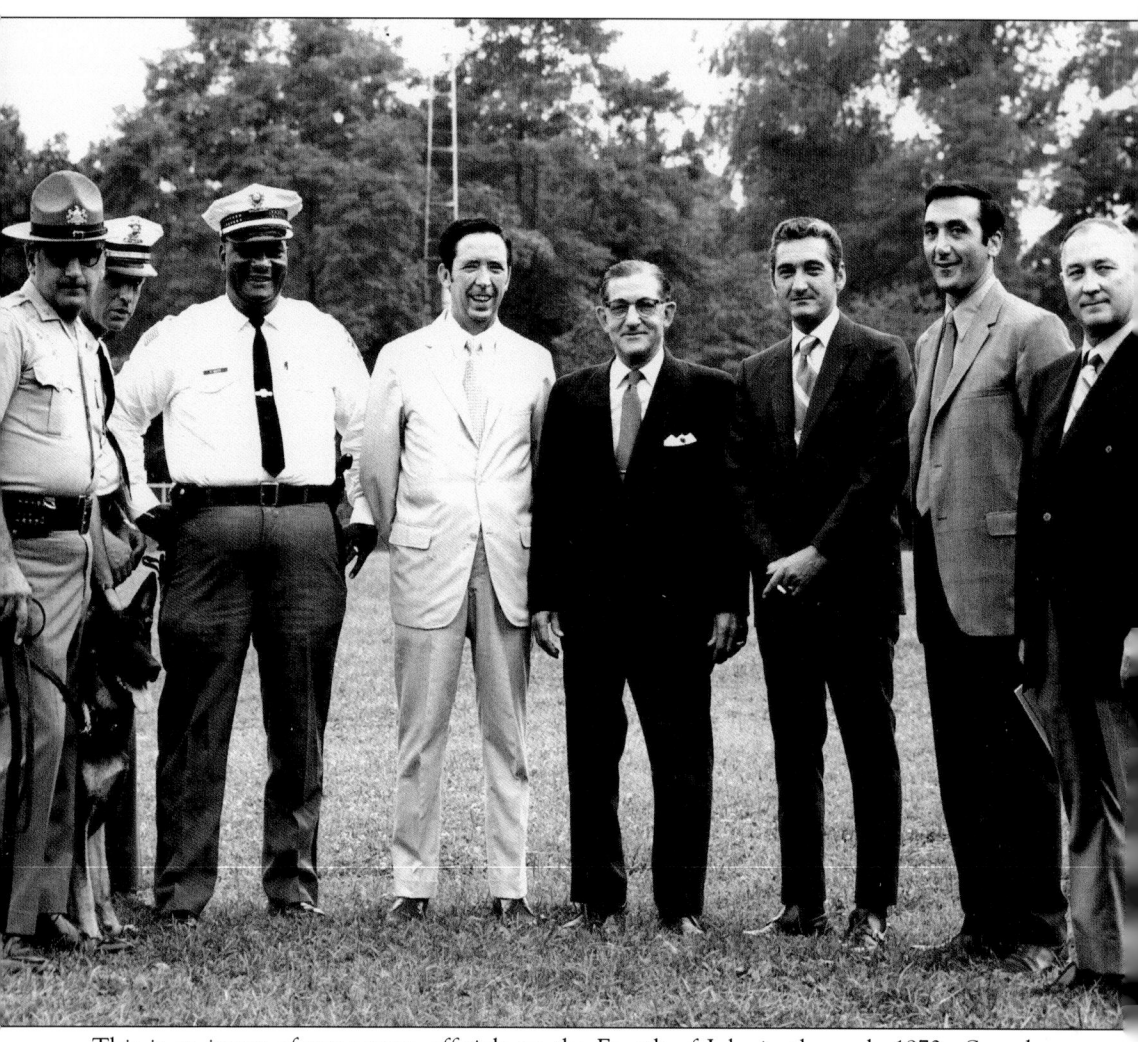

This is an image of some town officials on the Fourth of July, in the early 1970s. Seen here, from left to right, are the following: officer Lou Lucenti and Coraopolis canine police dog Prince, officer Don Fingerhut (in the back), Chief Howard White, Pennsylvania state senator Tom Lamb, Coraopolis mayor Dominic DeRusso, Second Ward councilman Fred Trello, Fourth Ward councilman Joseph DiVito, and Second Ward councilman Harold Gray.

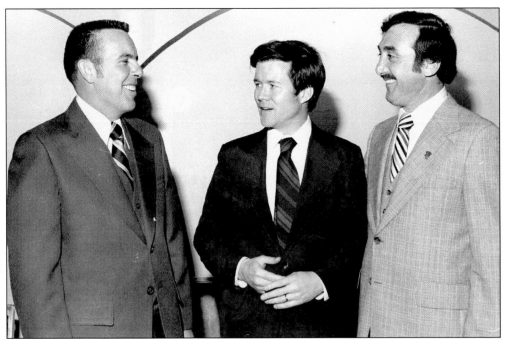

This photograph of, from left to right, Robert T. McBain (Fourth Ward councilman), Pennsylvania state congressman Doug Walgren, and Joseph DiVito (Fourth Ward councilman and president) was taken in the early 1970s while they attended a Christmas function.

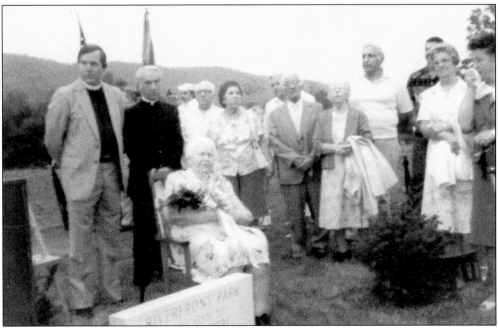

Susie Letteri was known for organizing continual spaghetti dinners to raise money for the football teams of Coraopolis. On behalf of her charity work, Riverview Park was dedicated to her, and a memorial was placed in her honor. As well as having Riverview Park dedicated to her, Cornell's school stadium is named after son Frank and is called today Letteri Stadium.

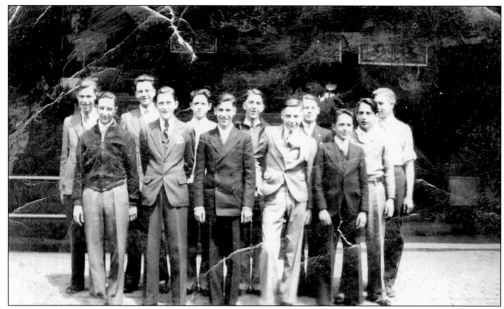

The unshakable Coraopolis newspaper gang of 1936 served the community delivering newspapers for many years.

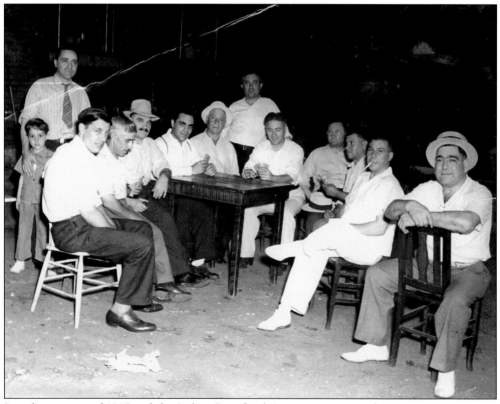

It is the summer of 1945 and the Italian Beneficial Association is seen here engaging in a very serious card game.

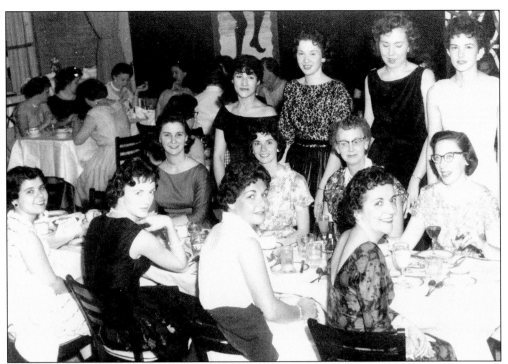

These ladies are seen gathered together looking lovely on May 28, 1959.

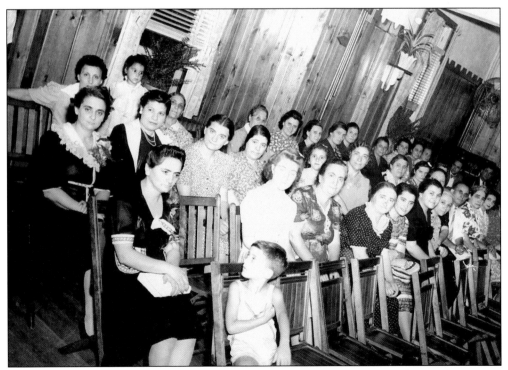

Once again, the Italian Beneficial Association is seen here, only this is ladies' night in 1946 (except for the little boy who apparently had no choice but to attend as well).

The Coraopolis Wolves Club gathers together for its yearly dinner banquet in the early 1970s. The Wolves Club has been known for its many scholarships offered to students from various schools such as Cornell, Moon, and Our Lady of Sacred Heart.

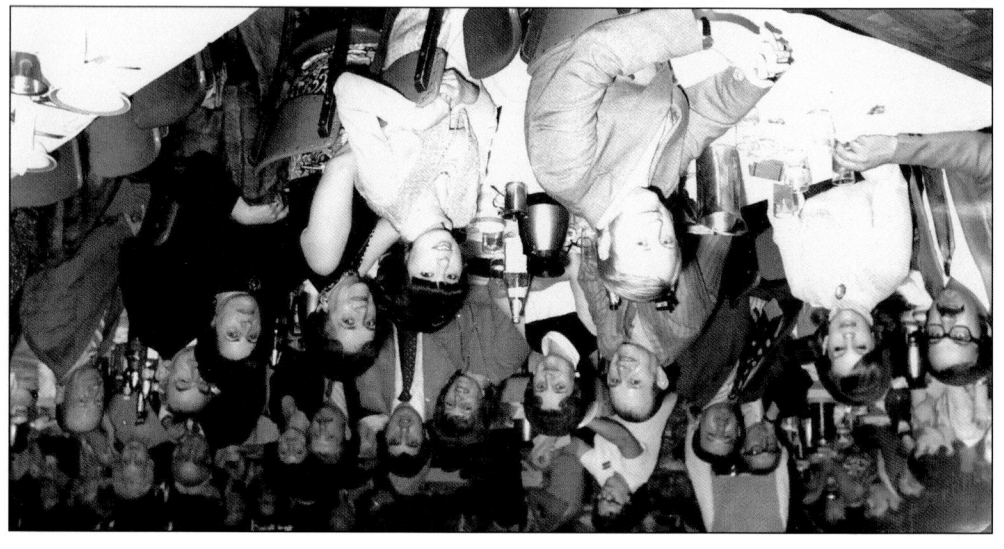

Seen in this photograph is the vibrant community of the charity-based organization known as the Lions Club. The Lions Club still meets monthly in Coraopolis today. It has raised much money for the visually impaired, as its mission and main focus is helping the blind and visually impaired. Both men and women are permitted to be members of the Lions Club, and there is even a club for children called the Leo Club. Most recently, the Lions Club has offered scholarship competitions to students, with community as its theme, as well as raising money for areas devastated by Hurricane Katrina. It is also in the process of merging with Moon Township Lions.

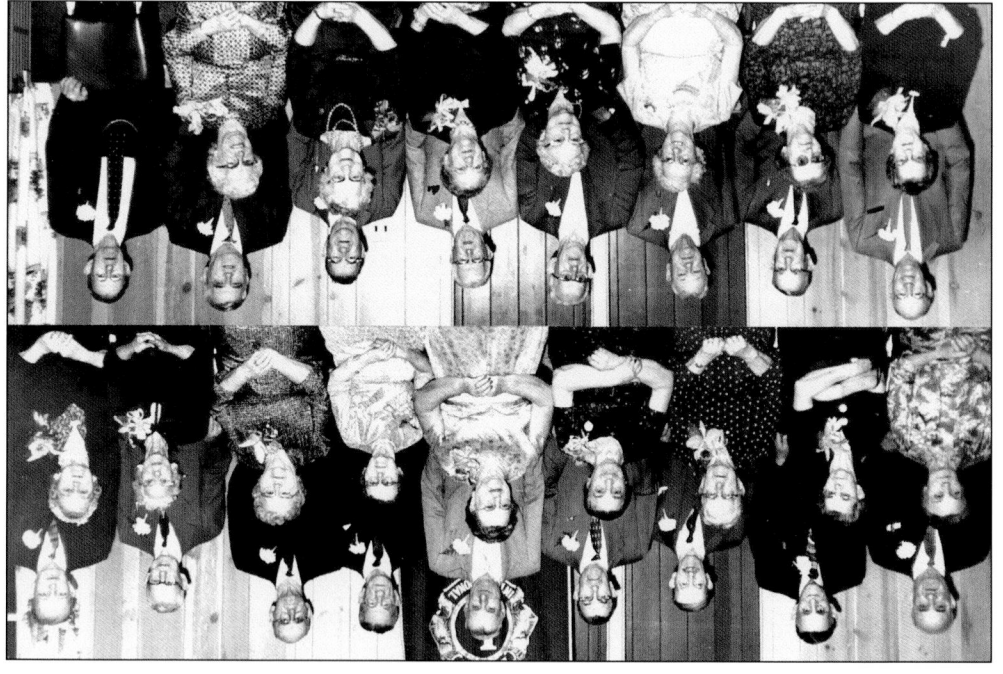

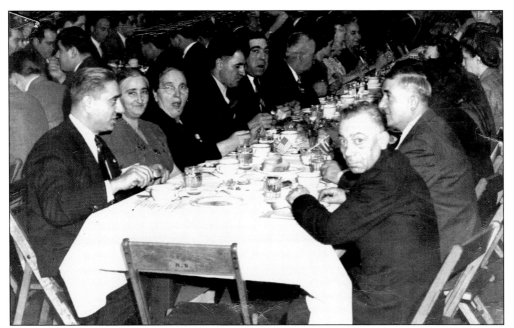

In the summer of 1946, the World War II veterans held a banquet in the St. Joseph Hall honoring their return.

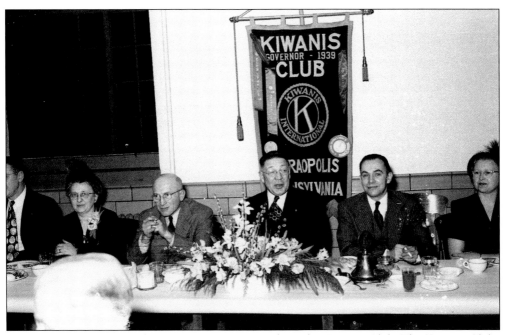

Another fine charity-based organization in Coraopolis is the Kiwanis Club. The Kiwanis Club's mission and focus is the community. Much money has been raised to benefit children, and many children's activities and sport teams have been sponsored by the Kiwanis Club. This is a photograph of a 1939 Kiwanis Club meeting. Reverend Poulson, who is pictured in this photograph, became the governor of the Kiwanis Pennsylvania District. The Kiwanis Club still holds monthly meetings today at a local area restaurant, Junior's.

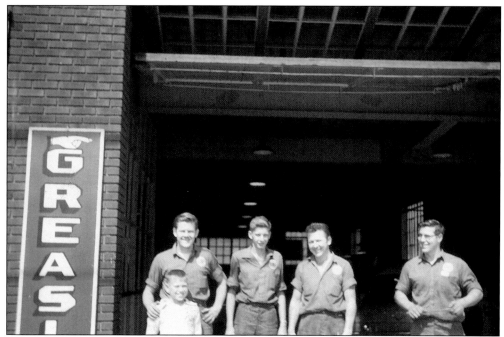

Hardworking mechanics and young Tom Myl take a break and hang around outside Pete Myl's garage.

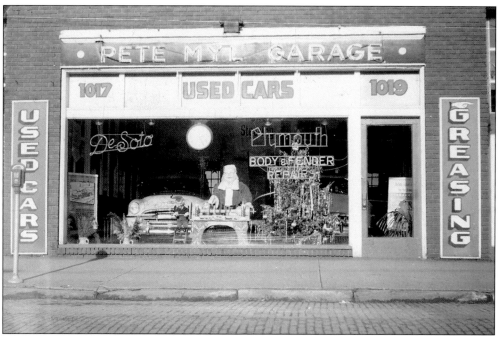

A seasonal display is placed to celebrate the Christmas season in Coraopolis. This building sits where the Cash Market stands today.

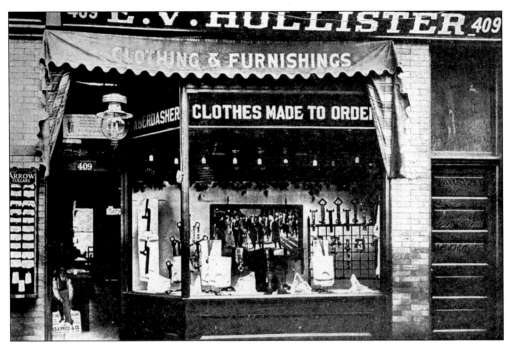

In the 1920s, the whole community of Coraopolis would go to 409 Mill Street to E. V. Hollister's to have their clothing made. Hollister's nickname was "Toppy." He was known to be a pleasant man who, in addition to making clothing, sold shirts and ties.

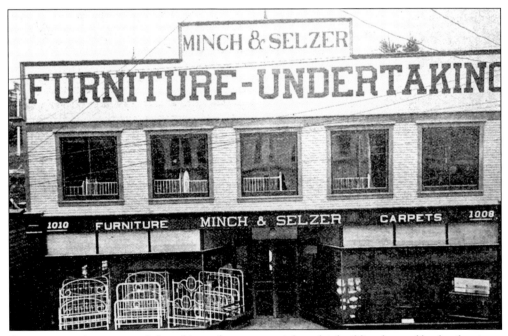

A strange combination and the subject of many town jokes, this building housed both a furniture store where beds could be purchased and an undertaking store in which coffins could be purchased. Seen here are beds in the window to the left and coffins in the window to the right.

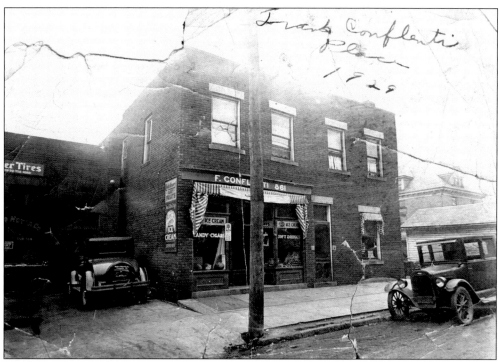

Frank Conflenti had this picture taken in 1929. He named the establishment Courtesy Bar, and it was located on 861 Fifth Avenue.

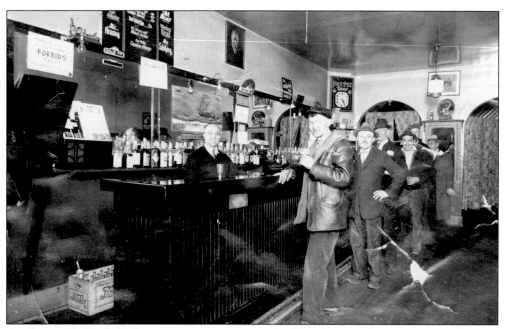

Conflenti is behind the bar serving customers in the formal attire that was commonly worn during this era. Notice the sign in the upper left corner that notes the Pennsylvania Liquor Board forbids the cashing of checks. In the far right corner of the bar observe a clock that tells the time is approximately 4:25 p.m.

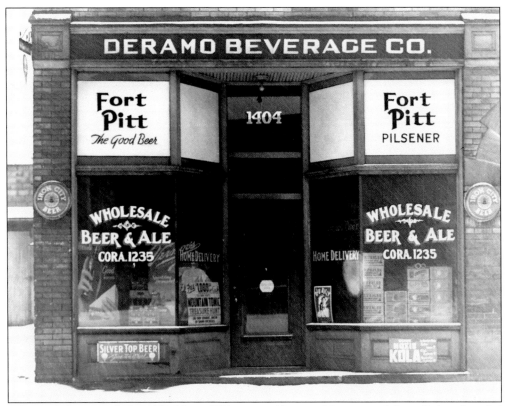

After Prohibition ended in 1933, Victor D'Eramo and his sons Vincent and, later, Robert founded Deramo Beverage Company.

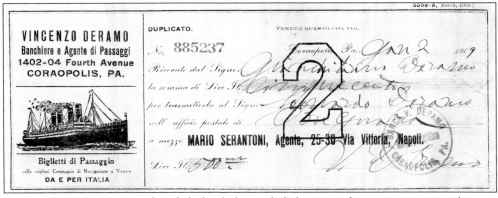

In the early 1900s, Vincenzo founded a bank that included a service for immigrants to send money back to their families in Italy. He also acted as a travel agent for people traveling from Italy.

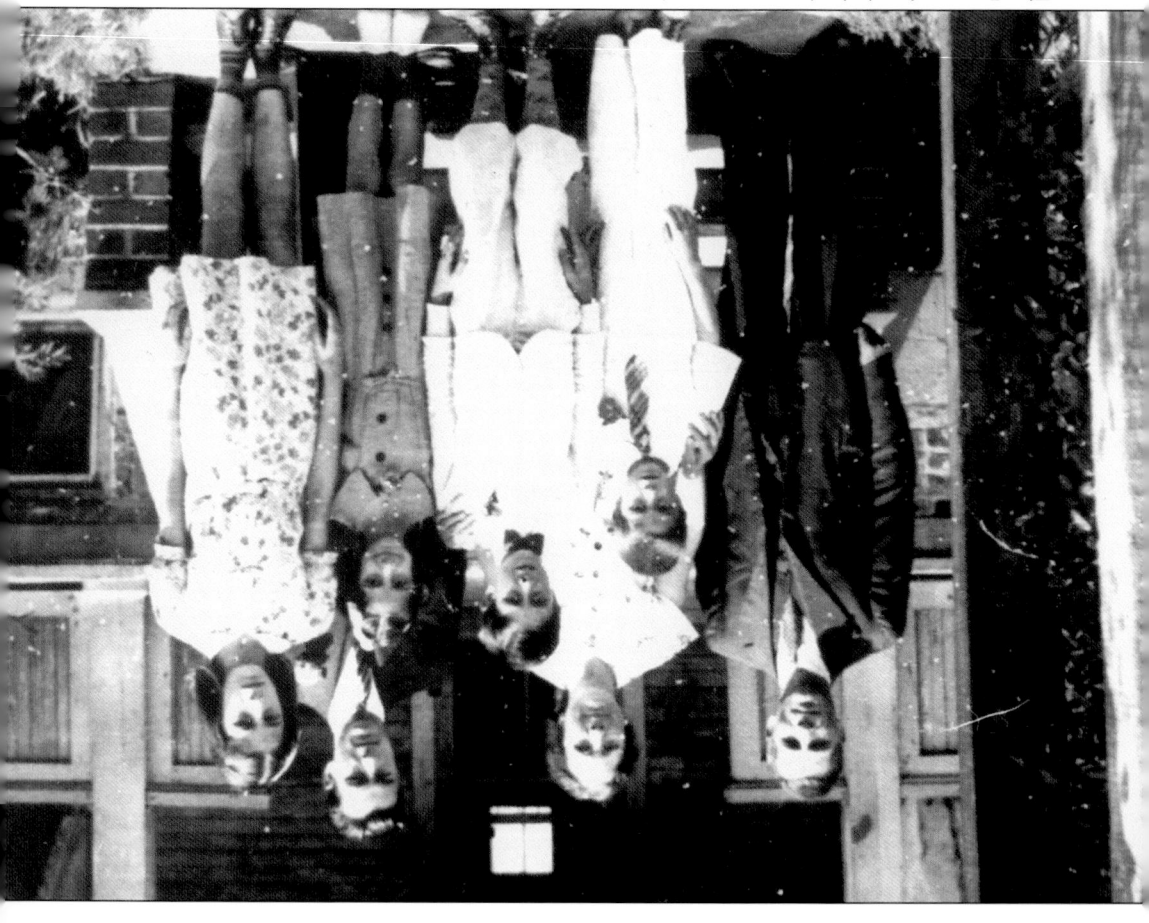

The Barone family had its picture taken on Easter Sunday 1940, a beautiful sunny spring day in Coraopolis. The family members are, from left to right, (first row) Robert, Ernest, Livia, and Carmelita; (second row) Anniable (father), Sylvia (mother), and Casper. The children are standing soldierlike because they were told to be serious since it was Easter Sunday. No fooling around was permitted on this sacred day. Despite that, however, as told by Robert Barone, he and his brother could not help but to argue over one getting to wear long pants and new tennis shoes and the other having to wear knicker pants.

Here stands the first borough building. It was erected in 1887 on State Avenue. The new borough building is now located on Fifth Avenue in the center of town.

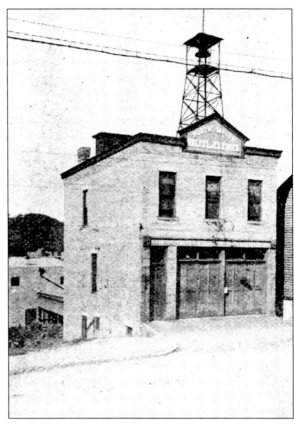

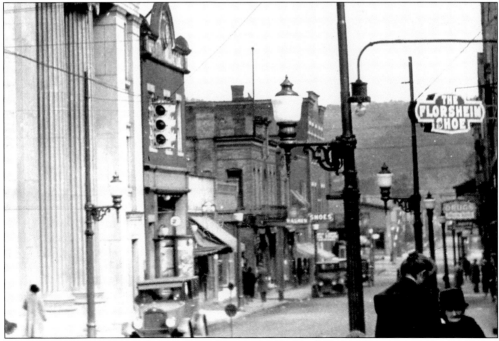

This photograph captures the Roaring Twenties in Coraopolis on Mill Street.

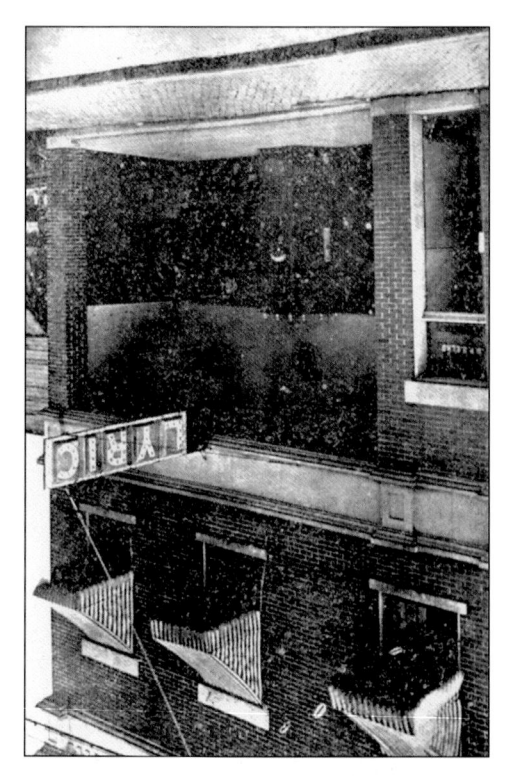

The Lyric Theater was located on Mill Street. Popular shows were serial reels such as Buck Rogers and cowboy movies. After every show, the audience would be left with a cliff-hanger to be continued the following week.

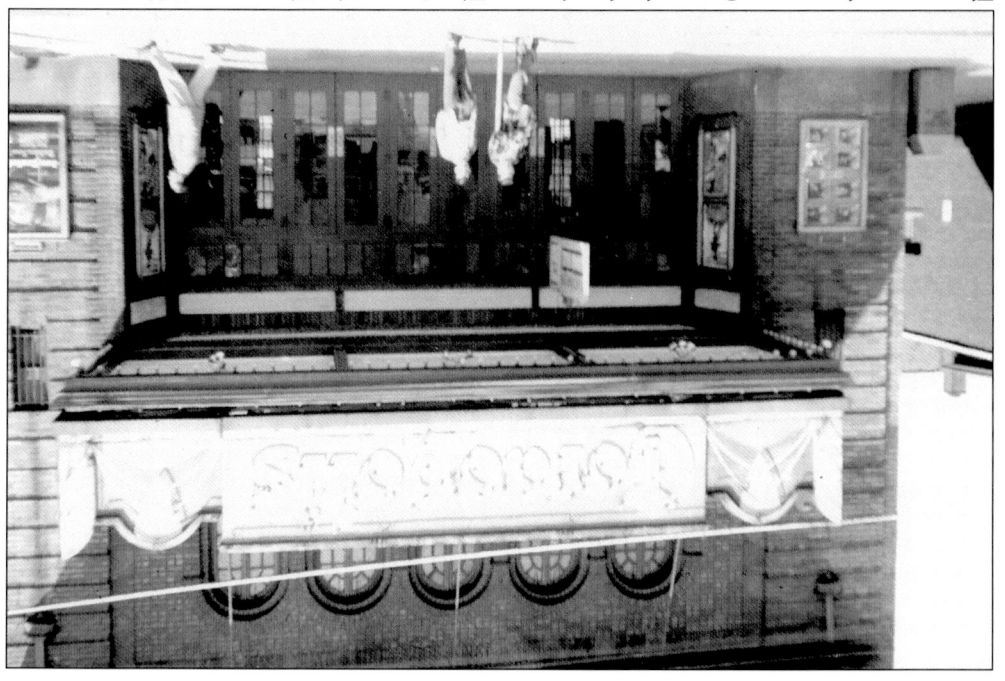

Theater was thriving in Coraopolis decades ago. The Coraopolis Theater on Fifth Avenue was known for its Tarzan and sword fighting movies. This particular theater had an alleyway next to it that made it accessible for youngsters to sneak inside through the back. Today in its place stands the beautiful town gazebo and clock.

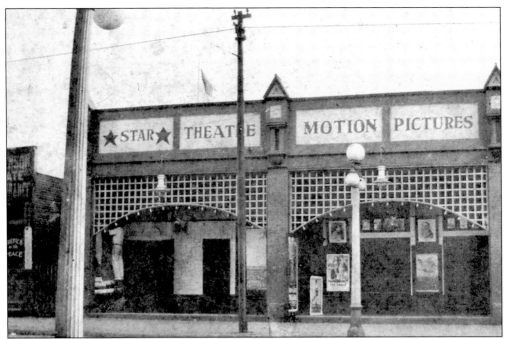

Most of the motion pictures played at the Star Theatre were silent films. The Star Theatre was known as the Mirage Theater until its named was changed in 1910. During the silent films, a piano player would be inside playing music to enhance the suspense of the movie.

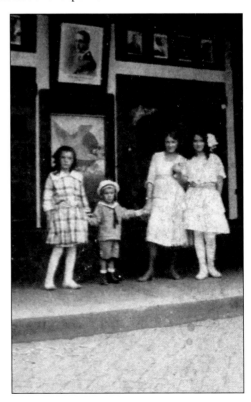

An unknown family is seen here leaving the Star Theatre after the show.

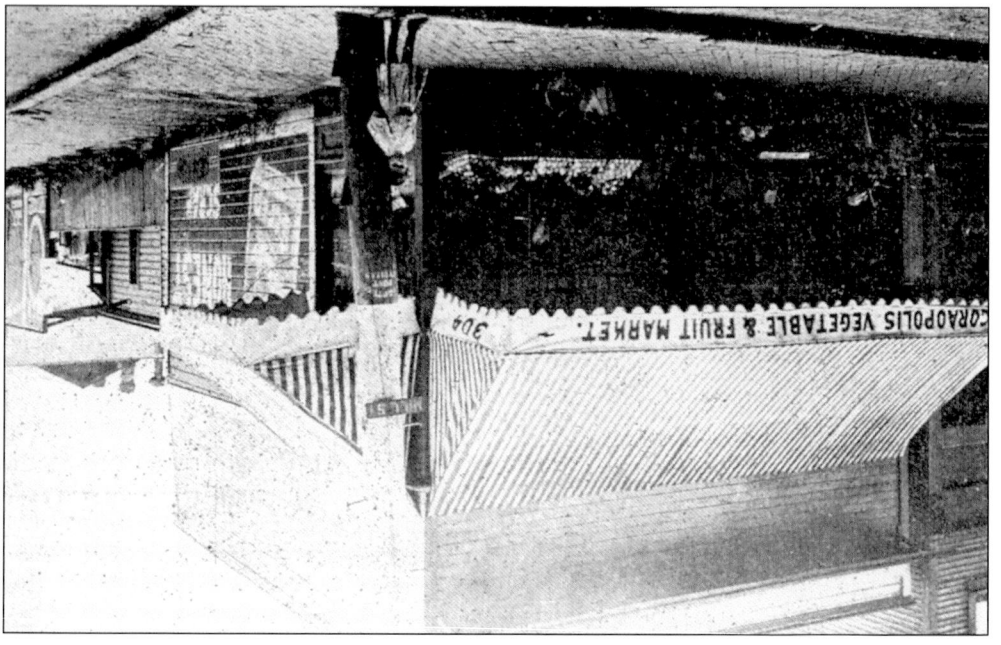

A small child stands by the Coraopolis vegetable and fruit market in the 1930s. On the pole the child is leaning against, the sign Mill Street is visible.

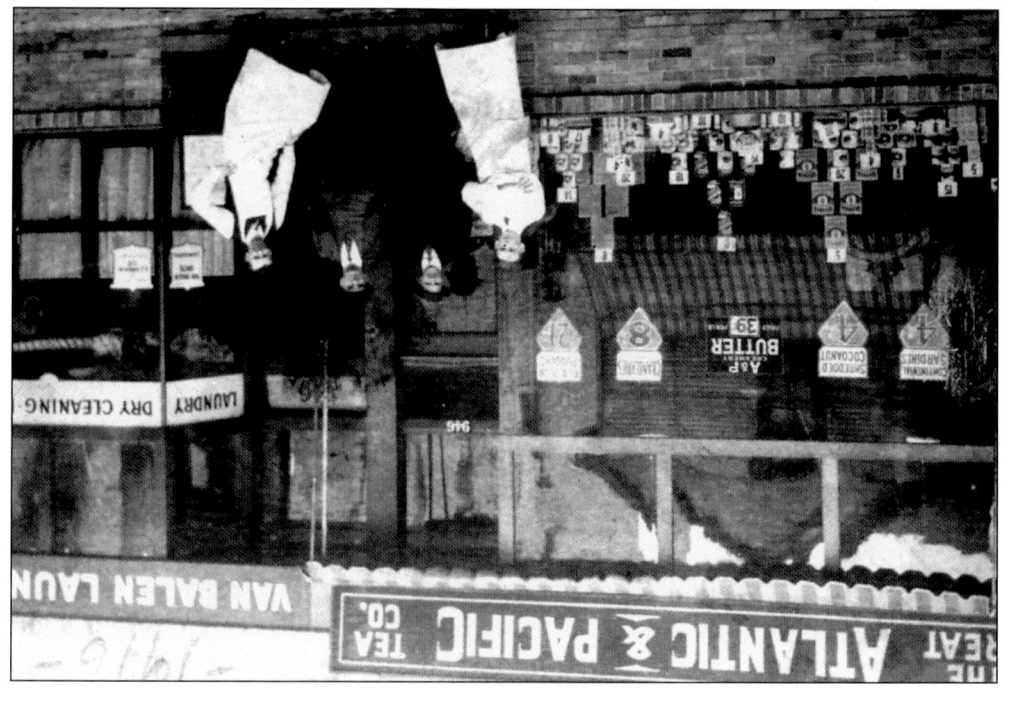

The general stores of Coraopolis were filled with all kinds of goods for people to buy. These gentlemen posed for this picture in 1927.

Automobiles were loaded up by local farmers and taken to the street corner to be sold to the community. The building in the background marks the area where the original St. Joseph Church would have stood.

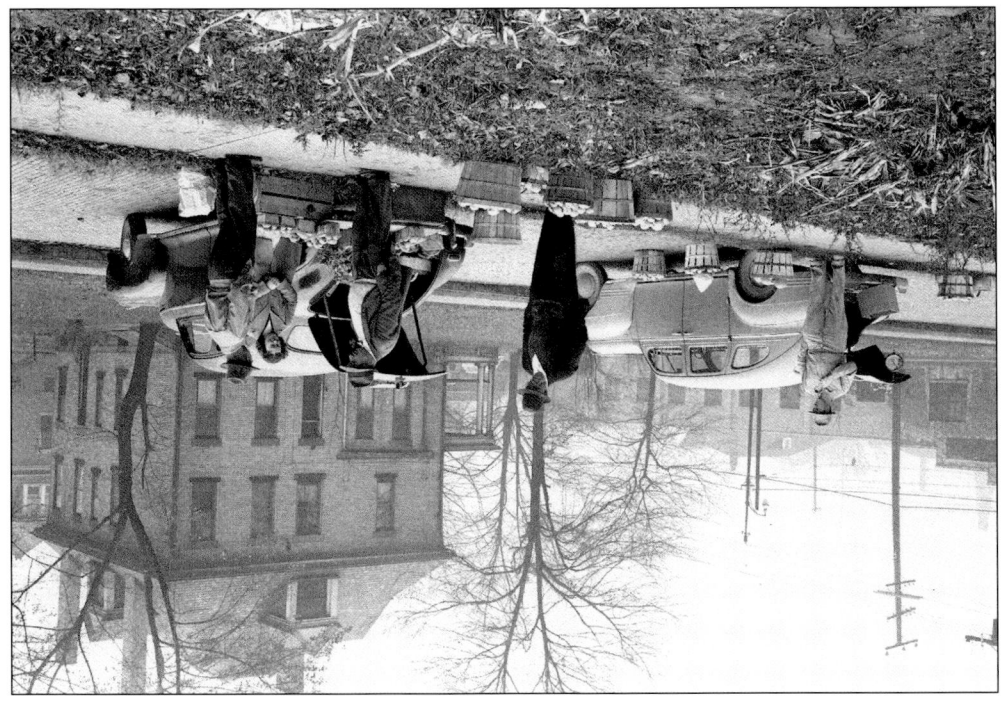

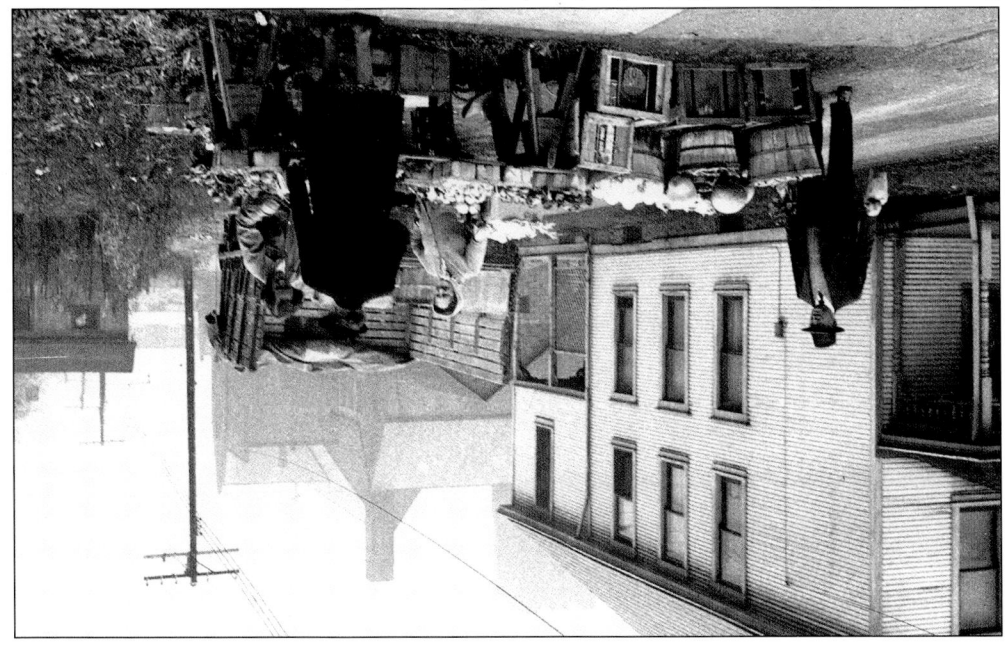

Fruit and vegetables were sold abundantly by local farmers in the area.

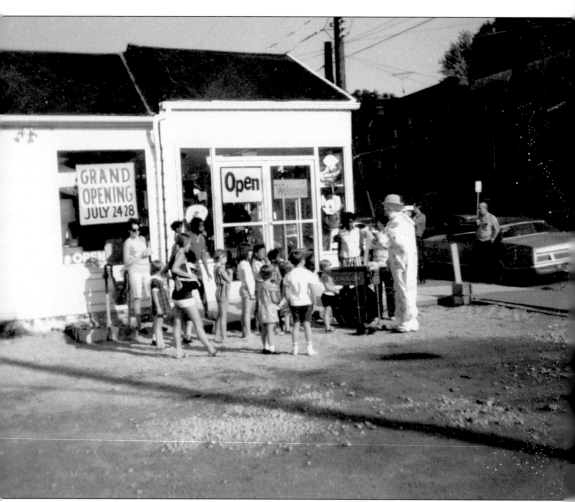

The grand opening of the Coraopolis Dairy Queen on Fifth Avenue was in July 1973. Proud owners Ed and Ann Dorsky arranged games, activities, drawings, and all sorts of fun for the celebration. This grand opening not only brought joy and entertainment to the community but was a day that gave the children of the community a chance to be highlighted as well.

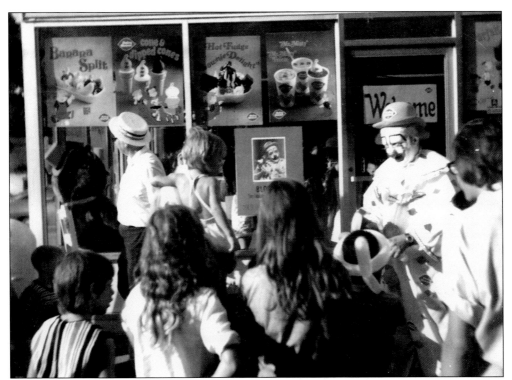

Ed Dorsky is seen here, in the white shirt and hat, overseeing the crowd as Blossom the clown entertains the children of Coraopolis.

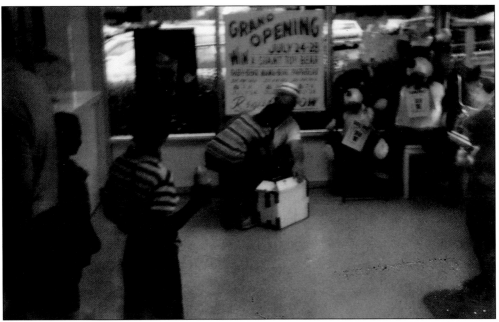

Inside the Dairy Queen, drawings for prizes were held. Children eagerly reached into the box to win the grand prize of a giant toy bear. The Dairy Queen on Fifth Avenue quickly became one of the town's favorite spots.

Isaly's was no doubt another one of the town's favorite spots. Children would frequently buy candy here to take into the Lyric Theater across the street. Isaly's was also well known for its ice cream, chipped ham, giant pickles, taffy, and chewing gum.

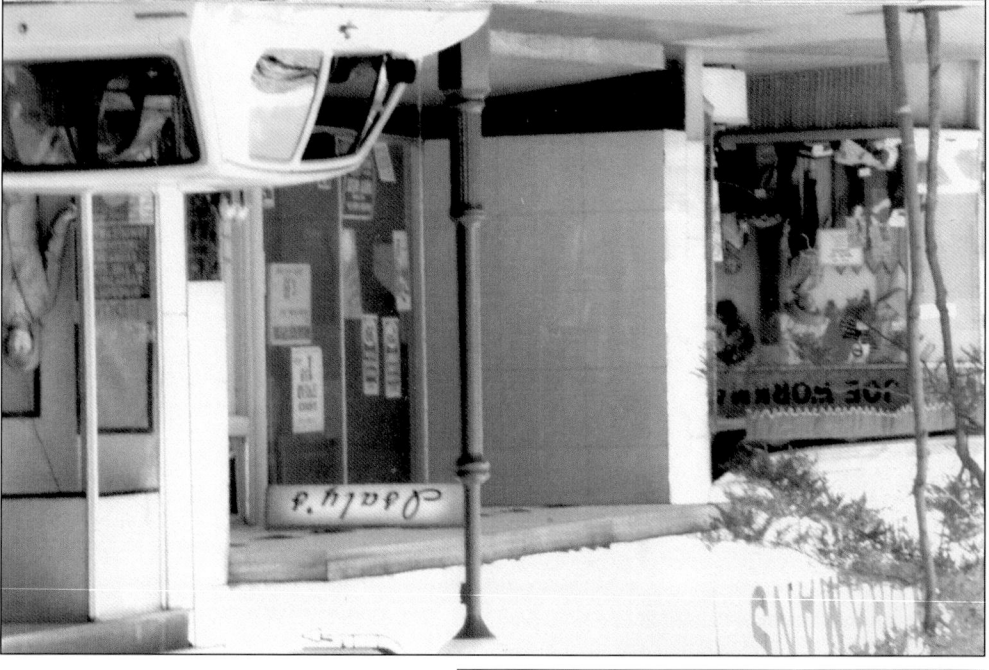

In 1975, McKinley Elementary School participated in a Thanksgiving Day dress up. These delightful children are dressed as pilgrims celebrating America's heritage. From the bottom left and clockwise the children are Richard Betsch, Karen Hessert, Mark Yocum, Erin Walsh, Glenn Potts, Michelle Landa, Andrew Stahl, Daniel Soza, Dorothy Steffler, Gerri Volchko, Alan Spriggs, Patrick Hobbs, and Jamie Dorn. Teacher Judith Sike is standing in the background.

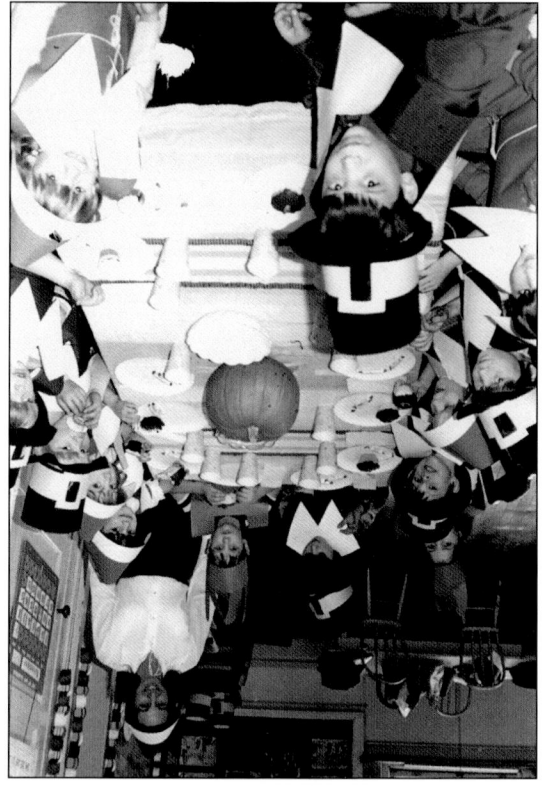

The direction of Fifth Avenue used to run both north and south, as seen here in this 1940s photograph. This rare picture captures the cars facing north on Fifth Avenue heading toward the Sewickley bridge. The Atlantic station no longer stands, and the brick building across from it is currently the VFW building.

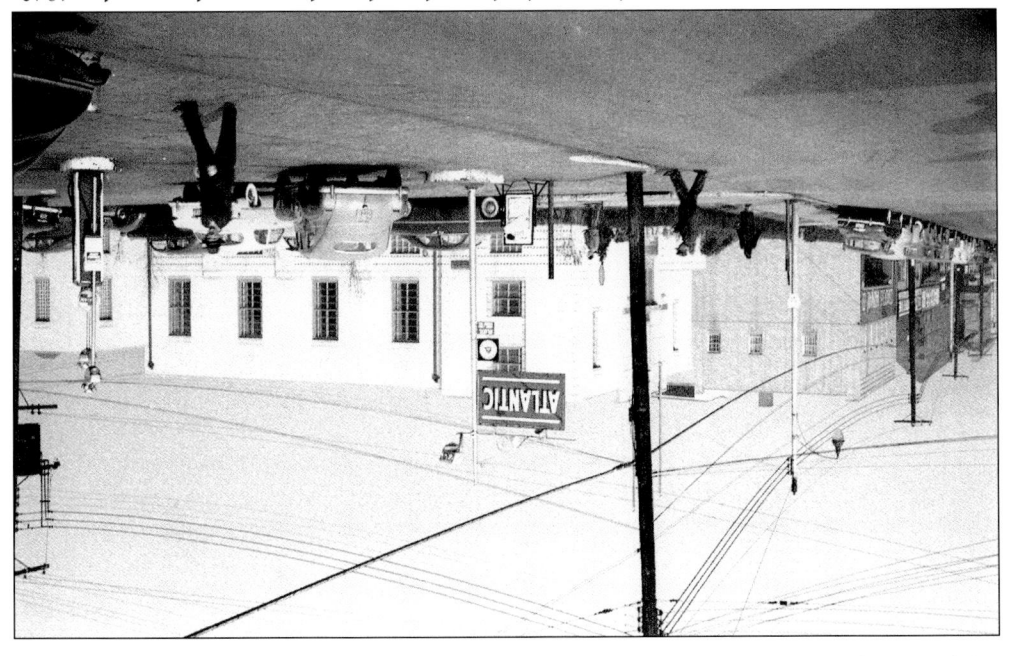

The ground was broken and the cornerstone for the YMCA was laid on April 26, 1910. The building was completed in 1911, and the total cost was $70,000. Quickly becoming a spot for enjoyment, by January 1913, this YMCA had 571 members.

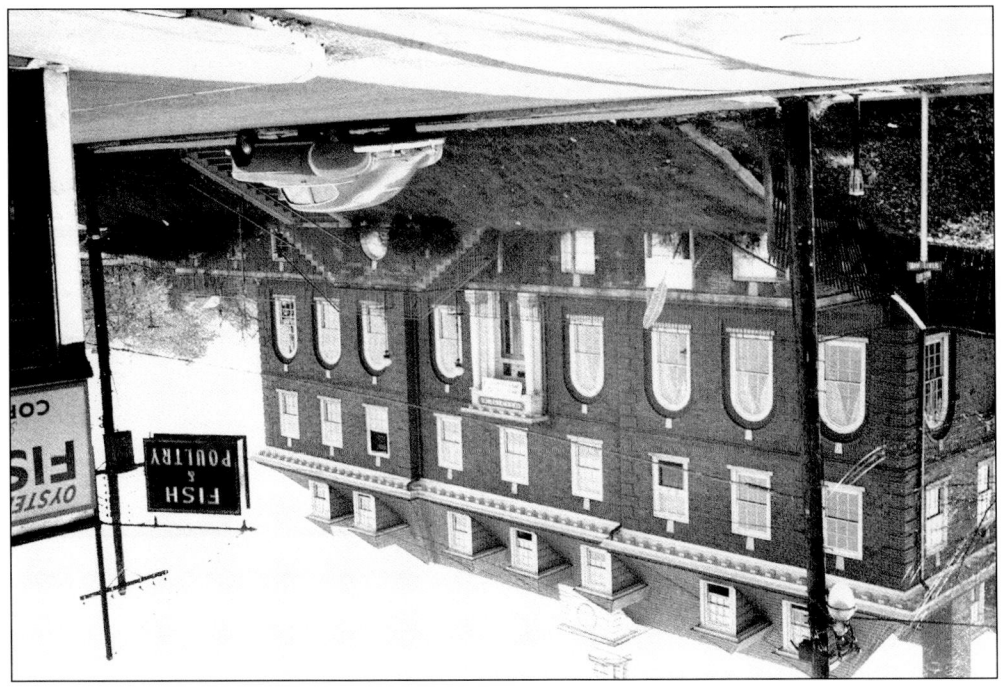

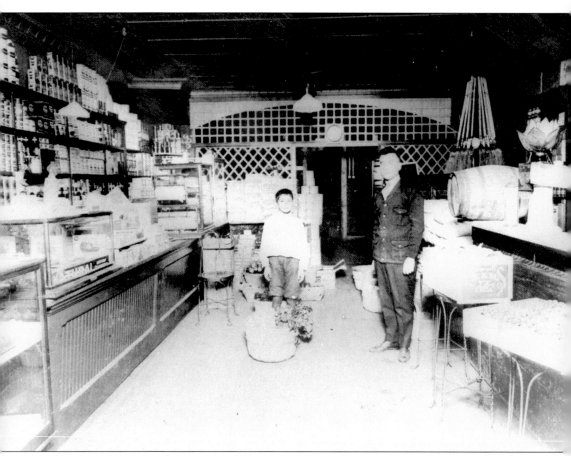

This is a rare picture of the inside of a local general merchant store owned by the Palaio family in 1933. Seen here is the classic layout of the local store and how it operated during that era.

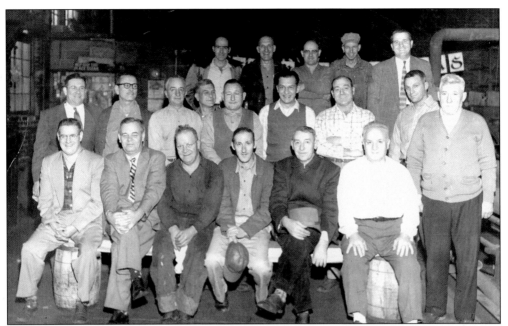

Here is a 1950s photograph of the Montour Railroad workers' Christmas party. These workers held very diverse and challenging jobs. A lot of these gentlemen had jobs such as blacksmiths, laborers, air brakemen, foremen, boilermakers and boilermaker helpers, machinists, pipe fitters, hostlers, general foremen, and master mechanics.

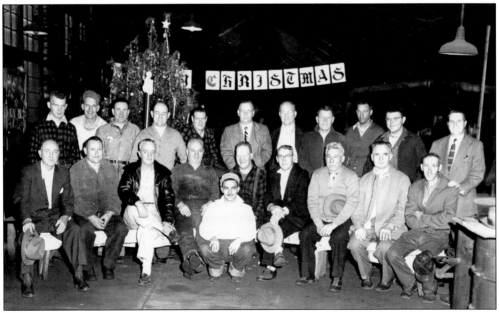

Again, these railroad workers engage in a Montour Railroad Christmas party, also in the 1950s. Among those pictured are Jim Kelly, Marion DiVito, Hugo DiMasso, Marco DiCicco, Tony Googlemier, Ed Wittman, Cesidio DiVito, Tofi Witowitz, Charlie Dawson, Larry Hallstrad, George Gebharf, Howard Harper, Bernie Miller, Ernie Ward, Joe Kelly, Evert McClurg, Chick Lanigan, Frances Malarkey, Vince Shulin, Freddie Rauschart, and one unidentified employee.

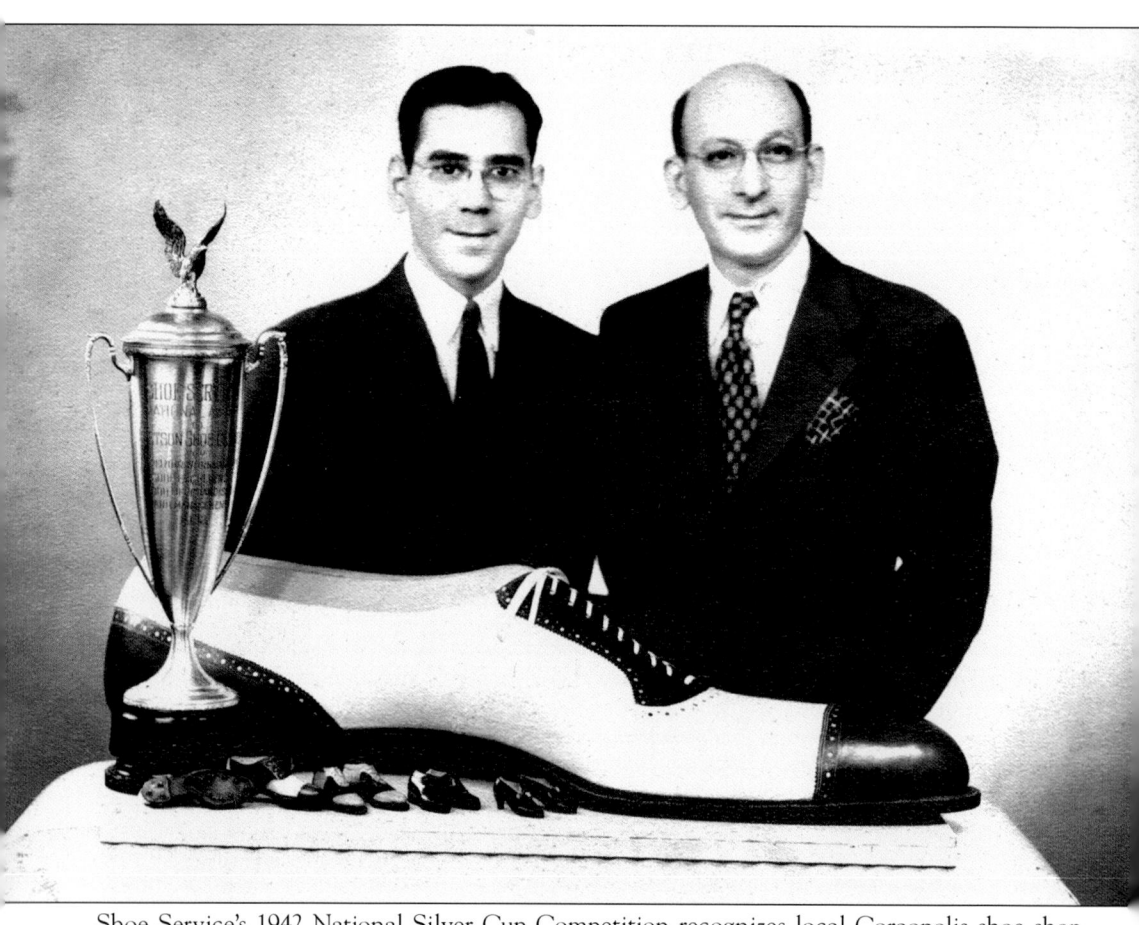

Shoe Service's 1942 National Silver Cup Competition recognizes local Coraopolis shoe shop owners the Gilberti brothers as the winners of the grand National Silver Cup for superior workmanship, shop excellence, good merchandising, and good management. These gentlemen were distinguished among 70,000 shoe shops in the United States.

Four

CLASSIC SPORTS

The town of Coraopolis is not shy of engaging in sporting events. The community has supported many sporting events of all kinds. The town has seen football teams, baseball teams, Little Leagues, and many other sporting events and teams. Many were sponsored by local social and charity clubs. The field where most of these games were played was known as Ewing Field and was dedicated back in 1935. Most recently, in 1999, the field's name was changed to Ronald Bliwas Field. Bliwas grew up in Coraopolis and moved to Chicago as an advertiser after graduating from college. Once there he did some work for a man named Arthur Frito and they became friends. Bliwas would continually tell story after story to his friend about his beloved treasure town, Coraopolis. Frito recognized Bliwas as being a good man and wanted to do something for his cherished town. Frito contacted the town's mayor and paid a visit to Coraopolis. It was during that visit he decided to pioneer a renovation project for Ewing Field and rename it Ronald Bliwas Field. In 1999, the project was completed and Frito flew Bliwas on a private airplane to Coraopolis without him knowing anything about the project. Once in Coraopolis, Frito took Bliwas to show him the field. Approaching the field, a train went by as if on cue. Once past, the string was pulled and in front of Bliwas was the completely renovated field with its new name.

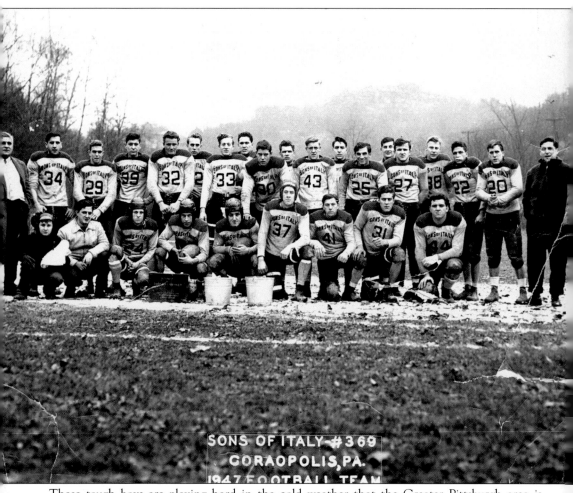

These tough boys are playing hard in the cold weather that the Greater Pittsburgh area is known for in the late fall. Featured in this photograph are the Sons of Italy No. 369 Coraopolis 1947 football team.

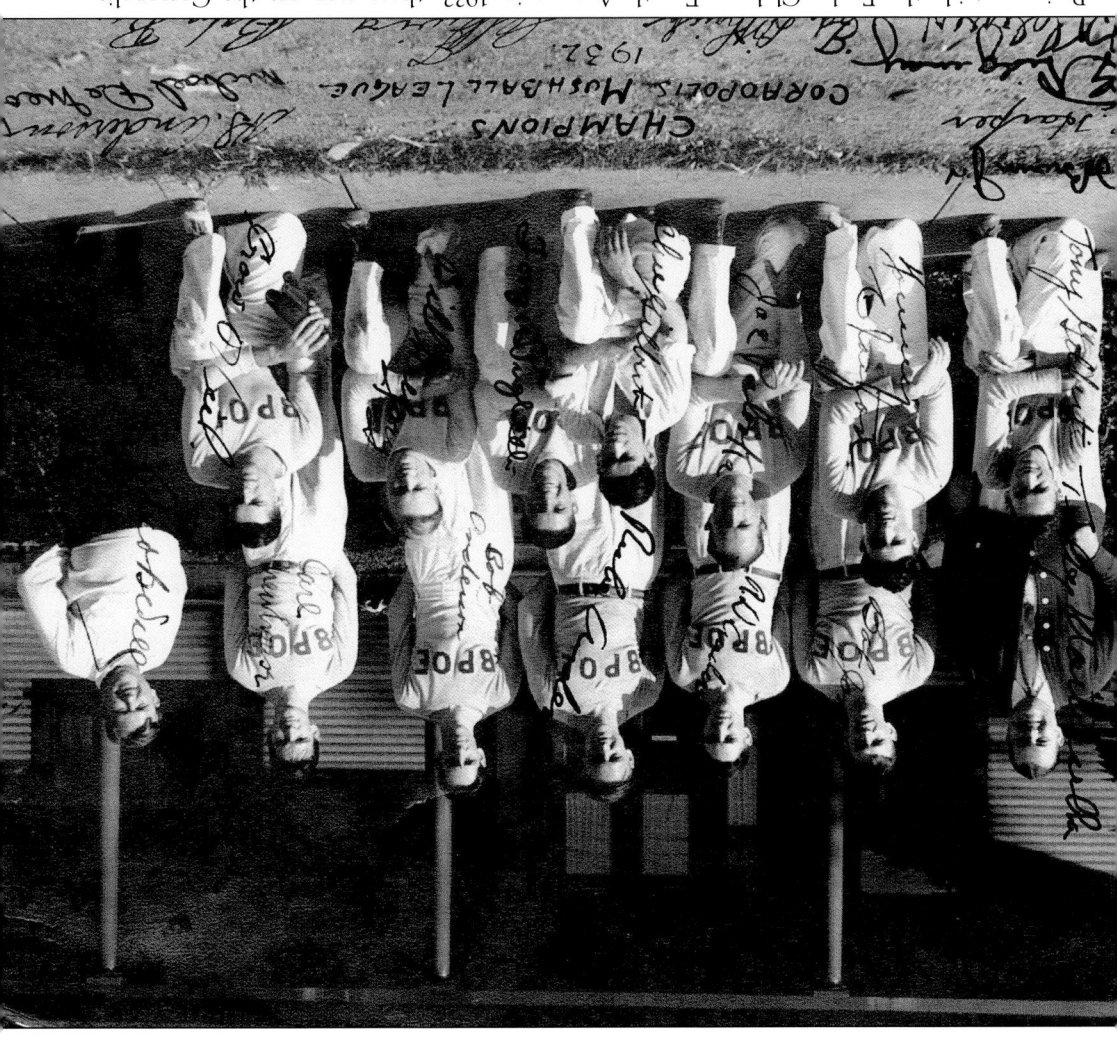

Posing outside the Eagles Club on Fourth Avenue in 1932, these men are the Coraopolis Mushball League champions. The sportsmen photographed here are, from left to right, (first row) Tony Gilberti, K. Claitton, Joe Palooka, Frank Gilberti, Fonzi Puglielli, Bill Gregory, and Crow O'Neil; (second row) Tubby Martinella, Bob Jones, R. D. Anderson, Rube Anderson, Bob Anderson, Carl Newhouse, and Ted Besall.

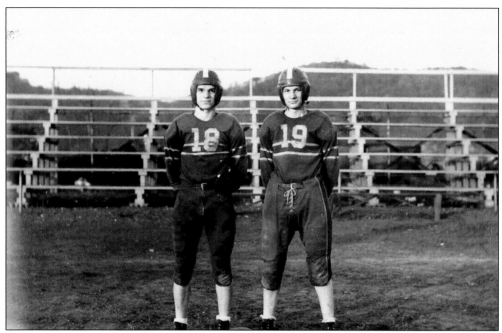

Photographed in their football uniforms in 1946 are Russell (left) and Pat Musta at Coraopolis Senior High School Ewing Field.

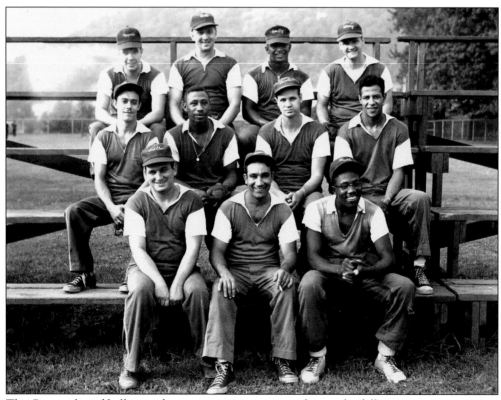

The Coraopolis softball team demonstrates its sportsmanship to the fullest.

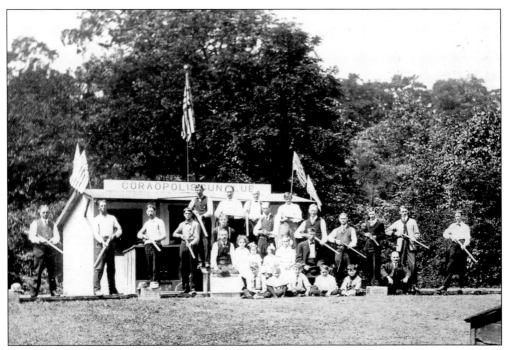

Featured in this photograph is the Coraopolis Gun Club. The club was located off Devonshire Road on the wooded hills of Coraopolis. The area has since been developed as a home site.

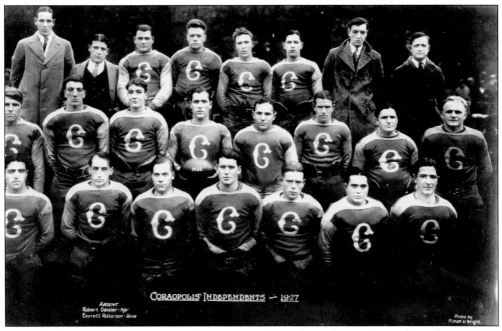

CORAOPOLIS INDEPENDENTS ~ 1927

ABSENT
Robert Geisler - Mgr.
Everett Patterson - Back

Photo by
Hanon & Wright

Seen here is a classic photograph of the Coraopolis Independents. The Independents were a football team, and this team photograph was taken in 1927.

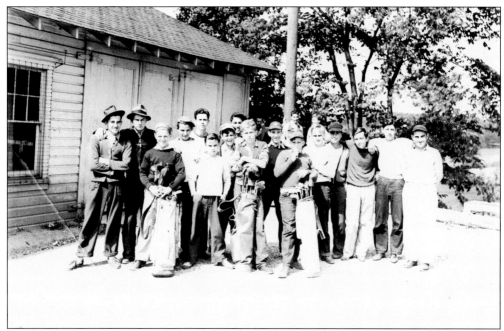

These Coraopolis boys are earning extra money as caddies for the golfers of the Montour Country Club. This photograph of aspiring golfers was taken on September 20, 1940.

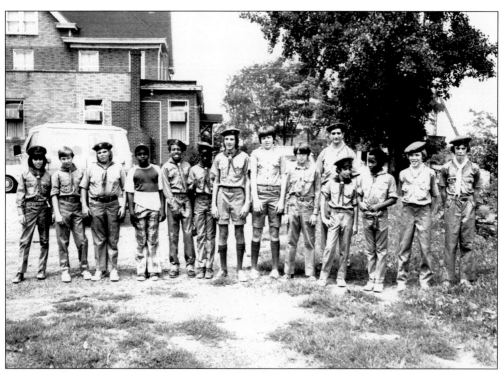

The true adventurers and sportsmen can be found in these Boy Scouts. On July 28, 1974, these young sportsmen of Boy Scout Troop 308 are preparing to go on a camping trip and venture into the wilderness.

Celebrating its 75th anniversary, the *Coraopolis Record* put out a special edition. History would not be complete if it had not been for this local newspaper reporting all the facts and details of everyday life in the town of Coraopolis. As well as being fine reporters, the staff members have made themselves excellent historians and storytellers of the town.

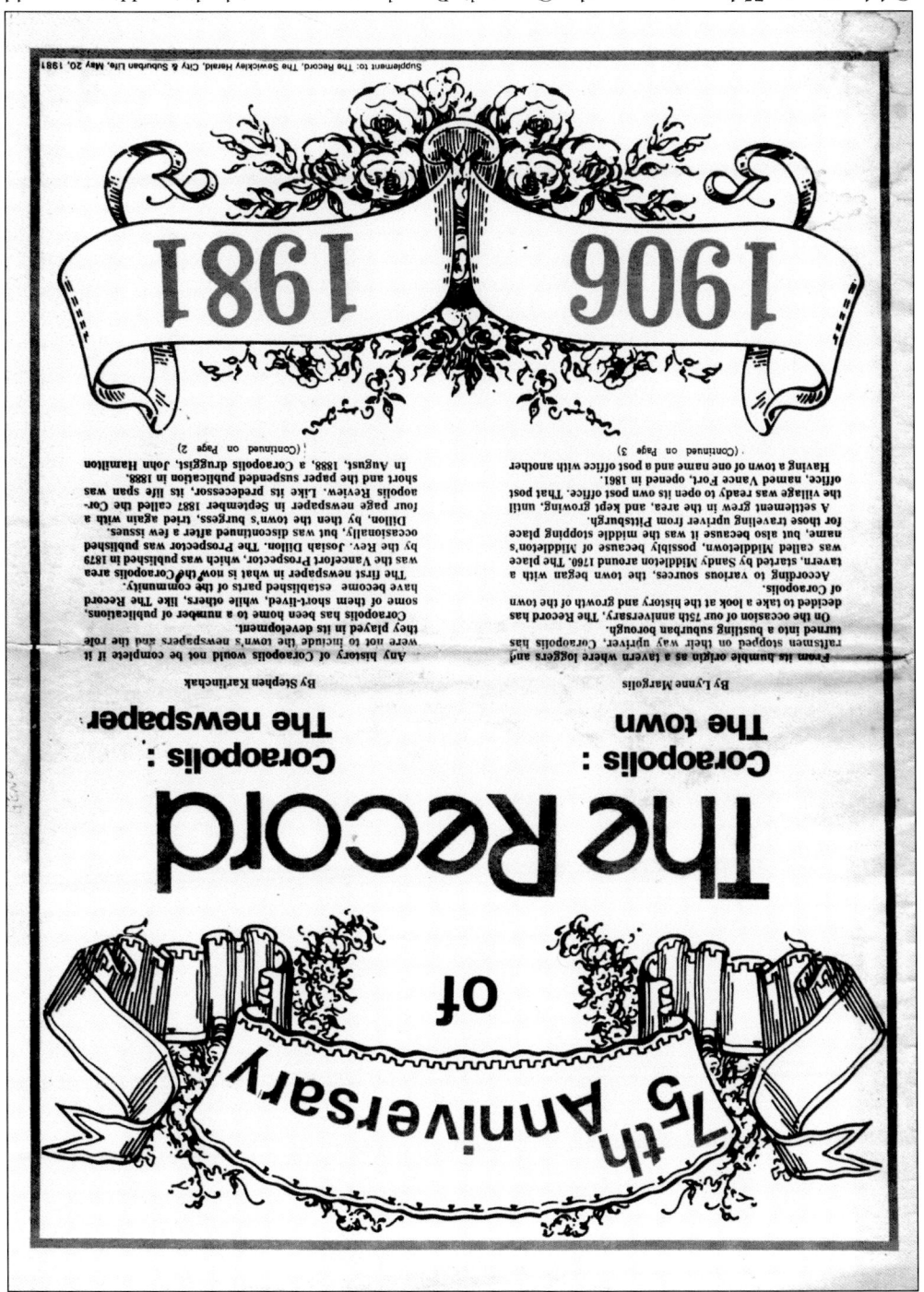

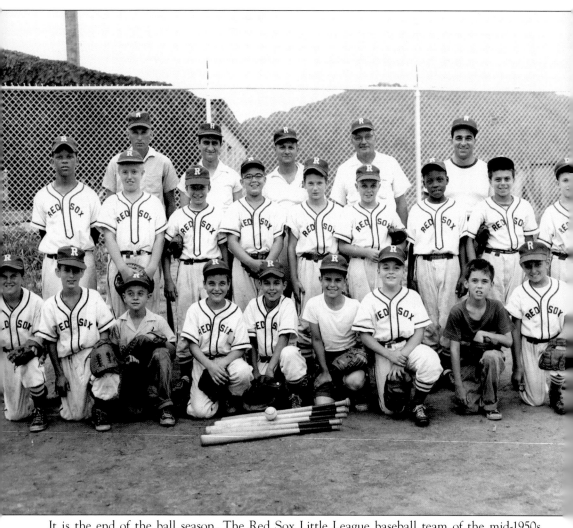

It is the end of the ball season. The Red Sox Little League baseball team of the mid-1950s has been sponsored by the Kiwanis Club and gathered together for a team photograph by Hendel Studio. The team is at Ewing Field, which has since been renovated and renamed the Ronald Bliwas Field.

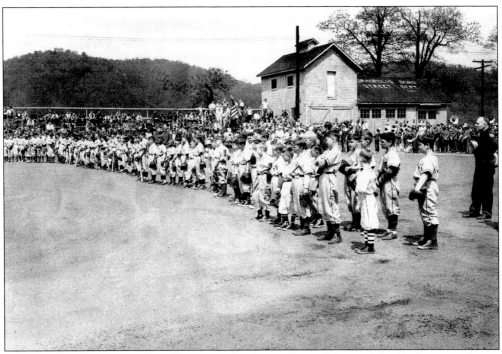

The Little Leaguers are singing the national anthem. The Red Sox and the Yankees are playing against each other, around the late 1940s.

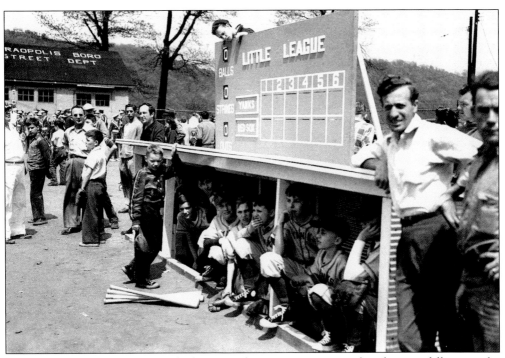

The Little League players and their coaches are sitting in the dugout, following the game in anticipation.

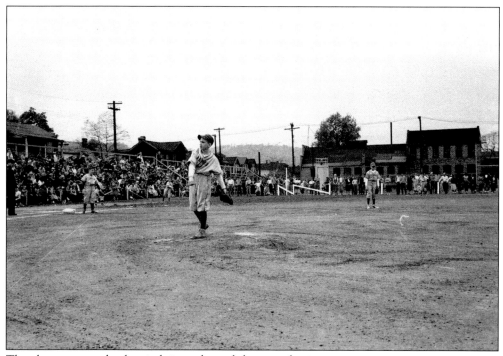

The players are ready, the pitch is made, and the game begins.

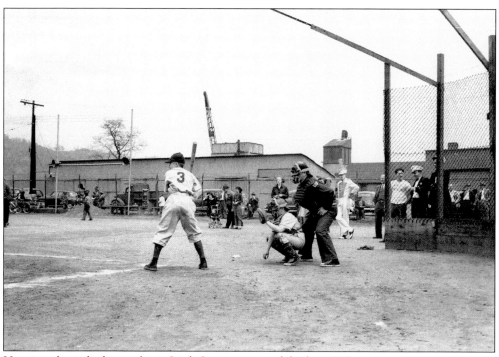

Here is a classic look at a classic Little League game of the late 1940s.

Five

READING, WRITING, AND ARITHMETIC

Coraopolis has always prided itself with being able to offer its children optimum education. As Coraopolis began to settle as a community in the early 1800s, education was primarily given at home. Around the year 1840, Coraopolis, not yet named but known as Middletown, had grown in population. Thus the first brick school was built and stood on what is now Fifth Avenue. The building was relocated due to the building of public roads and boundary lines. It served as a schoolhouse until Middletown outgrew it in the early 1870s. Shortly after becoming a borough and taking the name Coraopolis, the Coraopolis School District began to organize its first school board directors. In 1904, Pennsylvania legislation required a student to study and complete four years of schooling in order to obtain a high school diploma. Education began to boom, and many families began seeking education for their children beyond eighth grade. Because of the demand, the school board approved the building of a separate high school that would be located on State Avenue. Religious education has been widely sought and available in the town of Coraopolis as well.

In 1972, the Coraopolis and Neville Island school districts merged into one new school system. This school system combined all grades from kindergarten to 12th grade into a new and beautiful complex. The name Cornell is a combination of Coraopolis and Neville Island. Cornell believes all students should be treated fairly and with respect. It has become a fine district with superior educators and among local school districts is held in high esteem.

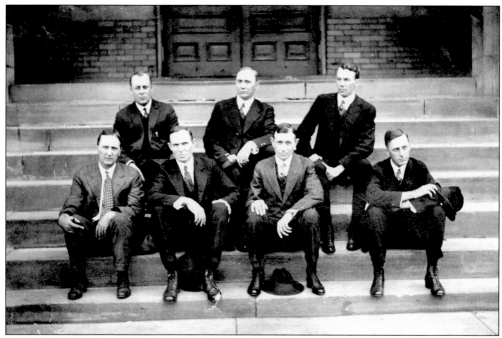

This is a classic photograph of the school directors of long ago. Seen here are, from left to right, (first row) directors J. M. Smith, C. E. Stone, C. A. Young, and C. C. Clark; (second row) principal J. C. Werner, president J. E. Haynes, and superintendent C. E. Hilborn.

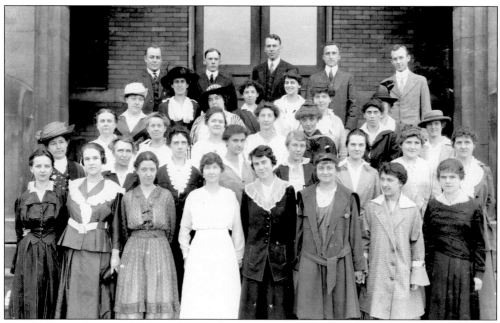

Seen here is a photograph of the Coraopolis public school teachers in 1916.

This is an original copy of the commencement exercises of Coraopolis Senior High School from May 26, 1903.

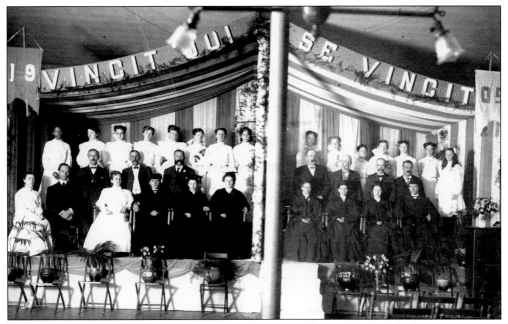

Courtesy — Mrs. Burim Troutman
Box 87 — Centra

Commencement Exercises

OF THE

Coraopolis High School,

Bank Hall, Coraopolis, Pa.

Tuesday Evening May 26th, 1903.

PROCESSIONAL MARCH..
"Swing Song,"...Lohr.
　　　　　　　　Pupils of School.
Invocation,..Rev. Jessie L. Cotton.
"Summer Days,"...Abt.
　　　　　　　　Pupils of School.
Buried Treasures,..Mary Byers.
A Retrospect..Bertha Magnus.
"O Pretty Red-Lipped Daisy,".................................Wekerlin.
　　　　　　　　Pupils of School.
How Nations Grow and Decay,......................Alice Phillips.
Evangeline,...Belle Buzza.
Sleep, Sleep, My Little Baby, Sleep,...........................Geible.
　　　　　　　　Prof. Richard Griffith.
Myths,...Jessie Harper.
No Discharge in this War,.................................Ethel Heber.
"Hunter's Song,"..Kinross.
"The Monk's Magnificat,"..................Claribel Shryock.
"The Signs of the Times,"....................Joy A. Goff.
"The Holy City," (Cornet Solo)...........................Adams.
　　　　　　　　Oscar McCormick.
Address to the Class,....................Rev. J. D. Moffat, D.D., L.L.D.
"Ring On, Ye Bells,"..Abt.
　　　　　　　　Pupils of School.
Presentation of Diplomas,...........................T. F. Watson.
Flower Girls..
"The Lost Chord,"..Sullivan.
　　　　　　　　Pupils of School.
Benediction,................................Rev. W. E. E. Barcus.

The Floral Decorations by Mrs. E. J. Ruth, Mill Street, and the Electric
Display by Mr. John Weible, Mill Street.

The class of 1905 is celebrating graduation on the second floor of the bank hall.

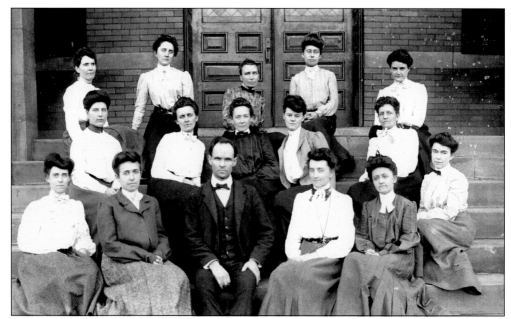

The principal is seen here having his picture taken with the Coraopolis schoolteachers in 1905. The building behind them is Central School, which was built in 1897.

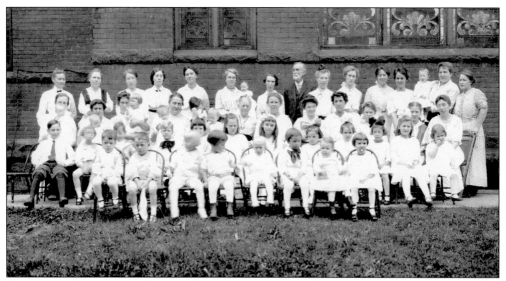

Captured in this photograph is a Presbyterian Sunday school class in the early 1900s. According to the *Coraopolis Record* on February 9, 1910, it is said Bohemian, Magyar, Italian, and English were all spoken in class.

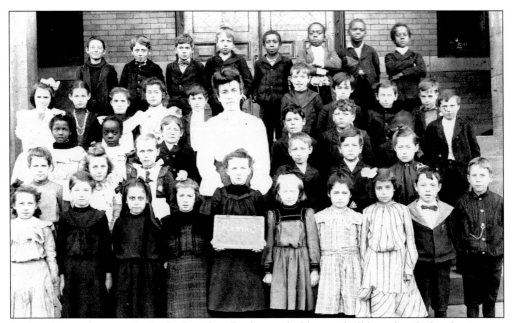

In this classic photograph, the little girl in the front is holding a chalkboard with the class's room number on it. In this case, these are the students from room five in Central School.

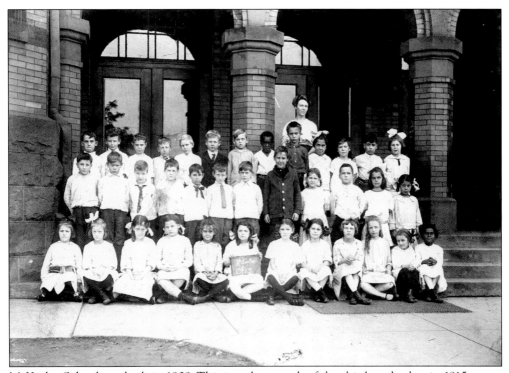

McKinley School was built in 1909. This is a photograph of the third-grade class in 1915.

In the early 1900s, this Presbyterian Sunday school class depicts the loveliness of Coraopolis in its earliest days. The building behind the class is an Episcopalian church. The building was owned, however, by the Presbyterian Church. The first church built in Coraopolis was a Methodist church of Episcopal denomination in 1849. Fifth Avenue would be on the left side of the class members, and they would be facing Broadway Street and the Presbyterian church if this photograph were to be taken today. Notice how everyone is dressed in beautiful white clothing. It is a unclear why the woman on the far right is in black, but back in this era, women were known to wear black for a year when in mourning.

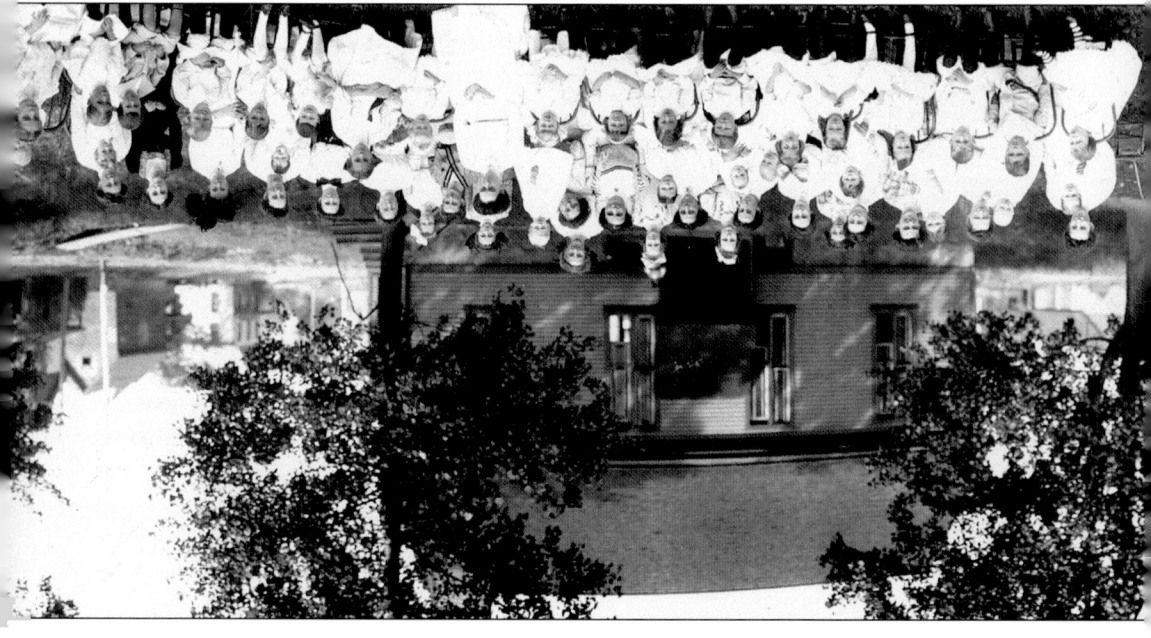

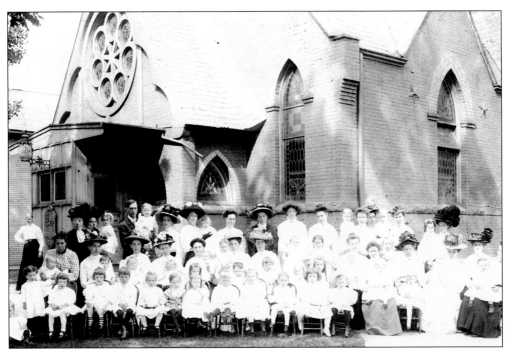

Seen here is a photograph of the Coraopolis Presbyterian Church Sunday school in 1905. The Presbyterian Church congregation in Coraopolis originated in 1882, and the church was developed in 1886.

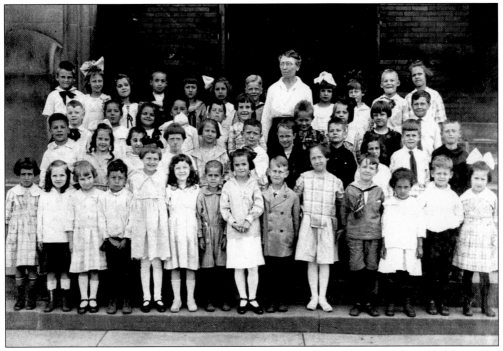

Notice the difference in the look and clothing attire as presented here in these children. The year is 1920, and the school is Central School.

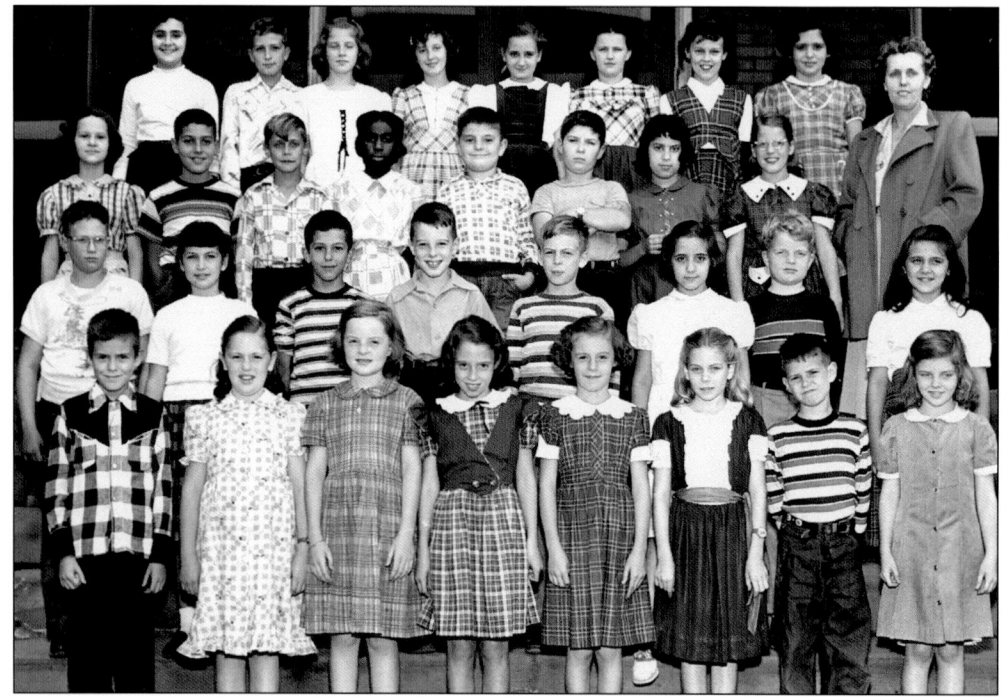

Even more updated than ever is the 1957 sixth-grade class as presented here. The teacher is Margaret Gray. Notice she is wearing a warm coat on what must have been a chilly day. By looking at the jubilant faces of the children, it is apparent they are not thinking about the cold.

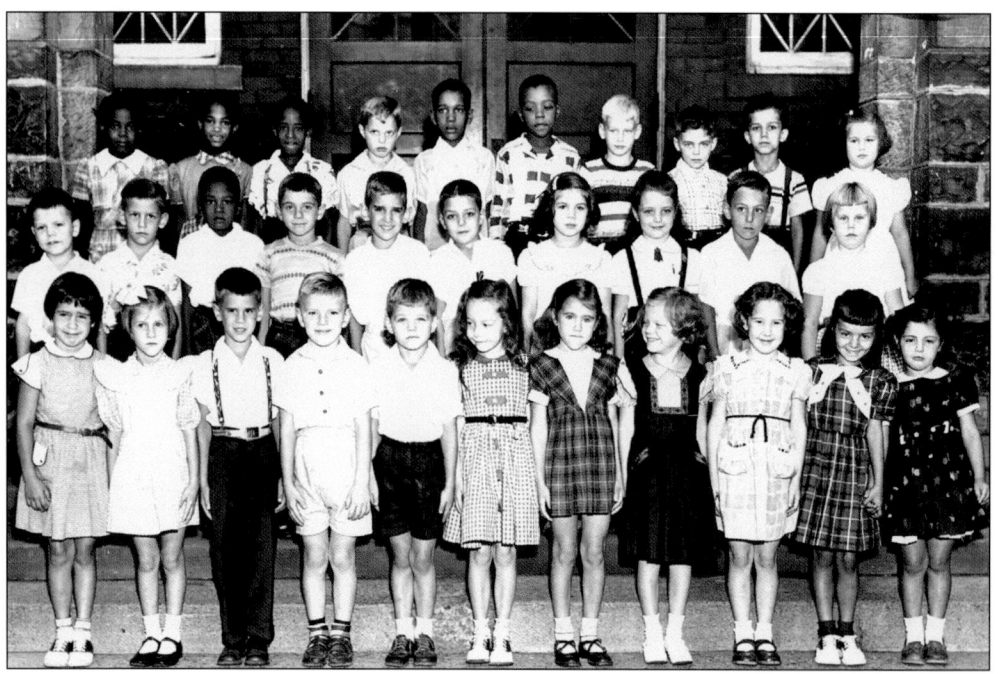

This annual elementary school class picture was taken in the 1950s in front of Lincoln School on Ridge Avenue.

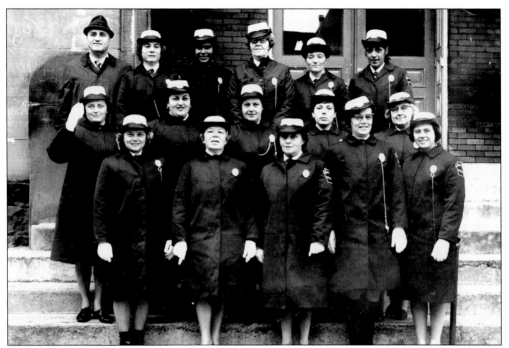

These women are standing in front of the borough building in 1967. Their primary focus was acting as the school crossing guards for the children.

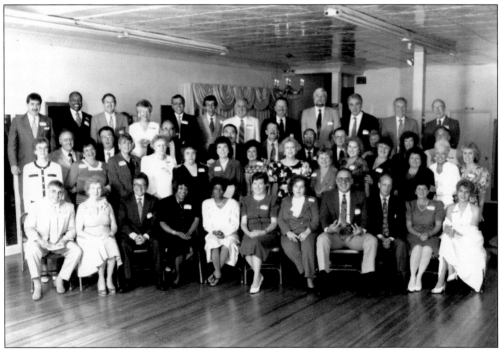

Celebrating their 35th high school reunion, this class graduated in 1955. In 1907, there was a total of 870 students in the Coraopolis schools combined. On May 21, 1913, Coraopolis Senior High School had a graduating class of 19 students.

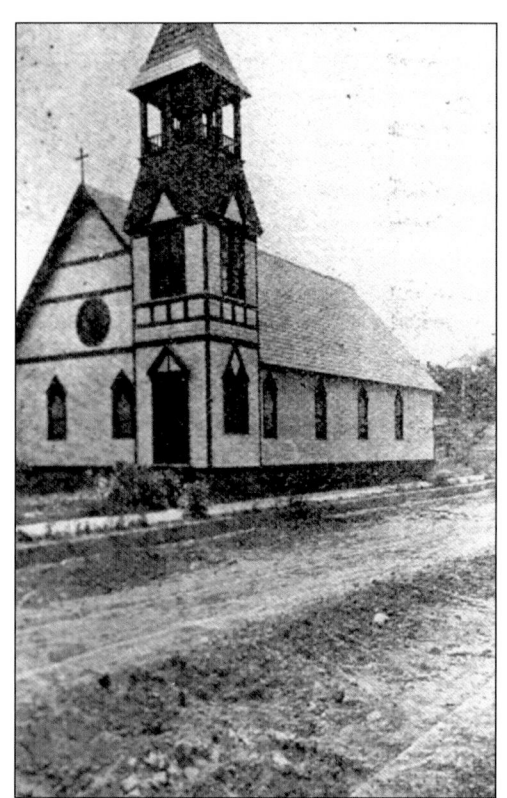

Two years after the congregation became established, St. Joseph Church was built, in 1890. It sat facing Fourth Avenue on the corner of Chestnut Street. Today St. Joseph Church has been rebuilt and currently faces Fifth Avenue. The first mass was held on First Avenue in the home of Mr. and Mrs. Patrick Kelly.

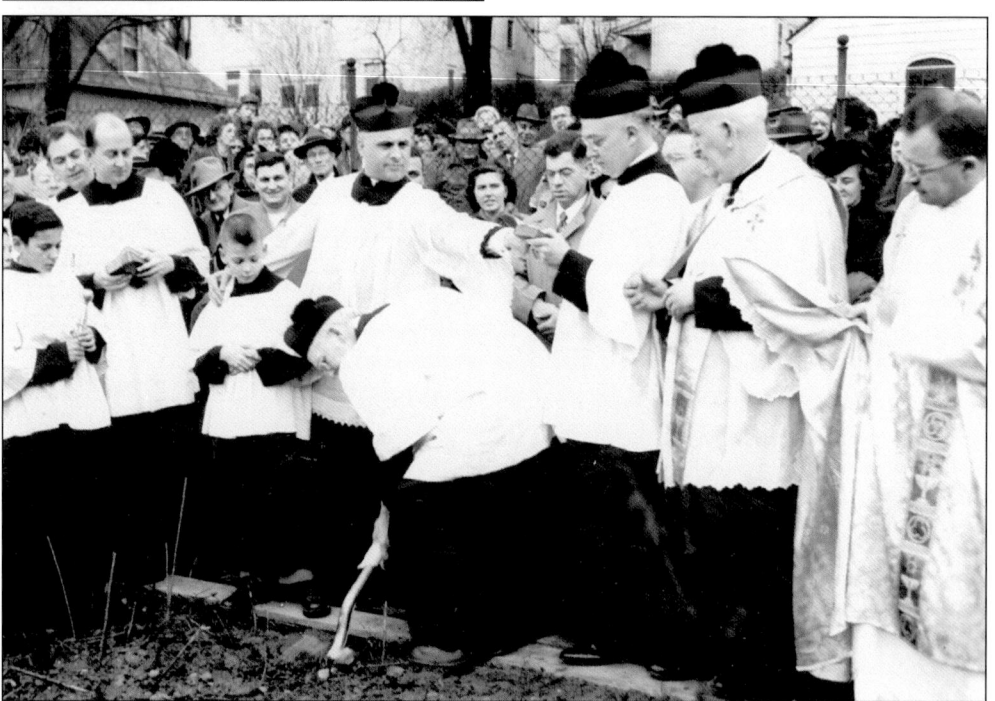

Groundbreaking ceremonies were held in honor of building the new St. Joseph School on February 15, 1953.

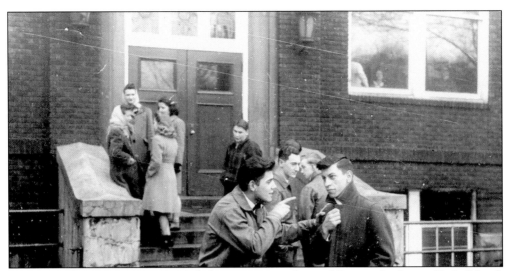

Students are creating memories while hanging out in front of Coraopolis Senior High School. Two young gentlemen, Sam Jampetro Jr. (left) and Roland "Cuss" Casasanta, are being typical 10th-grade teenagers in the year 1944. Coraopolis Senior High School was dedicated in 1915.

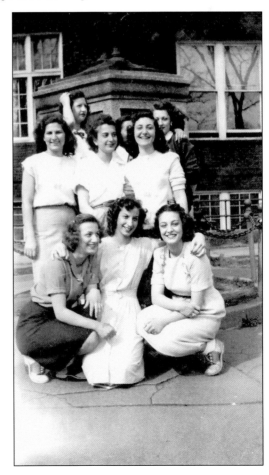

These delightful ladies pose in front of Coraopolis Senior High School in April 1948. They are, from left to right, (first row) Nancy (DiLisio) McAllister, Alma (Casasanta) Bafile, and Elinor (Iacobucci) Musta; (second row) Lillian (Trello) Ricci, Molly (Ventrusca) Wickline, and Olga (Santucci) Lacenere; (third row) Anna Michali, Marie (Thomas) Pressley (hidden), and Grace (Hendel) Colarossi.

cornell educational center

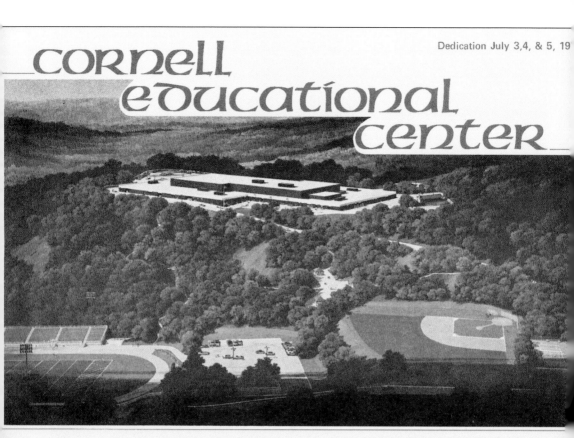

In July 1976, Cornell Educational Center was dedicated and officially became the education center for all students in Coraopolis kindergarten through 12th grade. Coraopolis merged with Neville Island, thus the name Cornell. This building consists of a generous floor plan that includes a gymnasium, pool, library, auditorium, cafeteria, planetarium, and media center. New programs are being implemented each year as the school continually strives to meet its optimum potential to the community.

Six

THE GREAT FLOODS OF CORAOPOLIS

In 1907, 1936, and 1972, Coraopolis endured great floods. The worst occurred in 1936. The entire town was engulfed in water, and many businesses, as well as homes, were lost. Unlike today, flood insurance was not a relevant thing people living next to the Ohio River had or could afford.

The first flood occurred on March 15, 1907. However, it was not until 19 years later that the worst flood in Coraopolis history occurred, on March 17, 1936. It was to be the town's semicentennial celebration, and plans had been in the works for a great length of time. The town was also in the process of writing its first published history book, *Semi Centennial*. All came to a halt for an entire year as the town, with great strength and deep devotion to itself as a persevering community, gathered together for a giant cleanup and restoration of the town. Within one year, despite the horrific and depressing devastation and loss that occurred, the town celebrated its 50th anniversary and decorated the town to its fullest, showing the healing and recovery.

In 1972, heavy rains from Hurricane Agnes once again flooded the streets of Coraopolis. History repeated itself with the community pulling together and cleaning up. Coraopolis has proven itself to be not only a town of integrity but a town of survival and rebirth as well.

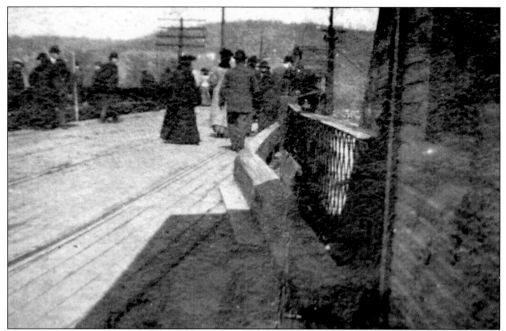

It is the great flood of 1907. Seen here are Coraopolis townsfolk standing near the tollbooth on the Neville Island Bridge on March 15. They are overlooking the devastation caused by the flood.

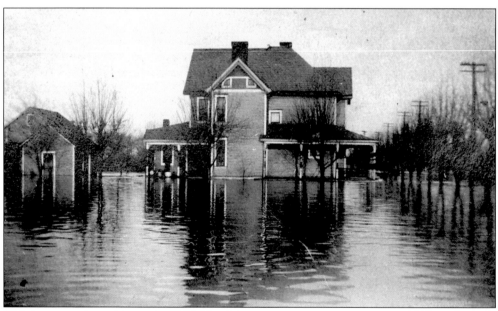

This is a water-logged home in 1907. Flood insurance was not an option in 1907, and people had to find their own means of flood cleanup. Local news to these families would have consisted of stories reported in the *Coraopolis Record*. One story is that of a boy who was hurt when his bicycle crashed into a horse and buggy on Mill Street on July 31, 1907. Also reported would have been news of things to look forward to in 1907, such as the annual corn roasts and various summer celebrations.

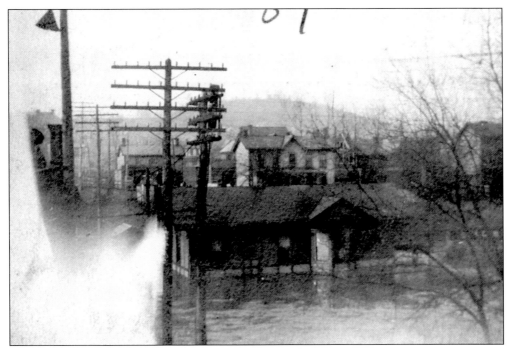

Floodwaters endanger the Montour train station in 1907.

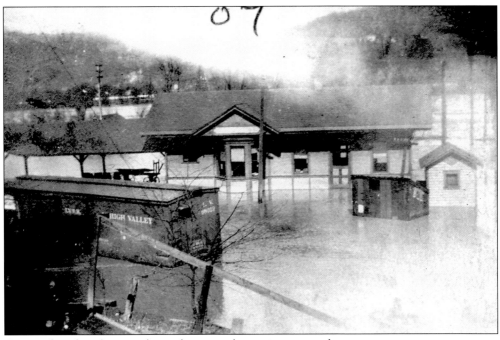

Captured in this photograph are the waters beginning to recede.

FLOOD EDITION

THE CORAOPOLIS RECORD

Vol. 31, No. 3   Coraopolis Pa., March 20, 1936   Free Distribution

FLOOD PERILS TOWN

In the wake of worst flood to hit Coraopolis and surrounding sections, health authorities here guarded closely against an epidemic outbreak. Every precaution has been taken against the spread of contagious disease, and citizens are warned to employ every sanitary precaution.

Flood stages were reported at Mill and Fourth at 5 feet, 9 inches; 6 feet, 7 inches at Neville and Mill, and 15 feet, Fifth and Locust.

CLEARING FLOOD DEBRIS

The flooded area of Coraopolis began to assume some stages of normalcy when the water receded Thursday afternoon. The flood relief committee, under the direction of Col. E. M. Iland, said persons whose homes were badly damaged by the flood were permitted to return to them but only long enough to clear away the debris in the flood wake. Fortunately there were no fatalities reported.

There was only mud, slime, broken store fronts, a foot of debris, and sad-eyed merchants, faces drawn and pale, standing ankle deep in the wreckage in front of their shops.

The streets that ordinarily blaze out in lights were dark and deserted as night fell except for the many volunteer workmen, grimly at work, and those on official business. A cordon of National guardsmen units barred every entrance to the flooded area of Neville Island and Coraopolis, and the ring they threw about the western section of Coraopolis was as unyielding as steel.

WATER LIKELY TONIGHT

There is a possibility of the community getting water by nightfall. Electric current is being supplied to several churches, YMCA, borough building and pumping station.

(Editor's note: Due to the absence of electric current for operating typesetting machines and presses, the regular issue of the Record will be omitted this week, marking the first ommision in over 30 years. The issuing of this sheet was made possible by hand typesetting and a foot-power operated press.)

SANITATION WARNING

Harry M. Lee, chairman of sanitation under the emergency organization, issued orders that water must positively be boiled before drinking, and unpasteurized milk must be boiled. "Raw" milk, in other words, cannot be used unless it is boiled.

RED CROSS ASSISTANCE

Red Cross authorities of Pittsburgh arrived at the flooded scenes of Coraopolis Wednesday afternoon and found a complete organization set-up. They brought blankets and food to care for the 1,000 or more refugees, who will continue being fed and lodged in the YMCA and various churches as long as necessary. The emergency hospital in the Coraodd Temple will be kept open indefinitely.

Councilman O. W. Cleaver, public safety chairman, organized the preliminary plans, as the flood began to reach alarming proportions.

HUGE LOSS REPORTED

A half-dozen homes at Groveton were washed downstream but no loss of life was reported. At the Montour railroad yards two houses were found overturned at the railroad tracks. The Montour shops were flooded and most of the machinery ruined. Several freight cars undergoing repairs were found on their side as the rushing waters lifted them from the tracks.

The Canfield Oil Co. suffered losses expected to reach hundreds of thousands of dollars. Huge tanks were moved from bases and upset. The Standard Steel Spring Co. also sustained losses which are expected to mount steadily as the debris is cleared away. The Duquesne Steel Foundry Co. was hard hit, as was Russell, Burdsall & Ward, Pittsburgh Forgings Co., Carbo-Oxygen Co. and other plants of the Coraopolis area.

Neville Island, especially the populated part of the western section, was left a mass of wreckage. Houses were loosened from their foundations. Neville Island's schoolhouse was badly damaged, water seeping into the gymnasium and first floor.

CHURCH SERVICES SUNDAY

At a Ministerial meeting held this morning it was decided to hold a "Community Service of Humiliation and Prayer" at the United Presbyterian Church, Sunday morning at 10 o'clock. All Sunday Schools and other regular services were cancelled on account of relief work.

It was announced that masses would be said at the usual time Sunday morning at St. Joseph's Church.

Here is a look at the flood edition of the *Coraopolis Record*. The date is March 17, 1936, and Coraopolis has been hit by its second devastating flood, on St. Patrick's Day. The *Record* did not publish any newspapers until this one on March 20 because of the great flood and a lack of electricity. However, it came out with this special edition by hand typesetting and a foot-power operated press. This special edition reports huge loses, saddened merchants, broken storefronts, depressed faces, and ankle-deep wreckage everywhere the townsfolk go. Homes also were reported as washed away, and the Red Cross brought blankets and food for refugees.

This photograph was taken looking down Mill Street toward the train station. The water is deep and everywhere, slowly destroying all in its path.

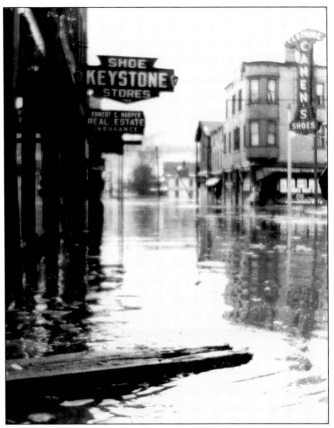

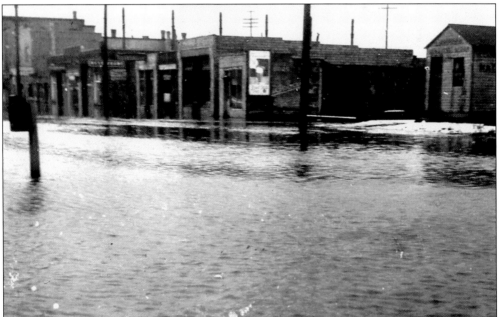

Floodwaters make their way through and completely overtake the town of Coraopolis on March 17, 1936.

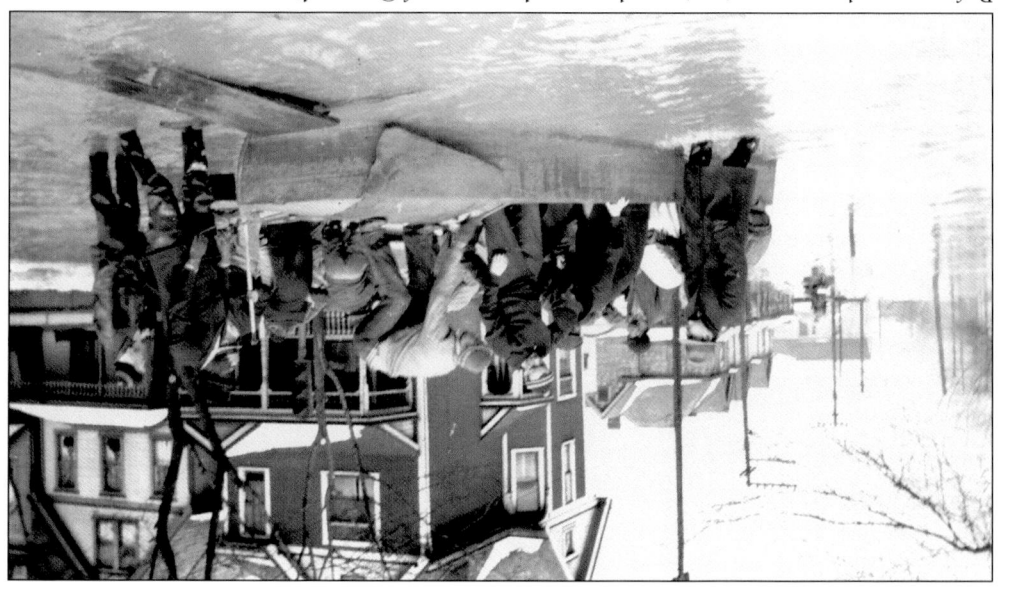

Refugees can be seen getting into a boat on the streets of Coraopolis.

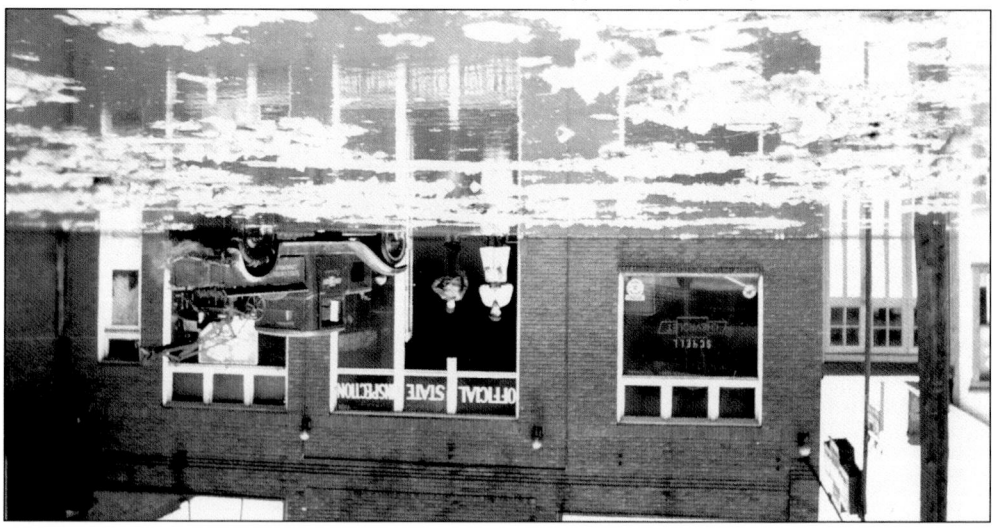

It is not yet spring and is still very cold. Ice can be seen floating on top of the floodwater at Schills Garage on Fifth Avenue.

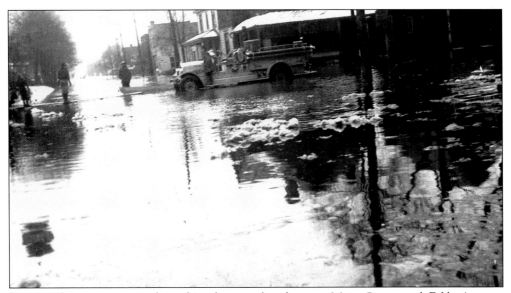

Snow and ice are captured in this photograph taken on Main Street and Fifth Avenue. Floodwaters were bad enough to have to deal with. Snow and ice along with freezing weather and no electricity made things all the worse.

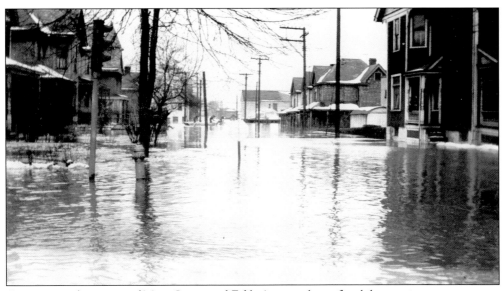

Once again, the corner of Main Street and Fifth Avenue shows flood devastation.

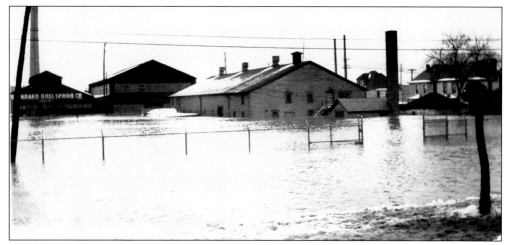

The Coraopolis Armory is largely underwater. The armory was established in 1910.

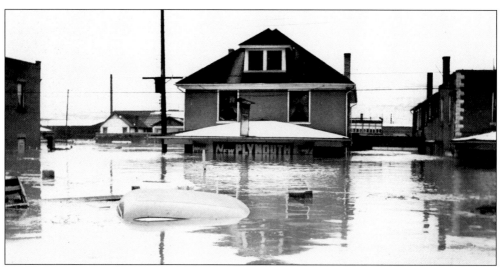

The water was estimated as deep as six feet or more in some areas of Coraopolis. Notice the car floating on Fifth Avenue in the front of this picture.

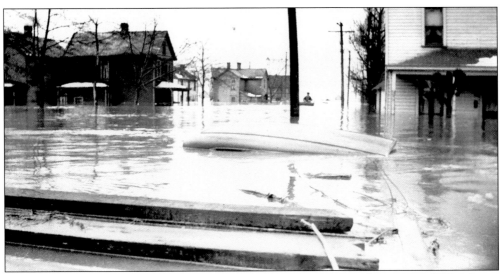

Vehicles and homes are shown at this waterlogged intersection on the corner of Watt Street and Fifth Avenue.

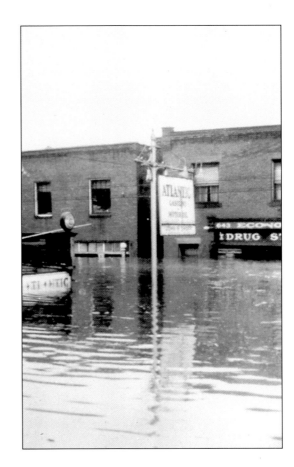

A view of Coraopolis, overtaken and submerged by floodwaters below Locust Street and Fifth Avenue, is seen here.

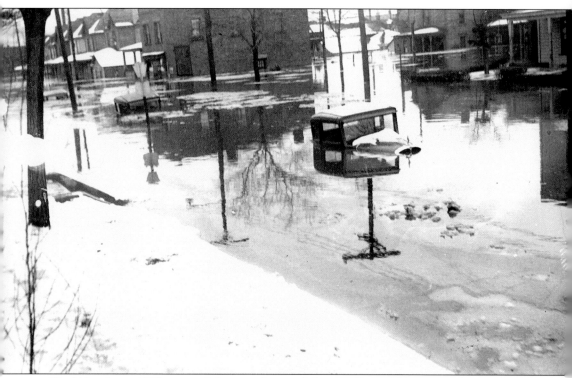

Would-be classic 1930s automobiles are submerged, floating down Fifth Avenue, lost and ruined. The depth of this floodwater in 1936 demonstrates just how destructive it was to the community. Businesses were in complete ruin and homes were destroyed. Many victims of the flood endured the bitter cold, ice, water, and loss of electricity.

People scurried to save what they could from their homes and businesses, but much was destroyed and lost.

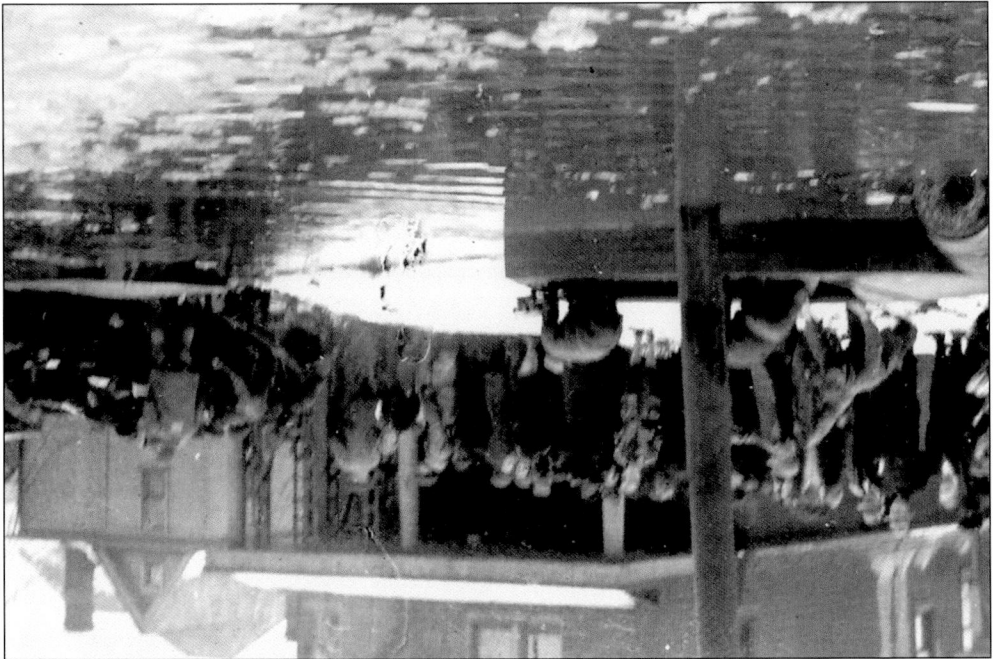

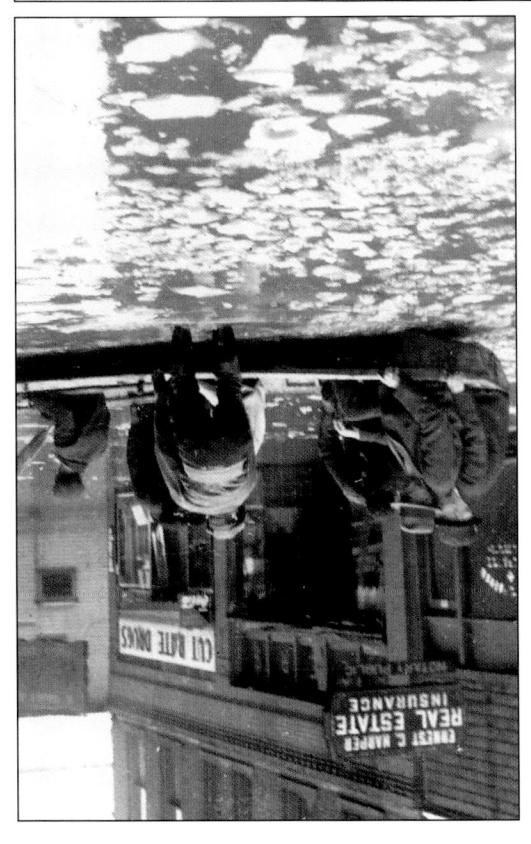

Local business owners are situating themselves in a small boat to go through the icy waters to inspect damage.

Floodwaters and debris can be seen looking down the Pittsburgh and Lake Erie Railroad from Ferree Street. The Consolidated Lamp and Glass Company can be seen in the distance on the right, and the metal crossing bridge can be seen in the center of the photograph. The little crossing bridge is still standing today.

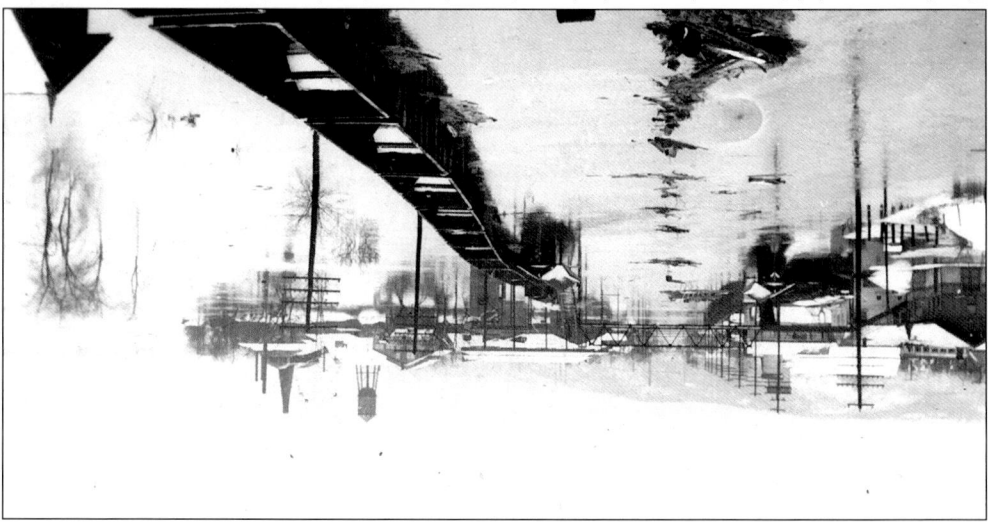

The old Neville Island Bridge can be seen on the left side of this photograph, and the Consolidated Lamp and Glass Company can be seen in the distance on the right. In the front center of the photograph are the Pittsburgh and Lake Erie Railroad cars submerged. Their rooftops are barely visible.

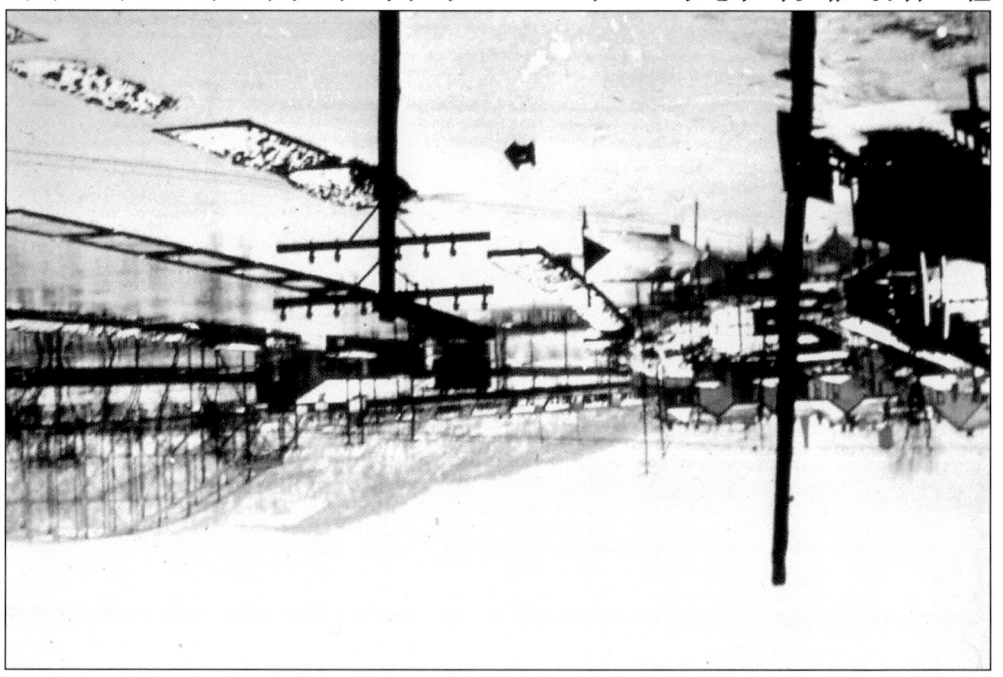

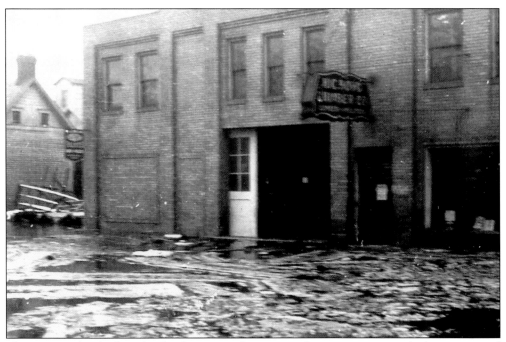

This is an earlier look at the floodwaters as they are just beginning to overtake businesses and homes; the water quickly rose and was much higher later in the day.

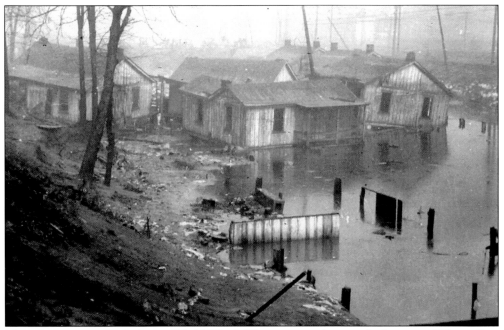

These houses were built during World War I. They are seen here at the bottom of Thorn Run Road all jammed into one another and completely destroyed by the 1936 flood. Each family belonging to these homes became homeless due to the devastation of the flood.

Coraopolis went on to endure a third flood, decades later, as a result of heavy rains from Hurricane Agnes in June 1972. These headlines discuss and show still another picture of evacuations and damage done to the town as a result of this flood. Once again, the community of Coraopolis demonstrated persevering spirits and overcame this devastation.

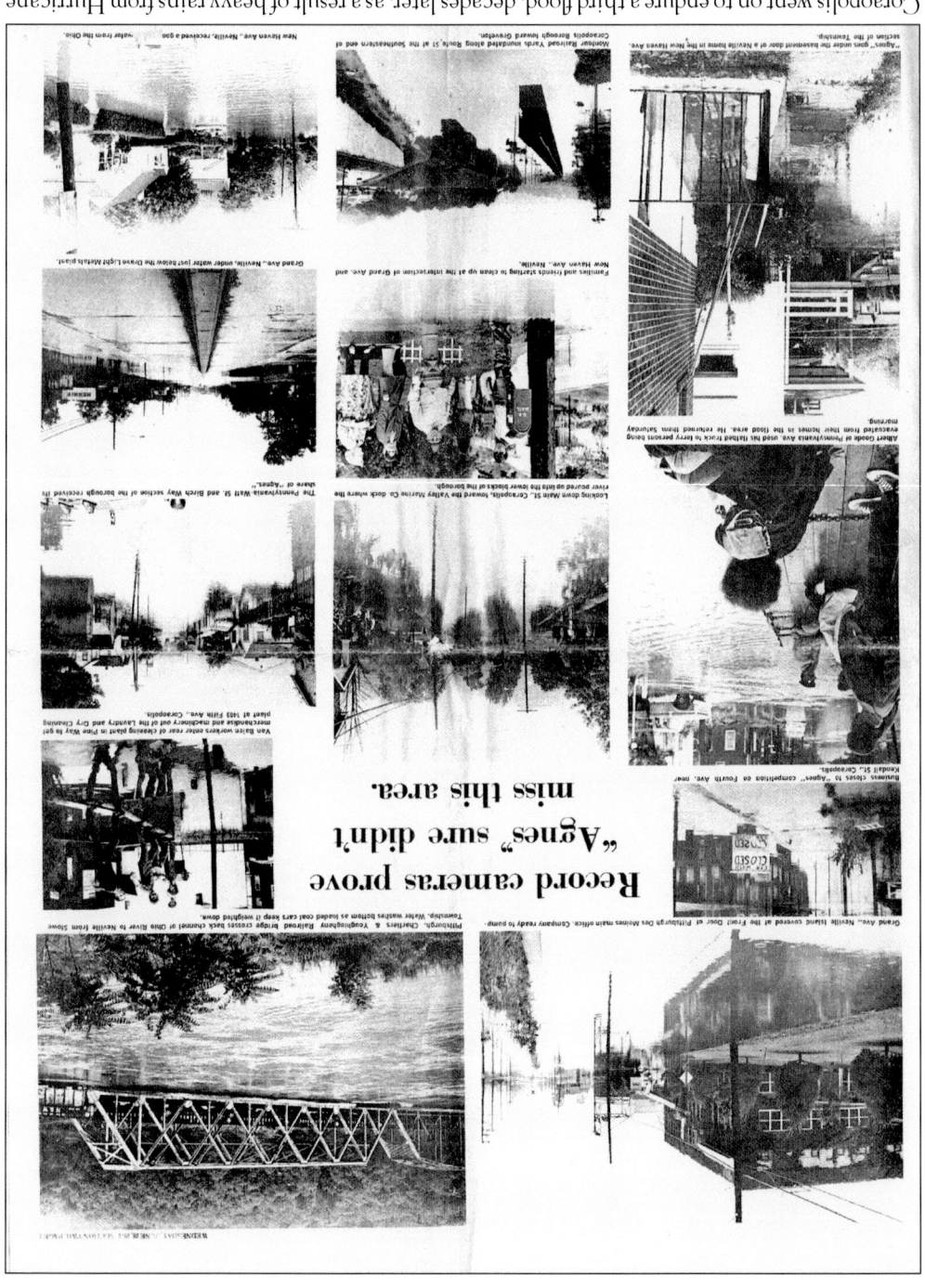

Seven

CONSOLIDATED GLASS

The Consolidated Lamp and Glass Company came to Coraopolis in 1895 from Fostoria, Ohio. Coraopolis was interested in bringing in an industry to help boom its economy. The Consolidated Lamp and Glass Company was interested in coming to Coraopolis but asked that it be given the land. Plans to obtain land at first failed. But through a second attempt the town found a way. In hopes of raising the economy, local companies donated a lot of land that could be used by the town to sell and pay a loan made through a Pittsburgh bank. Coraopolis then purchased land near the Ohio River and gave it to the Consolidated Lamp and Glass Company. The Consolidated Lamp and Glass Company moved from Ohio and began production. As business boomed, the town quickly grew, and with in a year, 350 jobs were created. As people moved into the town and bought the various given lots of land, the town was able to pay off its debt.

The Consolidated Lamp and Glass Company, referred to by the community as the Glass House, closed permanently in June 1963. Today, thanks to author Jack Wilson, the gems and treasures of magnificent glass that were produced by this company have been discovered to be extremely valuable. Thanks to his research, a simple paperweight that would have been originally sold for perhaps 50¢ at a garage sale can be sold for well over $100 today. In July of each year, many folks come from around the country to the Embassy Suites located in the local neighboring town of Moon Township for the Consolidated Lamp and Glass Company convention.

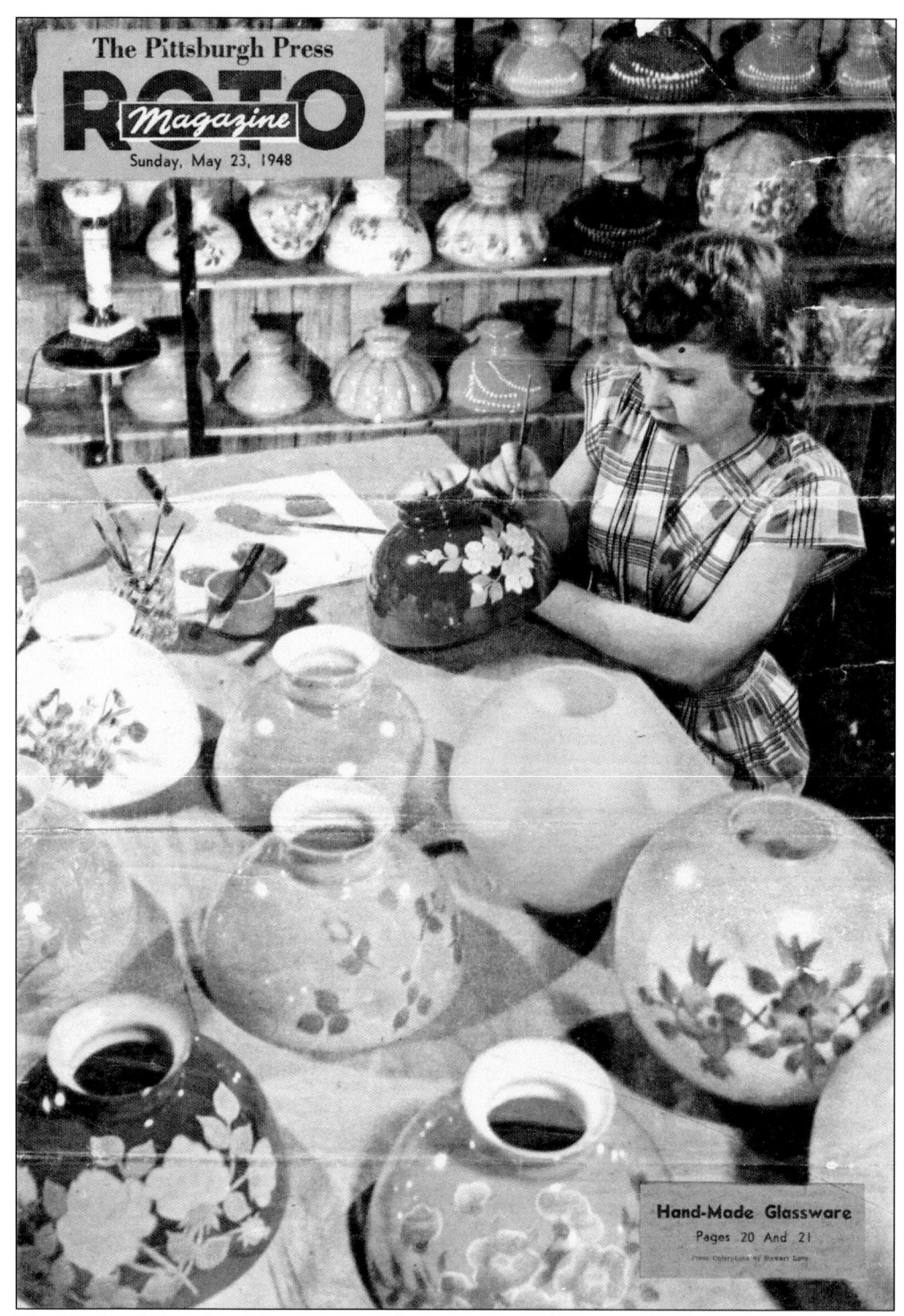

The Pittsburgh Press
ROTO
Magazine
Sunday, May 23, 1948

Hand-Made Glassware
Pages 20 And 21

This *Pittsburgh Press Roto Magazine* cover shows a woman who artistically designs and hand paints the beautiful glass that comes out of the Consolidated Lamp and Glass Company. The women of the Glass House worked elegantly and precisely, making each piece of glass painted unique.

114

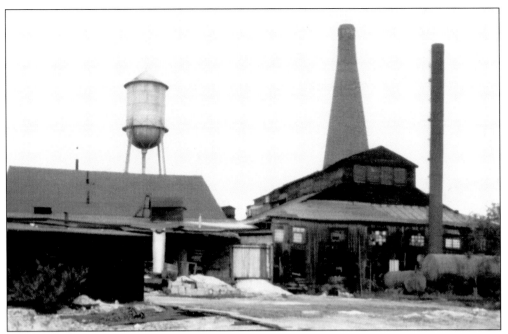

The Consolidated Lamp and Glass Company is shown here and recognized as a thriving business in the town of Coraopolis. Shortly after production began, the Glass House employed 350 people at the beginning of the 20th century. The town of Coraopolis began to immediately thrive and grow.

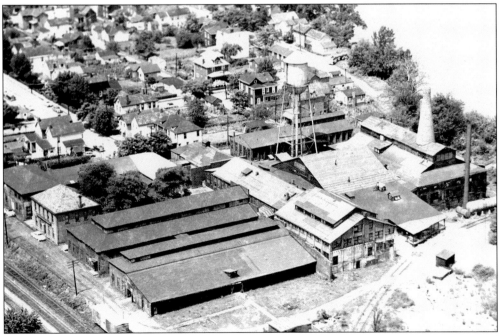

The Consolidated Lamp and Glass Company came to Coraopolis from Fostoria, Ohio, and began operation in 1895. This aerial photograph of the Glass House offers full detail of the factory and maps out all its facilities in Coraopolis.

This stunning photograph shows a worker next to the large furnace used to melt the sand and other ingredients that made the glass. Notice in the center of the furnace is a glory hole. Inside, glass would be melted. A carrier would then take it to a fellow who would be sitting and ready to blow glass. Next to the furnace, observe the rods that were used to transport the glass from out of the hot furnace.

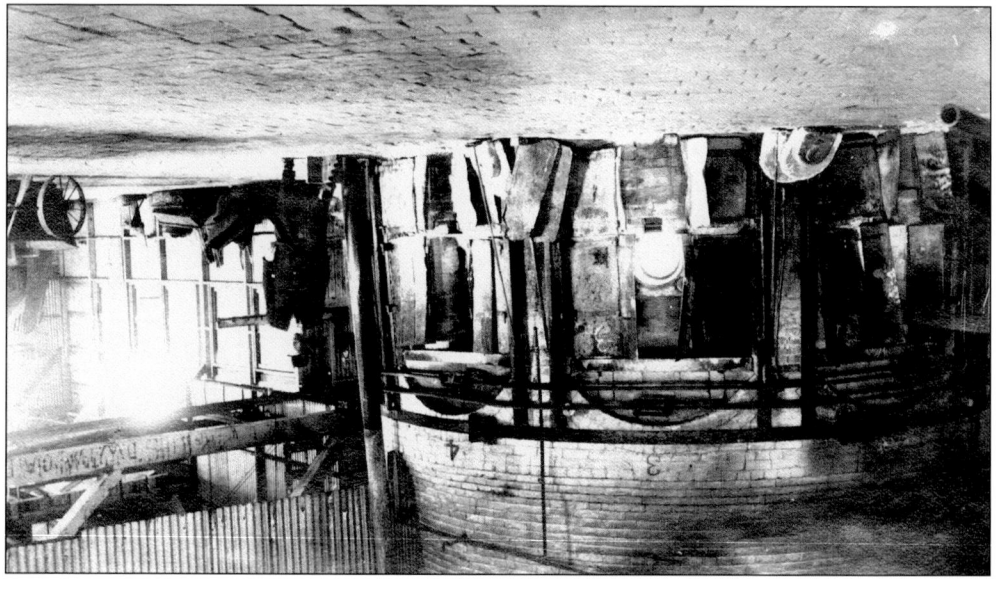

This photograph shows the interior of the Glass House in the background.

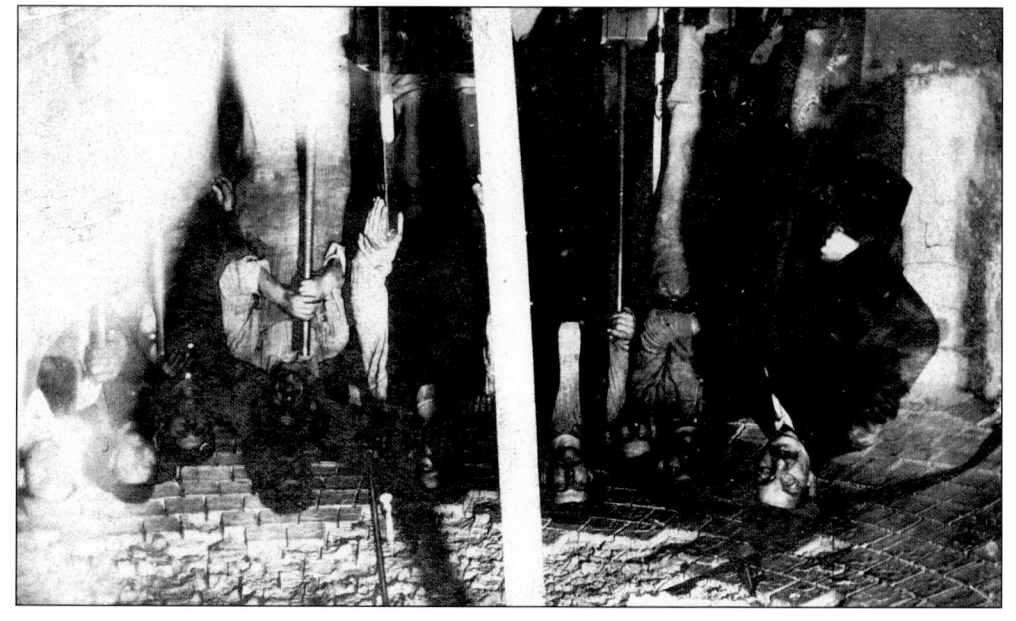

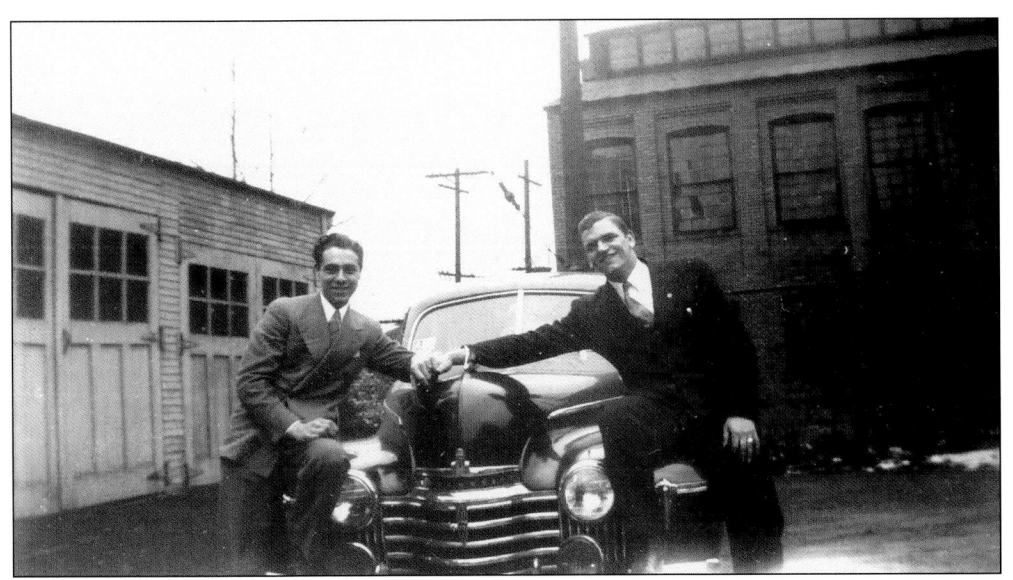

Joe DiNell (left) and Gus Agostinelli had their photograph taken in 1943 at the Glass House the day before leaving to go into the army.

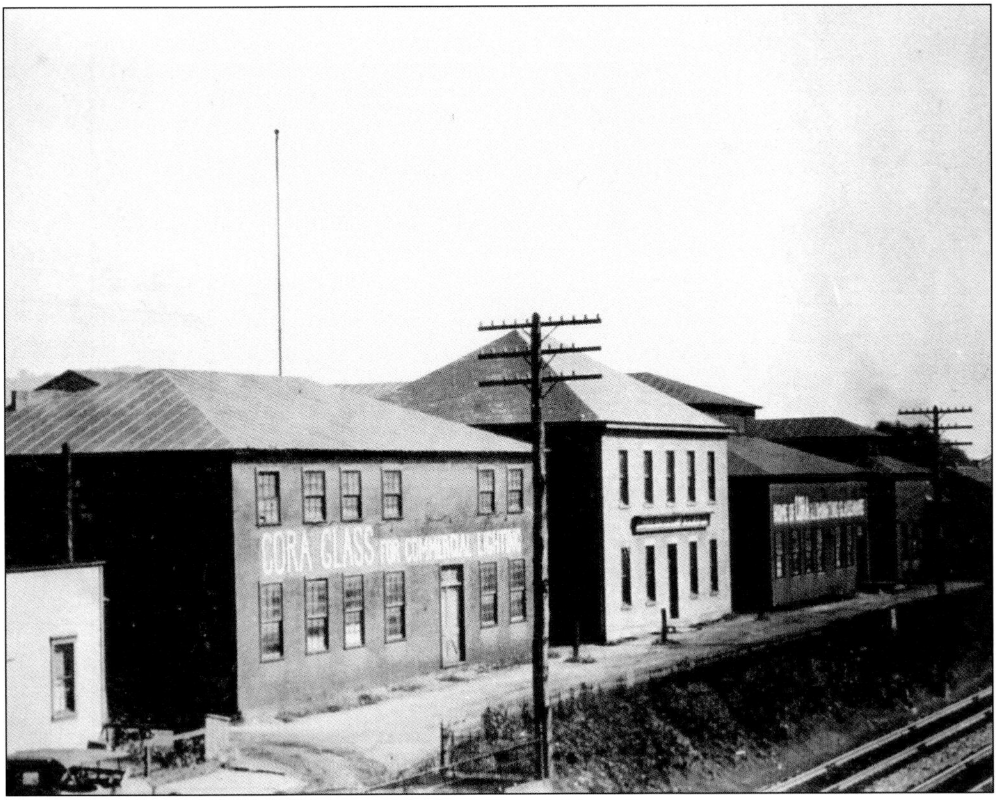

Here is a perfect look at the Consolidated Lamp and Glass Company.

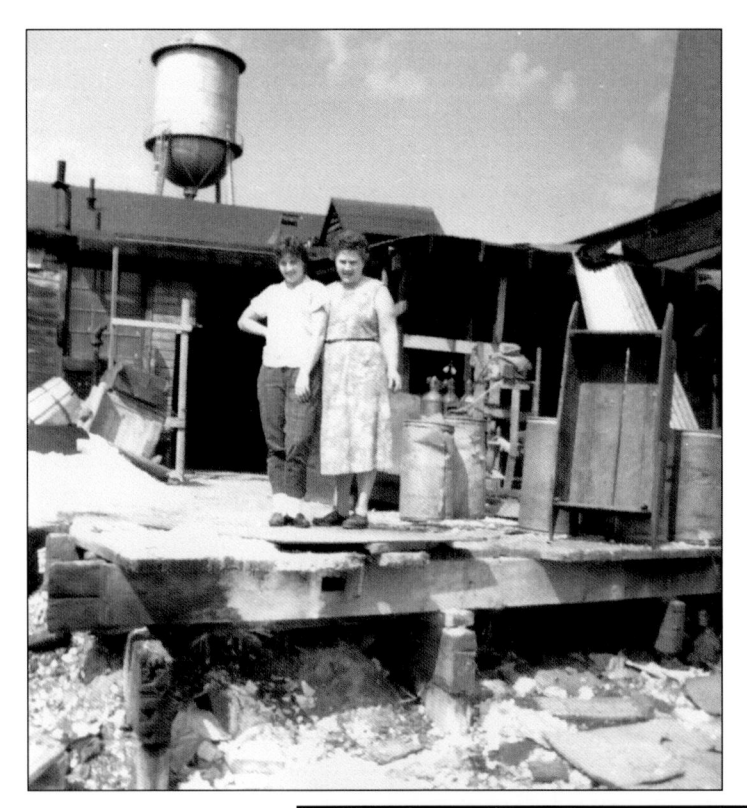

These ladies pose in the midst of the factory. Notice all the piles of broken glass. Glass shards remain deeply buried like fossils at the original site of the old Glass House today.

These beautiful glass vases were especially hand painted delicately and gently by mostly women workers of the Glass House. Today these items are considered precious treasures and sold expensively.

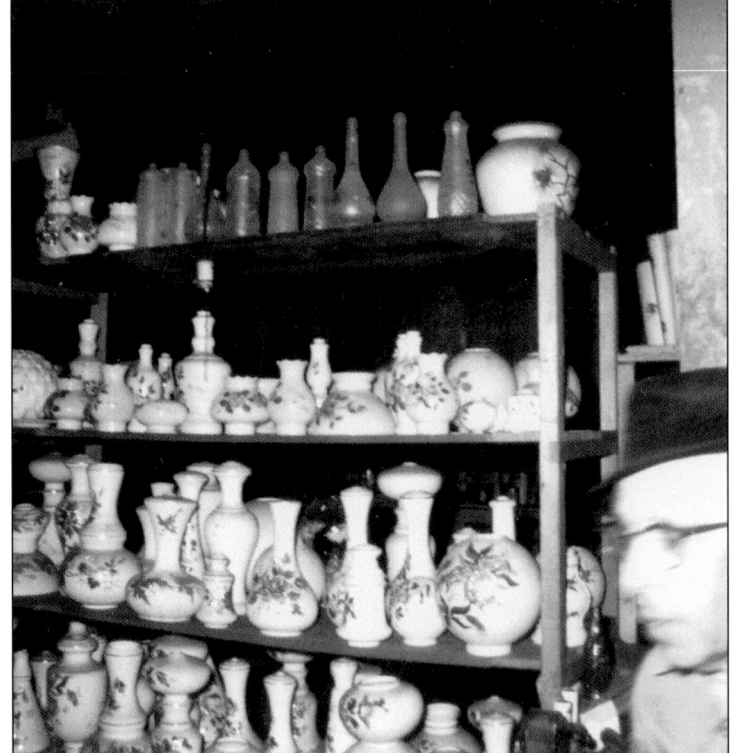

Eight

RAILROAD ARCHIVES

The railroad in Coraopolis was the absolute heart of the community in its day. The railroads that pass through the area of Coraopolis are the Pittsburgh and Lake Erie Railroad and the Montour Railroad. The Montour Railroad Company was connected to the Pittsburgh and Lake Erie Railroad at the Montour junction. Progress and growth in the town of Coraopolis is largely due to these railroads at the beginning of the 20th century. The Pittsburgh and Lake Erie Railroad began in 1875, a year before Coraopolis became a borough. It was officially completed as a single-track railroad in February 1879 when the first train passed through. The railroads hauled coal, steel, and iron ore, to name a few. The workers held both diverse and challenging jobs. They would go years without missing a day's work. Some of the jobs these gentlemen held were that of blacksmiths, boilermakers, machinists, pipe fitters, foremen, hostlers, and air brakemen.

The railroad was one of the main means of transportation in the early 1900s and remained that way over the decades. The stations of Coraopolis were actively used by the townspeople and by the neighboring communities to commute in and out of the city of Pittsburgh. During the war, many young men would head off to the army via the railroad. But the railroad is best known for putting the town of Coraopolis officially on the map, becoming known to all, and therefore making the town thrive.

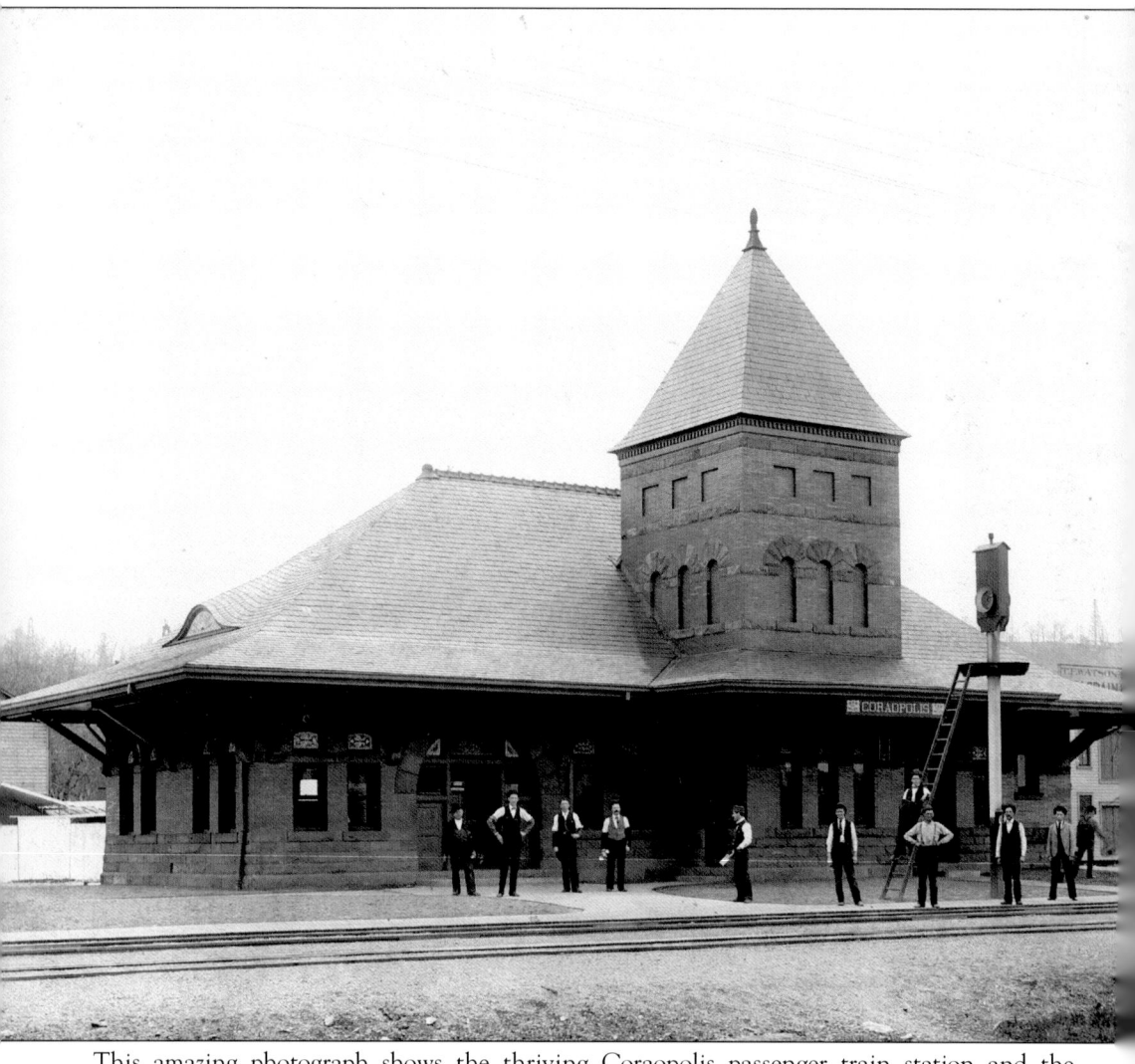

This amazing photograph shows the thriving Coraopolis passenger train station and the Pittsburgh and Lake Erie Railroad around the late 1800s. Several things are noticeable in this early-20th-century photograph. The hills behind the train station are still undeveloped as no homes have been built yet. The employees are shown here with sport gaiters on their sleeves to keep their cuffs from falling. Elegantly demonstrating the magnificence of this station, this picture shows the beginning days of great services becoming available to the Coraopolis community through this means of travel.

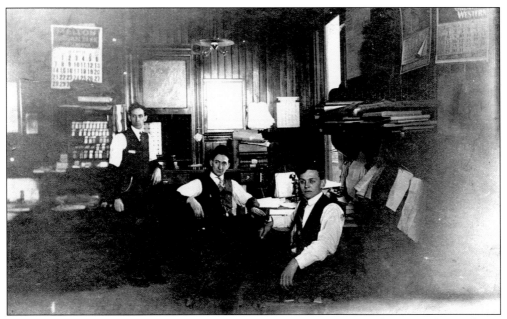

Here is a 1890s inside look at the Coraopolis train station. The magnificent wooden walls are easily visible and this particular station was known for its beautiful Richardsonian Romanesque design. These gentlemen are busy at work. Several calendars are visible in this photograph as well as the ticket booth and window.

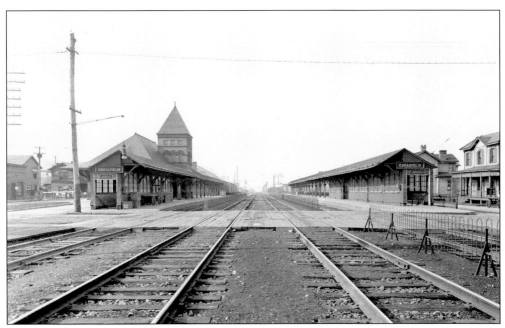

This is a long view of the very tracks that were instrumental in making this town thrive. Mostly used as a passenger station, this railroad station brought in lots of people, jobs, and business to the town of Coraopolis. In 1890, the population of Coraopolis was slightly over 900 people. By the 1930s, the population increased to nearly 11,000 residents. Today the population stands around 7,000.

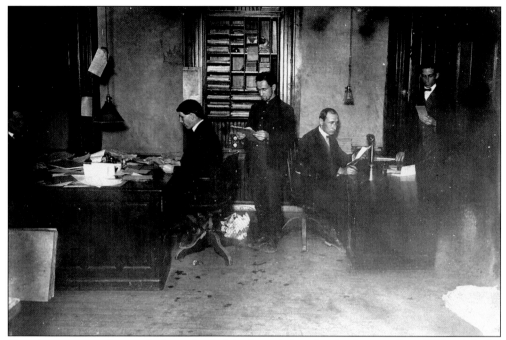

Here is an extremely rare look at the freight house's interior in the very late 1890s with the railroad crew at work. All these men are focused on their jobs, and many would go years without missing a day's work.

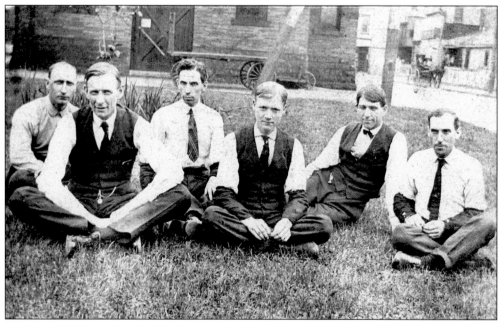

The freight house gang, as they referred to themselves, is seen sitting outside just across from the passenger station.

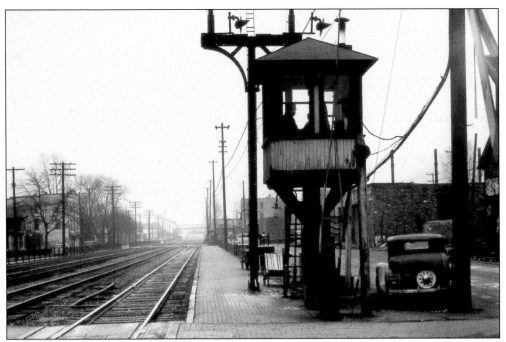

Captured in this photograph is a man in the railroad watch tower, across from the Coraopolis station, overlooking the Pittsburgh and Lake Erie Railroad tracks.

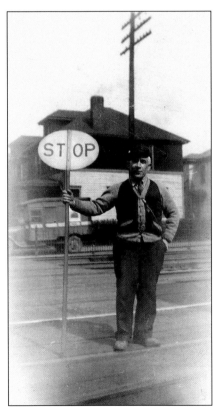

Rocco DiLisio is on duty for the Pittsburgh and Lake Erie crossing at the intersection of Broadway Street in 1945.

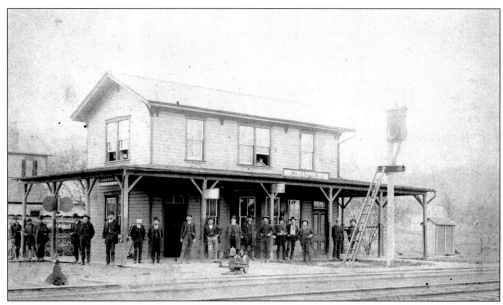

This photograph of the Montour Railroad station was taken in the late 1890s. Much activity is featured in this picture, demonstrating the liveliness of the railroad. This side of the Montour station is facing the railroad tracks. Working the railroad station consisted of jobs such as boilers, machinists, and foremen. These jobs were frequently challenging and difficult.

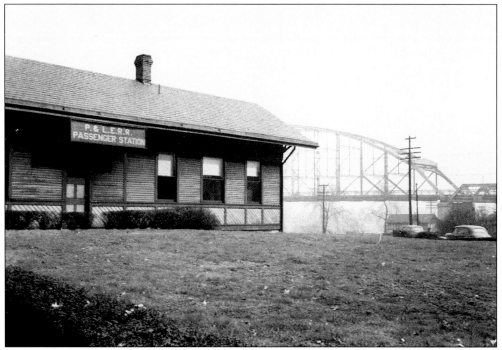

Here is a glorious photograph of the Montour station facing Fourth Avenue. The Neville Island Bridge is visible in the background.

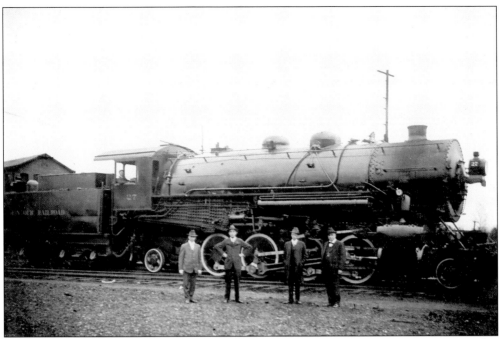

In 1915, these four men stand proudly in front of this new and impressive Montour engine. It takes water 212 degrees to reach a boiling point at which steam is created. Once steam is obtained, it is strong enough to make an engine move. The first Pittsburgh and Lake Erie Railroad engine to pass through Coraopolis was on February 24, 1879.

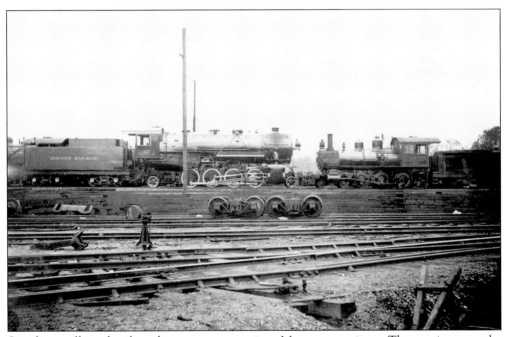

Standing tall and vibrantly are two amazing Montour engines. The engine on the right was an old Montour engine, and the engine on the left was considered a new and thriving Montour engine.

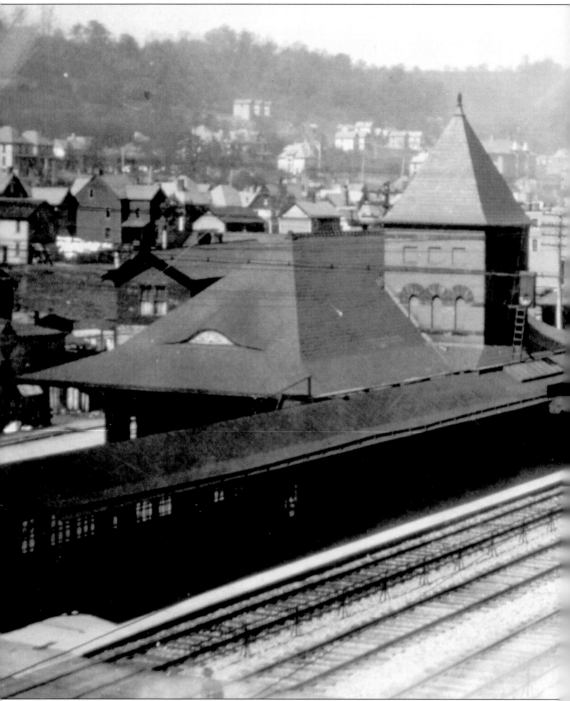

It is apparent here the illustriousness of this mighty train station. This aerial photograph distinctly depicts the generous activity of this station serving the Coraopolis community at its height. According to the commemorative ticket, the last passenger train ride through the Coraopolis station on the Pittsburgh and Lake Erie Railroad was on July 12, 1985. This station, although inactive, is still barely standing today. Inside, the splendid Richardsonian Romanesque

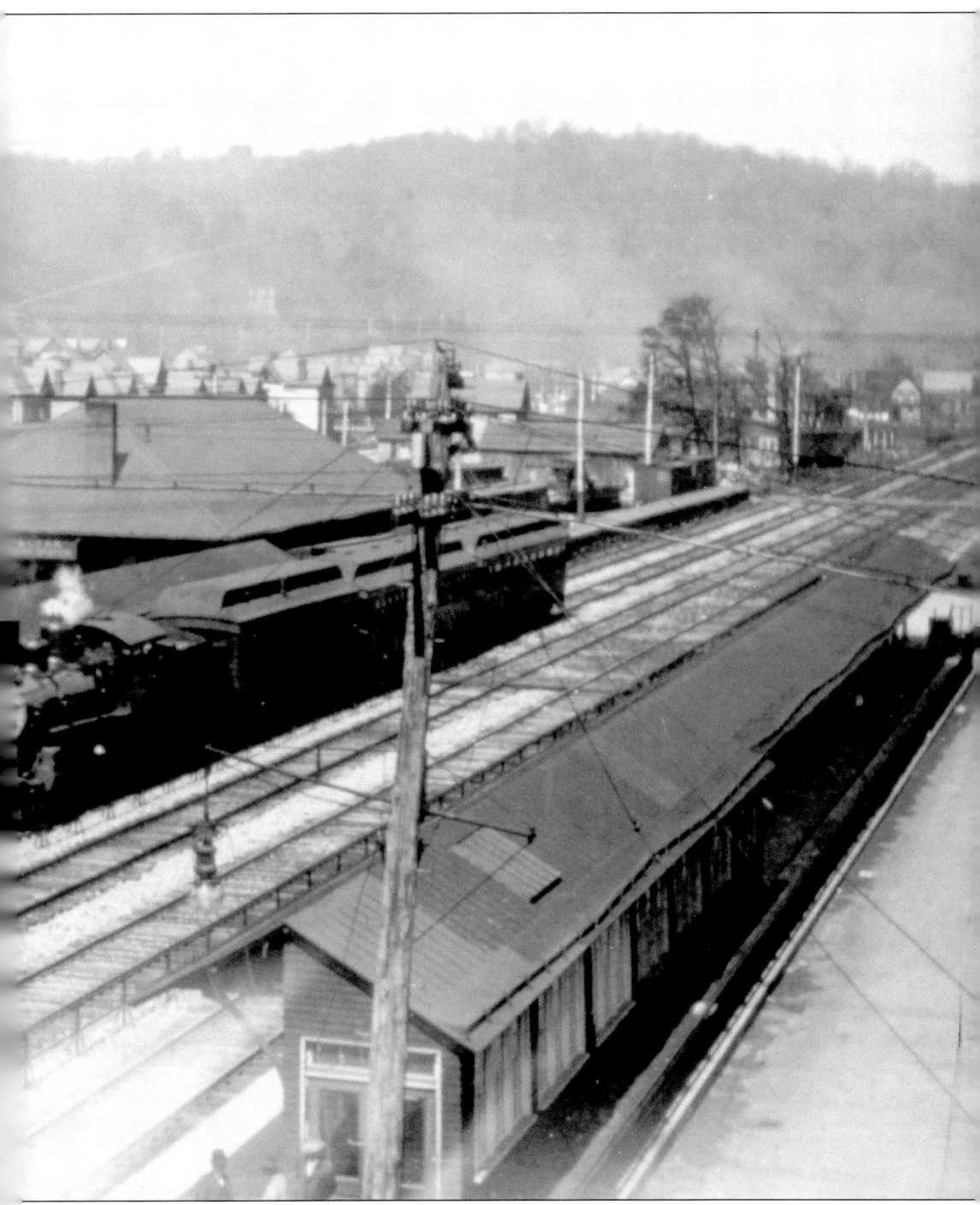

ceiling structure and design can still be seen but is incredibly delicate. A major renovation project is currently being pioneered by Rev. Sam Jampetro as an initiative of the recently formed Coraopolis Community Development Foundation. Together with volunteers of the Coraopolis community and its neighbors, perhaps this sleeping giant will awaken and become a heartbeat for the community once again.

Discover Thousands of Local History Books
Featuring Millions of Vintage Images

Arcadia Publishing, the leading local history publisher in the United States, is committed to making history accessible and meaningful through publishing books that celebrate and preserve the heritage of America's people and places.

Find more books like this at
www.arcadiapublishing.com

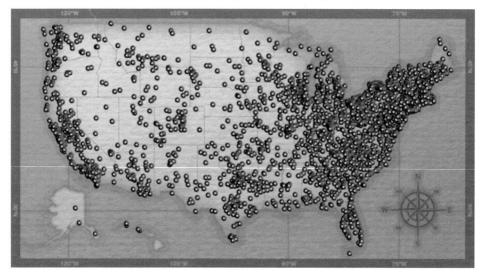

Search for your hometown history, your old stomping grounds, and even your favorite sports team.

Consistent with our mission to preserve history on a local level, this book was printed in South Carolina on American-made paper and manufactured entirely in the United States. Products carrying the accredited Forest Stewardship Council (FSC) label are printed on 100 percent FSC-certified paper.

MADE IN THE 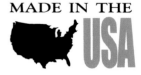 USA

Made in the USA
Monee, IL
01 December 2022

Kicking Butt
in Khakis

RON KRIT

ISBN: 978-1-7370303-1-7

Any reference to historical events, real people, or real places are used fictitiously. Names, characters, and places are products of the author's imagination. Cover design and book formatting by Joseph Grisham.

This book is dedicated to my boys
...
with a special thank you
to my editors (Erika & Jim),
family, and friends.

BEGINNING

"We are gathered here today to celebrate the life of Jerry Waters. Jerry will never truly die, for his spirit will continue to live on in all of our hearts ..."

The cemetery is an ironic place; the perfectly cut grass, the flowers centered evenly on the graves, the sun hits the grass and causes a beautiful glow, yet it houses hundreds of decaying bodies.

My navy blue, button-down suit multiplies the hot-humid June day. Realizing the last of my extended family has passed away, I wonder who's next. Cousin Jerry died three days ago, six months after his dad, Jay, left us. People said he couldn't live without his father and best friend; personally, I think someone murdered him. My overactive imagination sees a short, fat man with a beard and not much hair driving right into his car and then driving away. Jerry would not drink and drive, that's more a me thing—but not anymore, of course. And he wouldn't be in the hood at night by himself.

My thoughts are rudely interrupted. "Jack? Hello, Jack? You okay son?" The insurance man Dave Heeder, a close buddy of my uncle's, has been trying to talk to me for the past three days about a job with his company. Dave works for a financial conglomerate,

Trust No One. Sorry, I mean Trust One—a pretty odd name for a company that screws people over daily. Dave just looks like an insurance salesman: five-nine, skinny, receding brown hair, and he can have that fake "I'm sorry" look going in less than a hundredth of a second.

"Hi Dave, I think I will go on that interview."

"The job would be perfect for a new college graduate. You would work in your field—Marketing."

Marketing. Shit—I thought I'd be a teller or insurance agent. "Marketing? Wow! How did you know that was my major?" I'm starting to think Dave is a little creeper.

"That's the business. I know everything. Plus, your uncle and Jerry gave me a copy of your resume when you were looking for an internship, which I gave to my boss. He liked the minor in finance and philosophy." Dave's voice began to bore me. That and all his insincere bullshit. I would really love a job with Trust One; they pay quite well. Dave began to speak again. "Ten o'clock Monday, downtown, 118 West Madison. Stop by my office and I'll take you to see the big man."

Dave shakes my hand and puts his other hand on my shoulder as if he wants to console me.

The funeral service ends as Dave walks away. I see a herd of people in black suits and black skirts quickly walking past me; I want to say, "Who died?" (Bad joke.) All the voices blend together, quietly apologizing for my cousin's death, "Sorry Jack ... Sorry Jack ..." Finally, everyone has left the gravesite but me. I feel the need to talk to my cousin's grave. In my head I sadly whisper, "I love you Jerry. I'll be talking to you." Jerry always offered me advice on life, school, investments and women. He was a cooler version of me. When my parents died, he treated me like a brother.

My sister surprisingly starts honking the horn of her red Toyota Celica. I forgot she was my ride. I slowly walk through the grass with my head down, trying to hold back the tears. I look at the sea of cars driving through the burial ground, realizing my sister and I are the last to leave.

Opening the car door, I feel the heat from the black interior causing sweat to form on my forehead. The metal on the seat belt burns my hand as I quickly snap it in place.

"You don't fucking honk in a graveyard, Alexis." I did not intend to be mean about it, but that bothered me.

"Yeah, I know, I just want to get out of here. Sorry." For the rest of the ride we say nothing to each other. We were both very close with Jerry, and with our parents gone, all we have is each other.

Our parents died three years ago, on their thirtieth anniversary. After working thirty-five years designing furniture, my father saved all his money for a vacation in paradise. Our parents were headed to a private island off the Pacific Coast near the Philippines. They were going to stay in the Hotel Golden, an extravagant hotel with beautiful-large-straw huts where all meals and drinks are from local farms served by natives. My dad heard of the island from my uncle Jay who gave my father a matchbox from the island as a joke. The joke became a goal. A goal that ended as a small plane lost an engine flying over beautiful blue water. Now all I have is a matchbox and nightmares. Alexis has dealt with their death by pushing it out of her mind.

Alexis turned twenty-six in May, and I've noticed a change, a maturity level she didn't have before. Lately she has been very self-conscious. She is getting married in two months and wants to look perfect for her day. She has long brown hair that curls up in humid weather. I look forward to her wedding. Maybe my friends will stop hitting on her. She owes me. I introduced Alexis to Mark Ladd (her fiancé) when I was sort of dating Mark's sister Terry. I stopped seeing Terry because she got pissed that I hung out with Mark more than with her. Like Alexis, Mark works in marketing, and I always hoped they would hit it off. Alexis does creative work, designing campaigns for low carb foods. The paleo diet is her best friend. Mark works as an account executive. He keeps his clients happy and his advertising associates happy. I want his job. I like it when all sides are happy. Mark says he got the job because they needed a big man for their corporate basketball team. Mark looks like a tall version of Antonio Banderas.

I'm glad he's tying the knot. Women never looked at my rosy cheeks, thin frame, or admired my Jewfro when we would hit the bars together.

The trip home ends quickly and quietly. Alexis manages to make a forty-five-minute drive a twenty-minute ride with no accidents. I keep thinking of stupid death expressions, like, "At least we made it here alive." (I keep those thoughts to myself.) Alexis lives in the apartment house across the street from me. We live two blocks away from Wrigley Field in refurbished apartment houses. I moved out of her creaky wooden floor, bright orange walls, Monet pictures-filled apartment a few weeks ago. My new roommate is my best friend from elementary school, John Gold. He bought the place and offered me a great deal.

John looks a little like me, but taller, broader, and somehow skinnier. For a mathematician, he has this dumb guy grin always tattooed to his face. He looks like an H&M model who got in a fight that ended his career. John's a little more introverted than me. He gets shy around pretty girls, has a mind that works like a calculator, loves to run, and pays more than his fair share of the rent. He works at his cousin's accounting and finance company with the title "analyst." All in all, John is a great guy that somehow manages to deal with me. We have been workout partners since high school and still dream of looking buff.

As Alexis squeezes into the tiny space behind her apartment building, she quickly spouts off, "Jack, tell your whores your new number."

All of a sudden, my ego comes into the picture. "Who's been calling—ratty-whore or trashy-whore," I ask nicely.

"Both. Did you sleep with them, too? What happened to that nice girl Amy?"

"No, I'm waiting for marriage. As for Amy, there's no love there, but I haven't given up yet."

"Whatever Jack. Come on over, we'll hang."

As much as unpacking is a necessity, I need some family time. "Cool. Let's catch some quality TV. And then I'll make you some dinner."

Inside Alexis's apartment, an assortment of French impressionists hit you at each wall. The wooden floor cracks in certain spots I try to avoid, and the smell of peach potpourri fills the room. We sit on her gray couch and sink in six inches. Alexis and I discuss nothing for hours as *Mr. Belvedere* and *Family Ties* reruns follow each other in the background on her tiny, blurry RCA television. I think it was a gift when she graduated high school.

Around eight, I decide to start cutting up vegetables for this recipe I saw the other day on a cooking show. I cut up onions, mushrooms, green and red sweet peppers, and zucchini on a brown cutting board shaped like a pig. "I cannot believe you saved my cutting board. Shit, this was made in sixth grade."

The aroma of vegetables fills up the room as I toss them in a frying pan with olive oil and garlic. Twenty minutes later, voilà—vegetable pancakes and salad are served. After consuming too much food, I hug Alexis and head home.

Alexis and I are lucky we have each other. She shows me the ropes, and I loosen them for her. Until she and Mark get married, I have a feeling we will spend a lot of time together.

MY PAD

Entering my home feels like driving a new car for the first time. I want to fill each wall with cool (and cheap) art, have sex in every room but John's, tear up the wooden floors with rollerblades (yes, I still rollerblade), play video games, and melt into the oversized couch Gold's mom gave us.

We live across the hall from "the dudes." They smoke a lot of weed (we think) and are very laid back. We do not know their names, so we call them "the dudes." Rarely do they make an appearance. Every once in a while, twenty people will leave their place as silently as they arrived. We never hear any noise escape from their place except for some Dave Matthews Band. One of them has the height of a basketball player, wiry, with greasy rocker hair. Think glam rock. The other guy comes up to my chin with a stocky build and crunchy dreadlocks. I invited them to our first party on Saturday. We could have much worse neighbors.

Interrupting my thoughts, John yells, "Darts! Your room, now!" I am up for the challenge; if there was one thing I learned in college, it was how to kick some ass in darts.

"For-shizzle!" John has always been better than me at video games and ping-pong, but with darts I hold the edge. It's the only "sport" where I feel comfortable, maybe even a little cocky, when I play.

As the game begins, John has no idea some of my college friends are about to enter the bachelor pad. I wanted to surprise him and pick up my spirits, so I called Cholet. Cholet Taylor is a beautiful girl with legs that could wrap around a man twice, gray eyes, dark skin, and a Julia Roberts smile. Sara and Stacey are the other two girls. They look like sisters, with blond hair, light blue eyes, voluptuous figures, and smiles bright enough to light up a room. Their secret? Crest White Strips and no coffee.

As the game goes on, I explain to John that he needs to hit each of the following areas on the dartboard three times: 20, 19, 18, 17, 16, 15, and bulls-eye (center of the board). Even though he went to college I'm not sure John ever played darts, or for that matter most bar games.

My last throw signifies my luck or excellence: triple 20s, double 18s, and one bulls-eye. "I hope you do as well on your interview as you're doing right now. No wonder you never made the dean's list in college, you were too busy on the pro darts circuit." Suddenly we hear "beep-beep-beep" from the security system.

I slide across the floor to the voice monitor, "Come on up ladies," and buzz them in. John's eyes light up like a Christmas tree.

"Jack, you're a playboy—"

"No, I'm not," I quickly interrupt. "I think you have to be rich and have an accent. You never hear about an American playboy. You always hear about the French or Italian playboy."

John interjects "Maybe when you're rich and well-traveled. Jerry would be very proud." As I open the door for the women, I quickly whisper, "I wouldn't even be in the running."

John takes one look at the girls, turns to me and says, "Oh yeah you would!"

"Wow, this place looks great! We are really sorry about your loss. We all loved Jerry. I remember him telling me how he was a map major."

"Thank you, Cholet. I remember when he told me he was going to get a degree in geography. I thought he was joking. Good thing he double majored."

The girls enter the apartment one at a time, and all stand next to each other on our Nebraska Cornhuskers red and white doormat my friend mailed us. I introduce the girls to John. Introductions lead to Sara whipping out a bottle of spiced rum yelling, "Jacky baby, let's do some shots for Jerry!"

Jerry always drank Captain and Coke. He never turned down a shot but was never drunk. I remember his drinking rules: no mixing beer and liquor, shots before midnight only, and water between every drink. While watching John give the quick tour, all I can think is, "Who killed Jerry? Why was he on the west side that late?"

John seats the girls on the slightly used leather couch. There is room for four, and no matter the temperature outside, the couch is cold. I run into the kitchen and go through each dark oak cupboard until I can dig up five shot glasses and five cocktail glasses. Using a circular breakfast tray, I bring all the glasses into the den without spilling. I sit in the La-Z-Boy across from John, who is sitting on the other La-Z-Boy. Before I can defend myself, Stacey finishes telling the story of the time I took some girl home from the school library and starts describing the time I stole a test by simply going to another class's final. Forgetting I have an interview at 10 a.m., we drink till the sun pops up and then pass out. I think John passes out with Cholet ... in his bed. Sara and Stacey sleep on my bed, and I get the couch.

"I wanna rock and roll all night, and party every day ..." The alarm in my room goes off—set, of course, to the '70s station—at 8:30. Sara and Stacey, out cold, do not hear a thing. I turn off the alarm, jump in the shower and attempt to wake up. Worrying that I might still be drunk, I drink some water as it sprays from the shower head. A throbbing and pounding sensation in my head indicates that I am entering the hangover stage. Multi-tasking, I brush, apply shaving cream, and toast an egg bagel. Running from kitchen to bathroom to bedroom, I eat, dress, smell good, but cannot find dress socks anywhere. I run into John's room. He's sleeping on his back with Cholet's arm over his chest. She happens to be laying on her stomach, on top of the sheets, naked!

"Nice ass, Cholet. Hey, John. Wake up, wake up."

"Jack, you got me drunk and she took advantage of me, it was great. No sex, but great."

"Okay, I don't want to know. Socks. I need dress socks."

"Sorry, Jack. I don't have to work today, but I have to do laundry."

"Fuck! No socks," I shout at the top of my lungs. "Oh, well. No one will know. Have fun John. You have three girls in an alcohol-induced coma."

"Good luck, Jack. Thanks for letting me borrow one of your ..."

"Shut up. I'll see ya later." A yawn squeezes out as I lock the door. Hopefully coffee will remove ample layers of brain fog.

Running to catch the train, stomach cramps and acid reflux burn my insides. I tell myself not to puke until the celebration after I get the job. The moment I step into the train, the doors slam shut. The "L," which runs above the wonderful city of Chicago, is packed with young and old commuters. I'm hoping the rank odor of the train is from someone other than me.

To mentally prepare for the interview, I try and think of my strengths and weaknesses. I never have a good answer to "What's your weakest skill set?" I suppose "everything" is not an acceptable answer.

I know I have a drinking problem, because all I can think about is how much this train looks like the train in the Coors Light Silver Bullet commercials. The seats are a little too close for comfort, and today it looks like I'm going to have to stand. At least they have handles at the top to grab, as my balance is a little off today. The yellow, shiny seats look like they were made of cheap plastic that melts in the heat. I never feel like a germophobe except when I sit on the train. Another commercial enters my mind as I determine the nasty smell is coming from the dude behind me: "Don't you wish everyone used Dial?" How do you stink at 9 a.m.?

The conductor announces each stop with incredible zeal. "Chicago, Chicago, next stop, Chicago," he sings across the intercom with so much personality you would think he works for

the late show. The conductor's voice wakes me up, "Last stop, everyone to work, last stop! Kidding."

A little disoriented, I walk toward Madison trying not to be nervous. My first interview for a real job, not a campus lifeguard. The thought excites me. I'm filled with positive energy as I whisper, "I am going to get this job. Let's go! Focus, Jack!" I'm just that odd, that I believe chanting and visualization works. I am hesitant to work for Trust One, but they pay well, and my secret mission is to find out what happened to Jerry. This would fulfill a few bucket list items: get a real job, work as a PI, solve my cousin's death, and travel business class. Maybe I need to have higher aspirations.

Walking into the Trust One building, a gloomy black and gray carpet and sea of people welcome and speed-walk by me. All I can think of is my crazy finance professor.

I visualize him standing at the front of the class, filled with enthusiasm. Dr. Powers would emphasize his points using all the energy his small beer gut and middle-aged frame would allow. I remember watching his full head of gray hair shaking as he yelled, "Everyone's an assistant vice president at a bank, but if you really want to be at the top you have start in the credit department! Get all buddy-buddy with your clients, and then they'll hire you away and give you a cushy job with a big title!" I can still see the small amounts of spit traveling out of his mouth as he yelled. I wonder if I'll be in the credit department.

Two security officers work at a large black desk ten yards past the front doors. The officers, both large black men, stand erect, wearing secret service-like suits, with the industry standard white button-down shirts. I walk up to the desk and witness them gawk at this woman in an elevator. The woman, a beautiful blonde wearing a tight white dress that makes her boobs look huge, is checking out her behind. She turns her head towards her back and looks in the mirror at her rear. Shaking her head in approval, you can tell she's thinking all the years in the gym paid off—and they have. As the elevator doors open, she walks past the desk and realizes she was just on candid camera. The two guards and

I give her the old two thumbs up. That's right, not even on the clock and I'm already sexually harassing the staff. While the three of us giggle like teenagers, I ask, "What floor do I go to? I'm Jack Waters for Trust One?"

Simultaneously, "Thirty-two, thirty-three, and thirty-four, west side." The larger guard adds, "So you might have a few meetings, son. No starting room sorry." Walking towards the elevators I thank them.

Wandering to the west elevators my arms begin to shake. Thoughts shoot through my head: "Will I land the job? Will I ever get a job? Is John having sex with Cholet? And will my heart stop beating so fast?"

I remember Dave stating how he works on the thirty-fourth floor (Walter Peyton's old number). I press the button, the light pops on, and off I travel to the music of Kenny G. The dark elevator quickly shoots to my stop. The doors part in slow motion, as if I am famous, or it's just an old elevator. As I step out, I hear a robot-like voice.

"Thirty-fourth floor."

THE INTERVIEW PROCESS

Black tile peeks out from a blood red carpet. It looks like they used this to mop up after an accident. I can smell deodorizer; it's like Mr. Clean just left. Yes, this is the big leagues! All the associates are dressed formally, the office furniture looks expensive, and I'm pretty sure I see an original Picasso! I hope to blend in with high society like scotch and soda (smooth, yet powerful, I think; I'm too young and poor for scotch).

The office seems dark for such a powerful company. The dreary environment scares me. Rows of gray cubicles give the office a maze-like atmosphere. In front of the cubicles sits a large white desk with black annual reports, a computer monitor so big a blind man could read it, and a phone with several lines flashing red like a phone emergency vehicle. Behind the desk sits a very pale man with a shaved head, a gray mustache, and scary blue eyes. The man looks at me, displaying no emotion on his face, "Good morning, Mr. Waters. Please follow me." (Great, I might get to work with Vincent Price. Maybe he didn't die.)

More afraid than nervous, I'm guided to Dave's small office. Now that I have sweated through my shirt and nearly peed in my pants, I feel confident.

"Jack, relax. Are you feeling all right?"

"Just fine, Dave. How are you?"

Dave gradually forms his insincere smile and starts to lecture me. "Follow me, Jack. You're about to meet the VP of operations, Bob West. I told him what a great kid you are. I said I informally interviewed you before. Not a complete lie. We did talk when you were looking for an internship. The position is an excellent opportunity for you. Trust One continues to grow …"

As usual, my short attention span and dislike for Dave forces me to stop listening. We walk through a section of gray cubicles, then white ones, then blue, and finally black, before we reach the VP's office. Did I just enter the dark side? I feel sweat flowing from my armpits down my side, a pretty disgusting feeling. Mental note: purchase new deodorant.

The floor resembles Charlie Sheen's office in the movie *Wall Street*—open and busy, except for Bob West's office. A huge wooden door separates his office from the rest of the world. None of the other offices connect to the ten-foot ceiling, but Bob's does. As Dave slowly opens the door after a double knock, my heart moves at double the normal rate and sweat continues to flow freely. So maybe I'm a little nervous and slightly smelly. Hopefully the office aroma will cover my odor.

Suddenly, I forget how to breathe without shaking. Sweat continues to pour out of me, and all the liquor from my wild night is gone. I cautiously study the office as if making a major purchase. The dark room contains a giant desk with a rolodex the size of a basketball. It takes up more space than the computer. Maybe this guy needs a cell phone. The circular window in the back of the room resembles a large peephole, and I can't help but be impressed by a large, thick, padded chair on wheels. This is the chair of greatness, something rich men sit on and poor migrant workers spend hours making. Behind the desk, an old school CD player softly plays rain sounds.

A hand suddenly appears on my shoulder. I jump, startled, as the hand's owner begins to speak. "Sorry. I didn't mean to scare you, Jack. Hi. I'm Bob West. It's a pleasure to meet you. Dave

tells me terrific things about you." As we shake hands, my heart is still pulsating through my skin. I try to relax as he continues to praise me. "Please sit down. Incredible resume." I see it lying in the center of the massive desk. "First, I want to offer my condolences. Jerry was a great man."

"Thank you, he will always be a great man in my memory." Gaining some confidence, I sit back in my chair and take a brief look at Bob. Bob does not look like he sleeps, ever. Under his eyes sit great big bags colored black and blue. He is short, fat and tan, with a dark brown beard and not much dark brown hair on his head. The dull light from above reflects off his shiny head into my eyes. I feel like I'm sitting in the devil's office. The air feels thick in the room; the smell of glass cleaner and cheap cigars builds a weird atmosphere.

My mind stops wandering when I hear another comment on my resume. "Your resume piqued my interest."

"Thank you—I think—Mr. West."

"Please call me Bob. Market research intern, financial consultant intern, creative marketing assistant, and Red Cross instructor. Very impressive. Three-point G.P.A., social group president, dorm treasurer, intramural coach, self-defense club ... and the list continues."

Bob continues to read out loud, as if I've written a Pulitzer Prize-worthy article. I never thought anyone would believe all that bullshit. In college the only thing I did sober was attend class and workout, which I did hungover. My eyes circle the room: IBM computer, laser printer, shredder, wireless headset, gray carpet, and a few pictures of ducks. Yes, ducks. No VP's office is complete without them. I think I'll go back to listening mode.

"So how was your semester in London compared with your summer in Mexico?"

Not thinking at all I respond, "Mexico was all about tequila and Squirt. London was all about LIBOR (London Interbank Offered Rate)."

"So, you drank a lot in Mexico, and studied the exchange in London."

"No, I drank a lot in both places." I continue to speak to him like an old pal. Maybe next I should tell him who was better in the sack (I wish I really knew the answer to that). I decide this man could offer me a large salary, so I open up a can of intelligence with a side of charm. "Just kidding. I studied diligently while absorbing the culture. The two cultures were completely opposite. In Mexico I studied marketing, realizing they could use a lot of help in that department. In foggy London I studied finance, realizing I could use a lot of help in that department. Besides picking up a plethora of information, I learned about people." When I realize I'm rambling, I force myself to stop yapping for a minute. It's hard to listen when you're a chatterbox.

Bob seizes this opportunity to chime in. "Great, Jack. Now I'm going to ask you a few questions." I think he means: enough chit-chat—let's see what you really know. As I fear that I'm a moron, this frightens me. Bob takes a serious look at me and opens his small mouth, "I think banks are trying to cash in on our business. Banks want to compete with us. I have no problem with competition, but society needs the safety, which the banking industry supplies. Explain your opinion on the deregulation of banks."

Staring directly into Bob's overworked eyes, I adopt the thinking-man pose, with my legs crossed, one arm across my legs, and my other hand stroking my chin. I know what Please-Call-Me-Bob wants to hear—that deregulation takes away the safety and how it might hurt the public. I give him what he wants to hear, only because I agree.

"Bob, deregulation was okay in the beginning. Banks tried to supply the customer with better services that were secure. As the regulatory dialectic continued (he eats that expression up; thank you, Professor Powers) and banks tried to get around the law, a line had to be drawn. The purpose of a bank, to the consumer, is to provide safety for their cash and hopefully some interest, while loaning out money. People know that they can put up to a hundred thousand dollars in an account and their money will be secure. If banks keep trying to compete with a company such as Trust One, banks will no longer provide the most liquid account.

Trust One is there to provide people with investment opportunities that will earn a greater return, with greater risk. An account at the local bank should be risk-free!" At this point in the interview, I feel like I could discuss nuclear fusion with Einstein and sound somewhat intelligent. I hope my jabber is making sense.

Bob leans towards me, shakes his head approvingly and asks, "Do you think this company takes advantage of people?"

I think, "No, you get sued all the time because you help families too much," but I don't think I'll say that. The question stumps me, but I give it my best shot: "To be honest (never a good start to any question boss—or a girl—asks), I cannot really answer that question without talking to customers. If this company helps people to retire in Florida, sends kids to college, and covers people's claims—while charging a competitive fee—then Trust One does not take advantage of people." As my BS increases, so does the moisture on my forehead and lower back. I lightly brush off my forehead waiting for Bob's response.

"Good answer, Mr. Waters," Bob says, yawning. Bob's mouth opens large enough to fit an apple and a sack of nuts. (He must have done some hard time.) "Sorry, Jack. I had a rough night. According to Dave, you already know all about our operation. We are a financial conglomerate. Trust One does it all: insurance, stocks, bonds, accounting, advising, and research to keep every sector successful. In fact, you would be working in the Market Research department. The position that's open is very challenging and an adventure!" All of a sudden, I feel like I entered the Army recruiting office and no one told me. "You'll be out in the field researching investment opportunities and claims firsthand. You'll almost be a private investigator." (Bucket list item!) "We'll supply you with a camera, tape recorder, and laptop with all the bells and whistles, email and fax. Since you'll be in the field, we will also supply you with an Acura MDX!" Suddenly my heart stops and my jaw drops, and the words "Big Time" ring loudly in my ears! All it takes is technology and a car.

Then I wonder: Why a tape recorder and camera? "Great. But why the camera and recorder?"

"Mr. Waters, for a deal worth over eighty-five thousand dollars, we might want a few pictures. The tape recorder is more for you, so you don't have to write everything down in meetings and whatnot." Bob's calm voice and low tone disappeared with his last sentence. Sensing his own hostility, he takes a deep breath and continues speaking. "Now Mr. Waters, before I can offer you the opportunity to join us, you need to interview with the man who would train you. Sydney Phelps is that man. Sydney has been with us for eight years, first as an intern while attending Northwestern. Currently he helps run our innovation department. The marketing position requires a complete knowledge of his department."

All of a sudden: "Beep!" Bob's enormous computer dwarfs his balding head as he quickly reads an email message. He laughs and slaps his thigh. "That was Sydney. He says I need to hurry the interrogation. So that's exactly what I'll do. Sydney also began in the marketing department and knows the correct research procedures."

Sydney Phelps sounds like a solid guy who worked his way up, but Bob is killing my image of this character. While I try to visualize Sydney, Bob shoots out of his chair and asks me to follow him. Walking with Bob feels like following a politician. Every corner we turn, he shakes someone's hand, asks them a personal question and barely stands there long enough to hear a response.

"Judy, how's your son doing in first grade? ... Great!"

Heading back to the front of the office, we pass the elevator bank and keep walking. There's another side to this massive floor. We use Bob's key fob to get a locked door open. More cubicles fill the all-white room. This room appears brighter and more open than the other side. No secretary sits at the front of this office, just a water cooler and fridge. The white walls are covered with motivational expressions. Quotes from Einstein to athletes are either handwritten on whiteboards or stuck to the walls. One banner reads, "Dream, Believe, and Achieve." I think that was my high school's slogan.

As we reach the end of the first row of cubicles, I see the desk of Sydney J. Phelps. Sydney currently is on the phone. Judging

by his tone, I think it's a personal call. He speaks softly with a deep voice, "Jessica, I leave work at 5:30, baby. I'll get you then."

Sydney is sitting in a swivel chair with his slightly shaved head leaning back. Sidney might be the darkest person I have ever seen. He has a lean build with broad shoulders. Sydney's long legs sit on his desk, with his big feet, hidden in brown Timberland shoes, hanging off the side. To the right of his feet, sitting on his organized desk, is a giant plaque from Northwestern. The plaque reads, "Sydney J. Phelps, #81 Most Improved Player 1991–1992." While gazing at his computer with an old Chicago Bears screen saver of Walter Payton and Mike Ditka, Sydney realizes we are behind him.

"Bob, how you doing? Life treating the VP OP well?"

"Great, thanks for asking. How are you and your family?" Bob politely asks as Sydney springs to his feet and extends his hand to Bob.

"Work is great, the social life is a little slow." Turning towards me he continues," I guess this is Mr. Jack Waters." After exchanging greetings, Sydney adds, "Sorry about your cousin."

While thanking him for his condolences, I wonder how everyone knows about my loss. I should just accept regrets, but for some reason I feel awkward that everyone knows.

While thinking about Jerry I forget what Sydney says to me. With a serious look on my face I ask, "Mr. Phelps, what did you say?"

With a huge grin, and amazingly white teeth, "Mr. Phelps. I like that. Until I get that raise Bob owes me, you can call me Sydney." Without being rude, Sydney points Bob towards the exit, "I need fifteen minutes with Jack, and then I'll call you."

Shaking his head in agreement, Bob tells me what a pleasure interviewing me was and how he envisions us working together. Bob grips my hand tightly and winks, as if to say, "Good luck, kid."

"Thanks for your time Bob, I also hope we get that chance."

Sydney quickly interrupts. "Enough ass-kissing." Sitting back down he energetically says, "Let's get this party started, Jack!" Quickly skimming my resume, he looks pleased.

Immediately I like Sydney J. Phelps. He has this relaxed, honest attitude that you cannot help but like. Even his dress is casual yet stylish. His outfit for the day is straight out of a magazine: khaki pants, a white button-down shirt with a large collar, no tie, and a navy vest (Tommy Hilfiger) with a couple yellow buttons not buttoned.

Using his deep soulful voice, "Please, sit down Jack. Just grab the swivel chair from the desk in front of mine. There is only so much Bob I can handle. I don't mean it in a bad way. Dude is intense."

I immediately start to laugh. "I almost died when I walked into his supersized office. When do you get that?"

Without any hesitation, Sydney responds, "No shit, that office dwarfs the Oval Office. Bob deserves the office; he pretty much runs the company. He does a lot of the things no one else wants to do. That's why he," Sidney raps the rest of his sentence, "Drives a BMW, owns a Rolls Royce, lives in a mansion, vacations in Europe, eats quiche, and wears a fur coat."

After his little rap session, Sydney's face grows serious and I can tell the interview will start as he begins his next sentence. "Now that we have developed a good rapport, let's discuss the job. I want to warn you—like Bob, you'll be doing the things no one else wants to do." I wonder what exactly 'no one else wants to do' means, but Sydney starts talking fast and I just try to keep up with the barrage. "You're going to be busy. You'll investigate everything from insurance claims to investment opportunities. The company will want information you cannot easily obtain. The hours are flexible, but leave that social calendar open because you'll be busy. The upside is that the cash is kickin'! And your job will not bore you one bit. You will have a company credit card, car, computer ..."

Responding on pure excitement, "Well, I don't have the job yet!" I feel like I'm speaking to a motivational speaker. My voice cracks and my heart rate starts to climb with positive energy.

And then Sydney powerfully responds, "Yes you do!" As he nods his head in approval and shines that large smile I just want

to yell, scream, and jump up and down to let everyone know: Jack Waters has arrived! With my heart pulsating through my chest and endorphins exploding in my body (it's like a runners high), I feel incredible. Looking out the window behind Sydney's desk and listening to Sydney, I feel on top of the world.

With a serious look, "The interview process is two ways. You have to decide; do you want this job? Are there questions you have for me? I have no idea what Jerry told you about working here, but he liked it. The kid worked some serious hours. Although my schedule is flexible, I'm always on call. Are you cool with that?"

With no hesitation I answer, "Yes, sir!"

"Congratulations Mr. Waters. You were hired before you walked in the door. If you choose to accept the job, training will start as early as possible. Sounds like you will you join the wonderful world of Trust One?"

Trying to act cool, I cross my legs, lean back in my chair and stare Sydney in his excitement-filled eyes and answer, "I'll take it."

Within a second, Sydney jumps out of his chair, extends a hand and pulls me off my chair as if I weigh nothing. I get a hug. "Great! I can't wait to work with you. This place needs an infusion of young blood. Energy. And my man, you got that. You need to work on that sweat gland problem. Probably just nerves."

Normally a stranger hugging me after an interview would feel awkward, but it feels natural with Sydney. The genuine excitement in his tight but manly hug immediately removes him from my list of suspects. His voice follows me to the elevators, "When can you start?"

I flip through an imaginary calendar I pull out of the inside of my suit coat. "Well, let's see. Tuesday, Wednesday, Thursday and Friday I have a lot of nothing to do."

With a smile, Sid answers back, "I'll see you tomorrow at eight thirty."

"I was thinking more like noon."

Shaking his head yes, "Noon it is! Lose the tie and dress casually. I'll tell Bobby you took the job and enjoyed meeting with him. The fast-talking Jimmy Smits will take you through

compensation today on the phone or tomorrow, as he'll have you fill out all the paperwork." At this point the elevator arrives, yet we keep talking. After I stick my arm in the closing elevator door, we shake hands and say our goodbyes.

Fireworks of excitement, joy, and fear hit me as the elevator descends. I wonder where my desk will be. Or will I even get one? Can I do this job? The rush sets in as I realize I will be making more than I can spend. I can actually pay my half of the rent. With a small jump for joy, I realize I'm not alone in the elevator. Looking over my shoulder I see an elderly lady in a pink long dress. I turn to her with a psychotic grin glued to my face and exclaim, "I got a job!"

She smiles at me and says, in a grandmotherly tone, "Congratulations, young man."

Rapidly, I reply, "Thank you, young lady."

I hope Trust One never screws her over. While enjoying the moment, I notice the lady moving away from the corner of the elevator to stand near me. She gives me the "nice old lady smile," and I think for sure a lecture is on the way. Suddenly the elevator says, "Lobby," in a computerized voice and as the doors separate, I let the lady walk out first. Walking fast, I quickly head towards the exit, waving to the guards. Loosening my tie while stepping into the warm air, I think I might accidently be strutting.

While heading toward the train, I see a familiar red Celica. The license plate reads LW0457. Incredible! My sister's car. Her dazed face drives right past me without realizing she's passed her own brother. The next intersection is backed up, so I run after her. When I reach the car, I bang on the passenger side window. Alexis's whole body tightens in fear. I guess my excitement level translated into a serial killer knock. When she starts breathing again, I hear the power locks open and sit down.

While turning down the Beastie Boys classic "Brass Monkey," Alexis starts talking. "Jack, you scared the shit out of me! Did you get the job?"

Practically yelling, I answer, "Hell yeah! Lunch on me!"

"That's awesome! When do you start? Tell me everything. Are you making more than me? Before you answer, come with me to Oakbrook. I have a photo shoot at McDonald's."

I respond quickly, "Well, I'll tell you everything, but I want to go home. I'm beat, spent, tired, and hung over. The new job excitement masks my pain. I'll drive down there with you and take the train home."

"Okay, I can deal with that. Start with what you did last night. I called your place and Stacey answered the phone." She raises her eyebrows and looks at me as if I've been naughty.

"I threw a little gathering. John hooked up with Cholet. I woke up and the girl was naked in his bed." Alexis stares in dismay. How could innocent John be waking up next to crazy Cholet?

The new job excitement slowly dissipates as drowsiness sets in. As I finish describing the interview, we reach a train station. Paying no attention to the noise of an oncoming train we continue to talk.

Alexis offers to take me out tomorrow for dinner, "Come on. Mark and I will take you for dinner."

Offended by her offer, and not thinking she is about to marry the guy, I yell at her in a joking way. "Oh, Mark and you. I see—can't hang out solo with your bro because you got a man." Suddenly realizing the train is here I run out of the car. "Shit, I'll call you later."

Not even thinking, I run inside the train and the doors close. Then it hits me—am I on the right train? My guess is confirmed as the short fat conductor with a handlebar mustache yells out, "Next stop—Union Station!" I caught the right train.

"Wake up! Wake up!"

My eyes barely open as I try to focus. A large and smelly conductor is repeatedly poking my shoulder with his fat index finger. With blurry vision, I see a round, chubby face, with scruffy brown-gray facial hair and greasy brown hair hanging over his forehead, telling me something. Wiping a little crust from my eyes, I feel as if I am still dreaming. I walk off the train, taking

my time. Gathering my suit coat and leather case I exit the train station and fall into a cab. After telling the cab I live on Addison and Wilton, I pass out again.

"Where the hell am I?" Moving my head from right to left I jump up and check my surroundings. I have no memory of getting in a cab. The driver begins to freak out.

With broken English and a thick Indian accent, he starts yelling, as if I am deaf. "You are a block from your home! You fell asleep! You scared the life out of me! Get out here! Eighteen fifty!"

Recognizing my location, yet unaware when I entered the cab, I leave the guy a twenty and walk away. Holding my suit coat behind me, loosening my tie and thinking about my new job, I feel energized. The hot sun feels good; the humidity must be hiding for the afternoon.

The mixture between the bright sun and sweat is killing my vision. Reaching into the inside pocket on my suit, I whip out my roommate's Ray-Bans. The two hundred and fifty-dollar glasses feel great. Maybe in a few weeks I'll buy my own pair. The lyrics going through my now over-sized ego are, for some reason, "Stayin' Alive" by the Bee Gees.

A job can easily bloat your ego. Strolling up to my building, I slip the key in the lock—and nothing. Without losing my high, I take my credit card out of my wallet and go to work. Wedging my gray Visa between the door and the lock, the door pops open. I feel safe.

The large wooden door to my apartment is unlocked. Sure enough, Stacey and Sara are asleep in my bed. Cholet still lies naked in John's bed. A quick glance at the white clock above our big TV, I notice it's only twelve-thirty. The adrenaline is fading; it might be time for a real nap. I remove my navy-blue pants, pull off the paisley tie and let exhaustion beat enthusiasm. The couch never felt so great. Unexpectedly, I am in a place full of music and color. I am going through my first day of work in a dream, and it plays out like a music video. The song in the background of my dream is "Sabotage" by the Beastie Boys. Everyone is playing their music today.

Awakening, I realize the music is coming from the CD player in the kitchen. The girls are putting the rum in the freezer and burning toast for their three o'clock breakfast.

"Hey, sleepy boy," Sarah and Stacey sing simultaneously.

I peek at them through the small hallway. "You calling me sleepy boy, and don't you have homes? I've been on an interview, got a job, went to Oakbrook, and saw my roommate get a piece of her juicy booty." While I point to Cholet she quickly snaps.

"What are you talking about? Nothing happened."

Sarcastically I add, "Deny, deny, deny, deny. You just mysteriously woke up naked in John's bed, but nothing happened." Cholet shakes her head as Sarah and Stacey start laughing, calling Cholet "naughty."

Cholet immediately changes the subject, "Congratulations on the job." Being the brief and very personal girl she is, Cholet cuts right to the chase. "How much will you make?"

A little embarrassed of my salary for a new grad, "Enough," is all I say. The doorbell rings and Sarah begins to talk.

"Enough to pay for the pizza?" The girls surround me and give me a big old congratulations hug and kisses on the cheek. After all the kisses, how can I not buy the pizza?

"Sure, I'll buy the food." Behind the door stands our friend Joe from Charlie's Restaurant. Joe went to undergrad with us and puts himself through law school delivering and cooking pizza. Joe loves surprising people; to bypass security, he rings the wrong apartment. He's weird that way. Just looking at Joe through the peephole, you can tell he loves pizza. Besides a pizza gut, he's pretty lean—or maybe his tall, dark frame just hides his fat well. Joe skipped a year of high school, finished college a year early to visit (AKA party with) his relatives in Italy (and to party in Europe), and will graduate law school early, but refuses to act intelligent.

When delivering pizza, he uses a thick Italian accent; we call him Paulie because he sounds like Paulie from the *Rocky* movies. Usually, Joe conveniently forgets to charge John and me. The girls walk to the kitchen while I let Joe wait. After all my hesitation I open the door and greet Joe, "Hello, Joe. I got a job, so I can pay

this time. Oh, try not to work Friday night; we're celebrating. That's Friday night, girls."

Upon hearing the word "girls," Joe steps in, opens his big mouth and begins the Italian act. "You got girls here? What kind? Easy? Blond? Brunettes? Redheads? Tall? Short? Voluptuous? Hairy? What you got? Come on out—I brought pizza and beer."

Looking Joe in the eyes with an inquisitive look, "Do you always invite yourself into people's homes? Not like I mind; just curious. Doesn't seem safe, either."

Joe responds with his tough guy look, "Fuck you. I'm just trying to be friendly, you cheap, two-bit, pizza-eating, no pants-wearing, Beastie Boys-listening bum!" As the girls walk into the main room Joe loses the act. "Hi, Cholet. Hi, S and S. You three crash here? Cholet, did you touch his roommate?" Immediately we all laugh. Joe also has ESP.

Cholet innocently says, "Joey, would I do something like that?"

Without hesitation Joe spouts off, "Hell, yeah! Besides, you are wearing his running sweats." Joe proceeds to John's room and begins talking like super spy Austin Powers. I haven't heard that voice in years. Using his funny English accent, he continues his assault on Cholet. "You shagged him rotten. His bed usually looks neat, but today the bed remains unmade. You did it just for shits and giggles. You're the town—"

Cholet interrupts, "Okay, Einstein. We just kissed."

Sarcastically Joe adds, "Right—those are probably his underwear and bra on the floor. I always told him he looks stunning in lace pink panties. And if those are his, I could pull down your pants and see your—"

Again, Cholet interrupts, "Enough, you jealous little pervert. Let's join the kids and eat." At this point, Sarah and Stacey are deep in pizza and beer, on my new couch. Part of me worries: Will today be the day the couch gets irreversibly stained? The front door remains open, music keeps blasting from the kitchen, and I can see my neighbors—"the dudes"—walking up the stairs.

Peering my head out the door I yell, "Hey, guys! Come on in for some pizza and beer. You can also meet a couple of my friends."

Simultaneously, they nod their heads yes, and the tall one says, "Cool, we're starving." While walking in, they see a pizza man's jacket and the tall one comments, "Is that the pizza guy eating with you?"

The three of us in the main room yell, "Of course," as if everyone eats with the delivery guy.

The dudes laugh, and as soon as Joe walks in the room, "Joe, what's up man?" Both dudes shake Joe's hand and exchange greetings. More shocked than ever, I stare at Joe as he spouts off their names.

"Adam D. Bone and Stevey Kline, how the fuck are you?" Joe now explains a long story about how Adam (the tall one) goes to law school with him. Joe somehow knows everybody. Adam and Steve sit on the dark brown coffee table that houses magazines like *Muscle & Fitness* and my favorite—*ESPN Magazine.*

It's weird talking to the dudes, they work a lot at night and that explains why I only see them randomly. The two have their own computer graphics business, which they run out of their apartment.

Joe and I are happy just eating mushroom-Canadian bacon-green pepper pizza and drinking Riptide Rush Gatorade (it tastes like grape Kool-Aid). After last night, the last thing I want is a beer.

The girls and the dudes, on the other hand, are drinking beer and chatting it up. Joe grabs the last piece of pizza and gives me half.

For some reason, everyone stares at us, and I decide to speak up. Holding up the beautiful, thin crust, half slice like a trophy, I say, "You know what that is? Respect!"

Adam and Stevey stand up. Adam does all the talking as he thanks us for the food and drinks. He then invites us over to smoke weed. John and I were right; they do smoke a lot of dope. Joe and I decline the offer as the girls head for the door. I wouldn't call it maturity, but smoking weed feels like something I did years ago. My brain can barely function as is—no need to throw in drugs.

While walking out the door, Joe yells, "S and S, ASAP—a little S and M for the VIP and the VP!" He flirts with every woman he meets and wonders why he's single.

"Pick one girl, Joe. You can't have them all."

Resting in the recliner, I hear laughter in the hallway. Sarah and Stacey struggle to open the unlocked door. Why don't they just go home?

I let them in and they giggle their way to the kitchen. Stacey and Cholet tear apart my fridge while Stacey stares at me with her red, glossy eyes. She tries to speak but cannot form a sentence. This is why I do not do drugs. I feel like I am stuck in a bad after school special, the one with the anti-drug theme. "You guys need to go home." All three girls are now staring at me and laughing, as if I was telling a joke and not requesting some alone time.

Finally, Stacey makes sense as she slurs her words, "Jack, you got a job, a car, free pizza, and now I'm going to get you high!" Sarah and Cholet start choking on an apple while laughing at Stacey's comment. Everyone is laughing as if Chris Rock just put on a show. I just sit back on my kitchen table, shaking my head. The dopers now run into the main room. Afraid they might break something, I follow them. The girls plop down on the couch and I sprawl out on the La-Z-Boy closest to the door. Stacey usually surfs the stations for twenty minutes before selecting a show, but in her induced state she puts on the Discovery Channel. While we watch John Glenn walk on the moon, the phone rings and startles all of us.

The phone is on the coffee table, hiding beneath a few magazines. I grab the portable phone that no one uses. "Hello?"

"Hello, Jack. Did you get the job?"

I easily recognize my roommate's voice. "Let me put it this way: Some of us got lucky last night, and others of us got lucky during the day. This weekend we must celebrate. My first day is tomorrow."

John replies enthusiastically, "Wow—are you making good money?"

"I am making enough to pay half of the rent and food, and will be driving a company car."

"Awesome, I'll be home early. Running some errands and needed to catch up on some work. I'll take you to Charlie's for dinner. I made invitations for our party; I might adjust them and mention how the bum got a job. Do not forget to call Blake; he has to come to the party."

"Okay, I will. See ya at—"

John interrupts, "See ya at five." John hangs up so fast I have no chance to say adios. The girls, bored, spring to their feet and give me some bull about why they have to leave. "It's about time." After three hugs, I inform them of our party. Pretending to be sad, I frown and wave goodbye.

Cholet speaks for the group. "We'll be at your party, sir."

I immediately run to the kitchen.

The bottom drawers on the right side of the kitchen hold my personal phone book. The rest of the kitchen is filled with gadgets I've collected from a lifetime of cooking. I have a spiralizer that makes veggies into pasta, various knives, a zester, a grater, and my special pan. This pan has been in the family for years. It's cast iron, and I've used it to cook since I was seven. My grandmother taught me how to deep-fry chicken in it with schmaltz—aka chicken fat. A few years later, my mom and I made a giant apple pancake with it.

Digging through the bottom drawer I find my black book. The black book contains all my friends' and family members' phone numbers. Just in case my cell phone dies, I like to have a quick backup. The other book I have is the "Chick-tionary." Jerry had it labeled for me and encouraged me to make copious notes there. It's completely blank, because I'm not that horrible a person. I will keep all my notes to solve his murder in it instead.

My first notes: Bob West—seems shady. Sydney is cool. Not so sure what Dave Heeder is all about.

My ADHD brain goes back to party-planning mode. I need to call Blake, my best friend from college. He's in medical school at Nebraska, becoming an even bigger Cornhusker fan. After

dialing his number by saying, "Call Blake," I hear his goofy voice answer quickly.

"Halloo," Blake says; adding extra Os is his thing. It used to be referring to himself in the third person. I'm so happy that phase ended.

"Hey, big Husker! You're coming in this weekend!" Offering no alternative usually works.

With no hesitation, "Cool!" The typical Blake response.

"Do you have tests next week?" I do care. I want him to succeed, but I want to see him.

"Only two tests and a lab, but I'll study on the plane. I take it you got a job. My baby's growing up. Congratulations!" At this point, I am ready to slap Blake over the phone, but instead I decide to sweeten the offer.

"Thanks, I'm making good money, so I will pay for your ticket. No arguments. Now study, so you can reach a new level of intoxication this weekend."

"Are you rushing me off the phone? You have a job, now you can pay a phone bill." Blake is always busy, but whenever I call he pushes off studying for at least half an hour.

"Blake. Study, masturbate, and go to bed. You have a long weekend ahead of you." Sounding fatherly seems to work with him. He pretends not to listen, but hears everything. His memory is an unfair advantage.

With acceptance in his voice, he replies, "Sounds like a plan. Call Vanguard. They're the cheapest." And just like that he quickly says bye and hangs up.

Paging through the black book I search for people to invite. After the tenth call, I hear a honk and see John's coupe from the kitchen window. Taking my time, I lace up my old man Rockports (they are so comfy) and head for the stairs.

CHARLIE'S

Jerry loved Charlie's. Who doesn't? The food is excellent, and the service is even better. I am anxious to start working and investigating Jerry's death. Sure, a hefty paycheck is motivating, but I have a lot more at stake.

John immediately shakes my hand as if I just closed a million-dollar deal. "Jack, welcome to the workforce. May your job be fulfilling, challenging—and let you pay some of our bills. Cable is no joke." John's seriousness forces me to laugh. John lectures me the whole five-minute drive. Sometimes John forgets I started working in junior high. The only time I have not had a job was about a week in 1998. The restaurant I worked at closed because the owner skipped town. I got through it; cutting veggies was not the best job in town.

We drive to the front of the restaurant and let the professionals park the car. Charlie does not charge us for valet parking. The owner is a friend of ours. Joe, John, Alexis, and I helped Charlie turn the restaurant around two years ago when Charlie Senior passed away. Charlie was a chemist in Italy and moved to Chicago five years ago to help his father out. Joe's parents took us to the restaurant years ago, and when Charlie needed some help, Joe started to work there, John took care of the taxes, and

Alexis and I helped develop a successful marketing plan. Every other month Alexis and I develop a new menu with Charlie and his chefs.

Charlie in turn takes care of us. We always have a table, free drinks, parking, and we pay half price for all meals. He also puts on a show when we bring dates there. We try not to take advantage, but the drinks are so good. He uses his chemistry skills to make these amazing fruit drinks that people purchase by the gallon.

When he's not working, he takes English classes at Loyola University, in hopes of teaching chemistry at the collegiate level. His science background helps him when testing food for fat, calories, sodium, and cholesterol—which he lists on the menu. Along with the critics and neighbors, we love this Sicilian spot.

Besides the amazing food, the restaurant has a "Godfather-like" quality. The floor is dark oak, the walls are gray, and the room is dimly lit. Picasso-like paintings cover a few walls, along with framed pictures of famous people with Charlie Senior. The waiters look like waiters, with white dress shirts, aprons, and black pants. Frank Sinatra songs play quietly in the background and except for a couple of large tables, booths fill every side and corner of the restaurant.

Charlie always sits us in the back corner and joins us for a special drink. "Tonight, we drink apple-pineapple sensation. Now tell Charlie, how are you two silly kids doing? You see Joe? He left an hour ago to deliver pasta. Yesterday, he was gone for two hours delivering a pizza." John looks at me, and knows he stayed at our apartment for at least two hours. We both feel a little guilty.

"Charlie, he was at our place yesterday. Sorry. And I just got a job."

Charlie, sitting to my right, reaches over and hugs me, "Congratulations! Tonight—my treat!"

John, sitting across from us, shakes his head, "No, tonight is on me. I'll pay for the food, you cover the drinks, and Jack will just relax."

Charlie stands up, "Okay, lobster tail for two, house discount still applies. I will personally cook the food." Before Charlie walks away, he nods his head in celebration and winks.

John and I discuss everything from my parents' deaths to starving children in Rwanda, to the poem on the back of the wine list.

The fresh smell of vegetables fills the room. The freshly made bread with rich olive oil melts in your mouth. Jazz plays softly in the background and you can hear the person sitting next to you.

The aesthetics of the meal piques our excitement as we gaze at a Picasso on a plate! It's like heading to Italy. Everything is made in-house and fresh. The oil and parmesan are imported from Italy.

Charlie and I wrote the copy on the menu together after drinking a bottle of wine. I never thought he would use it. My version rhymed, and he told me, "This is not a children's restaurant." But after a few tweaks he really liked it.

Every five minutes the waiter brings us more drinks and another basket of soft buttery rolls. After fifteen minutes and more than three drinks, Charlie brings the buttery lobsters. My eyes water as I stare at the pink lobster tail; I have never seen so much lobster on one tail. The aroma of the garlic and butter sauce fills the booth, and before Charlie says enjoy, I'm already halfway done. Thanking Charlie as he walks away, John and I finish our meal without saying anything but, "So good!"

Charlie slowly does his rounds, talking to every customer, and then sits at our table. "How was the food?"

"Charlie, you are a genius! The next time I'm depressed, down on my luck, hating the world, about to end it all, I will think of this meal and be content." John interrupts my tangent.

He has a look on his face as if he's about to deliver bad news, "Actually Charlie, after that meal, I could die, and my life would be complete."

The three of us laugh loud enough to create a scene, but no one is about to kick us out. Charlie thanks us for the compliments. "We are having a party. Stop by!"

Before he can answer, our waiter rudely interrupts our discussion, angering Charlie. He's all about service and not rushing people. Charlie rips up the bill and leaves the table, guiding the waiter to the kitchen.

John turns to me with his serious look, "You think he's going to kill him?"

"Probably."

Charlie meets us as we reach the door. He has four large pizzas, two gallons of a mystery elixir and some sweet treats. "Please excuse your waiter, he's new and not too bright. Here is food for the party. The misses and I will stop by. Do not feel guilty about the meal, Joe paid for it. He called while I was cooking. Pop these in the freezer. Some jerk ordered four pizzas and just called saying he had to cancel. I think there's a mix of toppings." Walking us outside, the valet quickly runs for the car and opens the trunk, and Charlie again apologizes for the waiter. After a quick hug goodbye, John tips the valet and we drive off.

"Jack, our party might not be well attended but it will have some serious eats. Women, pizza, drinks, music, and probably a few too many dudes will be over, but I'm okay with that. I have high expectations after your last soiree." John's enthusiasm shocks me. I have never heard John so excited for a party. Ever since we moved in together, he changed from workaholic to pro frat boy. John continues, "I think I might have to make out with Cholet."

"John, when did you become such a pimp?"

Before I can add another word, John turns to face me, "The day I moved in with you!"

John is focused. He sets these ridiculous goals, like graduating number one in his class, and then he makes it happen. My focus is fun. Life is too short. Girls never flocked to me. I have fun and they join the party. I know nothing about women, but I know how to throw a party. The occasional beauty that walks in my life walks right out after a month or so.

Usually I'm stuck so far in the friend zone, not even millions of dollars could buy me out of it. Terry, Mark's sister, was the only girlfriend I've ever had over a month. We dated for four

months; it was a record. After listening to all her complaining about her perfect life, I started to hang out with her brother. The boomerang effect occurred as Mark began to spend more time with my sister and less with me. Maybe that's some twisted message, or karma. Next time I make a friend, Alexis just won't meet him or her.

Pulling into his parking spot, John still glistens with enthusiasm. "Jack, we CPAs know how to party. I can do some sick things with a spreadsheet. Anyway, do you think Cholet likes me? I have never messed around with someone I didn't date before." John's sudden seriousness indicates a major crush.

"Bullshit. New Year's 1999, you kissed that one girl in the tight silver skirt at Joe's party. I will not excuse that kiss because of the holiday. I thought the Cholet thing was a fling, but you have a crush!" John instantly shakes his head and dismisses the crush theory.

"See John, Cholet is like an old sports car; she's pretty, still moves quick when well oiled—as you already know—but she has a lot of miles on that small engine."

A little perplexed, John scratches his head for a moment before he speaks. "I like your twisted and perverted analogy. I'm in the market for a newer car, one that hasn't been driven so much. Any suggestions, playboy? What about your other girls?"

For some odd reason that offends me. "What's with this 'your girls' shit? What am I, some kind of pimp? Am I right up there with Superfly? I don't have girls. I know a couple, but I don't own any of them." Taking a deep breath, I let the anger go. I think about Jerry as I apologize to John. "Okay, my little rage has passed. I will set you up with a beautiful baby bunny at our party." Sadness settles in as I realize my cousin, one of my closest friends, won't be at my first bash.

Fighting off the loss of a loved one is hard. You would think I would be a pro by now. But there's something more behind his death, and I can't fully relax until I figure it out.

John quickly pulls the key from his car. He senses my sadness. "I'm really sorry about your cousin. If there's anything you need.

And the 'your girls' refers to all the beautiful women you somehow dated once, never slept with, and somehow keep in touch with. You've broken some record, for God's sake. You are a sucker for a pretty face; you meet a nice girl and immediately feel the need to show her a good time. Your whole game is to entertain, and you become fast friends and then move on to next girl that happens to sit behind you on the train. Oh, and sometimes you're worried they will not go out with you again."

Seeing how John analyzes me to a perfect T, I tell him he's right. Instead of taking the stairs behind the building, we walk around to the front to check our mail. As usual—no mail. Simultaneously we say, "No one loves us." Now the door inside the apartments is jammed. After three tries apiece, I take out an old hotel key (one of the credit card-shaped keys) and jimmy the lock.

Surprised, John mutters, "You are James Bond."

"I wasn't always a businessman." I learned how to jimmy certain locks in college. Teachers always tended to keep their doors locked, but who knew how easy it was to borrow an exam?

Luckily, the key to our actual unit works. John and I change into our shorts, brush our teeth and fall asleep without much small talk. A couple of Charlie's cocktails will knock you out every time.

"It's 3 a.m. and I'm lonely!" Searching for a clue, my head pops off the bed and my heavy eyes are half open. I arrive at one conclusion: time to hit the snooze bar.

"Wake up boy," John yells like a drill sergeant. My eyes, still out of focus, see a blurry version of John walking out the door. Taking my time, I turn off the Sony Dream Machine alarm clock, the small square one everyone owned at some point in their life. I don't have it in me to toss it. My parents got it for me freshman year of high school.

Forcing my way to the kitchen, I sit down and have a piece of untoasted wheat bread (the loaf was on the table), and stare at our white kitchen. I take the mornings slow.

Time for some orange juice and ESPN. Following my usual pattern, I pour some juice, limp to our large couch, and grab the

remote. Since we do not get a newspaper, we rely on television for major news. Turning on the most important news station, I watch in awe as *SportsCenter* replays the highlights from last night. With sleep still in my eyes, I try to wake up with some pushups and lunges. A little more energy hits me. I can now shit, shower, and shave. The S's are a ritual most men are genetically coded to follow every morning.

Tossing on a green polo, khaki pants, and brown shoes, I'm ready to work—and to start my unofficial investigation. Everyone is really casual in the office. Hopefully I fit in.

DAY ONE

The uneventful commute is tame compared to yesterday's journey. Not many people ride the train at eleven. I enjoy all the space, but soon I'll have a car. Visualizing the car makes me excited and nervous at the same time. I better not wreck my new ride. Maybe I'm not ready to join the workforce. I need more time to do nothing, which was my real major. What if I suck at work and nobody likes me, so they fire me? There's only so long I can live off John, and what about Alexis? How am I going to be able to buy a nice wedding gift? What women will want an unemployed-lazy-alcoholic-bum as a boyfriend? The train stops at Madison. While jumping out of my seat, I end my inner monologue and yell, "I'm no bum!" Since no one else is on the train—no embarrassment.

Confidence builds with each step toward my building. Walking inside the building, I see the same security guards as yesterday. They both greet me in unison, with a smile.

Entering the spacious lobby, I envision my parents. I know they are watching me. Holding each other's arms, wishing they could take me to dinner and celebrate. I wish the same. I think this job will help keep my mind off the hurt and emptiness I bury beneath a smile. I try not to display my sadness while I enter the

mirror-filled elevator. The only time I really broke down was when I found out at school. The phone rang at eight a.m. I knew something was wrong; nobody ever calls a college student before eleven. My roommate Sam answered the phone because he knew I did not move quickly in the morning. With an unusually serious voice he said it was my sister. She was crying the whole time, gagging as she told me they died. I just stood there with my eyes filling with tears. I couldn't even move my mouth, let alone speak. My heart beat erratically as I said I would catch the next flight out. The only other time I cried was at the airport when she picked me up outside O'Hare International. Holding each other, knowing we were all the other had was the saddest moment of my existence.

Just as my eyes begin to well up, the elevator opens, and there's Sydney with a smile. Grabbing my hand tightly he shakes it and states with enthusiasm, "Welcome to day one Jack! I'm so excited to finally have a partner! We're the dynamic detective duo; we're just going to hurt companies like Ike did Tina!" Turning my head from left to right, I look for Bob West. Sydney seems like one of the good guys, but I'm starting to wonder, did I just come to work for the Dark Side?

"Domestic abuse metaphors are never okay."

With a serious look, he apologizes. "Sorry. I went a little too far."

Walking toward his desk I ask, "Am I going to receive that greeting every day? You drink a lot of coffee, don't you? I appreciate you letting me come in at noon, it gave me a couple of hours to drink off the shakes."

Sydney sits down in his swivel chair and picks up the phone, apparently dialing Bob's office. While dialing and laughing he says, "The intoxication has not even begun!" With a change in his tone he begins to speak with Bob.

"Hello, Bobby. I have your new hire. Should I send him to Jimmy or Steve Smith in HR? Okay, I'll send him to the condo." Wondering what the condo is, Syd turns my way and scratches his semi-bald head. "Bob wants to see you. Since you're big-time, he'll handle your paperwork."

I turn to Sydney. "Okay, the condo is his office. I like that. Does the big man usually handle the payroll with the rest of his VP duties?"

Still puzzled, Sydney answers, "No, just for you, big-time." Sydney guides me to Bob's office. The familiar rainforest music did not relax my anxiety. After a quick knock, we walk in. Sydney winks and smiles at Bob and walks out, leaving me all alone. I feel sweat dripping down my side as I realize I do not deserve all this money, but I'll take it. While I try to relax, Bob stands up to greet me.

"Relax. You already have the job, son. Now you just need to keep it." A creepy smile leaks across his face as he gestures me to sit down. A woman in her late forties and dressed in a gray suit walks through the huge doors without knocking. She was at my Uncle's and cousin's funeral; she was their stockbroker. She's a real tycoon. She stands a little over five feet and has an average figure, pixie cut, and her dark blue eyes send chills right through you.

As she stands next to me, Bob introduces us. "Jack, meet Cynthia Rocks. She was your uncle's stockbroker, your cousin's, and now she's yours."

After exchanging greetings, Cynthia cuts to the chase. I zone out at first because who can concentrate on someone talking while wearing a diamond necklace the size of rocks. It's like what Wilma had in *The Flintstones,* but real diamonds. "Okay, I have some money for you and your sister that your uncle originally left for Jerry. The money is in top-notch funds, equally balanced for growth and safety. Your sister already gave me the go-ahead to keep everything as is and reinvest any dividends." As Cynthia rattles on so fast I see smoke leak out the corners of her mouth, I only pick up fractions of her sentences. "Take a look at these investments. Blue chip, no-load, A-rated bonds. All you have to do is add three hundred dollars a month to the portfolio, and in twenty years you retire a millionaire, like your sister."

I feel like I'm getting cornered into some plan by a devious, money hungry, Nazi sympathizer/hard-nosed broker. Rocks, an appropriate last name, already sucked in Alexis, and Bob looks

sold—and it's not even his money. Cynthia keeps handing more reports and analyses than I saw in four years of finance classes combined.

Reviewing all the reports, I see my old professor and hear his powerful lecture on reports. With his hands full of 10-Ks, annual reports, and other papers he yells out, "This is all green eye shade material, they can alter-adjust-average, and turn the geek into a prom queen. You must read in between the lines and compare reports. Some of you will have jobs as a two-bit analyst fixing reports and making them pretty. Well, do a damn good job, because if the Fed figures it out, one audit and it's all over.

"Mr. Waters. Hello? Are you in or out?"

"Sorry. You threw a large amount of information at me at once." All the stocks look like investments I would make, if I had any money. I still want to know what happens if I cash in my prize today. I know I'll keep the investments, but I want to mess with the Rock and there's something to controlling your own money. I try to control my sadness. All this death has a way of catching up on you, and money—although helpful—never replaces family.

Bob is really starting to bug me. Why is his face getting all red? He should not even be in this meeting. Between the two of them, the temperature of the room rises, and they both look in need of a laxative.

Cynthia glances at Bob, as if I ruined their devious plot. "Your assets are around ninety thousand dollars. With fees and taxes, I can write you a check for seventy-one thousand seven hundred dollars." She ended her sentence with a sudden calmness; maybe she knew I was just playing.

"I suddenly feel like I'm on *Deal or No Deal*."

Bob starts laughing, Cynthia Rocks wants to slap me, and I think I should take my act on the road. Cynthia stands up and pulls out a pen as Bob continues to laugh. "Sign here, smartass. Sign here for direct deposit, 401(k), stock options—and here's your checking account with four hundred and fifty dollars—eighteen hundred quarters—here's a debit card combo 1010, and if you

have any questions here's my card. Have a nice day, gentlemen." Leaving all the paperwork in front of me, she leaves the office.

She speedwalks away, so I have to yell out, "Thanks, Rocks!"

Bob, grinning like a schoolgirl, looks me in the eye. "Jack, you kill me. That woman needs a good you-know-what." I want to ask Bob to tell me how he really feels. Bob continues to bash women and explain what I'm signing. He starts telling me this joke about a whore and a Koala bear as I sign my life away.

"The Koala Bear asks the hooker for sex and all she can say is, 'But you're a Koala Bear.' The bear pulls out a dictionary and reads the definition of a prostitute. 'A person who does sexual acts in exchange for money.' Finally, she gives in and has the best sex of her life. She then asks for payment. He explains he's a bear. He has no money. As she keeps complaining, the bear again refers to the dictionary. He reads the definition of a Koala Bear: 'An animal that eats bush and leaves.'"

By the time he finishes the joke, I've filled out all the information, not knowing what kind of deal I just made with the devil. Luckily, he let me use the copy machine in his office, so when my attorney tries bailing me out of this, he'll have some background information. Bob, gleaming with joy because I laughed at his joke, refers back to my benefits.

"All your checks are directly deposited into your checking account. All your insurance, including automobile, we will cover one hundred percent. You will receive cards for everything in the mail." Reaching into his front desk he pulls out a credit card. The card has my name and the company's on it. "Use this wisely; we will cover all your business-related expenses, gas, meals, travel— use your judgment. 401(k), IRA, and stock options will all be handled by Cynthia. We do match your contribution up to eight percent on the 401(k), which does not start until your six-month review. I apologize for going through this so fast. If you have any questions, your best bet is to ask Cynthia." Bob finishes his sentence quickly and stands up, extending his hand. I follow suit, stand up, and shake his fat hand.

"Thanks Bob. I look forward to working with you."

Walking me to the door, Bob loses his smile and softly speaks. "Be careful in the field, Jack." Stepping out of his office, I notice a large leather couch and a full-size fridge. That place really is like a condo.

Heading directly to Sydney's cubicle, excitement fills my body. I have a job, an expense account, a paycheck, a small fortune, and no idea what is expected of me. Of course, Jerry's dad, my Uncle George, would pay me to solve his son's murder.

Images of expensive cars, large houses on the beach, and women explode inside my oddball brain while staring at the gray carpet, stained with blood or ketchup. Before my daydream ends, I feel a hand on my shoulder. Again, Sydney has found me.

"Jack, you ready to get behind the wheel of a brand-new, black, five-speed, sunroof, power everything, V8, fully loaded, lady-lovin' automobile?" Still with his large hand on my shoulder, he points to the elevators and keeps talking. "Today we're going to have some fun, Jacky."

I respond to his enthusiasm. "I'm ready for some fun, but what about this work thing?"

He smiles. "What work thing? Shit, you have two, three weeks before you have to do any real work. Just follow me to the garage. Oh, and do you know how to drive stick?"

After the elevator goes "ding," I explain how I learned how to drive stick. "It started with a few cocktails. Not me—my friends had a few too many. All we wanted was a patty melt sandwich, so after a few practice runs in the parking lot, I ventured out to Perkins."

"Great story," he says, sarcastically.

The third level of the garage houses my new car, my only car. At the fourth stall from the front stands my beautiful two-door Acura Integra. Turning to Sydney, placing my hand on his shoulder and pointing at the car, my excitement takes over. "Keys. And fasten that seat belt, bitch!"

Sydney fires back, "Why I gotta be a bitch? Who has the keys? Who hired you? Why you gotta have a problem with authority? Take the keys—I don't know how to drive stick anyway!"

Laughing, I stare at the car and click the keyless entry button to open the doors. "I love the noise of the door opening; you have to love keyless entry."

"Jack, I have been with the company for a long time, and I never got a company car." Sydney continues to speak as I step on the clutch and turn the key. "Either you're real smart and resilient or just real lucky. Either way, we are about to find out." Sydney ends his sentence while laughing. "Drive out of the garage and head east. We want to get on Lake Shore Drive."

"No problem." Leaving the garage, I can already feel the power. Since the only *Road & Track* magazine I ever saw had pictures of half-naked women in it, I know nothing about cars. "I wish I could describe the engine size, horsepower, or the tires, but I can tell the car handles real nice."

"Just like a young, lucky, wet-behind-the-ears rookie to not even know what he has."

I adopt a serious tone. "Do you know anything about cars?"

Sydney's face turns to anger. "Do I know anything about cars?" he yells. "Man, I could tell you things about cars, like, chicks dig red cars! The only *Road & Track* magazine I ever read was the swimsuit issue, but it was damn good reading!"

Shaking my head and laughing, I turn on the radio. After scrolling through the stations, I choose The MIX. Approaching Lake Shore Drive, Sydney points north and I enter the Drive heading toward Sheridan Road. The excitement that comes with driving a new car should be bottled and sold by doctors to cure various ailments. Speeding about twenty miles over the limit still seems way too slow. "I am Speed Racer!" I turn up the volume with a grin so large I look psychotic. This car has a lot more pickup than my grandmother's 1988 Buick Century, which had been my only other car. After my sister drove it for a few years, it was my car, and then it died while I was on the highway. The only lucky thing that happened that day: A nice cop was right behind me and drove me home.

Interrupting my high, Sydney tells me to exit at Irving Park and look for Mind and Soul Martial Arts Academy. After his

directions he lowers the radio and asks, "You got that, Speed Racer?"

Nodding, I start to wonder what sort of adventure will begin at Mind and Soul. Thunder interrupts my thoughts, the sun hides behind clouds, and rain pours from the sky, foreshadowing trouble ahead. Just my luck—a perfectly shiny new car and it rains. The trip leading up to the dojo is filled with levity and music; now the car turns silent as I park across the street from the school. Sydney begins to speak in a serious tone as lightning rips through the air.

GETTING LUCKY IN THE DOJO

"Okay fly boy, this is your first case. Your resume had some bull about self-defense, martial arts, kung fu crap. With that, Bob thought this would be an excellent case. Mind and Soul is ensured by Trust One insurance. Lately there have been several claims made by the school—too many. The reports on the dojo are in the office; we'll review them tomorrow. Most of the accidents are broken or sprained bones in the back, neck, shoulder, wrist and ankle. We have no proof of fraud, just speculation. We need you to enter the class and seek the truth. I registered you for the adult advanced class. That class filed all the claims. Now, if our suspicions are wrong, it's just one bad, tough, rough, ass-kicking class. Prepare for a beat down LAPD/Rodney King style." Sydney's face lights up as he continues his comedy act. "They might whip you like you got caught littering in Shanghai! Good luck!"

I interrupt story time. "Ok, Chris Rock. Anything I should know?"

"The class starts at 6:30 p.m., and I know what you're think-ing: Why did we arrive so early?" Syd's smile brightens the car as the rainstorm grows darker. Placing his hand on my shoulder, he continues, "You need to try out. I told them you have ten years

47

of experience and a black belt. They also think I paid for your membership as a graduation gift. Kick some butt and take notes."

With a serious tone I inquire what happens if I fail the try-outs. Still smiling from ear to ear, Sydney yells, "Bob West fires you, gives me this car, and I hire a new college grad. Relax. If you don't make the cut, the investigation takes a few more weeks. If Karate Kid can't kick it, they start you in the beginner's class."

The rain suddenly lets up, so we exit the car. Trying to fill myself with confidence, I visualize winning. We cross the street quickly, rain lightly hitting Sydney and me as we open the dark wooden door with a yin-yang sign and some Asian writing. Three instructors greet us and extend their hands.

Shaking everyone's hand, all I notice is the middle teacher. Wow. She has beautiful long red hair past her shoulders. Light blue eyes sparkle from her perfectly pear-shaped face. She resembles a young Elle Macpherson, the Australian model. Her skin glows a golden color, and for a thin tall woman, she has some curves.

The other two teachers are Asian and look like the stereotypical karate instructors. The Asian masters resemble each other, probably a father and son duo. The older of the two has short gray hair running along the sides and back of his head, leaving the rest of the area empty. The partially bald man stands a head shorter than me and probably weighs a little over a buck forty. The other man has the same defined face with a tiny-button nose, cleft chin, dimples, and beady brown eyes. Besides the younger man having hair and longer legs, the two look very similar. All three wear black pants that resemble sweatpants and white robes. After introductions, my assumption is verified—Chung is Bob's father. The older instructor begins to speak, as I try hard not to stare at Julie Stemp. Sydney, noticing my distraction, elbows me in the side. Turning my head towards Chung, I pay close attention to his voice. The three teachers block our view of the gym, forcing me to concentrate.

Listening to Chung requires full attention because of his thick accent. "Jack, in a minute we give you tour. Your friend gives

you wonderful gift. Congratulations on finishing school, and welcome to a new school."

"Thank you, Chung. Sydney has given me a great gift and I look forward to training with you and your staff.

Chung, Bob, and Julie lead us inside the dojo as we take off our shoes per their request. The inside looks like a gym where Bruce Lee could have worked out. The classroom is all white. White thick mats cover the entire floor like a carpet and mirrors hang from the floor to almost the ceiling, surrounding the room. Everywhere you look, a mirror copies your every move. Two silver swords, a long bamboo stick, black throwing stars, wooden nunchucks, and a two-foot blow gun hang above the mirrors circling the room. In each corner sits a different piece of exercise equipment. Starting in the northeast corner and moving clockwise lay a human-sized dummy, an Everlast canvas punching bag and a Wing Tsun dummy (it looks like a large round varnished stump with branches sticking out). And in the northwest corner a black medicine balls sits on the floor. The smell of Bengay and sweat permeates the room like a high school wrestling practice. Sydney and I follow the teachers to a swinging door between the punching bag and wooden dummy.

The door leads to a small, gray office. The funniest thing about the room is a *Garfield* fish tank. It's also odd that soft tribal music plays from oak speakers. The Enya-like music makes the room relaxing enough to soothe a prisoner on death row. I wouldn't expect Metallica, but this is a house of violence.

The office almost seems hidden; the door sits in the middle of a wall with no handle. A black desk with no drawers stands to the right of the entrance, housing a Gateway computer and laser printer. They are in desperate need of a technology upgrade. Behind the desk is the industry standard swivel chair, and behind that a brown bookcase stacked with books about everything from essential oils to pressure point techniques. The perfectly organized bookcase also stores supplies, and rubber sparring knives. I'm trying to find anything that sticks out among the usual office equipment. There is an extra-large first aid kit and a defibrillator.

I'm not sure if that makes me feel better or worried that, after this session, I'll need something from that case.

The walls remind me of a family restaurant. Pictures of instructors with various students cover the office. Most photos have an instructor breaking something: cinder blocks, wooden boards, bricks, ice blocks and even chairs—wooden of course. No wonder they have a lot of claims. Who breaks a chair?

Turning folding chairs toward the couch, Sydney and I sit down. The three teachers melt into the couch. Chung and Julie sandwich Bob in the middle of the love seat/couch. I keep staring at Julie. She has a beautiful smile that lights up her face, and it hits me—she's a young Julia Roberts. Taking my mind off Julie, I try to stop sweating. I am literally sticking to the chair with my wet pants. I hope I do not smell as bad as I look.

The warmth of the office, combined with the smell of the school and the wet feeling from the rain, puts me in the mood for a shower. Needing a shower before your workout is not a good sign.

Chung interrupts my self-disgust. "Mr. Waters, Mr. Waters." I turn my head away from Julie and stare Chung in the eyes. "Sydney has given you a great gift, but you must demonstrate your skill. Your tests will be mentally and physically challenging. You will spar multiple opponents and break certain objects deemed unbreakable. Few students have ever been ready for this challenge, and many have failed. We will not think anything less of your ability or toughness if you choose to start with a beginner or intermediate class."

As my stomach rattles and my nerves scream "Do it!" Sydney speaks for me. "Jack did not study all this time to start as a beginner. Jack's a bad man. He knows the way—kung fu, karate, judo, aikido—and he can cook a mean fried rice with no MSG!" With his smooth delivery and excitement, Syd brings the room from tension to laughter.

The laughter dies down and Chung repeats himself, asking me if I want to back out. "Chung, I'm ready when you are." Internally shaking like a leaf, I ask exactly how the test works.

Julie answers with a smile that says she's going to enjoy watching me fail. "You will break a variety of boards and one cinder block to start off. After that, you will spar with me, then Bob. And the last test will be multiple students attacking simultaneously." Julie finishes her sentence and leads Sydney and me out of the office into the gym. Bob and Chung come out of the office after everyone else, holding wood and cinder blocks. My insides churn as if I drank bad milk. I'm not even excited to fight Julie. Well, maybe a little bit.

Julie and Bob set up the room as Chung springs out of the office with a clipboard and a pen. "All you have to do, Mr. Waters, is sign the release form. We do have insurance for emergencies, but we won't let you get hurt." Turning toward Syd for his reaction, I see his "You're getting beat LAPD-style" smile. After I sign the form, Chung asks whether I want to borrow some clothes to wear. Sydney answers for me.

"No. Khaki pants from Old Navy are just as comfortable. Right, Jack?"

With an unhappy glare at Sydney I respond, "I'll be fine."

Chung interrupts before I can make fun of Sydney. "Do you want to warm up or stretch before this exercise?"

Trying to psych myself I respond quickly and upbeat, "No. Let's get this party started!"

With that comment I take my eyes off Chung and onto the rest of the dojo. I can barely even hear Syd commenting, "Stick and move."

The gym looks like a bad martial arts movie. Wooden boards are lined up all around the room. The center of the room has cinder blocks holding five boards, one wooden board beneath the other. Bob holds another board at face level and stands to the right of the cinder block arrangement. Julie, on the other side of the arrangement, stands with a board at knee level. And behind me, Chung now holds one at chest level. With his thick accent Chung tells me to start and follow my soul and empty my mind. I have no idea what that means, but I'm breaking that wood.

All this wood makes me think I could do a lot more damage with a match than with my body. Before I begin, I turn to my new best friend (as of today) for support. Sydney nods his head, and with a smooth and tough voice yells, "You got the fireplace, a beautiful baby, and bottles of Dom, now break that firewood and set the mood!"

Surprisingly, the motivational comment sparks something inside of me. I'm going to tear this room apart. Exhaling slowly, I envision myself breaking all the boards. I no longer hear music or the noise of the wood breaking, and I feel no pain. I finished the task. All the boards are broken, and I do not remember how I did it. My senses slowly come back as I hear Sydney yelling, "That's my boy!" My hands and elbows are red, and I feel a little stinging.

Next, Chung points to the cinder block. My eyes answer: okay. My mind, of course, is thinking, OMFG. My deep breaths are interrupted. "Nice concentration, but you no break block. Just like to see if someone will try."

"Chung, I could kiss you."

Chung and the others have a look of acceptance on their face. Chung speaks with a tone of joy hidden under a thick accent. "Very good. Now you will spar Julie. Do not underestimate her power and speed because of her beauty and grace. Julie, as well as the others, will not go easy on you." Chung then turns towards Bob and they gather all the wood and place it in a black garbage bag with a yellow handle. Chung runs the bag into his office and pops out five seconds later with three tiny folding chairs that he must have stolen from an elementary school.

Julie stands in the middle of the mats waiting to kick my butt. Chung, Bob and Sydney sit against the back wall in that order. Sydney whispers at me, "Float like a butterfly, sting like a bee."

Walking toward Julie, I tell Syd, "Thanks for the advice, Ali." Approaching Julie, I try not to think about ripping off her outfit. I wonder if she wears anything under those pants. (It's difficult to stop thinking with the little head when he wants something.) Before I can picture her naked, she bows, and I follow suit.

The room temperature has dropped, but sweat beads still form on my face.

Chung yells, "Begin!" My eyes focus on her eyes. Julie stands at an angle with her right foot in front pointing straight at me. Her back foot is perpendicular to her front foot, knees slightly bent and both fists are tightened guarding her perfect face. I form a similar stance and all I hear is the beating of my heart.

Staring with all my concentration, I anticipate her kicking my knee. I move back, grab her ankle and kick the back of her other ankle causing her to hit the floor. As she falls, I grab her left arm, move it toward her back, drop to one knee and pretend to hit her in the head. My hearing recovers slowly and a clapping nose fills the gym. Of course, the only person clapping is my number one fan, Sydney. Chung yells, "Again!" as Julie springs to her feet with a hand from me.

I expect Julie to be mad, but she smiles and whispers in a soft voice, "Good job, Jack."

While I thank her, we start circling each other and my trip into a bad martial arts film continues. She patiently waits for me to make the first move, like we are on a first date. Her smile still shines as she walks toward me and feigns a kick to my side, hoping I will lower my hands so her punch can connect. My hand slides down her arm, and I grab her wrist as the right cross comes at my face. Using her forward momentum, I move to the side and back and continue to move her wrist forward. All the momentum forces her to fall and land on her chest. Julie quickly rolls onto her back as I pretend to kick her in the side.

My heart rate slows as I slowly exhale and wait for further instructions. Sydney's clapping boosts my confidence, and I'm ready to kick more butt. Chung interrupts my karate zone when he points for Bob to stand up.

"Very good, Jack. Now you will spar Bob." My insides turn. I can feel my self-confidence, energy, and power fade as Bob stands up. Bob scares me. Even though he stands at chest level and weighs a buck forty, he has huge hands and stocky legs.

As Bob walks toward me, I notice a slight limp in his left leg. I'm going for the bad leg—easy in and easy out. Paying no attention to Julie thanking me, I stare into Bob's eyes. His dark brown eyes look almost black, and the wrinkles along his temples add to his tough look. Bob's eyes tell me he's ready to fight till I can't get up.

Taking my eyes off Bob and turning to Sydney, I read his lips. "Bob and weave." Shaking my head, it suddenly hits me: Why "Bob"? I can see "Rob," even "Bobby," as a bad dude, but "Bob"? All these thoughts float in my mind as Bob and I wait for the other to attack. Still pondering his name, I kick him in the hamstring area with my shin. His knees buckle, and he drops one hand and taps his side. Tapping usually signifies quitting in martial arts. Bob limps to the office, I made him a gimp. I am a horrible person. I feel like I just cheated on a test and hit a disabled a person all at the same time. Yeah, I'm going to hell.

"Are you okay, Bob? I'm sorry."

He turns toward me and smiles. "I'm fine; just getting some ice."

Sydney hollers, "You have a fridge in there?"

I shake my head at Syd. "What do you want—a drink or something?"

He jumps out of his chair. "Maybe I want a drink, some food, a yogurt, turkey sandwich, beer, Coke, an apple, greens and some chitlins! What—am I fat? Obese? Large? A whole lot of loving? I thought we were friends. Now I see how it is."

Julie, Chung, and Bob think the same thing I do: "You are crazy." As my eyes tear up from laughter, I wonder what will come out of his mouth next. Three people in karate uniforms enter the gym as everyone but me continues to giggle. Those characters must be my multiple attackers. As strange as this might sound, I've been waiting for this experience my whole life. The students walk toward us slowly, taking off their sandals before they step on the mat.

Bob disappears into the office as Chung introduces me to Daniel, Reggie, and Sara. Daniel looks like Captain America—on crack. He has dirty blond hair that partially covers his

bloodshot blue eyes and stands a couple inches taller and weighs less than me. Sara resembles a young Cher (as if there's any difference from the older version), with curly dark hair, dark eyes, pale skin, and long legs. Reggie looks the most intimidating. He has the same dark color as Sydney, a full beard, and muscles that bulge out of his uniform. He reminds me of Wesley Snipes in *Blade*. The three fighters wear blue belts around their waists, three belts away from black. I try to avoid nervousness by looking around the room and thinking of odd things, like "A Coke and a smile."

Bob reappears from the office with a Coke and a smile. Just kidding—he actually taped a bag of ice with clear wrap around his left hamstring and brought in another chair. Now the row of chairs goes: Chung, Bob, Julie, and then Sydney. The three students stand in front of the teachers, awaiting instructions. I stand by Sydney, waiting for more tips. Before Sydney can talk, Chung says, "Begin."

Chung further describes how he wants them to surround me, bow and then attack. Following Chung's orders, my opponents form a circle around me, with Reggie to my left, Daniel to my right and Sara behind me.

Adrenaline pumps into my muscles as I initiate contact by kicking Sara in the stomach. Reggie, now behind me, whispers in my ear that he's going to "fuck me up."

With no hesitation I throw my elbow back and hit his jaw. Reggie hits the ground hard as Daniel kicks the side of my stomach. I grab his leg, kick Sara in the stomach again, and pull him forward so he will trip over Reggie. Sara catches her breath and approaches me as Daniel falls. I watch her eyes as Chung yells, "Enough!"

"Very good, Mr. Waters. I will see you at eight tomorrow. I now must tend to my wounded students.

I stand, in disbelief of my luck, and watch Bob and Julie walk toward the entrance. Watching Sydney walk to the door, I snap out of my daze. Bob and Julie open the door and wish us a good day.

The moment the thick door closes, Sydney angrily asks, "Why did you have to knock out the brother? Didn't knock out the white folk, but the black guy had to hit the floor. I see how it is, you kung fu, khaki-wearing motherfucker! You probably just waiting for the opportunity to take me out!" Sydney settles down and starts laughing. "Anyway, how much ass have you kicked?"

Without cracking a smile, I inform him, "That's the first time I ever hit anyone."

Sydney automatically starts laughing. "You're not kidding, are you?"

Using the keyless entry on my keychain I unlock the doors and explain how I learned to fight. "I was a beat-up dummy for this guy who taught three different arts. Every once in a while, he would let me teach. I hit plenty of pads and heavy bags, but our sparring was very controlled. I never made full contact." The drive back to the office goes fast, we manage to avoid verbal altercations, and I slip in a comment about Jerry. "Did you know Jerry well?"

Sydney apologetically comments, "I saw him at the gym. He was there almost every day. Nice kid. He focused on the research end like you, but less field work. He did his research on a computer. Speaking of computers, we are going to pick up yours today."

The tech geek in me comes out, "ThinkPad? MacBook Pro? Acer is making some great computers these days."

My answer is sitting on Syd's desk. My IBM laptop lays flat on his matted desk. A surprised Syd: "Wow, you didn't even have to walk to Jimmy Smits or Steve Smith? Easy to confuse Smits and Smith, but different people. When most people join the company, Jimmy is their best friend, but Mr. High Class gets everything delivered first class. I had to sit through a two-hour class on diversity with Jimmy—and I am diversity!" As Sydney breaks into laughter I stare at my baby.

The fully loaded Think Pad has everything from standard Windows Office to Shareware (I do not even know what that means, but it's on a note on the cover of the computer) to Google Chrome. The note on the cover lists set up and password steps, and for any questions send Bob an email.

"Jack, let's get connected." Before the computer expert finishes his sentence, the computer is ready. "Okay, since you do not have an email address for the company yet, just use the account on your resume. Knowing Bob the way I do, you already have mail."

My account downloads quickly and all my emails are from Bob West. Bob sent two emails my way, one labeled "reports," the other "club." The first note reads like a book. There must be four pages on how to write up a report, info to research, and miscellaneous info. Scanning the letter, I wonder how I'm going to get all of this information. The message ends as follows:

> *If you have any questions/concerns, please send me a note. Tomorrow plan on discussing your current case with me at 1:00 p.m. Please prepare questions ahead of time.*
>
> *Your job is incredibly important to us and very challenging. Your contribution to this company will increase shareholder wealth as well as your own wealth. I look forward to working with you.*
> *—BW*

I turn to Syd before opening the next email. "Wow—Bob sure has a way of making you feel important."

"Just wait till your first review; even if he says that you need to work on everything, he still manages to make you feel like you could run for office—and win."

Opening the next note, "club," I become more and more excited. The "club" refers to Muscle's Gym, the new hot spot for working out. Trust One wants to invest in the gym and make it a franchise bigger than 24 Hour Fitness. We also buy data from them for corporate wellness. Besides all the reports, my main job is to test the gym out and compare it to other clubs in the area. I have a free membership for a month, guest passes, and guest passes for other gyms in the area. Sydney reads the email (he's been standing over my shoulder since I turned the computer on) and looks more excited than me.

"We're going to that gym tonight! That club has everything; my ex-girlfriend dumped me for that club. Yea, me, Sydney P. Phelps, dumped so she could work out more. She better hit the weights, that pudgy little ho!"

"Why don't you tell me how you really feel?" Laughing off his pain, Sydney asks me if I have a lifting partner, so I tell him about John.

"Call John and have him meet us at 6:15 with his gym bag. This is WAY nicer than the office gym. I have to catch up with the IS department for about an hour. Make some calls, work on your shit. We'll regroup when I finish my rounds." Sydney pats me on the back a little too hard, like we're teammates, rather than office mates, and then walks away. It makes me feel like I'm back in college, hanging out with the jocks.

"Thanks, Syd. This is the beginning of a beautiful bromance."

Leaving my new car in the lot, Sydney and I take the train to my apartment. Unlike Sydney I do not pack workout clothes on the off chance I might hit a random gym for a workout.

While slowly traversing the city by train, I ask again about Jerry. "Where did Jerry sit? Anyway, you could take me by his office. I never got to say an official good bye."

"I'm sorry. Jerry was cool. He worked from home, coffee shops, and those type of places. He did have a cube near Steve Smith but rarely used it. Dude was sick with numbers. He really dug the analytics. Once the company started paying for a few classes at DePaul we never really saw him."

As I step off the train I feel a little better. "Thanks. I like hearing about Jerry."

THE 'CLUB'

Just as Syd and I approach the front door, John pulls up to our apartment, rolls down his window and yells, "Grab my stuff, too!" Turning to Sydney, John yells, "Get in the car; we'll leave him." Running upstairs, I wonder what they are talking about. I hope they get along.

Running through my apartment, I grab my fluorescent-orange bag and John's black bag with "1985 Wilson's Athletics" written on the side in yellow. Locking the door, I gaze at the ceiling and wonder who's jumping around in the apartment above us. Must be some huge guy.

Approaching the car, I hear the trunk pop and toss our gear inside. Sydney plants his butt in the front seat, so I have to slide in the back. Sitting in the back seat of my roommate's car pisses me off. "Sydney, what are you thinking? You can't just sit shotgun in your coworker's roommate's car."

"You know, Jack, you say some odd shit. Try not to bring that crack-smoking attitude to the office. I sat in front because I have long legs, broad shoulders, and a dick that just doesn't hang well in the back!"

John butts in without cracking a smile. "It must have been hard growing up when your parents forced you and your immense penis to sit in the back."

"I'm still emotionally scarred."

Sydney cannot hold back his smile. Feeling left out of the conversation, I ask to change the subject. "As much as I would really love to further discuss Sydney's concealed weapon, I say we change topics."

Sydney drops the smile and looks at me with a fake pissed-off look. "What, are you too cool to talk about my penis? Does it bother you? Do you feel uncomfortable because your penis stands shorter than mine? Well you know what …" Sydney's face again forms a huge grin. "My penis really isn't that big, I just wanted to sit shotgun."

John and I simultaneously remark, "I knew it." I figure the conversation is done, but John keeps talking as if we're having a serious discussion. John wraps up his comments as we park in the lot. The health club has a valet—a little too ostentatious for me. I want a small club. No frills, no whirlpool, no tennis courts—just the weights. I don't even want to see a Stairmaster—just a jump rope and a heavy bag for cardio equipment.

The outside of Muscle's Gym resembles the outside of a small library. The square architecture and brick entrance seems a bit much for a gym. The valet guys don't even park your car; they just hold your keys and wear silly red tuxedo vests with no tie or jacket. After John pays the key holder two dollars, we head to the front door. Instead of walking single file, we walk shoulder to shoulder, carrying our bags and stepping in unison. The three of us have our tough faces tattooed on and refuse to smile till reaching the locker room.

Walking through the glass doors, I am truly amazed. The club looks so cool, maybe I could work out here. As we pass the entrance, our attention immediately turns to three cute girls seated at a long black table. We each go to a different girl. Sydney selects the muscular girl with short red hair, John chooses the skinny brunette, and I speak with the tall blond. I wonder if our selections are due to chance or preference.

After explaining that we have a corporate membership from Trust One, we sign a waiver and head to the locker rooms.

The gloss on the hardwood floor around the front desk adds an air of extravagance, not sweat. On our way to the locker room, we pass an aerobics room to our right, and another room to our left. One room is filled with stationary bikes, and the other contains little steps and twenty sweaty women bouncing around. One man hops around with the women. Syd comments, "Is he gay, or just smart? Maybe both."

Past the aerobics room, a staircase leads to a second level. After the stairs, we finally reach the locker room. Narrow wooden lockers, capable of holding only the essentials, stand next to each other in this large room. This place is for the vain—loaded with mirrors, hair creams, combs, and blow dryers. The showers are in the back of the room, where the sauna, whirlpool, and steam room sit, all of it impeccably clean.

The three of us take lockers next to each other. The guys standing around us range in age from twenty to thirty, with a few outliers around sixty. Except for the old men, everyone has a towel wrapped around them or clothes on. The two old men walk around naked, talking to each other as if their balls aren't flopping in the breeze. While discussing theories about old men and nudity, we slam our clothes in the small area, lock it, and leave.

Sydney and John start discussing running as we walk to the second floor. Sydney starts talking trash. "John, if you really want a race, I'll call my grandma Flo-Slow. And she'll still win!"

Before Sydney can make another stupid comment, John says, "I'll race her. Call her right now. I'll even take the motor out of my wheelchair." Sydney and John continue to trash talk as I closely inspect all the equipment. I'm here for business.

We walk to the to the weight room, which should be marked men only—not because women are not allowed, but because inside there are twenty dudes and one girl. Two wooden doors lead to row upon row of free weights, machines, and medicine balls. The most prominent machines are white Hammer Strength and gray FreeMotion machines. The machines sit on a black rubber carpet that covers the huge floor. All the equipment leans back to

back against other machines. Behind one bench, there's another bench. Whoever designed the gym spaced it out perfectly, with plenty of room to walk in between equipment.

Sydney interrupts my work as he taps my shoulder. "Wow! This place is awesome! We have benches galore, shiny metal barbells, racks of dumbbells, and mirrors all over the place." He shakes his head, completely in awe. "Jack, I'm sorry—I don't see a heavy bag, wrestling mat, or any samurai swords." Sydney turns to John. "Did you know Jack's a bad motherfucker? I saw him kick some serious ass today."

John responds, "Who do you think was his practice dummy? Every time he learned a new move: 'Oh, John! You got to see this move!'"

"Well John, you better buy a cup, face mask, football pads, an aluminum bat, some solid health insurance, and a fucking gun. There's some serious rage in that crazy motherfucker." After agreeing that I'm crazy yet have no real skill, we split up and start our respective routines. Syd starts his workout on a flat bench, John sits on the bench behind him, and I use the pull-up bar nearby. After every set we gather in the middle and talk about goals, girls and good food. After finishing my last set of pull-ups, I take over John's bench. John and Syd move on to different chest exercises, but we continue our discussions at the water fountain.

As the clock nears six, people file into the weight room. More men than women enter the area; grunts of pain and motivational exclamations drown out the background music.

After squatting until my legs shake uncontrollably, I'm done. Sydney and John are also ready to go. However, there's suddenly music—like, crazy club music—playing. We peek in the cardio room, where there's an actual DJ playing intense beats, and it energizes us like a shot of espresso.

Feeling adventurous, we walk around the cardio room. There are stationary bikes, treadmills, stair climbers, and different versions of elliptical machines facing a huge window where televisions jut out from the wall above. In front of the aerobic machines, mats lie across the floor with various tummy tightening gadgets,

like rollers and medicine balls. The amazement has nothing to do with the machines and everything to do with who's using them. Black, white, Hispanic, Asian, and other races are represented in this diverse room of beautiful women sweating in spandex. The popularity of the room leads to lines of gawkers.

John grabs Sydney and me and whispers, "I think we just opened up Pandora's Box. This might even be Nirvana." Sydney and I smile as John goes on. "We must never tell anyone of this wonderful room." John turns his head slowly, from left to right, looking for affirmation. "Are you guys with me?"

We pull John out of the room and walk out the door to the locker room. As we descend the stairs, a girl grabs me by the shirt collar. Sydney and John stand in amazement. I realize the girl works with my sister and her name is Erica.

"Jacky! I didn't know you worked out here. How have been you been?"

"Great! It's good to see you, Erica. This is my boss, Sydney. And this is John, my roommate. Hey! We're having a party Friday and would love it if you stopped by. We live in the building across from Alexis in apartment 102. Bring friends."

Weaving her fingers through her blond hair and staring with her puppy dog eyes into mine, she says, "I'll see the three of you on Friday. Nice meeting both of you."

We enter the locker room and John starts in. "Jack, you know more people than anyone I know. I'm happy most of them are girls! By the way, I called our landlord. He's cool. His only requests: invite all the tenants, and quiet the group down around eleven." I nod in agreement.

"I invited the dudes yesterday. I'll ask the floor above us, and you take the top floor. After we shower, let's hit Charlie's for a sandwich. We'll introduce Joe to Sydney, unless you have plans."

John turns to Sydney, "Do you want to join us for some grub? No pressure."

As we walk to the showers, I see something very familiar—a black lock with a white face. That has to be Jerry's lock. In high school, Jerry kept forgetting which locker was his. So one of his

coaches took white-out and painted the front of his lock. And I will never forget his combo: Walter Payton (34), Michael Jordan (23), and Jim McMahon (9).

"I'll meet you guys at the restaurant. My sinuses are totally stuffed; I need a good steam." It is easier to lie than to talk about my research/vengeance project. And I do like a good schvitz.

Jerry's locker is very clean. Even the clothes seem clean. You would think workout clothes left in a locker for at least two weeks would be nasty. I toss everything from his locker into an old-school JanSport backpack. The only thing of interest so far is a notepad. Thumbing through it tests my PI skills. The first pages have numbers on them with no explanation or letters: W 30, 32, 44, C 500, 33.5N 111W. My initial thoughts: Fantasy football players? Pages of the Bible? Swiss bank account? Regular bank account? Addresses? Measurements?

As I walk to dinner, reviewing these crazy theories, I start to think that maybe I watch way too much television.

"Joe, you studying? Where are the guys?"

"Why is everyone so shocked? I am in law school. I study between deliveries. I told Sydney he was way too cool for you guys and recommended staying away from you both. They are in the back."

"Study. And yes, we all think you are lazy. But we love you."

As I walk away, Joe gives me the one-finger salute.

Sydney greets me with sarcasm. "Did you have a nice steam? What about the facial? Massage? Microderm? Pedi? You look rested." Before I can defend myself, the attack continues. I think John is in love. Not many people are this quick-witted. "Joe told me you are lazier than him, and that if it wasn't for the urge to poop, you would never wake up." Sydney finally ends his Jack-bashing session, "I should go easy on you, you could kick my ass."

While the boys bond, I search my phone for football players numbered thirty-two. It seems like it'd be a running back or shooting guard. Magic Johnson? Too bad they did not offer a codebreakers class in college.

Joe tries to get off work as we scarf down honey mustard chicken sandwiches. He pops out of the back room shaking his head. "The man's holding me back." Sydney and Joe exchange numbers like a couple of high school girls. Joe's last words as the door closes threaten to ruin the relationship: "I have a dream … that one day, all pizza dudes, of all races and creeds, will share crazy bread."

The summer night feels cooler than normal, but no one complains. We walk around the block to a small bar with a pool table.

Shooting pool and discussing football is pretty much standard guy small talk. Syd decides to talk shop. "I've been at Trust One since college; they've never had anyone like you."

Curious, I ask, "That's a good thing, right?"

"It's cool. Good to see them trust some young blood with this shit. Anyway, I got to get home. I'm not young like you two."

John points out the Jack/Blake rule: Whoever wins the last game is the big winner. The rule emerged in college, when we were too drunk to remember who won all the other games. He holds up Syd's hand and announces, "You are the big winner!"

Syd is slightly embarrassed. "Um, thanks?"

As we watch Sydney leave the bar, John and I realize that we're the only ones in the bar other than the bartender. John and I contemplate leaving while we finish our second beer.

"Jack, let's go." After John's command, we bring our glasses to the bar and say good night to the bartender.

Speedwalking to the car, we discuss Sydney. John is not easily impressed, but I can tell he adores Syd. Besides being athletic and cool, he has this warm quality. That same quality also resides in John—and in most of my friends, for that matter. It's difficult describing that thing that makes you like someone. Whenever I meet someone new, I always think of my parents and how they always loved my friends. Sitting in John's car, I tell myself how lucky I am to have been blessed with such great parents, and how proud they would be of me. I know my mom would tell me, "Don't investigate Jerry's death. Enjoy life!" But I can't fully enjoy life until I know the truth.

Memories of playing with my parents and sister stir up emotions of sadness and joy. I vividly remember walking toward the gates of Disney World with my family. We walked in a straight line, all holding hands. My dad held my mom's hand, my mom held my sister's hand, and I held my sister's other hand. My sister and I wore matching Mickey and Minnie Mouse sweatshirts. Tears slowly drip down my cheek. The empty feeling in my stomach takes over. But before I can feel sorry for myself, John starts to talk, sensing my pain without looking at me. And before he turns toward me, he instinctively allows time for me to wipe the tears away. Then he tells a cheesy joke. "What does the man with five penises says about his jeans? They fit like a glove!" The joke brings a smile to my face. Even though it's horrible, it's straight out of my dad's joke book.

"Jack, let's hand out party flyers to the neighbors. Remember: you get the floor above us and I'll get the top." He continues in a militant tone, "We divide and conquer, to leave no partygoer uninvited!"

"What happened to the shy introvert? Now you got the jokes, you're hooking up with girls—and you even have a black friend."

"I ran track in college; I have about five black friends. I need a few Asians. I feel bad about that." John and I both have a tendency to go off on tangents, each tangent odder than the next. I pretty much surround myself with people who have a lot of personality, from Sarah and Stacey, to Mark, and now Sydney.

GIRL

Running through our apartment, we grab the invites and prepare to "divide and conquer." John's invites are simple and to the point. He used white paper and typed *Party—free beer, free food, free cocktails—Friday at 9*. He tried to make it snazzy by adding black and white pictures of people dancing. I would've added some bells and whistles, like color, but this will do fine.

First-party excitement ignites a bomb of enthusiasm in my body. I rush up to the steps and anxiously knock on the apartment directly above mine. I can see the party already, people scattered throughout my place just having fun. It makes me feel a little settled.

The door opens quickly, as if the person on the other side knows me. The door opens all the way, and my heart skips a beat. I stare Dana Sugar straight in the eye and my mouth drops.

She stares back at me, and as much as I want to speak, no words come out of my mouth. Standing there in awe of her beauty and a smile that lights up the dark hallway, I form a sentence. "Wow, Dana. You are still as perfect as you were in seventh grade."

Slowly stepping toward me, she hugs me like no one has hugged me before. Wrapping my arms around her just feels right. I had a serious crush on her in junior high. Right after she agreed

to go out with me, her family moved to Atlanta. I listen to her every word while trying not to stare at her breasts, which are barely contained by her green tank top.

"Jacky Waters, you're still a little charmer. Come in and let's catch up." Entering her apartment feels like a dream. Dana's apartment resembles mine but with pictures of nature and a grey couch. My eyes don't wander from her dark skin and light eyes. "Sit on the couch." I sit and sink about six inches into her couch, then hear a noise from the kitchen.

Hoping it's not a man, I ask, "Is that your roommate?"

Sitting next to me, with her tan, toned legs crossed, and taking off her trendy black glasses, she runs her hand through her shiny brown hair and answers. "No, I live alone. That's just my friend Adam." Turning toward the kitchen, she yells, "Bye, Adam!" She turns back. "He lives above me. Now what are you doing here, Jack Waters?"

"Well, Sugar, I stopped in to invite you to our party. John Gold and I just moved in below you and our big bash takes place Friday. I really hope to see you there."

Dana's soft hand touches mine, and my stomach fills with butterflies. "Of course I'll be there! I cannot believe you live with Johnny Gold!" As she moves her hand away, I notice she's picked up a sweet little southern accent. "Now Jacky, tell me what's happened to you since seventh grade. You still owe me a date from 1990. I expect ice cream, a walk in the park, mousse in your hair, a tie-dyed T-shirt. And we must watch MTV while eating pudding pops at your house. Seriously, tell me about yourself."

Time stands still as Dana and I tell stories about the past, present, and future. Hours fly by, and even though we seem to connect completely, I still walk down the stairs wondering if she has a man. She did hug me, with her thin arms tightly wrapped around my neck, when I left, and she kissed my cheek. Even though it was just a hug, it melted my heart.

Realizing John has locked the door, I whip out my keys and notice my watch; it's 2:30. Stepping into my bedroom, I see the outline of a person in my bed.

Terry is lying on my bed, asleep, with the TV on and lights off. I have to make a decision. Do I hop in bed, or sleep on the couch?

Terry lies in the bed wearing a red satin top—very tempting. Walking to the bed, I pull the covers over her, turn off the television, and walk to the couch. Yes, the couch. Two things keep me from sleeping with Terry: she's a little crazy, and I can't stop thinking about Dana. The main reason Terry and I broke up was because I like her brother better than her, and that bothered her.

After we broke up, she kept calling me and hanging up. When I confronted her, she apologized, and then we became friendly-ish. Since we broke up a couple months ago, we've messed around twice, and afterward experienced serious awkwardness. I cannot believe I have to rationalize not sleeping with a woman, and tomorrow, when I take care of my own business, I'll be regretting sleeping on the couch.

Before going to bed, I dig through Jerry's stuff. There are a few items in the bag:

- Clean-ish workout clothes
- Notebook with odd code
- SanDisk
- Business card for Leslie's Jewels

I plug the SanDisk into my laptop and impatiently wait. The only thing I can figure out is that there's a lot of data here. Each file is a different day, and lists a name, time, and "MM#." I'm not sure what that means, but I intend to figure it out.

THE MORNING AFTER NOTHING

Little kisses act as my alarm clock. My eyes slowly focus as I mumble, "Hi, Dana." The kisses stop as I realize I just fucked up.

A raised voice asks, "Dana? Who the hell is Dana? Is she the reason you slept on the couch?"

With a glance at the VCR, I see the time and figure that could be my excuse. "Terry, it's seven. I normally don't start thinking till at least eleven. Now stop yelling at me. If I remember correctly, you dumped me."

"You're right, Jack. I'll talk to you later!" Storming out of my apartment, Terry slams the door and John walks into the den.

"Dana? Dana Sugar? What made you think of her?" John is now standing in front of me mostly naked, eating a banana.

"I saw her last night. She lives above us. She looks fantastic. I think she's going to be my wife. We talked till two in the morning last night and I still do not know if she has a guy."

John's face forms a huge smile, "I swear Jack, you fall in love every day. Then again, in seventh grade you told me the same thing. Go back to bed, we'll talk about Sugar later." Closing my eyes, I agree to call John at work.

The phone wakes me just as I start dozing off.

"Hello?"

Clearing my throat, I listen to Patty Grace from Trust One transferring me to Bob West.

"Hello, Jack. I just wanted to see if we could meet at ten instead of one."

I respond without thinking. "One would be better for me. I want to prepare extensively for our first meeting." If I had not just woken up, I would have done whatever the boss wanted.

Bob continues the discussion as I walk to the bathroom and start peeing. What a great job. "Jack, you really do not need any preparation. This will just be a touch-base meeting. I want to tell you about a new project and I want to fill you in on travel arrangements."

Before BW can utter another word, "I'm going to travel?"

"Yes. I need you to go to Sacramento, Seattle, Minneapolis, and Phoenix. Now will you now be able to meet at ten?"

"One o'clock Bob. Take it or leave it." What am I thinking? It's too early to let him see my goofy personality. "Just kidding, I'll see you at ten."

"Thank you, Jack. I really appreciate your flexibility. I'll see you at ten."

Hanging up the phone, I turn on the shower and simultaneously brush my teeth, which is just one of my many talents. With each stroke of the toothbrush, my muscles burn. I love the feeling of sore muscles after a workout. But while I'm all for being sore, I can't tell whether I have to poop or my stomach is just torn up from the workout.

Pushing aside the red curtain, I step into the warm shower. A non-rushed shower takes fifteen minutes, but today the two-minute soap-a-dope and dry will have to do. I don't want to be tardy. I always try to be early, but my good intentions go unnoticed because I underestimate travel time. I also like to take my time in the morning: reading the sports section, eating a bagel and a banana, drinking some juice. And the three S's of course.

The wooden floor creaks as I run naked to my room, throw on clothes and then run to the kitchen for a banana. Running out the door, I remember where my car slept last night—the garage at work. Tonight, I'm driving home.

Mentally visualizing my day while walking to the train, I see my meeting with Bob, some computer work, and my first class at Mind and Soul. Bob or Chung probably teaches the class. I wish Julie taught the class. If we spar again, I'll let her win. I probably didn't win her over when I kicked her ass. The train zips past me as I reach the platform; maybe I won't make that meeting after all. Staring at my bare wrist, I decide that today will be the day I purchase a watch. Looking for a pretty girl to ask the time, I see Dana.

"Dana, what are you doing here?"

Without missing a beat, she sarcastically answers, "Just hanging out. I'm waiting for the 'L'! What else would I be doing?" She waves her hand, with its bright red nail polish, through shiny locks of brown hair. So pretty. She continues to talk as I try to look cool. "I heard someone yelling in your apartment this morning. Was that your girlfriend?"

My nervousness slowly fades, yet my palms sweat like a junior high student holding hands for the first time. I tell her the story about Terry, and she asks the obvious question.

"Why didn't you sleep with her?"

We step on the EL and sit next to each other. I take my time sitting down because I do not know how to answer her question. I can't tell Dana the real reason was her. Maybe that is what she wants to hear. First, I need to find out if she has a man. Before I can answer Dana's question, she answers it for me.

As her sparkling brown eyes gaze into mine with a smile so white I consider that she must never drink coffee, she says, "Because of me," and starts to laugh.

Feeling at ease, I follow her lead. "You found me out. I'm absolutely crazy about you. My every other thought, vision, dream, fantasy resolves around Dana Nicole Sugar." I wonder whether I've gone a little too far. Trying to save myself, I ask if she is surprised I remember her middle name.

Still giggling, she says, "Since you're infatuated with me, you should know my middle name. I know yours, Jack Calvin Waters." Okay, Dana knows my middle name! Maybe she likes me.

"Come on—we were Junior High sweethearts. I must have written your name in my Chandler's notebook a million times." Trying to play it cool externally, all I can think about is that she liked me! She really did! It wasn't as one-sided as I thought. Maybe there's hope!

We continue to flirt until the Madison and Wells stop, where we exchange goodbyes as I head to the office. I get my second kiss on the cheek in twenty-four hours.

I feel like I'm standing eight feet tall. I flash a peace sign to the security guards like a poor excuse for a rapper. What is the matter with me? I still don't know whether she likes me or is just messing with me. Before I step into Bob's office, I stop by Syd's desk.

He takes one look at me, shoots out of his chair and whispers, "Did you just get laid?"

"I wish. I just saw this girl I'm crazy about on the 'L.'"

"Did you get her number? Does she have a boyfriend? Shit, does she have friend for me?"

Heading toward Bob's office, I answer all Sydney's questions. He uses several vulgar words to express his disappointment in my skills. "How the fuck can you sit on a girl's couch till 2 a.m., flirt with her on the train, and still not know about a boyfriend? Kid, you need to ask the right questions, or you'll turn into the best friend—with no touching, no licking, and sure as hell no hardcore, nail-biting, sweaty-steamy, erotic, ass-smacking, booty-bouncing BANGIN'! Now go talk to BW." Sydney covers his face with his hands and shakes his head as he walks away like a father who just found out his son flunked shop class.

The amazing office of the VP/OP appears empty as I stick my head through the slightly ajar door. Bob unexpectedly pops out of a closet in the right corner of the office.

"Come in, Jack. I just had to put my hat away. Out in that sun, if I do not wear a hat, this dome gets cooked. Now sit down, son. I just want to touch base. You have two new companies added to your plate: First Sure Insurance and Big Bad Burger."

Bob continues to speak as I jot down notes. I feel like I'm back in college, prepping for a test. He signals with a hand movement

that I do not need to take notes, but I do anyway. "First Sure will need the following: full financial analysis, discount dividend model, P/E ratio, quick ratio, current ratio, and all that other good stuff. Steve Smith manages the HR team and is an actuary. He sits on the thirty-third floor. He'll help you compile the data and analyze it. A lot of the info is in the paper and online, but I need more. I want to know everything that this company doesn't want anyone to know. I want to know what kind of price discrimination they do, what their employees make, how they base their rates, who their target market is and why. Hell, I want a copy of their internal report."

"Can I get all this information legally?"

When Bob mentions internal report, I remember my old finance professor. Dr. Powers would go on and on, raising his voice, about how companies manipulate numbers—except the internal report. I still visualize the good doctor yelling, with spit coming out of the corners of his mouth, "You really want a true picture of a company, you need the internal report. All the bullshit and pretty pictures are in the annual report. But if you can get your hands on the internal report, you'll see the real deal!"

Bob notices the worried look on my face and stares me right in the eye as he attempts to console me. "Jack, we do not ask you to break the law; there are legal ways to obtain all the information we ask of you. If you ever have questions of legality, just ask me." Then he winks at me like I'm a little kid in need of encouragement.

Bob brings his hands together and claps. "Now let's discuss the travel. Big Bad Burger happens to be a healthy fast food chain. The restaurant uses lean meat for their burgers, low-cholesterol buffalo hot dogs, grilled chicken breast, low-fat tuna salad, and protein shakes. There are two BBBs in California, one in Seattle, Colorado, Des Moines, Madison, and one just opened on Clark Street here in Chicago. You visit a few of the out-of-state restaurants. We will of course pay for all your travel expenses. I want you to check out the restaurants for consistency, fat content, popularity, sales, profit, and other items that I'll email you.

You will have a partner for the project. Jeff Riley will help you investigate the company. He works for our consulting division. I want you to call Jeff today or tomorrow. He lives in Los Angeles."

Bob keeps talking without taking his eyes off a memo sitting on top of his desk. He also keeps fighting with a pen in his left paw and hands me Jeff's number with his right hand. His mind is somewhere else, which makes me lose my own focus.

My mind starts to wander as Bob surveys his desk for a lost paper while rambling on about Jeff and LA. "Jack, you will first visit the restaurant here. The owner, Tom Keefer, will be in town for three months and expects to see you tomorrow at 10 a.m. Jeff will be in town Friday. He needs you to pick him up from O'Hare at eleven. United flight 467. Don't forget. He could cab it, but it would be a nice gesture." I refocus as Bob finally makes eye contact with me.

"Take pictures of each store. You have some fancy camera. It's in your trunk. Have fun with it. Take pictures of the equipment at Muscle's Gym and then email them to me." While finishing his sentence, he opens a side drawer of his large desk and pulls out a cell phone, probably one of many. He's like a drug dealer.

He tosses the phone my way. "Here's your phone. Your number is 555-JACK. I figure you can't forget that. Now get back to work! I can already sense what a large impact you're going to have on this company. Stay on top of your work and keep that ear-to-ear smile lighting up rooms!" Bob stands up and extends his hand to make it obvious the meeting is ending.

Shaking his hand and smiling I wonder whether I can trust him. "One question Bob: What did Jerry do for you?"

"I am so sorry about that. Jerry was awesome. He ran a lot of analytic reports for us. He was a numbers—or, better yet, a computer—genius. He worked on bunches of projects at a time, impeccably tracking each one. You'll get this in your report about Muscle's Gym; but we buy their member information and sell it to companies. Some bank wants to know how often their employees exercise and whether that lowers health risks? We can do that for them. Jerry played with those numbers to show companies that

when more employees exercise, absenteeism drops. That way we can double dip—make money insuring the gym, and then get a discount when we buy data from them."

Somehow Bob could tell that this seemed a little shady to me. "It's not scandalous, Jack. It's corporate wellness. Talk to Steve Smith about Jerry. They were buds. And maybe talk to a social worker. It can't be easy to deal with all that death."

As I walk away part of me feels warm. This guy cares. And then uneasiness sets in. How did he know about all the death? Who researched me? This place is a little too "big brother."

Leaving his office, I pick up the fragrance of a Cuban cigar. The sweet smell almost makes me want to put the horrible cancer stick in my mouth. Heading straight to Syd's desk, I wonder if I'll ever have a cubicle. Sure, the cubes are small, dimly lit, and gray, but it would make me feel accepted.

Jamming on his keyboard, Sydney transcribes one computer language to another while simultaneously checking all the baseball scores. Sensing my presence, he turns around and shouts, "Cubs win, Sox lose, and Bryant hits another homer! Let's go to a game this weekend. Bob gave me five tickets for Saturday. Ask John if he wants in."

"John will come. Do you mind if I bring my buddy from out of town?"

"Sure. Are you talking about Jeff Riley?"

"No, but we should take him to the game, too. I was talking about my buddy Blake, who's coming to town for my party. With John, Jeff, Blake, you and me, that's five people—"

He quickly interrupts, "Cool. We'll have a blast. Now, Bob told me to take you to Steve Smith's desk. Let's go." Sydney stands up, stylin' as usual in black pants and black V-neck T-shirt, and quickly steps to the elevator. "Steve is a kiss-ass. His nose is so far up everybody's ass, he wipes it instead of blowing it."

I try to hold back my laughter, keeping a serious look on my face as the elevator doors close. "That's disgusting." We laugh all the way to the thirty-third floor, skip out of the elevator and take a right. Trust One only has offices on the right side of the floor.

The left side is an advertising agency. Two glass doors labeled "Trust One" in white paint stand in front of us with a keypad lock. But we get buzzed in. Behind the doors, a young lady sits behind a small oak desk. She asks us to sign in and calls for Steve. Within seconds Steve pops up next to Syd.

As he shakes Sydney's hand and reaches for mine, I think I can already see the brown on his nose. "Pleasure to meet you Jack. I received a heads-up email from Bob West informing me of our partnership. I started crunching some numbers this morning. Follow me. All the information I needed I received from other companies' web sites. I used the dividend discount model, the capital asset pricing model—"

I cut him off. "I prefer the Swedish model ..."

Sydney elbows me. "Listen to the man!"

Steve will not accept my apology. "Do not apologize for making a funny. Bob warned me about your sense of humor. Anyway, since you were a finance major, I'll use the abbreviations and that should cut a good twenty minutes out of our meeting. See, I make jokes, too."

Finally reaching Steve's office, Sydney and I sit down. His is one of those comfy chairs with thick black quilted pleather over it that leans back. In front of his black desk, Sydney and I sit on stiff wooden chairs. Steve does not have a window, but he has a corner office with not one but two computers. With a soft tone, he welcomes us to his office and begins to throw around terms that you never think you'll use after school. I only catch bits and pieces as he begins speaking rapidly. "I calculated NPV, APV, BV, CEQ, EPS, EX, PVGO ..."

Sydney and I turn to each other with the same look of complete and total ignorance. Steve starts to slow his speech after he has exhausted all his financial vocabulary. "Jack, the only information I need from you is in your email. Please take your time and ask questions. Research these companies. The more info you get, the better. Once you collect all the data, send me a note and I'll crunch the numbers. Bob will then get a detailed report."

Leaping out of his cushy chair, Steve leads us back to the elevators. On the short walk, I see a name plate that reads "Jerry Walters, AVP," outside an office. I need to get back up here.

Stepping inside the lift, Steve shakes our hands. "Pleasure meeting you, Jack. And Sydney, it's always a pleasure. You gentlemen have a good day."

The doors shut, and I immediately turn to Sydney. "Wow! You were right about the ass-kissing. Why would he kiss my butt?"

"That's what I was trying to figure out."

"Can we talk about his mustache for a moment?"

Syd remarks, "Someone needs to tell him that the Hitler look is never in. He's an odd guy, but he'll do a ton for you."

"Thanks. He seems to really break down everyone's work. Now all I need is an intern to do some of the day-to-day stuff for me, a little computer hacking, and send it all to Steve and I won't even have to wake up in the morning."

Syd doesn't hesitate. "One, you don't wake up in the morning. Two, I already checked out a few sites for you. Bob wants a lot of information that you just can't walk in and ask for. I receive a copy of all your emails. I'm still trying to figure out how to get a copy of an internal report. Is that just a joke? You might have to pull a little Jack charm to obtain that info. After the whole karate thing I won't doubt your skills, but if you acquire the internal report for First Sure without getting arrested, I will really be impressed."

My already-swelled ego starts to get the best of me. "This afternoon, I will walk in the office with a copy of First Sure's internal report."

Pulling out his black leather Coach wallet, Sydney hands me two hundred dollars. "Place the report in my hands by five, and I will give you a hundred more. If you fail, just hand me back my money."

We argue about the bet for ten minutes. I finally take his money, "You better hit a cash machine after lunch. I'm going to feel bad about taking your money. Oh, but if I do get arrested, I'll use it for bail and pay you back later."

THE INTERNAL REPORT

Before I take on the challenge of sneaking into a company and stealing information, Sydney and I leave the office for lunch. A hot dog shop called Frank's, on the corner of Franklin and Randolph, is where we dine. Frank's is practically a landmark—everyone in the city has been there at least once. The owner looks about ninety and works the cash register with a smile and a ready handshake. When I worked in the city one summer, I ate there three times a week. Frank still remembers me and that was two years ago. The restaurant looks as one might expect—Vienna Beef signs all over the place, yellow tables, yellow stools facing the window, workers in all white, and the aroma of grease hanging thick in the air. Sometimes a hot dog, fries, and a Coke costs three-fifty, and sometimes the same thing costs eight-fifty; either way, you pay Frank and smile back.

Sitting at a yellow table, Sydney and I eat our food and he tells me about The Wiener Circle. According to Syd, the workers swear and yell at you as you place your order. A regular, such as himself, walks in and starts cursing off the bat to receive faster, friendlier service. He agrees to take me there after my party on Friday. Lunch draws to a close as I help Sydney with the last of his fries.

The restaurant has done nonstop business from the moment we stepped in till now, but Frank still takes the time to say goodbye. The humidity hits us as we step outside. It's like entering a steam room. Standing on the sidewalk and waiting for the light to change feels like an eternity in this weather.

Sydney follows me to the garage and wishes me good luck on the mission. He then hands me a quarter. "Call me if you need more money for bail." Winking at me and smiling, Sydney turns toward the office, offers a fist bump and leaves.

First Sure is in the North Shore, near Wheeling. I grew up not too far from there, so I know the area fairly well. The company has three buildings on the same street. The building in the middle happens to be the corporate headquarters; I will start my journey in that office. GPS says I'll get there in fifty minutes. Hopefully I can drum up some confidence in that time frame.

While driving, I buy one hundred shares of First Sure stock on my phone. The price is low. And who doesn't want to help an investor?

My new car still has that new car odor. I think you can buy that smell, but why anyone would do such a thing is something I could not tell you. While driving, I start to daydream. All I need now is Dana in the passenger seat and I'll be set. Once the air conditioning and radio are at full blast, I feel ready for this mission.

Taking the express lanes, I speed all the way to Lake and take the westbound exit. The company is on Sampson Street, only a few blocks from the highway.

Turning left on Sampson, I see the three buildings and pull into the middle one. All the buildings look the same—black siding, tinted windows, massive parking lot, and guards. I was not prepared for the guards.

As I turn into the complex, a white gate and small guard stand greet me. Dressed in a black suit with a white shirt and red tie, an eighty-year-old grandmother/security guard approaches my car. "Yes, who are you here for?" I feel bad for her; she walks with a limp and cannot stand upright.

"I have an appointment to get a tour of the facility. My name is Ted Stickles." That's not appropriate at all, but I don't even think the lady can hear me. She lets the gate up and waves me in. At this point, I'm okay with the deaf, fragile lady for security. Heat stroke is about the only thing she could catch in this weather. And why am I making fun of her? She's letting me through the gate and smiling at me.

The size of the facility intimidates me. There must be at least six hundred cars in the lot. Searching around the lot, I find a spot near an entrance, in an enclosed area. While walking to the doors, I use my key fob to lock the car. A revolving door takes me inside, but I am still not in the clear. Another guard stands past the entrance behind a desk. Trying to be cool, I keep walking right past the guard. I even say hello and wave. My pulse shoots to about two hundred as I make it to the elevator with no confrontation. Unsure of what floor to select, I turn to my trusted phone. I check LinkedIn and search First Sure. Damn 3G is taking forever to list my contacts at First.

With my best million-dollar smile and a handshake, I go greet the guard. "Hi! How are you doing today? I was supposedly meeting someone for a tour of the facility and to get some investor information."

The guard, a black Fabio minus the Italian accent, speaks in a deep voice, with a Jamaican accent. "You want to see someone? I have the girl for you, man." He picks up the phone on the desk and dials 18523. "Hello? Halle Stevenson? I have a man here to see you. I believe his name is Ted Stickles." After hanging up, the guard points to the small television on his desk. "We have audio, too."

Trying to act cool, I just nod my head and wait for Halle Stevenson. Shit—I went to high school with Halle. Dumb luck works faster than my phone. Walking toward the desk, I realize Halle still looks like a cheerleader. Milk, running, lifting, and whatever else she does pays off. The last time I saw Halle, she was training for the Boston Marathon. Beneath the body of steel lies a golden heart and some serious brain muscle. Now the question is: What do I tell her? I really need a plan for these missions.

Realizing I'm "Ted Stickles," she comes and hugs me. "Ted! So great to see you. Let's go to my desk." Halle leads me to the three black elevators and presses the up arrow. "Testicles? That's the best you could do, Waters? You are so fucking lucky it was me. What was plan B? It's great to see you, I don't think we've run into each other in two years or so." Her tone softens as she starts her next sentence. "How are you?"

The last time our paths crossed we were at my parents' funeral. I remember her holding me tight, telling me to cry. Touching my shoulder, she asks me again, "Talk to me! And what are you doing at First Sure?"

"First off, thank you. You were great when my parents died, and I'll never forget that. Anyway, I'm doing great. I just started working for Trust One and they sent me here for some information. Plan B was you. I had no idea the security would be so tight. My new smartphone is a little slow, but it all worked out. To be honest, the boss told me he wants to invest in First Sure, but maybe they are just looking for some inside information. I came here for a copy of the internal report. I don't think you can really give that to me."

Finally, we reach the twelfth floor and take a left out of the elevator, and then a right down a narrow hall to Halle's desk. With a shocked look on her face and a sarcastic pitch: "Oh, let me just print you out a copy. I work with investor relations, so I really can give you a copy."

"Hey I'm an investor." I show her my phone.

"The only investors who have access to this information are those who own a block of shares or sit on the board, but I'll take care of you."

Excitement takes over my emotions. "Halle, you rule! Is this against any SEC insider trading? Thank you so much. Besides owing you big time, I want you to come to my party."

Before I can tell her who I live with, she starts talking. "I already know about the gathering. John emailed me an invitation. John and I run together occasionally. I told him not to tell you I was stopping by—I wanted to surprise you." Halle continues to

hand me information as we play catch up. With a quick glance at her watch, I realize I have to drive back now. "Jack this info in folder B is something we actually post online. We pulled it down because the CEO decided it has too much strategy. If anyone asks, you got this online. Everyone has been looking for this. It's your golden ticket, all because we screwed up."

"Halle, you are the greatest. I have to run and win a couple hundred dollars. Call me anytime." I write down my number, hug Halle, and head for the car.

Walking to the garage I hear, "Bye, Mr. Testicles," in a Jamaican accent. Using the keyless entry, I open the door and break most of the rules of the road as I race to the office. Parking in the usual lot that Syd informed me Trust One leases, I run out of the car and head for his desk. Breathing heavily, I make it to his desk before quitting time.

Hearing my breathing, Sydney turns in my direction and asks the hundred-dollar question. Raising his eyebrows and lowering his voice he eventually asks, "Did you get the goods?"

With a cocky attitude, I answer. "That's why I make the big bucks. Speaking of big bucks, did you hit that cash station?"

"I got your money, hustler. Tell me one thing: Was it easy?"

"I'll say this: I had to deal with multiple layers of security."

Laughing while he hands me the rest of the cash, I open my wallet and hand all the money back to him. Without hesitation he takes all the money back. "Shit, if you hand it back to me, I'm not going to argue. If it was just twenty dollars, I would say keep it, but this is a lot of twenties."

Unsure of the next step, I ask Sydney if I should run all the information to Steve's office. "Hell no! Call Steve and he'll run down to you." Indeed, less than thirty seconds pass before he pops by.

Grabbing all the information out of my hand, he thanks me profusely. "You are amazing, Jack. With all this information, I can finish the report by Friday."

Staring at Steve's ear-to-ear grin, I say confidently, "Just another day at the office." Steve thanks me again and disappears

within seconds to do the other half of my job. Bob will probably pull me into his office and ask why Steve does all the work. Guilt gradually creeps into my mind; I should have at least perused the information. I turn to Sydney for reassurance, but he offers little sympathy.

"You could've opened a book, read a paragraph, highlighted some info, or taken some goddamn notes. Lazy!"

I interrupt the slew of insults. "Okay, I get the picture. Can we go back to work now?"

Glaring at me with a fake look of disappointment, Sydney sits in his chair and hands me a laptop. "I snagged the computer from you yesterday, added a few enhancements. Please, handle with care." Sydney gently hands me the computer. "Grab a chair and check your messages."

Whatever adjustments Syd made seem to have worked. The computer loads up faster and gets the internet up quicker than before. Since I do not yet have a company account, I type in my old-school Hotmail information. Sydney watches me as I check my messages. "You like my adjustments?"

I briefly lift my head up from the computer to respond. "Yes." I have ten messages, and none arel business related. The most shocking message is from Terry. She apologizes for the scene in the morning and looks forward to being friends. There's also a message from her brother. Mark always sends ridiculous messages—either it's a random joke or a complaint about my sister's gas problem. Mark's joke of the day reads as follows: "What do you a call a hundred lawyers at the bottom of the ocean? A good start." He ends the letter apologizing for the bad joke and telling me he'll be at my party. The next message is from Alexis: she complains about how we never talk anymore. Tomorrow, I must meet Alexis for dinner or face the consequences. Instead of replying to Alexis's message, I reach past Sydney and grab his phone.

Quickly dialing her work number and telling Syd I'm calling my sister, I close the laptop and prepare for a tough conversation. "Hello, stranger. How are you?" Before Alexis answers my question, Sydney leaves to give us some privacy. Alexis and I talk

for twenty minutes about nothing and agree to meet at Charlie's around seven. Just as I hang up, Syd reappears.

Sydney sits down, puts his feet on the desk, picks up the phone and glances at me. "What's John's work number?"

Reopening the laptop, I spout off John's number. While reading my other emails, I eavesdrop on their conversation. Sydney begins the conversation blunt and rude. "John, since Ralph Macchio has to do his kung fu crap, you wanna hit the gym?" At that point, I stop listening and notice Bob just sent me a new email. Skipping over the other two messages from him, I open the most recent note.

Jack, I just want to congratulate you on a job well done. Steve sent me all the information I need; disregard my email entitled First Sure. You will receive a five-hundred-dollar bonus in the mail. Keep up the good work. Only two days on the job and I can already feel the mutually beneficial partnership beginning to pay dividends. —BW

The feeling I get upon reading Bob's email tops sex. (Well, at least sex without a partner.) Now I really wish I knew what I handed Steve Smith. I will call Halle tonight and find out what information warranted a five-hundred-dollar bonus. Internally glowing, I forget that I have half an hour to get to karate. Luckily, Syd reminds me.

"Jack, get going. You have thirty minutes before class. However, I am impressed that you worked till six."

Grabbing my laptop as well as the briefcase I stole from my dad during college, I run to the elevator. "See you tomorrow. Around eleven is good for me." Not waiting for a reply, I hop in the elevator and push L.

Turning the air conditioner on full blast while pulling down my seatbelt, a thought hits me: If you are late to a martial arts class, they make you hurt a little extra. It's a respect thing.

Speeding home and dodging pedestrians, I hit every red light. Double-parking in front of my building, I unlock the front door

on my second try and sprint to my apartment. Picking up a pair of sweatpants, a T-shirt and boxer briefs, I close the door and jump down the steps. Luckily, Mind and Soul's location is only a couple blocks from my house. The car clock reads 6:25 as I place the car in neutral and pull up the parking brake.

A mass of students exits the dojo as I step through the large wooden door.

LESSON ONE

The only instructor present is Julie. Her shiny red hair bounces around as she stretches her neck in the center of the room. Two other students stare at Julie as everyone else exits. Julie looks like she belongs in a *Sports Illustrated* swimsuit issue; her tight white uniform allows cleavage to peek out, and her pants are cupped at the knee, exposing her beautifully toned calves. Julie is just a sexpot. It's a combination of her confidence, red hair, and blue eyes. This might be wrong, but the fact she can kick butt only makes her hotter.

Trying not to strain my eyes, I move my focus away from the beauty queen. The room seems bigger today. Maybe it's because they added a row of chairs along the back wall. The heat from outside leaks into the dojo and adds extra humidity. I walk towards the sign for the locker room; yesterday I didn't even notice the plastic sign. Julie realizes I'm about to change. "Take your time, Jack. It's good to see you again."

The locker room has two showers, a urinal, a stall, and twelve tiny lockers on each side of the room. Quickly undressing and re-dressing, I place my belongings in a locker and run to the class.

Still only two people sit on the mat. The students look either Filipino or Mexican. Julie stands in front us. She stops stretching as I

sit next to the others. "Jack, this is Eric and Raul Ventos. Eric is Raul's nephew, they moved here from the Philippines three years ago."

The two relatives stand up and shake my hand. Both Eric and Raul have short, black hair, defined cheek and jaw bones, dark skin, and stand a head shorter than me. Eric speaks for both of them and says what a pleasure it is to meet me. Eric's other uncle, Tang, was injured two weeks ago in class and decided to take a month off. Tang sprained his neck and wrist when Reggie practiced a dangerous neck toss. Julie made it a point to tell me it was not anybody's fault. I wanted to ask, "Then why do you feel guilty?" but I restrained myself.

Julie swiftly changes the subject from Tang to stretching. "To further prevent injuries, we do more stretching and strength training. Please rotate your necks from left to right and follow my count. One, two, one, two ..."

Julie continues from one stretch to the next while mixing in some running in place. Fifteen minutes of warming up has everyone—including Julie—sweating. After a quick water break, Eric leads us through various kicks and punches. Julie allows us another water timeout and emphasizes hydration.

Julie runs to the office and comes back with a clipboard. Reading from the clipboard, she rattles off calisthenics and an outline for the class. "After sprinting, hopping, skipping, crawling, and walking on your hands, we will review choke holds and spar." Julie sits on a chair and yells out each exercise as the three of us react to her orders simultaneously. My shirt is soaked, as if I'd been caught in a monsoon. The temperature in the room seems to rise. Finally, we help each other walk across the room on our hands and take five. Sucking the water from the fountain as fast as possible, I feel like puking. Julie hands us small white towels as we walk away from the fountain of delicious cold water.

Before we start up, I ask to be excused for a moment. Lifting the toilet seat, puke flies from my mouth. Sweat, puke, and embarrassment make for a great workout. I wish I was not such a loud puker. I hear the others asking with worry in their voices, "Are you okay?"

Rinsing out my mouth with water, I respond, "I'm fine." When I step back on the mat, I convince everyone that I'm okay. After five minutes of arguing, they agree I can continue. Julie then asks if she can demonstrate a choke hold on me. I was surprised that after all my puking and sweat she would choose me. While choking me, she tells us that we each will practice this move and then show her a choke hold. I think the concept of us showing her something is very cool. I wish I knew a move to display.

As she applies pressure to my neck, there's no way I can pretend it doesn't hurt. Sensing my pain, she eases up. "Give it a shot." Julie lets me practice on her, my attempt to be gentle upsets her. "Harder, Jack!"

While strangling Julie with my forearms, I ask why she'd demonstrate on the sick kid. Whispering, she tells me I still smell better than the others. I answer back, "I thought it was because I'm the cutest."

She smiles. "Oh—that, too."

Eric and Raul insist I teach a move before their turns. I display a choke hold that I saw on *Monday Night Nitro,* and no one knows the difference. Eric and Raul demonstrate holds on the ground. They're a little technical for me, but with Julie's help I figure it out.

Eight o'clock quickly approaches as we stretch again. Julie takes us through several more stretches before the class ends. Eric and Raul jet out of the gym after bowing to Julie and me. With no hesitation, I ask Julie if she wants to grab a bite. Initially she resists, but I continue trying to persuade her by saying I have free passes at the hottest new restaurant.

"Come on. Join me for a quickie at Big Bad Burger. It's this healthy burger place; they use lean meat, quinoa, and skinny buns."

Nodding yes, she softly says, "This is not a date. And first a shower, then a quick bite."

I immediately answer, "Great! You bring the soap."

Julie shakes her head and walks to the lady's locker room. "Funny."

The white shower with a crusty blue curtain provides all I need. Two plastic clear tubes hold shampoo and body soap. All my thoughts revolve around Julie. You really can't blame me. She's a knockout who can knock you out. I still have the occasional thought about Dana. Julie's pretty, but I have a crush on Dana. Thoughts of Dana disappear as I tie my shoes and exit the room.

Walking toward the mat, I feel Julie tugging on the back of my shirt. Turning to face her, I notice three things: red sweatpants, white tank top—and a shiny engagement ring. Julie follows my eyes. "I'm engaged, not married. But even though you're the cutest, it's just dinner."

"Fine. Dinner and maybe some cuddling."

Stepping outside, I tell her the place is within walking distance, so we decide to throw our smelly clothes in our trunks and head to Big Bad Burger.

The discussion on the way to the restaurant revolves around Eric, Raul, and Tang Shin. Eric and Raul run a Filipino grocery store and bring fruits and vegetables to the class once a week. Tang, the injured relative, brings in baked goods a few times a week. According to Julie, these three relatives are the nicest people she has ever met, especially compared to a few new students that are incredibly aggressive. The Shins are also incredible martial artists. Julie goes off on a tangent describing their skill. "The three men have super quick hands and feet. You put fighting sticks in their hands, and forget about it. They're also acrobatic; Raul once flipped over Eric to kick Tang."

Finally reaching Big Bad Burger, I open the door and hold it for Julie. The inside resembles an old diner. The walls and tables are painted black and white. Old music plays in the background as I read the giant menu above the front counter. Next to each food item is the fat content, protein, and calorie count. The menu ranges from chicken and hamburgers to tofu and veggie burgers.

Julie orders a grilled chicken sandwich with onions, Muenster cheese, lettuce, tomato, cucumber, and grilled mushrooms. "I'll have the same, and we'll split some special spuds. What are the special spuds?"

The man behind the counter replies with a Spanish accent, "They are sweet potatoes baked with barbeque-honey sauce, and only have four grams of fat per serving. Would you like an order?"

Before I place the order, I check with Julie, "Would you like to share a serving, honey?"

"Yes, dear. I would love to. Should we get a shake with two straws?" Julie and I laugh as the man behind the counter looks confused. We tell him just the spuds, and I display my coupons.

The coupons also throw him for a loop. Turning to the back, he yells, "Señor, we have a coupon!" A tall, pale, muscular man wearing a stained apron and extra-large grin walks toward me.

"Hi, I'm Tom—owner and chef. Glad to see my promotions working! What's your name?"

"Well, hello! I'm Jack and this is Dana—I mean Julie!" Julie gives me a Who's Dana stare and laughs. Tom brings us our order, a receipt that lists the nutritional content of our food, and thanks us for visiting his dream. The food looks excellent: The sandwich barely fits on the bun—the chicken must be a double breast—and vegetables and cheese overflow, making a fork a necessity. Tom has sliced the massive sandwiches in half and placed a toothpick in each half. The potatoes look like they were fried, not baked. They're crispy on the outside and soft in the middle.

Since losing my lunch and burning more calories than two hours on a Stairmaster, I scarf down my food and three-quarters of the spuds. Julie also eats fast, but I still finish before her. While dipping a potato in ketchup, Julie realizes my meal has disappeared. "Wow—you don't have a gag reflex? Did you taste any of the food? That can't be healthy. After the purging during my class, I thought you would take it easy."

Embarrassment turns my cheeks red. "Sorry. I was just really hungry."

"Don't feel bad. I eat like a man. Not to change the subject or further offend you, but you don't look like a fighter."

With my best smile I reply, "I'm a lover, not a fighter."

"If you're a better lover than a fighter, you must be one hell of a Romeo."

My shy side comes out as I quietly thank her. We continue discussing fighting as I tell her she's way too beautiful to hide in a dojo all day and night. Julie tells me how she was a dancer and one of her teachers recommended karate, and the rest is history. She continues to question what brought me to Mind and Soul. "I can tell you and Sydney are great friends, but what made him choose Mind and Soul?"

"Here's the truth: It's for my job." As I come clean, I can tell she wants to help me. Julie opens up like a good book and tells me all the details. She tells me that everything truly occurred accidentally.

"I took over the advanced class after Tang injured his neck. Chung taught the adult class before. His style of teaching is brutal. That, combined with a few aggressive alpha males, led to some accidents. A Trust One examiner sat down with the three us after Tang's fall. He warned us that we were under investigation and might lose the current policy. Bob teaches with the same attitude as Chung—no pain, no gain. I work students out hard and always avoid injury. Chung is old school. He had me hitting and kicking trees, breaking cinder blocks, walking on hot coal, and sparring with men the size of bears. I took ice baths and anti-inflammatory drugs every day until pain meant nothing to me. When Chung beats a wooden stick all over your body, you break or the wood breaks. Usually, we just have a lot of students quit, but this new breed is almost looking for pain. Chung has altered his classes to prevent injury, and he asked me to teach your class until he feels ready. I have documentation on all the injuries—even letters from doctors with x-rays. I'll make you a copy of everything. Stop by around ten tomorrow."

I am unbelievably amazed that Julie is telling me everything. "I do not know what will happen, Julie. All I do is gather the information. Thanks for the input. Anything else to add?"

With an inquisitive look, "Building issues, but I'm not sure of the details. Chung owns the building and people always want to buy it. He bought in '83 when the area was ghetto."

I grab our trash and put it in the garbage. Julie and I have been talking for almost two hours. Only two lights remain on, and all the employees except Tom have left. Tom unlocks the door and tells us to come back anytime. We apologize for staying so late and walk fast to our cars. Before Julie enters her car, she runs over to my car and hugs me. A little shocked, I hug her back and invite her and her fiancé Paul to the Friday night bash.

Driving around the block five times, I finally take the spot in front of the fire hydrant. Quietly opening the door, John greets me. "Hello, stranger. Sarah and Stacey, your sister, Mark, and Blake called. Now I'm going to bed. See you Friday."

"I think we'll actually see each other tomorrow. You want to lift at six?" We agree on 6:15, and then I pass out. I'm so worn out from the class that I don't brush, floss, or take off my clothes.

JOB AIN'T NOTHING BUT WORK

[Ring—ring—ring] "Hello. May I speak with Jack Waters, please?"

My alarm clock reads 9:30, so I guess this is my wake-up call. "Hello, Patty. No, I was not sleeping."

"Please hold while I transfer you to Sydney Phelps. Have a great day."

Sydney tells me how sore his legs are from squatting, and that I should not forget about meeting with Tom Keefer at Big Bad Burger around ten. Sydney also transfers me to BW.

"Jack, hope you're feeling energized! Your jam-packed agenda includes a meeting with Larry Jones at four. Larry developed Muscle's Gym. If you have any information on Mind and Soul, just bring it to me. Steve has a full plate. Have a good one." The phone clicks and I don't even get a word in edgewise.

The clock hits 9:40 and I boogie. Taking off my clothes from yesterday and putting on a powder-blue, button-down, collared shirt, I feel professional. The only other pair of dress pants I own look clean enough to wear.

After a good two minutes of brushing, I gargle and grab a banana. Tying my Rockports and staring at my watch, I realize I have five minutes to meet both Julie and Tom. Since ladies always

come first, I peel the parking violation off my car and double park outside Mind and Soul. Hopefully I don't end up with another ticket.

"Good morning, Julie. You got the goods?"

The dojo is empty except for Julie and a box she opens in the main room. After a guy hug (grabbing my hand and slapping my back), she runs into the office. "Give me two seconds." Julie jets out of the office with an envelope labeled Jack Waters. "Here you go, mister. Thanks for dinner. I'd like Italian next time."

"No problem. Thanks again. I'll see you Saturday at three." (The advanced class takes place Mondays, Wednesdays, and Saturdays.) Julie lets me go, and I drive right to Big Bad Burger and park on the street. After popping my trunk and grabbing my camera and cell phone, I run to the entrance.

The lock on the door prevents me from entering the eatery. Tom eventually hears me knocking and lets me in. "Tom Keefer, it's a pleasure to meet you again. I'm Jack Waters with Trust One."

"Jack, it's nice to see you again. Wish I would've known you were the consultant last night; we could've discussed business over a drink. I met your partner Jeff Riley in LA. Great guy. I thought he would be here today."

So now I'm a consultant. I like the sound of that. "I actually pick up Jeff tomorrow. He couldn't make it today. Did Bob tell you what this meeting was about?"

Tom gives me the grand tour and tells me to click away. I snap pictures of the large grill, steel oven, meat locker, wooden cupboards, and checkered tables. When we get to the kitchen, he takes a large bag labeled "Jack & Jeff" and carries it to a table. "Please sit down, Jack." Tom starts to explain the story behind Big Bad Burger before we even sit down. "I wanted good food, reasonably priced, served fast, and I didn't want all the fat and sugar and nasty processed crap. I sat down with two buddies from college and we came up with BBB. Sure, the name is intimidating, but it piques curiosity. One of my partners was a chef for the Ritz hotel in St. Louis. The other was a personal trainer in LA. My background stems from a degree in Management and a history of low-paying

management jobs. When Dave, Chris, and I met in LA a year ago, we combined all of our experience to create a healthy fast-food chain. Right now, we lose money every month on this store and the one in Des Moines. Both stores just opened three weeks ago, so I'm not worried yet." Tom continues to explain the goal, vision, and history as another man brings out a sample plate filled with food.

The young man speaks Spanish and broken English. Tom thanks him in Spanish and tells him to continue prepping. I miss most of the conversation because my last Spanish lesson was in high school, but I understand the important parts. The worker walks away, and Tom invites me to go nuts.

"Jack, sample all the food. The bag I have behind me contains everything on the menu, frozen. You can take that to a lab and check the accuracy of our menu." Tom keeps yapping as I dig in. I sample everything.

The plate has three different types of potatoes; a piece of every meat on the menu; samples of tuna, chicken, pasta and vegetable salads; one chocolate shake; and a hummus pita wrap. Tom recommends only one bite of each and half the power protein shake, and I immediately regret not taking his advice. Feeling obscenely full and lethargic, I cut the meeting short. This might be the second puking event of the week.

"Tom, the food sucks. Just kidding! I wish I could eat more; it's fantastic. Will you have time to meet with Jeff and me?"

Tom stands and holds the door open for me. "I'm literally always here. At the moment, I'm renting a place across the street."

I cannot believe I just consumed a few pounds of meat, a quart of salad, and a shake. I place my camera under the seat and start to drive home, hoping the boss does not call.

Taking a quick detour, I stop in to see Charlie. Charlie's kitchen contains nutritional testing equipment; he tests his food once a month as his menu changes.

Carrying the bag directly to the massive kitchen, I find Charlie cutting onions in the back. "Charlie! How you doing? I have some business for you." Before I finish my sentence, Charlie puts down the knife and offers up a hand and a hug.

"So wonderful to see you. I am fine today. When you bring a girl here?" After explaining I will bring a girl as soon as possible, I ask him if he can test the food for me. Even though my company will pay him, he insists on not charging me. "Stop by tonight around eight. Bring Alexis. We will have dinner and the tests will be complete." Charlie walks me out and hugs me as I open the car door. "Beautiful car Jack, I will see you later."

"Thanks for your help. I look forward to dinner." The moment I turn on the air conditioning and put the car in first, the phone rings. The only person that has the number is Bob— I think.

"Hello, Bob. How are you?"

"Bob? Do I sound white, fat and bald? I am black, bald and beautiful, bitch!"

"Sorry, Syd. It'll never happen again. Now, what do you want?" Sydney asks me whether I've checked my email today. Evidently, Bob has assigned another case to my already busy schedule. He also wants the information on Mind and Soul ASAP. Sadly, there will be no nap time in my future. I really need a massage, too. That class crushed my body.

The new plan: Hand BW the information, check my email, go to the gym and, finally, meet Alexis at Charlie's. Sydney finally lets me go, and while driving down the Kennedy, I call Alexis.

Since Alexis never answers her phone at work, I leave a nasty message demanding her presence at Charlie's. Ten seconds after I hang up, my phone rings. Alexis whispers, "Okay, fucker. I'll see you at eight." Caller ID at work will be the death of my prank calls.

Soon Alexis will be married, and I'll have no one. We used to see each other all the time and talk daily when I went to college. Dumb me introduced Alexis to Mark, and now we rarely hang out. The summer after my parents died, we were inseparable. Last winter, the two of us went to Colorado, and then Mark started eating up her time. Okay, I'm done venting. I feel better now. My pity party lasts all the way to Sydney's desk. My therapist said it's normal to have a cry. Vent, bitch; just don't forget the good times.

"Hello, black, bald, and beautiful." Without saying another word, I speedwalk to BW's office. The immense door is slightly ajar. I knock and enter. Bob waves me in while speaking to someone on the phone. I place all the Mind and Soul information on his desk. He gives me the old thumbs up followed by the "I'll call you" sign. Either that or he wants a banana.

Sydney's desk is now vacant, so I sit down and check my email. Today I have three new messages: one from Mark and two from Bob. One of the messages from Bob is from the morning and the other message is ten seconds old. I check the last message from Bob first. The note thanks me for the information and informs me that Jeff Riley will also assist on the Muscle's case. His other message lists my new projects: Ace Investing and Kevin Slim. Ace Investing loans money to riverboat casinos in the Midwest, and Kevin Slim died in auto accident but still manages to cash checks. He ends by suggesting that I keep taking classes at Mind and Soul.

I feel like Magnum PI. Now I just need a fancy car, like a Lamborghini.

Mark's email is short but entertaining. "Busy. Have fun with my fiancé. My sister now hates you. Heard you have a new lady friend. Fill me in. Blow-up dolls do not count. Off to sell diapers."

Sydney stares at me, wondering what's so funny. "You wouldn't get it," I tell him.

He replies quickly, with a stern stare. "Oh, I get it—white boy humor. Something about frat boys and beer? You're real funny. Maybe you should go on the road! In fact, why don't you start hitting the road right now? I think Vegas, Nashville, Tulsa, and Tacoma need you. Now get the fuck away from my desk, funny man." Suddenly his straight face falters, and tears form as he tries to fight his laughter.

We laugh so loud together that people start to stare. Walking away from his desk before we both get fired, I tell him not to forget that 6:15 is gym time. Shooting down the elevator with a smile, I think about taking that nap.

The moment I step inside my apartment, my cell phone rings and I accidentally answer. I hate answering when I don't know

who's calling. "Hello. This is Jack Waters. Please leave a message. Beep."

"Hi. This is Jeff Riley, and that is the worst fake beep I've ever heard."

"Hi, Jeff. I will see you at eleven tomorrow at United. Two questions: Where are you staying, and do you want to go to a Cubs game?"

"Sweet! I'll go to the game. I'm staying at the Holiday Inn on Ohio. I figure we'll work in Chicago till Wednesday, and then start our west coast trip. Any other questions?"

"Friday I'm throwing a party. You are more than welcome to come—and even help set up after work. Any chance you want to help? You will get paid in nachos and beer."

He answers immediately. "I have no problem with that. See you tomorrow." I like Jeff already. I lay my drained body on the couch, and my other line rings. I decide to screen this call, so I allow the machine to answer. When I hear Blake's voice, I pick up the phone.

Having completely forgotten about picking him up, I lie when he asks if I forgot about him. "Of course I remember that I'm picking you up at six. I want you to take the 'L' instead because traffic is going to suck. Take the Blue Line to the Red Line and get off at Addison. You remember where the stadium is? That's the Addison stop. Call me when you get there, and I'll pick you up. Bring your hat—we're going to the game on Saturday."

We forgo the usual small talk. Blake lets me go and agrees to call tomorrow.

The clock on the DVD player reads 3:00 p.m. I close my eyes and pass out like I have never slept before. My eyes gradually open, and it feels like I have been sleeping for hours. Sitting up fast I start to freak out. What if I missed my appointment? Bob will fire me, I'll lose the car and John will have to pay all the rent again. Then I glance at the DVD player: 3:20 p.m. Gathering my workout gear and keys, I lock the door and head straight to the gym.

BEHIND THE MUSCLES

The parking lot resembles an empty playground. Then again, it's not rush hour. Pulling into the front spot while searching for my camera, I wind up stalling the car. It dies for the first time—a rookie mistake. Placing the car in neutral, yanking the parking brake up, and grabbing my camera, I head up to the front door. Every time I meet with someone, I feel like I'm leaving something out; and I'm constantly late. Entering the facility, I peek down at my watch. I'm twenty minutes early!

The front smells like someone just cleaned the wooden desk with a pine tree. The cute woman holding a dust rag behind the counter verifies this. The leggy blond drops the rag, smiles at me with a bleached-white grin, and offers to page Larry Jones. Shit—I left a pen, notepad, and recorder in the car. A large man hops down the steps with a name tag—"Little Larry"—on his chest. I decide not to run to the car to get the notepad as Little Larry extends his massive arm in my direction. He speaks with a very deep voice, "You must be Jack. Pleasure to meet you. I'm Larry Jones, otherwise known as Little Larry." His face forms a smile as I firmly shake his hand and respond.

"The pleasure is all mine, Little Larry. Nice to meet you. I arrived early to take pictures of the equipment and facility.

You have an awesome gym. I worked out here the other day, and I'm working on the guns today." Larry looks at my arms and shakes his head. As he leads me to his office, he suggests we work legs today. Larry towers over me as we walk; his bald head and muscular build cast a shadow that completely covers me. Larry's corner office is opposite the cardio room. He jokes about how he dreams of a quiet office as he ducks his head to fit through the door.

"Sit down, Jack. I want to show you some data on the success of my clubs in LA and New York. I met your partner Jeff Riley in LA a year ago. Great guy. He's seen the other clubs and said he'll be in town next week to meet with the two of us." Trying not to act surprised, I shake my head and make an appointment for next week: Tuesday, 10 a.m. Larry continues to tell me the company's vision of becoming the best "hardcore gym" in the country. I finally remember to use the recorder on my phone. Taping the conversation allows me to look Larry in his eyes and not worry about forgetting any details. He informs me that Jeff also uses a tape recorder, and takes lots of pictures.

"Hey—were you related to Jerry?"

"Yup."

"I'm sorry for your loss. He was here every day, twice a day. You guys buy our data, and Jerry downloaded it in person. I would've emailed it. We would love to do more corporate wellness. Right now, selling our data is step one. Jerry was really helpful explaining what info to capture, and how to do it without being intrusive. Thanks to Jerry, we have a few other companies that buy data."

That explains the Excel file. "Thanks. I really appreciate it." Larry continues to speak, but my mind wanders. Jerry liked to work out—but twice a day? He was a runner and biker like my roommate. I wonder if Jeff will have any info for me about Jerry.

Jeff does what I do, and he's called a consultant. I wonder whether he works for Trust One or a consulting firm. I have all these questions to ask Jeff: Does he have to find companies' internal reports? Does he ever have to lie? Bend the law? Has he ever

gotten in trouble? And does he make more money than me? I'll skip that last question, but Jeff is in for a full interrogation.

Larry continues to discuss his vision and goal as I return to listening. He emphasizes total training: eating right, aerobics, lifting, sleeping, attitude, and posture. All his members get free private sessions when they sign up, and then he randomly checks their progress. He personally works with a different individual every day. And Larry decides that today is my turn. "Now, Jack, today I'm going to measure your chest, back, arms, legs, calves, and waist. I will also calculate your body fat, target and resting heart rate, and your fitness level. We will tear apart your diet as well, and I will suggest some supplements to put some weight on your candy ass."

Since I need to have the last word, I respond, "Listen Scary Larry Jones, don't make me put the smack down on your over-developed ass!" We continue joking around as Larry whips out the tape measure and asks me to stand up. "Just don't make me turn and cough!" Insisting he'll be gentle, he slides the tape measure around my body and writes down my dimensions. Next, he hands me a machine I hold in my hand to calibrate my fat percentage. It reads 11.2. My ego slowly rises as Larry compliments me.

"See Larry, I'm a fit cat, a well-oiled machine, a specimen which others—"

Larry stops me mid-brag. "Yeah, that percentage is almost as low as Jeff's."

Now that I feel average again, Larry walks me to the locker room and tells me to change. Larry talks to me as I get dressed. Slightly uncomfortable, I listen closely to his motivational speech.

"Jack, I'm going to work you over. You will sweat and scream in pain, but when this workout is over, you'll feel like Hercules. Today, we'll tap into your immense strength, stretch your muscles, and lift more weight than you ever thought possible. Every rep, every set will tear your muscles apart. And then you'll drink some protein and supplements that will help your body grow! Now drop five of these under your tongue—anabolic steroids. Just kidding! This is liquid creatine, which will help you stay

strong. With this substance there is no loading stage, and it doesn't tax your kidneys. Post workout, you'll have a drink that contains L-glutamine, which aids in muscle growth and repair." Larry now has me ready to take on the world. Insisting I keep the supplements, he hands me a bottle of water, puts his hand on my shoulder, and in a deep voice he orders, "You will get big today!"

"Does everyone take this stuff?"

"No. I'm just hooking you up. Plus, Bob paid for you to get the A package, which includes blood testing, supplements, and training. Trust me—you will see some results! We only sell supplements that have been fully tested and approved by a third-party research firm. You gotta be careful. Some of this shit has arsenic, steroids, and other horrible stuff."

All the cheesy motivation is working; I am so pumped right now, I could tear the head off a lion. Well, a stuffed-animal lion—but still. Jones leads me to the bikes and sits down next to me. He tells me most people call him Jones (his last name) because Larry is more of a skinny guy name. I tell him Jack is more of a couch potato name and that, if he's up for it, drinks are on me after the workout.

After five minutes of intervals on the bike, Jones pushes me on. "Okay, funny man. Now it's time for active stretching and weights."

Jones is yelling at me like I'm a professional athlete training to make the big bucks, "Come on! Power up! Let's go! Three more. Good! GOOD! GOOD! Keep going, burn it out, come on, ONE MORE!" Grunting, screaming, pushing, and Larry's comments carry me all the way through to complete exhaustion. I can barely stand as Jones leads me to a bike for ten minutes of cooling down. He continues his coach-speak as I drink a milk jug full of water. "Shit, son! I've never seen anyone work that hard in Lincoln Park. You did a great job. How do you feel?"

"I felt like I just boxed twelve rounds with the champ, and he definitely won." After stretching and a protein shake, Jones recommends an ice-cold shower.

"When you finish your shower, head up to massage bed three. Carol is going to relax you for half an hour. The massage is free, but please tip her. And no—she isn't a hooker. After your massage, stop by my office to pick up some information on our last quarter."

I thank Larry profusely for my session, and he hands me another drink. "Banana, coconut milk, chia seeds, and chocolate hemp powder. I'm like a hippy." After a long shower, I dry off and see John and Syd in the locker room. I tell them about my experience and emphatically recommend they work out with Jones. I cannot believe I have been at the gym since twenty to four; it's now almost seven. Excusing myself from the guys, I run up to bed three for my massage.

The door to the room is open, only a candle keeps the room lit. Carol is wearing a tight white shirt, her chest looks like it might bust through the cotton. I'm beginning to understand why this gym makes so much money. Trying not to ogle her, I smile and lay down. I don't want to be the freak with a boner during my massage. "Hi, Carol. I'm Jack and this is my first time. Take it easy on me—I'm a virgin."

She speaks softly. "Don't you worry. I'll be gentle. Now take off your shirt and pants, and place this towel around your waist." I've waited a long time for someone to say that to me. She leaves the room as I change, but quickly reappears with a jug of oil. Carol covers me with a sheet and adds, "Normally, after you change, you hop under the covers. I know you're a rookie, so I'll let it slide."

I wake up half an hour later and pray I did not embarrass myself with any night toots or morning wood. "Jack. Jack. Wake up. Your time is up." Wow, I might have slept the whole time, but it was amazing. We walk to the weight room. Carol refuses to take any money. I introduce her to John and Sydney while they stare at her assets. Leaving them to talk, I collect my workout gear and run to Larry's office. He hands me the material and apologizes for being on the phone as I walk away.

My legs feel like jello. The simple act of driving proves difficult for my tired muscles. As I pull into the closest spot, I see

Alexis's red car behind me. She and Mark wave as I put the car in neutral and pull up the clutch. We exchange hugs before walking in. Charlie greets us at the front with more hugs. He hands me the results of the tests of Big Bad Burger's food. I thank Charlie while scanning the sheet: high-protein food, low sugar, low fat, average sodium, and above-average amounts of fiber. I technically have been working all night, so it's time to put the folder down and enjoy some food.

I sit next to Mark. "You fit in well with our family," I tell him. "My parents would have approved." He has this likeable quality that few people have and all people admire. He genuinely cares for others and openly discusses his feelings. I am happy Alexis met such a great person. They're like two peas in a pod. They even have the same cheesy sense of humor. Watching the two of them together makes me think of my parents. Even though my parents were polar opposites, they always had this glowing smile around each other. It never got old. I hope one day someone looks at me the way Mark looks at Alexis.

Once the food comes, I forget everything else. I can smell fresh lemon and rosemary as I devour my chicken and pasta dish. Alexis turns to me in awe. "Holy shit! Did you even chew?"

Mark adds, "Good thing you don't have a gag reflex."

"No joke: I just had a two-hour personal training session. This dude killed me. I can't really feel my legs right now."

Alexis offers some advice. "You need a hobby—and girlfriend."

Since the check never comes, the three of us pitch in for a big a tip and thank Charlie. I ask Alexis and Mark to drop me off, figuring I'd never find a spot in Wrigleyville at this hour. The minute I reach my bed, fatigue sets in; fully clothed and completely sober, I pass out.

FRIDAY

[Ring—Ring—Ring] I reach for my phone and realize it's my wake-up call.

"Hello, Patty Grace. Are you having a good morning?"

"My morning is great so far. Please hold for Bob. Have a great day!" Patty speaks softly, with an upbeat tone. Most people use alarm clocks; I have my own private wake-up call. I'm what you call incredibly lucky. I might not have an office, admin, or a six-figure-plus income, but I have a wake-up call. It feels early for some reason, but I feel well-rested. I glance at my alarm clock and do a double take. It's 6:30 a.m.

I attempt to focus as Bob starts talking. "Jack, keep up the good work. Monday, I would like to meet with you and Jeff. Is ten good?" Still half out of it, I say yes and write down *10 Monday* on a notepad. Bob again thanks me for all my work and asks me to stop by his office in the morning.

Before I leave the bedroom, I take Jerry's flash drive and plug it into my personal PC. I scan the Excel file with all the members. If Jerry worked out twice a day, he would be listed twice each day, and sixty times for the last month. His name only appears twelve times. Why would he delete his name? Or did Jones lie?

Curiosity consumes me as I begin my morning ritual. While washing my face over the sink, soreness sets in. My legs feel like they each weigh a hundred pounds, and every muscle feels pulled. The weird thing is that I love the pain. The more I ache, the better the workout, right? I still need to check out the paperwork and interview some of his clients and staff.

My mint-green polo shirt and linen pants help me withstand the heat; the temperature must be around 100 degrees. The humid air immediately forces sweat from my forehead. By the time I reach the car, I feel the need to change shirts. I watch the heat leave the car as I open the door. The car feels like a sauna; maybe it'll be good for my muscles. The air conditioner shoots out warm air like a stove. I'm going to need more deodorant. Glancing at the passenger seat, I notice I left my computer, camera and recorder in open view. Thank God no one stole anything. I should leave my car at the restaurant more often.

The car finally cools down as I pull into the garage. I take my usual spot on the third floor and remove all my valuables, plus the nutritional information on BBB. The security guards greet me with a wave and head nod, and I wave back and wish them a good day.

Walking straight to Sydney's desk, I remember that I need to pick Jeff up in twenty minutes. I drop off all my equipment on Syd's desk, then run to Bob's office. He waves me in and hands me a Montblanc pen—whatever that is. It looks fancy. I hand him the caloric and fat content of Big Bad Burger's food and thank him. Bob tells me that I am an asset to the company and to continue the good work. I run back to Sydney and announce, "I'm running because I'm late to get Jeff."

Sydney decides to answer with, "Okay. Let's jog. Follow me to the Batmobile." The running is actually loosening up my legs. On an unusually light traffic day, we reach the United terminal at 11:10. With a loose sheet of paper and my fancy pen, Sydney makes a quick JEFF RILEY sign. The moment I hold up the sign, I see a blond guy with a goofy grin walking my way.

"Nice sign, Junior. What—they don't pay you enough to buy markers?"

"Hey! We wanted to use crayons, but it wasn't in the budget. I'm Jack, and this is Sydney."

Jeff speaks with a slight Southern accent. "Nice to meet you guys. Can we grab some McDonald's before we go back to work?" He throws his green bag in the trunk and sits in the back seat. We drive to the nearest McDonald's as Jeff tells us how he only eats hamburgers from there. He never orders a burger from a restaurant, but once a month he needs a Big Mac, large fries, and a medium Coke. The three of us sit down like little kids, wolfing our food down without speaking. Sydney and I finish in two minutes as Jeff slowly and patiently eats his food, dipping his sandwich into ketchup with every bite. He eats everything in shifts: first the burger, then the fries and, lastly, the hot apple pie. Before throwing out our trash, we discuss life, work, and the pursuit of women. Jeff notices the time and wonders whether we have to work at all today.

Sydney explains that his day is free, but Jeff and I must meet with somebody. "Oh, shit—we have to meet with Tom at BBB." Though not even a drop of ketchup is left on his tray, I ask sarcastically, "Are you done, Jeff?"

"You guys are so funny."

Already I can tell Jeff is a good guy. On the way to BBB, Jeff and I discuss information we have attained for Trust One. As our discussion continues, I realize that he has never had to find an internal report or strategic documents. Even though we just met, I feel I can trust him. He agrees to read my emails and tell me if anything seems odd. Syd throws in his two cents. "Jack, they pay you a lot of money for a reason, and the company has a set of the best lawyers in the country." He laughs and adds, "If you bend a few laws, they'll get you off the hook."

"Thanks. I feel a lot better now. As the police read me my rights, I'll feel confident. I hope you both show up to my arraignment. Now let's discuss something of greater importance: my party. What do I need to throw a party Dallas Cowboys style?"

Jeff quickly answers, "Cocaine, cheerleaders, weed, hookers, and Michael Irvin."

I shoot back, "Done! But seriously, what should we buy? I want everyone to have fun, get lucky and dance.

Jeff and Sydney respond simultaneously, "Roofies and condoms."

"Okay, you two aren't invited. What—do you guys shower with your socks on? I'm not buying condoms." The laughter subsides as we pull into Big Bad Burger. I guess Syd will be working in the field today.

As we walk in the door, Sydney asks if we'll get free food. I answer yes, and a huge smile forms on his face. "It's not like you're getting a million dollars. Plus, you just ate, fatty."

"Wow! You guys get the cash, the car, *and* free food. I need to switch positions."

Tom greets us and asks us to sit down at a booth as he runs into the kitchen. Sydney and I sit on the same side, leaving Jeff to sit next to Tom. Jeff quietly complains, "Thanks. Put me next to the guy who smells like oil and onions."

Tom walks to the table carrying a plate full of food and three shakes. While handing a chocolate shake to Jeff, he asks what kind Syd and I want. I get the vanilla and Sydney takes the other chocolate. The minute Tom sits down, I whip out the recorder and begin taping our conversation. All I know is that Bob wants him to discuss growth strategy.

Two hours pass as Jeff and Tom discuss golf and Kansas basketball. Jeff and Tom both grew up in Kansas. Besides learning about the "best college program," I find out Tom needs help with his marketing plan. I see dollar signs and offer him help. We plan a meeting for Sunday night to evaluate his current plan and new strategies. "My sister and I have worked with other restaurants. We might be able to help you out."

As we make our way out the door, I invite him to my party. He agrees to come and offers to bring some food. With the pizza from Charlie and Tom's goodies, everyone will leave the party fat and bloated. Not quite what I planned, but who doesn't like free food?

After the restaurant we make another stop in order to take care of an important personal matter—booze. At the store we

pick up the usual: cups, napkins, garbage bags, a keg of Miller Light, ice, jugs of vodka, soft drinks, condoms, breath mints, and packs of Winter fresh gum. I hate the smell of beer on a girl's breath. The moment I pick up the gum, Jeff declares, "Now it's a party."

The second we set foot in my apartment, the phone rings. I hope it's not Patty Grace. "Hello! What's up, Johnny boy? I just purchased all the liquor; you owe me a hundred and fifty bucks." John and I continue to talk as Jeff and Sydney start arranging things, as if they live here. John tells me it must be nice to get paid to eat and shop.

"Start partying frat boy. I'm stuck here till seven. Save me a girl and some punch."

As John hangs up, the phone rings again. I'm never this popular. I recognize the voice. "Blake, walk three blocks away from the field. Turn right on Grace. The address is 1250." I hang up again and turn to Syd. "Syd, preheat the oven to three fifty. I'll be back in five minutes. Help yourself to whatever. I appreciate all the help." As I run out the door, I run into a new person opening the dude's door. The new guy is tall with long hair and a broad build.

"Hi! You must be Jack. I'm Tyler Brody. I showed the apartment to John when you were interning in Iowa. My uncle owns the building, and I just moved into Adam and Steve's place. They moved a couple blocks away. I do graphic design. I turned one of their rooms into an office. They worked out of the kitchen. I would weigh 400 pounds if I worked out of the kitchen."

I invite Tyler to stop over as soon as he has a chance, and we chat for a few more minutes. Eventually, he asks me where I was headed. I suddenly remember Blake, who's probably carting a huge duffel bag around the block. I excuse myself and literally sprint down Sheffield.

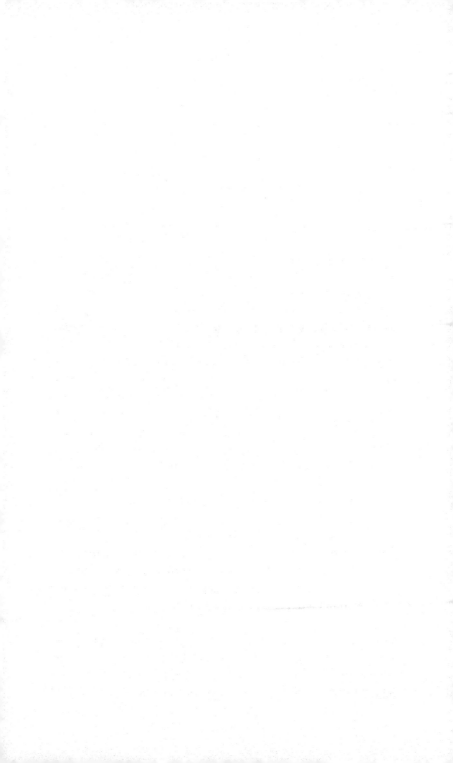

BLAKE

"Jack, you limp-dicked, pussy-whipped bitch! My mom really appreciated it when you left that message on my machine. She says the next time you visit you're going to church—even if you're Jewish. Now give me some sugar."

"Dude, you made it pretty far! If I hadn't run out, you totally would have found the place." Hopping up the stairs, I notice my opened door. I peek inside and smell pizza cooking. Tyler, Sydney, and Jeff are all playing video games while sitting on the couch with their feet on the coffee table. I feel like I'm back in college. I love that feeling.

"Hey, everybody. This is Blake."

The crew pauses the video game for introductions. I mix up some of Charlie's cocktails and bring them in the main room. Time flies, and before I know it, a few friends arrive. Still no sign of John. As eight o'clock approaches, John pops in. His eyes meet Cholet's and his face lights up. Everyone is munching on pizza except for Syd, who's enjoying the vegetables. At least there's one.

I pull Halle into my bedroom. "So the info you gave got me a bonus and a fancy pen. What the fuck did you give me? And did we break any laws?"

She smiles. "Relax, J. You are fine. We broke no laws. If Trust One invests in my company because of the information, they will have not broken the law. The shit's all online. Of course, most people would spend months searching in order to find it." As we continue our discussion of the law with Joe, everyone wonders what the three of us are doing.

Joe tries to ease my nerves. "Just watch your back. I'll read the info. In the meantime, drink heavily."

Halle adds, "His mouth is too pretty to go to jail."

We leave my room so we can get back to mingling. Alexis and Mark walk in and need drinks. While mixing drinks for the happy couple, I search for Jeff, Blake, and Dana. I hear absolutely nothing Alexis and Mark are saying as I spot Dana walking in the door. Like an obedient dog, I excuse myself and quickly make Dana a drink. Casually brushing everyone aside, I greet Dana with a drink and a smile. She looks fabulous in a pink tank top and tight black pants. The only downside: She came to the party with the guy who lives above her. I shoot him a quick "Hi," as I gaze into Dana's sparkling eyes. I point the guy in the direction of the beer and bring Dana into the living room.

While guiding Dana to the couch, Tom from BBB comes in carrying three trays. "Don't thank me. They're leftover mini veggie burgers." Dana sits on the couch as I run Tom to the kitchen. All I can think is that I hope no one steals my seat.

Tom places the food on the counter. "Unfortunately, I have other plans tonight. But I look forward to our meeting on Sunday!"

I run back to Dana and am happy to see her patiently waiting for me. She is wedged between Jeff and Blake, who are ignoring her. Jeff is talking to a tall brunette that I have never seen, while Blake talks to Halle. John looks my way as he tries to convince Cholet to stay the night, then does a double take upon seeing Dana sitting on our couch. Leaving Cholet, he heads to the couch with so much oomph, Jeff and Blake almost fall off.

"DANA!" Hugs are quickly exchanged. The three of us sink into the couch and stroll down memory lane. Most of the

memories involve me sitting in the observation chair in elementary school. John and Dana trade stories as if fourth grade was yesterday. I'm surprised they haven't forgotten the time I told my teacher why Dana and I would make a cute couple. They continue talking as Sydney walks by; he immediately senses this is the girl I've been talking about.

"Hello. I'm Sydney. I work with Jacky." Sydney's already-deep voice drops a bit more. "Oh, you live upstairs. You live with your boyfriend, right?" Internally, I'm shaking. I cannot believe he said that, but I appreciate it. Pretty smooth, really.

Turning to speak directly to me, Dana states, "No. I live alone, and I don't have a boyfriend." Sydney winks at me and walks away after telling her how nice it is to meet her. John also excuses himself. As he walks away, Blake stops by with two drinks. He sets them on the coffee table, smiles at both of us, and walks away.

I explain to Dana that every time I see Blake, he tries to get me drunk, and that he usually succeeds. Dana and I continue to discuss everything from college friends to future goals. The only time my eyes leave hers is when she goes to the bathroom. Half the people at the party have unfamiliar faces. I'm okay with that. There are no fights and no puking. So, overall, it's a success. People are dancing and chatting, and one drunk couple is making out in the kitchen. Dana and I don't even have to get drinks. Blake delivers a new glass every twenty minutes. I can tell he's already drunk—he's wearing a huge grin and having trouble walking straight.

Dana comes back from the bathroom, sits down and asks me if my old girlfriend is at the party. She asks her question nonchalantly, and her face lights up when I tell her she's not here. The party becomes gradually louder, which brings Dana and me even closer to each other. With every exchange, our faces touch as we talk into the other's ear.

Well after midnight, the noise starts to die down and most people have left. Normally that might offend me, but for the moment I'm more than content. Dana and I are extremely intoxicated at this point, and she asks me to take her home.

THE AFTER PARTY

The moment we stand up, Blake brings us two cups of water. He can always read my mind. I tell him I'll be right back and head out the door. I take a quick glance around the apartment and notice Jeff kissing a brunette, Sydney dancing in the kitchen with two girls, and the rest of the party has moved to the couch or chairs.

I hold her hand as we walk up the stairs. What will happen next, I don't know. I have never felt this way about any girl. Usually at this point my goal is naughty, but I'm too nervous to even think about that. My only goal is to not screw this up.

With a few unsuccessful attempts, we finally unlock her door. She stares into my eyes. "I want to thank you for one of the best nights I've had in a while." Her eyes sparkle. "I still remember our first kiss. Your little palms were so sweaty. I want you to promise me, tomorrow will not—"

Interrupting her memory, I kiss her. I take my time, brushing her hair back and placing my arms around her. After the most passionate kiss of my life, we gaze into each other's eyes, not knowing what's next.

Interrupting the silence, I speak from the heart and maybe a little from the booze. "Tomorrow, the next day ... will only be

119

better. You were my first crush, my first kiss, and I'm not letting you sneak away again." As I reach for her hand, she leans in and kisses me.

"I hope you feel the same tomorrow, because I will." Her eyes sparkle as she squeezes me as tightly as her small frame will allow. I kiss her hand and walk down the steps. I run up for one more kiss and then walk back downstairs. Tomorrow I will surprise her with breakfast.

On cloud nine, I open my apartment door to see that almost everyone has left. Sara and Stacey are asleep on my couch. Cholet is probably in John's room. Sydney is crashed out on a chair. Tyler (my neighbor and new best friend) is passed out on the other La-Z Boy, and Blake is probably sleeping in my bed. I hope he's alone. Opening the door quietly I see that Blake is still up. With a naughty look on his face, he raises his eyebrows. "I'm ready for you, big boy!"

"Go to sleep, you sick bastard!" He continues to joke around, asking me to hold him. Finally, he gets serious as he compliments me on Dana. "That's the first time I've seen you talk to one person all night. Somebody killed the social butterfly. About time!" With that said, we both fall asleep. The clock reads 11 a.m. as I hear the door buzzer. Since everyone is still out cold, I answer the door.

Jeff explains that he wound up sleeping at the brunette's house. He did not do much sleeping, though. I persuade him to sleep on my bed instead of going to the hotel. All his crap is still in my trunk, and I don't feel like driving anywhere. As we start toward my room to my room, Tyler wakes up and says Jeff can sleep on his couch unless he prefers sleeping with Blake. Jeff takes Tyler's offer and I run to the kitchen.

In the kitchen I cut mushrooms, onions, peppers, and tomato into a frying pan. Ten minutes later, I head out, carrying a tray with an omelet, orange juice, toast and some fruit. I hope Dana is still home.

After three knocks, I hear a voice. "Hold on. I'm coming." Wearing a red silk robe and an ear-to-ear grin, she invites me in.

Now I wish I'd put on some clothes. My outfit of a muscle tee and sweats does not have the effect as a sexy robe.

"Breakfast in bed! I apologize if I woke you." Putting the tray on her night table and looking around her room I notice two pieces of cucumber. I hold back my dirty joke.

"You didn't wake me, and I'm more than fine. But there is one thing I have to tell you." Oh no! Here it comes—she has a man. "I have a boyfriend." My heart stops. That little bitch! Now I'm pissed. She looks up at me with a big smile. "Just kidding!"

"That was not funny. You suck. Now you're in for it." With that, I jump into bed with her and tickle her toes, then lightly kiss her stomach. Her skin is smooth, and she smells like sugar. Her robe comes off in slow motion, and there's nothing underneath! This is like my seventh-grade dream coming true. Actually, it's much better. Now she has boobs and is a willing participant.

My first thought is to get up before I accidently have sex, but when she removes my shirt, I change my mind. She takes the tie from her robe and uses it to pull me closer to her. I move back to her toes and kiss her ankle, slowly working my way back to her beautiful face. The room fills with heat as we kiss. I reach over the bed and grab the fruit. I slowly feed her each piece and follow it with a sweet kiss. She glances at the omelet and asks what I put in it. After I list the ingredients she sighs, "What a waste."

Dana gives me a teasing smile, "I'm pretty hungry. But we can reheat it later." She digs her candy-apple red nails into my back. "Come here, Jacky Waters. I want to kiss you." I always wondered what would happen if we ever met again. Her olive skin and white smile glow as she lies on her crisp sheets and waits for me to make the next move. I kiss her on the cheek and stand up. She laughs. "It's rude to point like that, Jack."

Standing in the doorway, staring into her radiant eyes, I feel like I am in a dream. She stands up and walks towards me. Her robe is still untied, and wow—I can't help but notice her perfect body. Even Dana's curly hair, still wet from her shower, excites me. Placing her hands in mine and focusing on my eyes, she makes me melt without even opening her mouth. "Jacky, I am so

happy you came into my life a second time. I didn't know if you were going to come this morning. I woke up early in anticipation and showered. I was worried last night was just drunk talk." Dana leans in and kisses my cheek, and I'm surprised when her hands squeeze my butt. "I'm glad you're here. Now go and entertain your friends. PS, were you always that popular?"

Walking down to my place all I can think is, why did I leave? Naked girl versus passed-out friends should not be a difficult decision.

My apartment door is still ajar, but I sense movement. I close the door softly. Sydney calls out a hello as he sits in the kitchen playing on my computer. "Check this out: I found a couple sites that might help you track Kevin Slim." As I approach him, he sniffs me. "You smell like woman. Did you just—?"

"No. We just ate breakfast. I really like her—a lot. I'm going to take my time, and hopefully things will work out. Now if we can get to work, why are you viewing porn sites on my computer?"

Syd explains that Bob wants us to track down Mr. Slim, who starred in several skin flicks. His real name is Kevin Stottle. Most of his movies had the same cast. Liezona Boner—no joke—starred in three out of five of them. She also happens to live in Chicago. I start to search for information on her as Sydney raids my fridge. One by one, everyone wakes up and enters the kitchen.

John appears first, just back from an hour run. Sydney interjects before I have a chance. "If you were able to run eight miles today, then that tall skinny chick gave you no love. Maybe you need to quit running and work on your technique."

John smashes Syd's theory. "Maybe I'm just that good. Open my door." Sydney and I creep to John's door and peek inside expecting to find a passed-out Cholet. At this point Sarah and Stacey awake and peep inside. Nothing—no Cholet, no panties on the floor, and the bed is even made. Trying to help John out, I add, "Wow, she even cleaned the room before she left!"

Sydney adds his two cents. "You're better off solo. She looked pretty used." Everyone in the room agrees she's been around the block as Sydney tries to make John feel better. "Shit, she's been

around the block, down the street, through the woods, up the creek, and back again! Now let's eat some leftovers and rehydrate." Sarah and Stacey walk over to the keg to follow orders. "I meant juice, milk, water, or coffee; there's no beer at breakfast. You two have problems." The kitchen turns into a comedy forum as I escape to the living room with my computer.

In the midst of my tracking down Liezona Boner (aka Kitty Cleveland, from Chicago), Jeff and Tyler enter the apartment. Tyler goes to the kitchen and Jeff sits down next to me on the couch. "I love this couch. Are you working on Saturday? They don't pay us enough for that. Let me check out the messages BW sends."

After I open up my email and hand Jeff my computer, he puts on his oval-shaped glasses and makes odd faces. "Maybe I shouldn't be reading this. See—you work for Trust One, I work for a consulting company. My job is more to analyze and develop procedures. My emails tell me what to do for a client and what Bob thinks of my suggestions. You gather information, and probably give it to Steve Smith. I receive the information from Steve and then work with the client to help generate more profit. I also have never had to find a missing porn star, but I'll help you look. You're like Remington Steele!"

"Nice old-school reference. Thanks for your input, Jeff. Now go to the kitchen and get some food. You're more than welcome to use the shower. And I strongly recommend a shower; you still smell like cheap perfume. Oh, and I have never seen that girl before in my life. Does she know John?" Jeff laughs as he explains she's temping at John's office and lives around the block with her twin. "So, did you have a chance to sleep with the whole family, or just one this time?" He walks away leaving me to use my imagination.

The clock hits three and everyone seems ready for the Cubs game—even the people who aren't going. Tyler takes the keg, Sarah and Stacey to his place, and we agree to meet after the game. The rest of us walk to Wrigley Field. The game has already started—and, yes, the Cubs are already losing.

After a few minutes sitting in our nosebleed seats, we finish our first beers and make our way to the Trust One box seats. Apparently, Bob told Syd that his guests are more than welcome. The Trust One box is awesome. Gourmet food and free liquor surrounds us. The only people in the box are Bob, his ten-year-old son (who is almost taller than Bob and luckily has a head full of hair) and a couple people from Accounting. I sit down and watch everyone drink themselves silly.

The Cubs lose, and nearly everyone seems drunk. Even Bob's ten-year-old drank a few beers, I think. He keeps bumping into the window, and his speech is slurred. The room fills with laughter as one of the accountants tells a joke. Bob, the only other sober person, pulls me aside as Sam from accounting prepares to tell another joke.

"Jack, keep up the good work. Do not get behind. With every successful report, there will be a bonus. There is no time frame. I want the information ASAP. The quicker the results, the larger the bonus. Good luck. And please call if you ever need anything." With a handshake and a pat on the back, Bob says goodbye and leaves with his drunk son. Blake, Jeff, and Sydney decide we should visit a strip club tonight and find Liezona Boner.

THE NUDIE BAR

The troops literally run home in anticipation of gawking at naked women. Their competitive nature is on display; each wants to be the fastest. Jeff ends up winning, with Sydney and Blake not too far behind. John and I are sober; we walk home like normal people.

Browsing the internet, we find that Liezona (Kitty Cleveland) works at Club Comfy in Bucktown. The plan is for Jeff and Sydney to go home and come back at nine. Blake and John suggest I invite Dana over. Two things keep me from following those orders. One: I only see Blake a couple times a year. Two: I don't want to rush things. However, I head upstairs anyway; I just want to see her.

Dana answers the door in jeans that perfectly fit her heart-shaped butt, and a white T-shirt. I sense she has company over and immediately hope her guests sit to pee. Questions race through my brain. Why am I jealous? Why do I want this girl so bad? How will she introduce me? With a kiss and a hug, she invites me in. The company happens to be a girlfriend who is in the bathroom. I invite both of them over for food. "I would love to, but we're going out for Chinese. Leave your friends and come with us. Or just stop by whenever you come home." We kiss

125

again in the doorway and I grab her hard bottom. She must work out. "Remember: Anytime," she says with a smile.

Anytime? Does that mean sex later? I ask the guys as they watch baseball highlights. Tyler is the first to weigh in. "Anytime means get drunk with your friends and then come upstairs so I can violate you."

"I think I can handle that."

Blake shouts, "You think you can handle that? I know you didn't go to college to study. You better be able to handle that! Opportunities like that don't come often. Shit—I remember back in the day, girls wanted me to violate them. Now they demand dinner, dessert, and wine first. A 'relationship.' What a bunch of crap! I'm in med school, a poor student—I can barely afford toilet paper, let alone the cheap Italian food in Nebraska."

John turns to Blake. "Are you done yet?"

"I'm sorry for offending you. I'm going to shut up and eat for a while." Blake helps himself to leftovers, and the rest of us follow suit. We all gorge ourselves on pizza and veggie snacks. The little fake burgers burst with pepper, basil, and oregano.

The doorbell rings at nine and everyone seems ready. The only person missing is my neighbor and new best friend Tyler. We send Jeff next door to gather the last member. When Tyler and Jeff pop back into the apartment, Tyler has on black pants and a T-shirt. "Jack, you have any hair gel?" I take Tyler to the bathroom and tell him to go nuts. With his long hair, he'll probably finish the tube. I watch him lather up the gel and grease his brown hair back. He turns back toward me, smiles and winks. "How you doing?"

"It's a strip club. You just need cash, Rico Suave."

Before I can enjoy myself, my car alarm goes off. I run downstairs and see someone running away down the street. And there's my new car with a busted window. Well, that's what insurance is for. I call my insurance company while running back upstairs to share the bad news.

Blake has taken over as bartender and hands me a drink. "Sorry, dude." We decide a few drinks might help us loosen up before

heading to the strip club. We finish the last jug from Charlie's and stumble to the street. Sydney is sober enough to drive, and he has a Range Rover that easily seats all six of us. He blasts some rap music and drives to the club as if he's been there before. The Range Rover is awesome: black exterior, leather seats, speakers with enough bass to set off a car alarm—and tons of cup holders.

"I'm drinking a forty out of the bag, asking the grocery girl if she wants to shag ..." What happened to music? I miss the end as Sydney finds a spot right in front and turns off the car. The only parking spot on the block, and it's right next to the club.

We pay twenty dollars and walk past two huge Latino door-men dressed in cheap tuxedos. The moment I step inside, I feel extremely dirty and guilty. Openly staring at breasts and thighs as if I'm about to order some chicken makes me feel like the devil's child. The rest of the group does not feel the same way. I can tell John feels awkward as he sits down at the back of our table, cross-es his arms over his chest, and says nothing. The others point, cackle, and pull out dollar bills.

The place looks like any other strip joint, with a long, mir-rored stage, metal poles at each end, lights flashing all over the room, topless women walking from table to table, and bad music playing in the background. The girl on stage has '80s hair (big bangs), pretty blue eyes, huge fake boobs, a tiny waist, and legs that could wrap around the pole twice. Around the stage sits a bunch of single chairs, filled with horny men with cash in their hands. The dancers make their way to all the bills while pushing their breasts or legs around the guys holding the cash.

I search around the bar and immediately spy Liezona Boner— or is it Kitty? The pictures online do not do her justice. She has short curly dark hair, green eyes, a thin frame, a round chest that just stands up, and a dark tan that is probably sprayed on. She stands at the opposite side of the bar, talking to the bartender. I walk right up next to her and give her a huge hug. Here goes nothing.

"Oh my God! Liezona, how the hell are you? I haven't seen you since you and Kevin did that movie in LA a couple years ago!"

My heart beats super fast as I try to maintain this lie with a table full of friends watching me. She looks me up and down, trying to place my face. "You probably don't remember me. I'm friends with Kevin. We all went out one night and partied pretty hard. I never forget a face, and that stage name was awesome. I can't remember your real name. I'm Cal Smooth. It's a pleasure to see you again." The whiskey is starting to kick in and the lying is starting to come easy. She might not remember me, but she is being extremely sweet and giving me a look you give a long-lost friend.

Liezona speaks bluntly. "You know, the last five years of my life were a blur. I just started getting my shit together. But I think I remember you. You used to be a lot skinnier. You look great!"

"Well, thank you very much! You look fantastic as always. I feel awful. I have not seen or talked to Kevin since then. You wouldn't by chance have an address?"

"To be honest I never really liked that cokehead. He goes by Jason Murphy now; he legally changed his name. He lives in Arizona, somewhere in Phoenix. No number, sorry."

I can feel a huge adrenaline rush. I did it! I have a lead! This makes up for my busted window. What a high. I feel like deception shouldn't feel this good. "Hey, I'm here with some friends, come and meet them." I walk her to the table and warn everybody, "Yes, Cal has found the hottest girl in the joint! Introduce yourselves while I run to the bathroom."

While walking to the facilities I bump into Tyler. He places a hand on my shoulder, "Your money and change neighbor. Money and change." Without another word he struts to the table and joins the others.

The bathroom stinks. Not like someone did a number two—it's more a mixture of pee, urinal cakes, and cheap perfume. The table now has three women. One sits on Blake's lap, another on Jeff's lap, and Kitty sits next to a nervous John. After three shots of tequila, we stagger back to the car. We don't turn the radio on. It's more of an interrogation for Cal Smooth—until my cell phone rings.

I have no idea what number this is, but it's my work phone and figure maybe it's the insurance company. "Hello." I sober up quickly as I hear a familiar voice.

"It's Bob. We got pictures from your car break in. The security company will email you soon. Sorry. We'll discuss Monday. Lay low."

"What the fuck, Bob?" I'm a little buzzed. "Camera in the car? Are there any other James Bond features I should know about? I don't want to accidentally eject Sydney."

"SOP, Jack. All company cars for VPs have them. Ask your buddy on Monday. If anything else suspicious happens, call me."

Sydney interjects the minute I hang up. "Relax, dude. All company cars have cameras. I forgot about that."

As we approach my apartment, Jeff, Tyler, and Syd make plans to hit another club. John, Blake, and I opt to go home. As I close the door to the Range Rover, I hear one last "Good night, Cal Smooth!"

John adds, "I'm not surprised. You've been pulling stunts like this since the fourth grade. Now you get paid for it." Blake and John continue to bolster my ego and attitude; I ignore the comments and run upstairs. Since it's early, I bring a pen, paper, and tape for a little love note.

My phone buzzes again. This time it's pictures of a man wearing a black hoodie. His face is distinctive: blond goatee, chiseled jaw line, and he looks broad. This is not your average car thief.

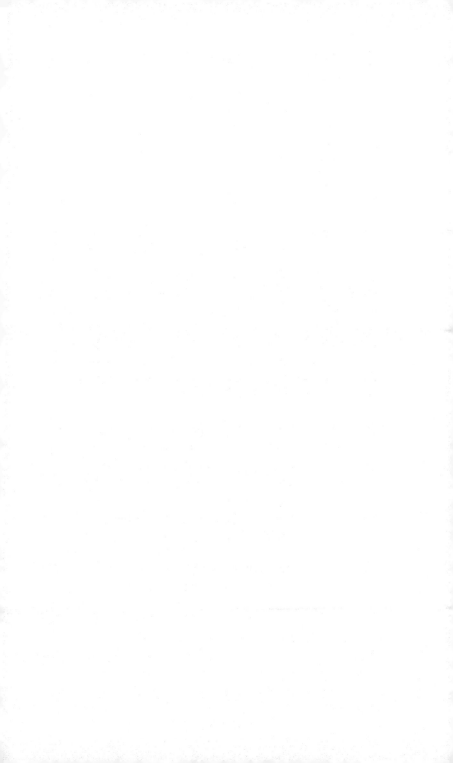

SUNDAY

Dry mouth wakes me up early. My eyes open, and I see a body under the covers. My first thought: Why didn't Blake sleep on the couch? My second thought: That's not Blake. I lift the covers and see—Dana! She's wearing shiny pink panties and no top. I carefully hop over her and step silently into the bathroom. I brush my teeth and grab some water. On my way back to my room, I notice Blake has passed out with the Playboy station and a smile on. I turn off the television and softly close my door.

Again, I hop over Dana and get comfy. She springs up from the fetal position, smiles, places her head on my chest and falls fast asleep. A couple hours later, water drips on my face. Cold water.

Blake stands over me in his boxers, wearing a goofy grin and holding a cup of water. Dana remains out cold as I slide out of bed again to put on cargo shorts and a Bears T-shirt. Blake's plane takes off in three hours, so we decide to spend some quality time together. Blake quickly throws on shorts and a red Nebraska shirt. We jam all his other clothes into a massive duffel bag and drive to a diner for some breakfast.

Our conversation revolves around Dana, med school, and my job. Blake orders strawberry pancakes and I choose a veggie

omelet. According to Kitty, I've put on some weight. When the food comes, I give Blake half my order in return for some pancakes. We eat slowly as Blake warns me to be cautious with my job. "Your job sounds amazing, but you better watch yourself. You always worked some magic in college with classes and an occasional girl, but that was Des Moines. If you ever think you're breaking the law, you probably are. I know you'll be an asset to any company and that you deserve the big bucks; just be careful."

"Thanks. I'll be okay. I'm onto something. I'm going to find out who killed Jerry."

"Again, be careful. It's not worth your own life. Maybe it really was a DUI."

We decide to wash down our breakfast with a chocolate caramel shake. It's almost ten. As the waitress pours the dessert into two glasses, our topic changes to school. Blake manages to stay at the top of his class, make new friends, and work out six days a week. He downplays the fact that he is at the top of his class.

From the time we leave the restaurant to the time we arrive at O'Hare, we discuss women. Blake always has a couple women chasing him. With more confidence than cockiness, he says he will start dating the girl that lives in his apartment complex. He also compliments me on Dana. They talked till four in the morning last night, mostly about me. She knocked on the door around two and Blake stopped studying to talk. His approval means a lot.

Blake is more like a little brother than a friend. We both learn so much from each other and know the other like a sibling. After a quick hug, Blake grabs his duffel and heads inside the airport.

"See you in a few," we tell each other simultaneously.

Driving home takes no time at all. As I unlock the door, I hear television and voices. I hope one of the voices is Dana. The door faces the couch; I glance over and see Tyler, John, and Dana watching a movie. Tyler and John are both wearing Adidas sweatpants and T-shirts. Dana wears cutoff grey sweats and one of my college shirts. Tyler turns to me first, "What did you bring us, Dad?"

"I brought you an apartment next door. Check it out! John, I brought you a room in the back. Take a look-see!"

Dana runs her fingers through her hair and butts in. "What about me?"

Ignoring Tyler and John's suggestive comments, I wave Dana toward me and lead her to the bedroom. The moment I close the door, she pushes me against it and kisses me so intensely I feel butterflies. I ask what that was all about, and she said it's because of her talk with Blake. According to Blake, I have never been so crazy about a girl. And he's right.

Ignoring the person knocking on my door, I kiss Dana's neck. Then all romantic thoughts immediately cease when I hear my sister's voice. "Jacky, stop whatever you're doing and come out. Actually, take your time. I like Dana. Mark and I will be watching *The Breakfast Club* with your roommates." I love that movie.

"Dana, my life is a little crazy right now. Some dude smashed my car. And maybe that guy also killed my cousin. My boss told me to be careful. I don't want something bad to happen to you. You didn't sign up for this crazy shit."

With a smile so warm it could probably cure hyperthermia, Dana suggests, "We could be like *Cagney & Lacey*!"

"Those are two women detectives."

"I thought that was *Kate & Allie.*"

"Different show."

Dana places her finger on her temple, thinking. "*Moonlighting?*"

"That works for me. Cybill Shepherd was a fox. Should we join the others?" Dana agrees we should socialize, so we leave my room. Alexis lied; the movie was not *The Breakfast Club*.

Alexis turns to me with a smirk. "I knew that would work. We have a meeting in a few hours."

Alexis and I prepare for our meeting with Tom from BBB, as the others watch some terrible Lifetime movie. We jot down simple marketing concepts:

- Corporate referral program
- Frequent buyer ticket/app
- Social media plan
- Blog schedule

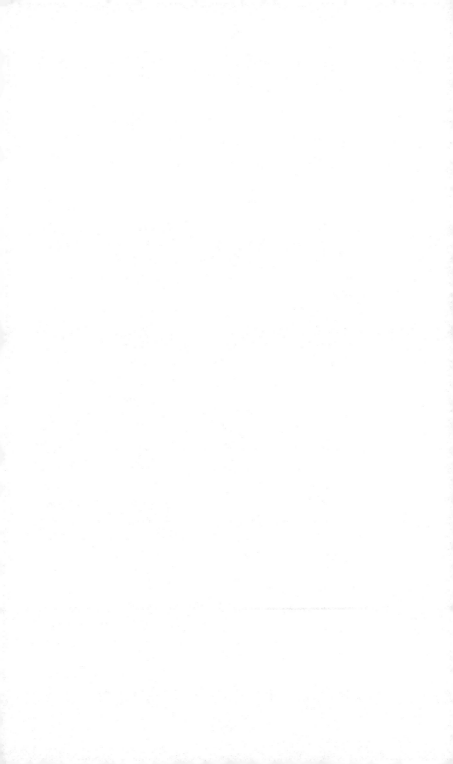

CONSULTANT

My cell phone buzzes, and I answer it. "Hi. It's Tom. I'm sick of sitting in the diner. Cool if we chat at your place? A coffee shop? Anywhere that doesn't smell like food?"

About five minutes later, the buzzer goes off. There is a quick quandary. Alexis asks, "Where are we going to meet?"

Tyler offers his apartment and free graphic design advice. "I'll cut you in, thanks." As Tom walks in, we guide him across the hallway.

Alexis starts the meeting by talking about some similar projects she's worked on. Tyler pulls out his portfolio. Lastly, I show the work my sister and I did for Charlie's. Two hours pass as we discuss BBB's target market, vision, pricing strategy, menu design, promotions, advertisements, and media plan. Alexis, Tyler, and I throw around other marketing jargon as if it were a competition—one I would definitely lose.

After working out a payment method, the four of us cross the hallway again. The apartment now has another guest: Joe is sitting on the couch with pizza and chicken sandwiches. "Hi, guys. Big order paid and then canceled." Dana makes a comment about how we never pay for food. Tyler asks John and me why we bother grocery shopping.

Tom leaves after a slice of pizza and a beer. The rest of us watch a lot of nothing on TV. The entire time, I'm wondering who busted my window. This is an area where people might smash and grab something, but no one just smashes a window. Did this asshole kill Jerry? What does this have to do with those numbers in Jerry's notes? What did Jerry do at the gym twice a day, every day?

Dana notices my distraction. "Jack, you need to relax a little. And I need to prep for the week. Dinner tomorrow?" I kiss her goodnight and then fire up my laptop. As I research Leslie's Jewels, all I can find is a blurb in the local newspaper. Owner shut down after fire. Half a million dollars in jewelry lost. Insurance claim. Insurer: Trust One.

After some stalking on Facebook and LinkedIn, I find pictures of Leslie's Jewels. She is on Facebook for one reason—to stay in touch with her grandchildren. All her pictures contain either a cat, a kid, or her Prius. I message her on all her accounts. I'm trying to appeal to her heart—and her business savvy.

Dear Leslie, I am so sorry for your store closing. My cousin was a huge fan of your store. He recently died, and I wanted to see if there was anything he had on order. All I need is a few minutes.

WORK, WORK, WORK

I hear John leave at seven and decide to start my day. I turn the radio on while I run through my morning rituals. During breakfast I fire up the computer and send a note to BW. I tell Bob about Mr. Kevin Slim changing names and residing in Arizona. I also mention that BBB has a new and improved marketing plan and a fantastic staff assisting him at a low cost. I ask him to send me everything he wants to know about Ace Investing. Toward the end of the note, I get a little cocky. "If you have any questions about companies, people, or life, I am happy to assist."

Sitting in my boxer shorts, eating cereal, and checking out my stock portfolio on the computer, I realize what an amazing job I have. A few minutes later, as I'm putting on a black, form-fitting polo and khaki pants, I hear the phone ring. "Hello, Patty. I'm up, dressed, and ready to work."

"Great, Jack. Have a great day. Please hold for Bob." Bob picks up quickly and thanks me for my message. He tells me to be in the office by ten thirty, and to pick up Jeff as soon as possible.

Ten minutes later, I call Jeff from the lobby of the hotel. I run up to room 310 and watch ESPN while Jeff spends ten minutes on his hair. We make a pit stop at McDonald's on our way to Syd's desk. Jeff and Sydney describe what occurred at the club

they went to Saturday night, and how they met these beautiful women and went to Jeff's hotel room. Sydney adds, "We had to switch girls. Turns out country charm and black Stallone had no luck. But then we realized the girl that liked Jeff was the one I was talking to, and … you get the picture."

"I'm glad you explained that. A 'switch' sounds like you were shooting an adult entertainment film. Sounds like a good night." Jeff then complains that nobody called him Sunday and he just stayed in his hotel room all alone. "Whatever, Jeff. You know my cell number. You were with the brunette and her sister last time I saw you."

They start laughing. Both spent the day with the sisters, but only Jeff made a love connection. Sydney makes fun of Jeff as I realize how late we are for our meeting with Bob.

"Jeff, let's run. I hate being late."

"Junior, quit worrying."

The meeting with Bob starts smoothly. He tells us to leave on Wednesday for our trip. I only need to go to Seattle and Kansas City. Jeff will visit all the BBBs and spend time in New York helping Larry Jones set up his next gym. Bob asks Jeff to leave as the meeting dies down.

My leg starts to shake as Jeff closes the door. Bob offers me a cigar while congratulating me on a job well done. He tells me I do not have to track down Kevin, as the police are looking for him. The ten-thousand-dollar reward for information on him will be invested for me by my broker. "Kevin is on the hook for millions of dollars. He said he only ran up a few K in fraud. He had the nerve to say someone stole his identity."

My mind wanders. I see a ten-thousand-dollar check! Wow, what a great job. BW is just throwing money at me. Is this legit? While thinking about the spending spree that will commence as soon as I leave, I overhear Bob talking about confidentiality. He warns me not to get too close to clients or coworkers. Another concern was Mind and Soul; all the information I gathered pointed to no wrongdoing. I should still work out there and be careful. He wants me to take part in a class led by Bob and

Chung. BW recommends I take a private lesson taught by the father-son team.

Bob also details the information Trust One needs from Ace Investing. "I will send you an in-depth questionnaire detailing all the information we need. Jeff will accompany you when you stay at the casino hotel. When we proposed a loan to The Grand a year ago, Jeff helped figure out the payment structure and other details with Steve Smith. Grand rejected our proposal and went with Ace. We booked you two into beautiful suites. Enjoy Friday night at the casino on us. Take notes on how many people are there, how often people win, and meet Saturday morning with the manager and director. I'll send you a note with more questions tomorrow. The bottom line: I want Grand to refinance with Trust One. You will help us gain a major account. Check your email later this afternoon; a new case developed this morning. Good luck and have fun. Oh, I was kidding about the reward. Enjoy this bonus and have a great day."

Bob hands me an envelope and shakes my hand with his claw-like grip. "And we will catch that asshole who broke your window. Be very careful. That martial arts training might come in handy."

My imagination returns all the toys and clothes I purchased while not listening to Bob. I close the office door and flip the envelope open. Five hundred dollars—pay to the order of Jack Waters! Not ten thousand, but very nice. A cashier's check? Weird, but I'm not complaining.

"Jeff, you ready to take a break?"

Jeff nods his head yes and Sydney shakes his head in disbelief. "You two deserve a break. You came to work at ten thirty, sat in a meeting for ten minutes, and Jeff emailed all his women while you got head from Bob. Please, get out of my cubicle. What the fuck do you guys do? Take the day off!"

Jeff smiles. "Sounds like a plan! I remember somebody taking off Friday to hang out. I think it's our turn." Jeff prints all his old files on Grand Casino and I find the paperwork I signed when I started. All my information sat in a drawer in Sydney's desk.

He noticed it sitting in BW's office and grabbed the stack. "Jacky, Bob wants me to show you my consulting report-writing software," Jeff continues in his slightly southern accent. "You have it on your computer. It's easy to use and makes your work look pretty."

Since we do not want to start our day off on an empty stomach, we visit BBB. Tom puts us behind the counter. Jeff and I spend an hour serving people and grilling. The lunch hour dies down and we make ourselves massive buffalo burger sandwiches. Tom tells us how excited he is about his new marketing team—he even gave his buddy at Better Burrito my sister's business card.

Next stop: Michigan Avenue. Jeff and I drop some cash in three stores: Banana Republic, Nike Town, and Barnes & Noble. Jeff spends a couple hundred in Banana and we both purchase new basketball shoes at Nike. I buy a couple books on baking. Jeff makes fun of me as I buy the ingredients to make a chocolate raspberry truffle cake.

After a full day of shopping, Jeff relaxes on my couch and I start baking. We discuss Jerry while I melt dark chocolate. Jeff starts yelling over a sports reporter. "He was a good dude. We didn't work together too much. I usually send info to Steve Smith. Jerry worked with me on a few cases. A few jewelry stores."

Leaving my dessert to cool, I run into the living room. "Jewelry stores?"

"There were a few fires and Jerry was gathering the data. Jewelers Row on Wabash has a ton of stores, so one fire is a big deal. Fire department is still trying to figure it out. Big losses. You can ask Steve about it. He can tell you more."

Diamonds. All I can think of is that movie with Leonardo DiCaprio and how shady companies are. If your price undercuts one of the monopolies, they burn your house down. "Do they think that some crazy diamond broker was behind it?"

We head back into the kitchen as Jeff answers. "No idea. Don't get all conspiracy theorist on me. A fire started at the end of one building. It ruined a few stores. No one was hurt."

The cake looks amazing. Jeff drools as I pour fudge and raspberries down the sides. The aroma of chocolate fills the apartment. Even the hallway smells edible. I toss on clothes for the dojo as Jeff dives into my dessert.

"This is great! One day, you're going to make some lucky man very happy." Jeff continues to make fun of me as someone knocks on the door. Tyler opens the door and demands some cake.

"I can't work, so I took a nap. While sleeping I walked here. You remember those cartoons where the scent drags the character to the food? That's what happened." Staring at the cake, he wonders aloud, "Where to begin?"

"Okay; I have to run. Please save a couple pieces." Running to the car and speeding to Mind and Soul, I pay no attention to the clock. When I pull up the parking brake I glance at the clock. I'm early!

I spend fifteen minutes watching Bob and Chung teach. The students range in age from fifteen to eighteen. Bob and Chung yell the whole time. Each scream motivates the kids to kick harder, hit faster, and ignore any pain. I think this is how they raise Olympic athletes in Russia. The teens spar, stretch, and kick the punching bag while I watch. The class ends with no casualties. The children run to their cars as I stick my head in the office. The sound of the ocean pours from the speakers inside.

"Shit, you scared the crap out me!" Julie grabs me from behind just as the sound of waves starts to relax me. After an insincere apology, I ask for Reggie's phone number.

"I'm thinking he and his buddies are the ones hurting everyone. Maybe there's something to it." A few people start to file into the class as we speak. I peek outside while she digs up his contact sheet.

Annoyed, she blurts, "Nothing! He put down Evan as his contact. Evan is in this class. And Evan put down Reggie."

"Jot down numbers, last names, whatever else might help me." Scoping out the guys in the room, I feel like someone stabbed me. I feel my heart beating through my neck, as if it's going to burst out. "Does Evan look like Thor?"

"If you mean tall, extremely muscular, with greasy hair, then yes."

"He broke the window of my car last night. Wearing a hoodie and all black clothes."

BIGGER, STRONGER, AND FASTER

When I sparred in college, my instructor had an expression for every fictional situation we would throw at him. I remember him yelling, "When some crazy WWE-sized frat boy wants to fight, and he's bigger, stronger, and faster, fuck him. Hit him when he's not looking and throw in a little extra pop." He always recommended breaking some appendage so that bigger, stronger, and faster doesn't matter.

And that's what I think as I beg Julie, "Please! Please let me demo a move early on."

"Jack, don't hurt him in our class. We cannot handle any more claims."

With a nervous smile, I ask incredulously, "How the fuck am I going to hurt the blond hulk?"

My phone buzzes as I stuff everything into my locker and try to calm my nerves. I wonder if this guy killed Jerry. And who is texting me? Glancing at my phone I see a text from Laurie the jeweler. "Dear Jack, thanks for the email. I would love to talk. I'm sad about 30 Wabash, but until I have a new location, I can meet you anywhere."

I pop out of the locker room so fast it surprises everyone. "What's the address here?"

Julie, puzzled, answers. "Five hundred Cornelia."

Addresses. Jerry left me addresses, and maybe Thor can put the pieces together for me.

As class starts, I try not to think about it. Talking to myself like some self-help guru or Seinfeld fan, I repeat "serenity now." I even shake Thor's hand and fake a smile. I should call him Drago, as his Eastern European accent reminds me of *Rocky IV*. The only other people in class are the Filipino guys from last week.

Julie tells us we will break boards, practice hip throws. and use fighting sticks. The class starts with jumping jacks and stretching. We break boards for half an hour. I use my head, elbow, shin, foot, hand. and knee to break six boards. My confidence grows with each break. I feel no pain until we take a water break. As I sip water, everything aches except my back.

For the rest of the class, I flip people over my hip and back. And now my back is sore. I'm not sure if I'm sore from flipping, or from getting flipped. I need painkillers, a massage. and a shower—but that will have to wait until I demo a move for the class. My adrenaline is pumping out of control, and I feel like the minute I throw Thor's arm around, I'm going to break it.

The move starts out with him holding my shoulder. I pull him forward and then flip the position of his arm. I have his bear-like wrist in one hand and my elbow is pressing into his arm, right above his elbow and near the funny bone. As his huge body lunges forward, I take him to the ground holding his wrist and arm. I drop my knee onto his back (more like his ribs), and hear a light crack. He's so thick I have no idea if that was my knee cracking or a rib. I turn and tell the class, "Once he's down you can put some pressure on him. That okay, buddy?"

I don't wait for a response. I grind my bony elbow into all the muscle and nerves under his arm. He winces as I whisper into his ear, "Why my car? Who do you work for?"

Trying to be a tough guy, he fights it for as long as he can—until he begins having trouble breathing and feels tingling up and down his arm. He winces more and finally blurts, "SG Diamond. Security. Security."

Julie is now yelling at me, "GET OFF HIM. JACK, YOU'RE HURTING HIM! GET OUT!"

"Call the police. I think he killed my cousin. He definitely broke my car window. I have the pictures."

Before he can finish saying, "Cute girlfriend," I completely lose control; and the sound is deafening. It's like a gunshot—POP!—as I rip his massive shoulder blade off the bone. I feel puke coming up the back of my throat. The cops can call me. I need to get out of here.

RUNNING

After puking in front of my car, I speed home and double park. I run up the steps to Dana's so fast I'm out of breath as I open the door. Dana shoots me a look of concern. "You look like hell. Are you okay?"

"You need to go. Pack up some stuff. Stay with a friend. Bring mace, a gun, whatever—but you need to go."

"Jack, you are overreacting. We're a team. Plus, I can't leave someone who bakes like Betty Crocker. That cake was like crack."

I manage a quick smile as my phone starts to ring. I answer quickly. "Bob, I'm sorry. Fire me."

Dana eavesdrops as Bob yells, "FIRE YOU? FUCK THAT! YOU SHOULD'VE KILLED THAT MOTHERFUCKER! FUCK HIM! Are you okay? This no fucking coincidence. You get on that plane with Jeff and get away. Tell your family to watch out. We can send over a few off-duty cops. I'll call you later. And talk to no one. We'll get you a lawyer."

Looking more startled than before, Dana asks, "Jack, what just happened?"

I text my sister to stay with Mark and work from home for a few days as I start to breath normally again. "Long story short: I broke a bad guy's arm—and maybe a rib."

Alexis texts me right back as Dana looks at me like she fell for a convict. "Downstairs at ur place. Stop down w D."

My hands shake, and my left eye is twitching like I'm about to have a seizure. Dana holds my hand tight as we walk down the stairs. John, Jeff, Alexis, and Mark are watching TV and eating my cake. Joe runs into the main room from the kitchen. Everyone is staring at me like I'm about to tell them the meaning of life.

"Tonight, I broke a guy's arm in class. I popped out his shoulder. It was the loudest sounding pop I've heard in my life. He's the same guy that broke my car window. He said he works for SG Diamond. And before I popped his shoulder, he told me to watch out for my cute girlfriend. No one is safe. We're getting an off-duty cop to hang around downstairs tonight. Alexis, stay with Mark. Joe, I have a file folder on the counter. Put your law school skills to the test."

The room is quiet—too quiet. It's like everyone is watching a foreign horror film and reading the subtitles as I speak. "I have no idea what the fuck is going on. We might be bugged, tracked … this is some serious shit. I'm sorry you are all involved. I'll fix this. But first, I need one piece of that cake." As I walk into the kitchen, the past few weeks fly through my head. I mentally jot down the clues: still a few addresses left, fraud, fire, insurance claims, SG Diamonds, security. I feel like I have mental Tourette's—images keeping popping into my head. Where can I research this?

Dana interrupts my thoughts. "Stay with me tonight."

"Listen—we just went from *Moonlighting* to some *Die Hard* shit. No way I'm letting this turn into *The Sixth Sense*."

Dana forces a smile. "How are you still making jokes? This is not a movie. No one is coming here to shoot us."

Suddenly, we hear noises from the street. "FUCK YOU! YOU FUCKING D-BAG!"

Everyone, more paranoid than me, runs into the kitchen and looks out at the alley. Jeff speaks first: "Fucking Cubs fans."

"No debate—Dana, pack a bag and stay with Mark and Alexis. Mark has an awesome apartment in the Gold Coast. You can walk to work—but take a cab. Jeff, you stay here with John,

and meet me at the gym tomorrow." I hug everyone and disappear as if I have a plan.

John looks stunned. I am unfortunately the person that brings unwanted drama to his otherwise happy life. I steal a shirt, shorts, and a hat, and change into John's clothes. "Jeff, pack me some shit for our trip. Joe, take me to Muscle's Gym."

Jeff asks, "Are you going to sleep at the gym?"

"No idea."

After another round of hugs, we hear police sirens becoming loud enough to shake the glasses in our pantry. "Joe, pick me up at Sheffield and Addison." I run out our back door to the alley and sprint toward the crowded streets of Wrigleyville.

PART II

Against his will, Joe agrees to get me a bunch of phones from a shady Radio Shack-type store. The phones that drug dealers buy—no plan, just minutes that you pay for in cash. "Jack, you're overreacting—but I'll do it. And why am I dropping you off at a gym? Didn't you just work out?"

"I'll stop by the restaurant tonight. Distribute the phones for me."

These days, gyms have computer labs. If I'm going to do some research, I need better than my home computer. That's why Jerry came here so much. He did research on computers that got cleaned every day. And I need a shower. I smell like a mixture of sweat, puke, and Old Spice.

My mind is spinning out of control. Is Trust One fucking with me? Is it this diamond company? What are all the other addresses? How do I go from tracking down a porn star to investing in a burger joint? My old martial arts instructor, now a dentist, would be so proud. Is Jeff a spy?

In an attempt to organize my thoughts, I research one item at a time. One of the addresses was 33.5N 111W. The other addresses are all jewelers, except for the dojo. What's .5? Google answers my question: Those are the coordinates for Scottsdale,

Arizona. The porn star is involved with this? Irrational thoughts drag me to Midway Airport.

"Can I use frequent flier miles to get to Arizona right now?" One of the many great gifts my parents left my sister and me: millions of miles. They transferred all their credit cards to our names so we could use the miles whenever we wanted to come home from college, visit family in California, etc.

"Sure, Mr. Walters. When are you coming back?"

"Let's do the redeye."

ADULT ENTERTAINMENT PART II

The adrenaline that carried me through the night wears off the minute the plane takes off. Landing fails to wake me, but the flight attendant takes care of that. "Mister? It's time to wake up. We landed. You're in Arizona." I yawn so hard I feel like my face might flip inside out. All of a sudden, the young redhead appears startled.

"Mister, your hands are red. Swollen." And now the pain hits. Breaking all those boards has caught up to my hands. Like a pro, she hands me Advil and a tiny water bottle. "Hold on; I was a nurse." She quickly covers both my hands with plastic wrap and some ice, and I look like a boxer after a fight. "Listen: twenty minutes on; forty minutes off. Take another three pills in four hours."

"Thank you." With no luggage and no clue where I'm going, I turn to Google and Enterprise Rent-A-Car. I speed down the highway, find Canyon Ranch Road, and circle the perimeter. The exact location leads me to a ranch home that looks like all the other homes in Arizona. Here goes nothing.

Before walking into the house, I check out the mailbox. All the mail is addressed to Jason Murphy. Could it be this easy? What the hell am I going to say? "Hi. You used to work in porn.

The FBI and Trust One want you in connection with fraud. They took you into custody because of me. Sorry." Heat and fear build up inside of me, and I'm sweating like I need Botox shots into both armpits. And I thought people didn't sweat in dry heat.

As I peek into the garage, a light tap on the arm scares the crap out of me. "Hi. I'm Ron, the neighbor, and saw you poking around. We already spoke with cops."

"Hi! I'm Ron, too. Nice to meet you. So you don't know anything, I suppose?" My only thought process: Go on the attack and maybe he'll think I'm an investigator.

He responds in a monotone voice. "I said my name is Ron." Ron does not look me in the face. He's fidgety, and looks more nervous than I feel.

"Do you know something, Ron? Is that why you aren't looking me in the face?"

"No—I have Asperger's. Don't take it personally. I know nothing. He's been MIA for weeks. Cops and some other guys came here two days ago." Interesting—exactly when I find his real name and location, Trust One sent people here. Man, they don't waste any time.

"Here's the truth. I found Jason Murphy. I tracked him down from Chicago. Two days ago, I told my company that he lives here, and now he's gone. Is that fishy? Can you let me inside? What's your theory?"

Looking down the street and away from my face, he continues, "He was in the porno business for years. He's been on the straight and narrow. He disappeared a few weeks ago. Someone came to town, he looked like you. The next day: gone. No goodbye. Nothing. And we were friends."

I pull up a picture of Jerry, and Ron nods his head. "Yeah. That's him. He was in a cab. I'd just gotten home from work, and thought, 'That's odd.'"

Either Ron is an excellent liar and actor, or he's telling me the truth. "Really?" Ron beats me in the spy game.

"Look at my phone." And—sure enough—there's his photo of Jerry getting into a cab. In the meantime, my phone and

hands are blowing up. Not my spy phone. "Why do you have two phones?"

Ignoring my new friend, I read my messages. It hasn't been five hours since I broke a man's shoulder, and Bob is sending me work requests—questions for this casino I'm supposed to visit with Jeff. I scroll down to the bottom. Cops want to talk with you ... Thor's car is dented ... suspect in Jerry's murder ... died before EMT arrived. My eyes lose focus.

"You got any ice in your house? And what about vodka?" We walk across the street, where ice is promptly served. My hands start feeling better, and I stop sweating. Ron's house is interesting: pictures of insects and nature fill his coffee table and walls. A ceiling fan cools me off, and a shot of booze settles me down. I cannot shake Thor's death. Did I kill him? No way! I go back to Bob's email. Died before EMT arrived. Resisted arrest when cops came to the scene. Used stun gun.

"Okay—back to you, Ron. Thanks for the ice and drinks. I gotta catch a flight, but first I need to ask you some questions. What do you think happened, and—do you have more pictures?"

"Jason managed Organic Grocer. It's like Whole Foods, but smaller and only deals with fruit, vegetables, and meats. They have five stores in Arizona. Very popular with the rich crowd. Jason was fucking a bunch of the wives that shopped there. No one knew besides the women, Jason, and me. They had a fire in the store Jason managed. He was helping with the rebuild after his time in the hospital."

I'm beginning to believe this guy. His level of detail is amazing. And he has no tact. "Hospital?"

Ron goes on to explain that Jason worked the night of the fire. He tried to put it out, but it was a chemical fire and the water only made it worse. He thinks one of the husbands found out and started the fire. He was stupid; he used to give all the women this stupid diamond ring. "It was a joke. They were stackable rings, and it was, like, for each blow job, they got a new one. He had a friend that worked in jewelry."

Either Ron is an amazing liar with a gift for Photoshop, or he's just a weirdo neighbor infatuated with his porn star friend. He has too many photos to look at right now. "Can you send me these files? Email? Did you tell the cops all this?"

"They never asked." After giving Ron my email address from high school—biggiesmallsfan@bsf.net—I'm ready to head back to the airport.

Ron drives me to the airport in his rebuilt, eco-friendly, green Corvette from the '70s. As I thank him, he tells me, "By the way, I think he's dead. Someone killed him. Check the pictures."

NO SLEEP TILL CHICAGO

All I want to do is sleep, but I can't stop searching through picture after picture after picture. My eyes are blurring together as I go through Ron's Flickr account. Man, does he love birds. And the thought occurs to me: should I trust someone who's taken over 200 pictures of sparrows?

Why did Jerry pay the porn star a visit? It just doesn't add up—all the fraud in Chicago was tied to the diamond company. And then I hit picture 2,302: Reggie. I need to find Reggie. How the hell does a guy from Chicago, working security for a diamond conglomerate, become connected to a porn star? I might be the worst private investigator ever. As my eyes begin to close, I make a mental note: view the other 2,000 images.

My short-lived nap is interrupted by a horrific landing. As the wheels hit the ground, the plane bounces up and down like a pogo stick. The oxygen masks all fall out of their overhead compartments, and everyone is up in arms. Too tired to be pissed about a bad landing, I head for the train. Hopefully I can sleep before my workout with Jeff.

Jeff looks like he's still sleeping as he walks into the locker room. Taking his time, he throws an old-school leather gym bag on the floor, takes off his black Kenneth Cole glasses and refuses

to workout. "Shit, we have to meet Larry in twenty minutes. I'm not working out. I'm still sore from a month ago. He made me do these crunches on this machine and it hurt to laugh for three weeks. I couldn't tell if I had to shit or if it was just soreness. And when I did use the bathroom, I felt pain." Jeff pulls down his sweats and shows off a pair of Kansas shorts, white socks and a white T-shirt labeled Polo Sport in blue. I question his manhood, and he changes his mind. "Fine, I'll work out with Larry. After the workout, we're getting an hour massage. I'll bill that to your company if Larry doesn't hook us up."

Jeff does a double take as he finally looks me in the eye. "You look like shit. Where have you been the last twelve hours? You disappeared—it was radio silence. Not even an email. And that's your thing."

"It's been a night. Did Dana go to Mark's house?

"Yes. Your girlfriend is safe. Cops stopped by. Just wanted to make sure everything was okay. That guy's death is not your fault. P.S.—we told the cops you went for a jog to clear your head."

"Thanks. Let's do this before I pass out on this remarkably white ceramic tile."

"The locker room isn't as nasty at the crack of dawn. Hey— your hands are really red. You okay?"

The ice really worked. My hands are no longer swollen, but everything is sore. Even my fingers are fatigued.

Larry greets us in a sleeveless shirt. His arms are the size of my legs—maybe bigger. "Good morning, men. I want each of you to have an energy drink before we lift. And smell this salt. I know it's odd, but afterward you'll be ready. Here you go. Follow me upstairs." Jeff and I walk behind him making faces while drinking the cough medicine-like drink. It's a little odd we just do whatever Larry tells us. It's not his arms or his PhD in nutrition science—he's just genuine.

"I have some files put together for you both. We'll look at them and then lift. Today I'm going to help you pump up your arms!" His pure excitement and energy helps Jeff and me wake up. The smelling salt is also incredibly energizing.

Larry stands behind his desk (he has no chair), and Jeff and I sit on two padded chairs in front of the desk. Larry explains the difficulties associated with owning a gym. He set the price high to keep the gym from overcrowding, and memberships have been slow. He used a formula to calculate the maximum membership without overcrowding the gym, and the magic number was twelve hundred. The formula takes into consideration people not showing, members exercising at different times, and other miscellaneous factors.

As he goes over his membership demographics, we notice that he hasn't tapped into the college market in the immediate area. Two hours pass as we discuss promotional campaigns and what made his other facility profitable. Larry now wants me to put together a marketing plan to help reach the younger market. Jeff laughs, "Stop moonlighting and concentrate on your full-time job. You know—busting skulls." He immediately feels bad. "Too soon. Sorry."

Jeff and I run to the locker room as Larry hands us another drink. The drink tastes good, like grape Kool-Aid. The locker room talk consists of Jeff warning me, "Tonight, this afternoon, tomorrow, the next day, and a few more days will pass before the soreness goes away."

Taking our time up the stairs, we follow Larry into the basketball court. Larry lets Jeff and me warm up with a game of Twenty-One. The object of the game is to score twenty-one points before the others. Every man plays for himself, and many people can play at once. Larry joins the game. It's hard to rebound over his enormous body. Jeff and I talk trash, and Larry just laughs. Larry shoots the ball like he's throwing a baseball and bounces every jumper off the rim. Jeff, on the other hand, does not miss. He hits all his open shots and never really takes it to the hole. He goes in for one layup, and Larry slams both the ball and Jeff to the floor. My shot is a little off today, so I move close to the basket and try to move away from Larry. My head is spinning with other thoughts; I am more than okay with Jeff beating me.

"Today, you two are going to get big! I'm talking huge, huge! Today we start with the triceps-bicep double burn!" I have been lifting since high school and have no idea what we are about to do.

Thirty minutes pass, and it feels like an eternity. We use rubber grips called Fat Gripz on the bars and dumbbells. My arms are on fire. It feels like a ghost is giving me an Indian burn. Every exercise entails two exercises—one for the triceps and the other for the biceps.

"See, all it takes is thirty minutes and we busted out two muscle groups. Grab some water."

While standing in line for water, a creepy dude in spandex shorts and a striped biking shirt approaches Jeff. With a lisp, he tells Jeff, "You've done some tri's, now do some bi's!" The man walks away smiling, as we realize he meant bisexual. Jeff looks shocked as Larry and I laugh.

"Be careful in the shower, Jeff. Don't drop the soap!" Jeff isn't as amused as we are, especially since his new boyfriend is also headed for the locker room. Luckily the stranger heads to the bathroom. Larry follows us into the locker room as well. "Clean up. Make the shower hot and then cold. Helps with muscle healing. I'll have some protein shakes waiting for you."

The protein shake is like a Frosty with a hint of banana—delicious. I could drink this for dessert every day. It's a mixture of chocolate protein powder, bananas, peanut butter, and milk. Fatigue sets in as we walk out into the humid morning. I am so happy Jeff took my car. "I could not be happier you stole my car. Drive us home."

As I walk into my house, I can feel anxiety and fear growing. We are going to have to move. Luckily my email inbox is filled with work. "Toss me my phone, Jeff."

The phone rings a minute later, and Jeff looks at me like I'm psychic. "Hey, Bob. I'm much better today. A little shaken, but okay." Bob interrupts before I can tell him the truth.

"I'm so sorry. We'll keep you busy so you can forget this craziness. Looks like you might have solved your cousin's murder. I am so sorry. I wish I could give you a motive. Or at least a

guarantee you got the guy. The case is re-opened. Jeff has the travel info. Work hard and have some fun."

A company called Travelman.com has taken care of our travel arrangements. You enter in where you're going, what airline you want to fly, your frequent flier numbers, hotel preferences, and rental car company and it does everything for you. Jeff explains, "BW sends me a message a couple weeks before a trip and tells me where he wants me to go. He wants us to stay at a casino for a few days. Sounds like you play more than you work. Since I've been here you've been paid to workout, eat, bake, stare at strippers, throw a party, and kick ass. It's like being paid to be a frat boy. You're about to start earning some of that fat paycheck."

I take all Jeff can dish out and then show him an email from BW. The details and questions shut Jeff up.

"No, I don't work hard. It's easy to find this information out. I usually just call up a company and have them send me a fax of all their private and confidential news. I've been hustling, every day."

Jeff asks, "So what are you going to put on your resume? Do you put hustling down as a work-related experience or a skill? Maybe you could add a bullet point that says 'Lie to porn stars, hack into computers, and have friends give you confidential material.' I've got it—the bullet point can read 'Industrial Espionage.'"

Jeff laughs as I stand there motionless. What's happened to me? I used to be moral and ethical, and not violent. "Jeff, do you think I'm breaking the law?"

Still laughing, Jeff assures me, "I was only joking. Relax, junior. I don't think deceiving a stripper counts as a criminal act."

Jeff sends me files on different cases and tries to lighten my mood. I see his lips move but don't hear to a word he says. My mind dances in worrisome circles. Am I headed to jail? What would my parents think? Will Dana break things off? Will Alexis kill me? Would any jury really convict someone with this face?

Jeff notices my lack of attention and starts Googling Liezona Boner. My eyes regain their focus on her enormous breasts and,

suddenly, I feel better. Amazing. "It's like visual anti-depressant medication."

"See, all it takes is a little porn to cheer anyone up. I can't believe that woman helped you find a criminal. Now let me take you out for a drink, Jacky." Jeff also believes a cocktail can cheer anyone up.

"Jeff, do you realize it's not even noon?"

"Shit, it's getting late." Jeff turns his head, flashes his million-dollar grin, and winks. Minus the wink, that's the look he uses on women. At my party, at the Cubs game, and at the strip joint, women approach him. If I had that power over women, I would probably use it for evil. He doesn't even brag; I like that. Since there's a Cubs game today, people are drinking everywhere. I tell myself that one beer won't hurt, and drink two.

While walking back home, my secret cell phone rings. "Hello?"

A sexy whisper orders me, "Go to your room." Dana's hiding in my bedroom? Part of me is upset; I don't want her getting hurt. Another part of me forgives her quickly as I approach the apartment.

My room has been transformed from boring guy room to romantic haven. How did I miss the smoke of twenty-plus candles? Brazilian jazz lightly hums in the background, and the place smells like sugar and cocoa butter. And then there's Dana. She is full-on lingerie model. Her hair is separated into two braids, and her brown eyes and red lipstick sparkle in the darkness. Her black outfit is hot: garter belt, lace garments, and a sheer bra.

"I know you want me hidden until you figure out what's going on, but I just had to see you before you left. I wanted to console you. I wanted to hold you last night and tell you everything is going to be okay."

Despite the air-conditioning, the room is getting very warm. Looking into her eyes brings me back to seventh grade. It was the last day of school, and we all knew she was moving. She came up to me and kissed me. I had never been kissed like that before. And she told me, "Everything is going to be okay." A decade has

passed since we last saw each other and, like last time, I'm not sure if she's right.

"You look amazing. This might come off wrong, but you, this room—it's a fantasy." Before I can take off my shirt, Dana does it for me. She unzips my shorts and, with one swift pull, takes off all my clothes. Her warm kiss covers me like a blanket.

"I'm not trying to ruin the moment, but you are really good at this. I'm a little nervous."

She grabs me with both hands. "This doesn't feel like nervousness." Without letting go she kisses my stomach, and I don't think I've ever been this hard in my life. The next trick will be to stay that way. She guides me to the bed and lays on top of me. I slowly remove her bra, transfixed by her perfect breasts. Her nipples rub against my chest as she wraps her legs underneath mine, kissing me the entire time. "I am definitely going to do this in two shifts. But I promise you—I will not quit until you are satisfied."

ROAD TRIP

As big as my smile is, Jeff's is bigger. He's very happy for me, "Jacky!!! I think you're in LOVE! That smile isn't just good sex— it's 'I made LOVE.' She has you whipped!"

"Okay, relax. Were you videotaping us or something? I just hope she stays clear of trouble."

My cell phone rings, and Jeff holds it up with a nervous smile. "Jacky, trouble finds you." The number is not familiar, but the caller ID reads "Chicago Police Department."

"Shit. Here goes nothing." I leave it on speakerphone, because at this point I want someone to know how crazy my life has gotten.

"Jack Waters? This is Detective Riley, CPD. Don't freak out; I just have a few questions in regard to Mind and Soul Martial Arts. You got a minute?"

"I'm actually at the airport, but fire away."

With a deep voice, and big-time Chicago accent, he proceeds. "What do you know about the man you injured? What was your business at the class? How did you know he broke into your car? Do you know about an investigation into Jerry Waters?"

Nervously, I answer, "I call that giant 'Thor.' I work for Trust One. They wanted me to investigate the studio. There have been

a lot of insurance claims, and they wanted to rule out fraud. My car has a camera and I was sent Thor's picture through the security company. Before I injured him, he said my girlfriend was cute. Someone is watching me. I think that guy killed Jerry. And he works for SG Diamond."

"Mr. Waters, thanks for that info. We are still working on a motive for your friend Thor. His car recently had work done to it. He could have killed Jerry. Do you think Jerry was suspected for fraud?"

I can't help becoming defensive. "No way! Jerry's not a criminal. He was onto something. I just haven't figured it out yet."

"Leave the investigating up to us, sir. We have a few beat cops watching your place. If you come across anything or feel unsafe, you call me ASAP. Have a safe flight. Domestic, correct?"

"I'm not leaving the country. At least not yet." Before we say our goodbyes, Riley hangs up the phone. Jeff begins to play detective and quickly impresses.

"Alright, Jacky: Someone was trying to frame Jerry. I sent him some info a few times, but usually Steve Smith took my info, or I sent it straight to Bob. You need to have a frank conversation with Bob about SG Diamond."

I never thought about someone framing Jerry. It makes sense, though. Before he mysteriously dies, frame him as a criminal. Since I've been on the job, there's been no fraud in the diamond business.

Before we board, I take out my secret cell phone. Joe answers after the second ring: "Batman."

"Joe, do me a favor—investigate who runs SG Diamond in Chicago. See what claims they have filed. Anything on my paperwork?"

"Dude, that was one day ago. Give me some time. Your financial advisor works at Trust One, and that seemed shady to me. Looks like you don't have to make a lot of money to retire and live well."

"Let's hope I make it to retirement age. Thanks, man."

We both feel cramped in our cabin seats. Jeff winks at me before starting in on the flight attendant. "Hi! Anyway, can we

move up to first class? I saw two open seats; and this way you can let a few standbys on." Jeff concludes with his toothy grin, and suddenly we're sitting in fully reclining leather seats, drinking free scotch. Unfortunately, I don't like scotch.

My email inbox is completely full. I read message after message from Bob West requesting info from our casino trip. This will not be fun with a lot of gambling and girls. Who knows? Jeff might wind up sleeping with this flight attendant. She's checked on us three times and we haven't even taken off yet.

While reviewing Bob's requests, I get a text from my old martial arts instructor: "Forgot to tell u. Got a reference call. Asked about u teaching and martial art skilz. All good. Told them great guy, watch out for his elbows." I wonder whether it's normal protocol or more shadiness. I would understand them calling my internship employers—but a guy I worked out with and taught a few classes with in college?

I respond back, "Thx. And thx for being my Mr. Miyagi."

Trying to escape reality, I read Mark's email, hoping for a joke. Mark, as usual, does not let me down. "Bro, how are you? I'll keep an eye on your girls. Try not to stress too much. Quit your job. I'll help you find a new one. Here's your joke: Three brothers are sitting on stools at a bar. A man comes up to the guy in the middle and says, 'I'm hooking up with your mom later!' A little later, he approaches the guy in the middle again. 'I'm going to fuck your mother tonight!' The three men shake their heads, and the old man wanders off. An hour later, the same man approaches the guy on the left and this time says, 'I'm going to make your mom give me a blow job!' With that, the guy in the middle gets up and tells the old guy, 'You've had too much to drink. I'm taking you home, Dad.'"

Mark also explains how his sister found a new man, and how Mark hates him. Usually, I'd feel bad if someone I dated found a new man, but I'm happy for her. At the end of the message, he asks me if I'll meet with his one of his clients. Alexis had told him about the work we're doing for BBB, and Mark wants us to help one of his smaller clients. I reply that I will meet with them as soon as possible, which probably means a week.

My work emails are crazy, and all from Bob. The incredible list of info he's requesting makes me feel like he's trying to keep me busy to avoid thinking about reality. The first message has a ton of questions about Ace Investing:

- What is the rate on the Hotel Grand loan—points, floating rate, flat rate?
- Expected payoff?
- Do they have a line of credit?
- Term and amount?
- Why did Grand pick Ace instead of Trust One?

At the end of the email, Bob asks me to tell Grand we could offer them an evergreen credit. An evergreen credit is not a very common loan. I remember my finance teacher yelling, "You do not offer Joe Blow an evergreen credit! This is the granddaddy of all credit! There is no maturity, and it has a revolving credit! The downside is that companies usually have to pay a hefty premium on the amount they don't use, and they may have to keep a balance ..." All this random knowledge comes back to me when I least expect it.

Bob has somehow arranged a meeting with Ace and me for Friday afternoon. Mr. Sam Kohl will spend a couple hours discussing his company and their investments. Jeff will meet with someone from the local government to find out how much revenue the casino generated for the city last year. Friday night, the two of us will spend time gambling and "researching." Saturday Jeff and I will talk with the manager and director of operations for the Grand. We'll also need to interview casino staff, dealers, waitresses, and security. He wants to know all the actual payouts, the number of winners, frequency—and other gambling terms I need to consult a dictionary to understand.

In Bob's second email, he asks me to wrap up my report on BBB after I meet the Seattle staff. He also requests a report on Muscle's after Jeff and I research membership rates and personal training revenue. Finally, he needs me to research two more companies

ASAP—Bank People and E-teller. E-teller is an internet startup that will go public in a couple months. Bob wants me to find out the true beta (risk) of the company. He's attached a file with all the financial data Steve found and wants me to visit the company and dig up whatever else I can. Bank People recently merged with another bank. Bob says he will discuss the questions on that case when I return home. And I have no idea what any of this really means.

Grabbing our luggage, I ask, "Hey, Jeff—on the road, do we sleep in separate beds?"

"Aw, come on, Jacky. What's the matter with a little inter-league play?"

I laugh and give him a wink. "Let the games begin!"

The pink hotel sneaks up on us. Adjacent to the hotel stands a white and pink sign for the strip club next to the hotel—very convenient. The hotel is right off the highway and five minutes away from the downtown area. Our rooms give us a nice view of the Space Needle. We both have suites on the twenty-fourth floor, and our rooms connect. The rooms have king size beds, doors separating the bedroom and den, huge flat-screen TVs, pull-out sofas, love seats, large desks, and—best of all—little mint candies on the nightstands. I sit in awe as Jeff begins to plan our schedule for the next couple of days.

Jeff hammers out the itinerary on Excel and shows me. We basically have no free time until ten every night. He typed in Hooters for tonight.

"Hooters? What's up with that?"

Jeff takes the defensive. "On the road, you get lonely. At Hooters, the girls are paid to flirt and look good. Sometimes you even get lucky!"

Being a Hooters virgin, I ask, "What kind of food do they serve?"

Jeff replies inquisitively, "They serve food?"

We both sit on my pink couch laughing before agreeing that it's time to visit BBB.

We discuss business while driving to BBB. Seattle was their first restaurant and does the most business. Word of mouth

spread fast and the restaurant became the local hot spot for teenagers and college students. Groups of kids hang out there till 2 a.m. BBB classifies itself as a late-night spot. The primary advertising medium is radio. Their slogan is simple: "Grab great grub at the spot—Big Bad Burger." The restaurant is situated in a suburb just outside Seattle. Josh, one of the partners, runs the shop. Josh works the weekend shifts until at least two. He has a bed in the back and sleeps there when he closes. During the week they close whenever business dies down. Most of the employees are high school students. On Friday and Saturday nights, college kids and locals take the late shift.

I'm not sure what Bob what really wants me to do with this case. All the information they need has already been gathered by Jeff. And we already tested the nutritional content. Jeff thinks Bob wants to arrange a buyout and that he wants my opinion on the company. Last year, the Seattle chain made a net profit of 250 thousand dollars—pretty high for one spot. Tom plans on opening six to ten restaurants a year, hopefully bringing them to three million in profits. If Trust One is their primary bank and insurer, six locations could happen really quickly. Bob wants the company to invest heavily in the health industry: fitness, health food, and pharmaceutical companies.

The Seattle weather (rain) forces us to put the top up on our rented convertible Mustang. Traffic starts to die down as we pull into the parking lot and park among a handful of other vehicles. The restaurant is relatively packed compared to the Chicago location. Families and teenagers make up the customer base. Seventies music is blasting through the speakers as we walk through the glass doors. A man in his late twenties with a tray of food greets us at the front.

"Jeff! Jack! How you doing?" Holding the tray in his left hand, he shakes my hand firmly and then places the tray down to hug Jeff. Jeff looks at me with surprise; the hug apparently surprises him. Jeff had spent months working with the three owners—Josh, Tom and Tony. Jeff and Josh exchange stories as I whip out the recorder and camera.

Josh leads us to the VIP booth in the back. Every table has a label. Including ours, there's: VIP, Hangover, Grunge, Scoopers (in the middle of the restaurant), Weak Bladder (next to the bathroom), Talkers, Date Night (complete with flower and vanilla candle), and PIGS (with extra napkins and bibs).

Josh had suggested the label idea to Tom. He initially laughed it off, but the novelty gives people something to talk about. I like the labels. Right now, each partner has their own store, and they meet once a month to discuss changes. Josh used to be a chef, so most of his innovations come from the kitchen. He tells us how his love for food fuels his cooking. He speaks proudly of his belly. "Do you have any idea how hard it is for someone as skinny and active as me to obtain a belly? I have to eat sweet potato fries and a shake with each meal to grow this nice, round gut." Josh continues talking about getting fat as I begin to observe what's going on around us. I pay attention to the flow of traffic, the amount of food on each plate, the average time spent dining, the ages and ethnicities of customers, and the design of the restaurant. Bob had asked me to watch for twenty different things, but I could only remember those six.

I refocus on Josh. He stands on the top of his seat and yells hello to customers as they sit down. He knows most of their names. You can tell everyone likes him. Adults and teenagers come over to our table to shake hands and hug Josh. He spends most of his time hanging out in the restaurant with kids. Josh sponsors baseball and basketball teams for elementary and high school students. Most of his business comes from the parents of children on those teams, and from college kids looking for late-night food.

Josh points to pictures on the wall of past teams as one of his young employees hands out samples. Whenever business dies down, workers walk around with small bites of various foods. He encourages his staff to create new things and get reactions from their customers. Today, the sample is a veggie burger burrito—a tomato tortilla stuffed with bits of veggie burger, cheese, lettuce and tomato. The kids load up on giveaways.

Many just order protein shakes and wait around for samples. Since customers have a tendency to hangout, Josh charges them a small fee for Wi-Fi. And there are no free refills, except for water and coffee.

After a few shakes, Jeff and I decide to leave. Josh walks us to our car and thanks us for coming. As I get into the car, I feel a sharp pain in my side. Deep breaths seem to make it worse. I wonder whether the pain is from martial arts, Larry, or flying.

I close the car door, and my phone rings. Who would call me now? I don't recognize the caller ID. Answering the call with a simple "Hello," I hear Bob's voice. He apologizes for calling so late, but needs me to visit Engineer Outfit (EO). The company designs equipment for outdoor sporting events. They also build paths, climbing walls, hills, and golf courses, and often work as consultants for televised exhibitions. Bob wants Trust One to invest in the company, but first needs a few questions answered. Tomorrow at nine I have an appointment with the vice president, Barry Gordon. Jeff will visit BBB solo while I meet with Barry, so he also has to chauffeur me there and pick me up at noon. A three-hour meeting with engineers—how fun.

I tell Jeff the news, and he laughs. "Did he end the conversation with 'This phone will self-destruct in thirty seconds'? You're every Tom Cruise movie wrapped into one—The Firm, Mission Impossible, and, tonight, Risky Business and Cocktail. We won't stay out too late."

"Sure, Jeff."

Jeff drives us straight to Hooters. He spots the orange sign in the distance, and follows it until we hit the owl in front of the restaurant. Pulling into a tight parking spot way too fast, he yells, "Home at last!"

We debate between sitting at the bar versus at a table until we both notice the waitress working the back tables. She has long brown hair, dark skin—and Jeff immediately likes her. The moment we sit down, she runs over to our table and joins us. "What do you guys need? Drinks, dinner, or both?" Jeff takes care of the ordering, and asks for two of their strongest, biggest beers.

We quickly knock down the beers, and I ask for a glass of water. Jeff laughs and starts riding me. "Who's going to drive us home?" I ask.

He attempts to reassure me. "I've been driving drunk since eighth grade."

"Great. That's something to brag to your kids about. Maybe we can put that on your tombstone."

"No—I want pepperoni and cheese."

The waitress joins in on the fun at my expense. She brings me a water, offers me a highchair, and tucks a bib under my shirt collar.

"Real funny, Hooters. You two are a riot. Maybe you guys could get your own act. Take it on the road. HBO, Showtime, Vegas …"

The waitress ("Courtney," according to her nametag) interrupts. "After I finish my degree in Engineering, I'll be open to travel." Jeff and I glance at each other; is she lying? "Look—just because I have big breasts, wear tight shorts and like to flirt, it doesn't mean I have no brains. I work twenty hours a week here, intern at Engineering Outfit and take sixteen hours …" I stop listening after "Engineering Outfit," pull out a chair, and ask her to sit.

Courtney sits down. Jeff looks at me and shakes his head. "Social engineering, that's Jack's job!"

"Thanks. Courtney, what can you tell me about EO? I have an appointment with the VP tomorrow."

Courtney's dark brown eyes light up like a Christmas tree. "Barry? He's the best. He's the only bigwig who skipped getting an engineering degree. He taught physical education before joining the sales team at EO. His fantastic people skills landed him in management, and then on to vice president. I teamed up with him and a girl from the IS department to develop an amazing simulation program. The project finishes testing in a couple weeks, and the system is going to revolutionize our industry. Barry's currently trying to get the patent …" Courtney continues as I struggle to remember all the details. Another waitress brings

us our drinks and flirts with Jeff. She's short, cute and spunky. It's odd how tan these girls are for living in Seattle. I compliment them on their glow and make a comment about the rarity of good sun in such a rainy climate.

"Even in Seattle we get some sun," the other waitress—"Natalie"—says. "It's the middle of summer; all I want is a tan and good lemonade."

Jeff turns on the charm. "Sounds good to me. Nothing beats a tall glass of lemonade on a hot summer day."

I chime in. "Simple pleasures are the best. That's why this place does great."

My comment seems to have upset the girls. Natalie cuts in. "What do you mean? Are we simple? Stupid? Just some T&A for your pleasure?"

Jeff smiles and answers in his southern accent. "There you go again, Jacky—getting yourself in trouble."

I try to save myself by making compliments. "Watching sports and talking to fun-loving, beautiful women is ten times better than some stuffy steak house." Slowly but surely the girls come around—before I mess up again. "Please don't get your skimpy shorts in an uproar." Thankfully, my phone rings, and Jeff takes over the talking.

Glancing at the caller ID, I recognize my home phone number. I pick up the phone. "Excuse me, ladies. Johnny boy, how the hell are you? You okay? Cops are watching the place."

I hear Dana's soft voice and hope she missed my "ladies" comment. "Where are you, Jack? Making some new friends with Jeff, huh? I'm just kidding, but I am a little jealous. You do spend more time with Jeff than me. I just called to say hello and that I'll see you Saturday. Can you have dinner with me? I don't want you to be jealous, but I'm staying at your place—giving Mark and Alex a break."

All of a sudden, I feel evil, dirty and guilty. Do I tell her where I'm at, who I'm with? I haven't done anything wrong. Does she really need to know everything? The more we talk, the more open I become, and I suddenly forget where I am and who can hear me.

"My whole day is filled with thoughts of you, and I miss you." Suddenly I hear "Awww," and see the girls making a "what a sweetheart" face.

As I hang up, the girls ask Jeff if he's taken. He responds with the player's line: "Tonight I am."

Turning my attention away from the girls' bulging breasts, I check out the restaurant. Everyone has left, the kitchen lights are off, and, besides the ladies, only one employee is still working—standing at the register, counting money. Jeff continues to work his magic as the man yells for us to leave. He must be the manager. I think he resembles Chuck Woolery from Love Connection. The girls change into jeans and T-shirts before walking out with us.

You can tell the tall older dude tries to sleep with all the girls. He winks at Natalie and Courtney as they walk out the door. "Stay out of trouble," he advises, as the girls jump into our sporty silver ride.

Courtney sits up front and directs me to the "Cool area." We park at the end of the first block, near the bars and next to a pizza place. Jeff and Natalie walk shoulder to shoulder and lead us to a small bar around the corner.

"Stay away. Stay away from the boobs," I tell myself, as Courtney and I walk next to each other. I make it a point to keep a little distance between us. I pull out my tape recorder and ask her if she minds telling me about EO again, so we can keep the conversation on business. Jeff turns to me with a smile as the four of us squeeze into a booth. "Are you pumping her for information?"

Courtney looks at me and answers his question. "Not yet." It's not the response I expected, but it's very flattering. If I'd met Courtney a couple weeks ago, this would have been a hell of a night. Instead, I'll just live vicariously thru Jeff—he looks quite comfortable with his arm over Natalie's shoulder.

We move from booth to pool table, to dart board, to bar. I keep myself sober with water and pretzels as the rest of my friends drink an impressive number of shots. The bartender hollers, "Last call!" but instead of ordering more drinks, we head for pizza.

The pizza joint stays open till 4 a.m. The bar side closes at one, according to the sign. Peeking thru the door, I see a few beers still floating around. The aroma of basil fills the room. A glass case displays the fresh food. The pizzas range from interesting combinations like tomato-spinach-chick pea to the classic pepperoni and cheese.

Jeff and I stand in a short line to place our order while the girls run to the bathroom. We discuss the women while we wait. Jeff insists I hook up with Courtney. "You started dating Dana not even a month ago. Live a little!" I ask Jeff about Natalie. "Come on, Jacky—I'm not like that." He gives me a grin and a wink. The girls approach as Jeff orders a pepperoni and cheese slice. I buy a chicken, mushroom and turkey bacon slice. The pieces are huge, like two slices in one. I share my monstrous slice with the girls. The vultures tear apart my meal with their fingers, leaving me with only a few small bites.

We walk back to the car—but it's not there. A quick survey of the scene confirms my initial conclusion: a red and white sign reads "No parking past midnight/Tow zone" in very small letters. Running into the middle of the street, I flag down a cab. The others are still trying to put the puzzle together as I yell, "Get in, drunks!"

DAY TWO ON THE ROAD

We drive to two different impound lots. Jeff spends forty-five dollars on the cab, and I spend seventy-five at Bob's city lot on the shady side of town. We stumble into the hotel around four. The girls crash in my room, watching Bravo (just a guess) and sleeping on the sofa bed.

I wake up at eight and throw on my navy-blue suit, a powder-blue shirt, and a silk tie with a little Polo logo. "I look good, right?" The girls show no sign of life as I quietly grab my laptop and cell phone. Before closing the door, I take one last peek inside the room. Natalie opens her eyes briefly and smiles.

As I walk to the car, I feel the soreness from Larry and the martial arts. I think I may have cracked a rib—or it could be from last night.

Bits and pieces of last night replay in my mind. I remember Jeff repeating, "I can't fucking believe this!" and, "Jack, this is all your fault." He kept smiling with a drunk, cheesy grin, like we've known each other forever. The Indian cabbie had also commented as we left each lot, exclaiming in his thick accent, "Not this lot? Oh, no! You crazy kids!" Occasionally, he would turn to the girls and mutter, "Pretty, pretty, pretty." It had been really awkward.

Opening the car door, I remember Courtney drawing a map and writing directions to EO. I pull out my wallet, find the map, and wonder what happened to all my cash. I'd probably had five drinks, and most of them were water. What good is money if you don't spend it—right? My grandparents died with money, which helped put me through college, but most of the cash went to greedy Uncle Sam. Last night, greedy Bob's Towing thinned out my billfold.

Following the map and weaving in and out of lanes, I make good time. Turning sharply into the parking lot, my tires spin out on the wet pavement and I feel the power of the Mustang. Even though it's an automatic, it has some serious pickup. I park in the lot closest to the VP's building.

The company has around 300 employees, split between two brick buildings. The buildings are separated by two softball fields and a small walkway just big enough for the golf cart the VIPs use to get around the campus. I snap a few pictures of the area: the parking lot, the softball fields, and the golf cart parked outside the main entrance. Walking past the cart and inside, a red carpet leads me to the front desk. The tallest woman I've ever seen greets me. "Hello, sir. Who are you visiting today?" She walks over to a water cooler and brings me a glassful.

I read her name plate. "Hi, Shelly. I have a nine o'clock appointment with Barry Gordon." She clicks away at her keyboard behind her enormous monitor until she finds my name.

"Follow me, Jack Waters." Passing pictures of golf courses, stadiums, and various sporting events, we walk across stretches of synthetic dirt, grass, gravel and pavement. Carpet lies below our feet as we reach Barry's office. Popping her head inside, she announces, "Barry, this is Jack. Jack, this is Barry. Have a good meeting."

Barry's office is pretty big, but not close to the size of Bob's. Barry has no chair for himself. His desk is a treadmill. He stops walking to shake my hand. His office smells like rubber, like burning rubber. Smoke is coming out of his University of Wisconsin garbage basket. "Oh, I was just testing this new synthetic fiber. It's not quite ready for the consumer public."

After gesturing toward a table with multiple chairs, Barry officially welcomes me with an energetic "HELLO, Jack! How are you today?"

With a firm shake, I surprise him: "I'm tired; you got a synthetic bed in here? Just kidding—I'm great. How are you today?" He towers over me, with the body of a defensive end. His stylish blue striped suit blends in perfectly with the office and matches mine, even down to the label. He invites me on a tour of the facility.

I mention that I've met Courtney, and how much she admires him. He cannot say enough good things about her. "She's a bright, enthusiastic, beautiful person. I really enjoy working with her."

Okay, Barry likes Courtney. Now that I have that figured out, I start the tape recorder—with Barry's permission. I can't help noticing the positive vibes flowing from each room. I meet several employees; they are all friendly and seem motivated. Even the old janitor—with his few teeth, eye patch, and foul breath—smiles as if seeing old friends, and greets us with a head nod.

The big boss leads me outside, and we hop on the golf cart and drive to the other building. The sun keeps the cart nice and warm; little fans above the seats help lower the temperature. The next building houses the R&D, marketing and customer service staff. The R&D team is comprised of chemists, physicists, engineers and athletes. The computer staff and upper management work in the other building.

By the time we reach the copper statue of Einstein, I'm thoroughly impressed. "This place is awesome."

Barry tells me how they constantly test gravel, artificial turf, and other materials. My short attention span drifts; I'm recording everything—why bother listening? Instead, I consider all the things I have to do: check my email, pick up Jeff, fill out reports for Bob, continue playing secret agent, call Blake, protect Dana, hope Mark protects my sister … and I think that covers it.

My mind shifts back to Barry as he's showing me rain-proof grass. I feel like I'm at a museum—all the rooms have huge glass

walls through which you can see scientists attacking different surfaces. In the last room we pass, a basketball player is repeatedly slam-dunking on special hardwood floors. The spring in the floor adds at least two inches to a person's vertical leap, Barry explains. Cool—I could maybe touch the rim. Barry introduces me to the basketball player and lets me attempt a dunk.

Running as fast as I can, I jump using both legs and reach the rim! I guess my broken rib was just indigestion; this feels okay. I hang from the rim as Barry takes a picture with my camera.

I feel energized as Barry drives us back to his office. He hands me folders of information and a SanDisk that had been sitting on top of his adman's desk. As we walk out the door, he thanks me, I thank him, and we exchange business cards. "We are at the edge of technology," Barry tells me. "Our scientists are going to build safe helmets, turf that won't screw up your knees, and rubberized skate parks—so when your crazy kid thinks he's ready for the X Games, he won't crack his skull." I can see why Courtney likes him. He has passion and makes you feel like you can dunk a basketball. And that feeling is awesome—especially given my athletically challenged genes.

BACK TO THE AIRPORT

The drive to the hotel takes no time. I park the car quickly and run to my room. Jeff might be in the middle of a threesome, I think to myself. Maybe I should knock loudly. I open my door slowly and creep inside. The door to Jeff's room is open and I can hear the television. I feel like the father coming home after a hard day's work, though it's not even noon. The girls are wrapped up in some movie and Jeff is packing. "Hi, kids!" The girls pop out of bed and kiss me on the cheek, while Jeff winks at me as if to tell me that something amazing just happened. Courtney asks me how it went, but all I can think is: Did Jeff just sleep with two women?

Jeff looks as if he just did something naughty. I ask him to help me with something next door. He shakes his head as he walks toward me and laughs. I throw everything in my suitcase and take off my suit, all in thirty seconds. Jeff starts talking before I can even ask what happened. "Nothing happened last night. Natalie popped in bed with me, but I was out cold! I just remember her saying, 'I'll be back.' Or was that Arnold on TV? I fell asleep with the idiot box on. We woke up about an hour ago and I got one kiss—and room service."

"You kissed the room service guy?" I laugh. "Whatever. You're holding out. I know that I-just-got-laid-in-the-shower grin."

181

Jeff's eyes widen and he nods his head yes. "Why so nosy and pushy? Maybe if you got some action you wouldn't be in everyone's business. We hit it in the shower while Courtney watched a pay-per-movie in your room. You think I had a threesome? I can barely satisfy one woman!"

Jeff and I giggle like we're in junior high as we walk back to the room. The party comes to an end as we checkout and drop the girls at their apartment. Jeff receives a big wet kiss and I get a kiss on the cheek. For the rest of the car ride, I rip on Jeff for his indiscretion. "You're a pig, a male slut. You're the reason women hate men, you dog. Why am I so damn jealous? I hope you're using protection. How many kids you got?" Jeff just sits there and takes my bashing, telling me how he's innocent and pure. By the time we reach the airport and return the rental car, we have thirty minutes until take off.

We run through the terminal like O.J. Simpson before he was a criminal. Just as first-class seating begins, we arrive at the gate and board. I want to call Dana, but I don't know her secret phone number. Jeff finds this entertaining. "You didn't hook up with a hot Hooters girl because of Dana, but you don't even know her number." I decide to call home and check the machine.

John, Mister I Never Take a Day Off Work, picks up the phone. "Hello, Jack. You missed the party!" John goes on to tell me about the party he threw—without me! What a bunch of crap, how can he throw a bash without me? Dana is sleeping on my bed right now, Sara is on the couch, Sydney fell asleep on the La-Z-Boy, and Joe is on Tyler's couch. Apparently, my sister and Mark also stopped over. "Jack, don't feel bad. After working out with Syd, my Uncle called with tickets to the Cubs game. When the game ended, we invited people over. Yes—your friends are now my friends."

"I'll try to forgive you. Will you wake my girlfriend?" Of course, the second Dana says hello, the message over the loudspeaker tells us to turn off our cell phones. "I'll call you when we land. I need your other number." As I end the call, I hear her say she wishes I was there.

Jeff begins drinking Sprite and vodka as I catch up on my sleep. My dreams revolve around work and breaking the law. Federal agents take me aside and question me, warning me that any violation of SEC laws has serious repercussions. I awake and hear the loudspeaker again. "Welcome to Kansas City. Thank you for flying ..."

The biggest benefit of first class: first to board and first to exit. The doors open, and within five minutes Jeff and I are headed to baggage claim. Jeff leads the way; airports are his home away from home.

The wait for our luggage takes fifteen minutes. While waiting, I call to say a quick hello to Dana, and verify our Saturday night extravaganza. Jeff gets the rental car, a green Sebring convertible, and I grab his suitcase and mine. We connect outside the terminal. The moment I shut the door, Jeff slams on the accelerator and we fly to Westport. Jeff apparently knows the city; he has no problem locating our Holiday Inn Express.

While checking in and organizing our belongings, I connect my computer to the wi-fi. Bob has sent me forty messages in the past two days. Since Jeff and I again have adjoining rooms, he comes in to watch television and work from my bed as I work at the desk.

My drug-dealing phone rings, and Jeff stares at me like I'm a criminal. "Hey—it's Joe. I'm still digging through your work stuff. You are not an employee of Trust One. You are paid as a contractor."

"This is so fucking crazy. Joe, am I breaking the law? What about my insurance?"

"You have a policy set up; they cover it. You aren't doing anything illegal regarding getting paid. However, it's time for a discussion with your boss. Maybe this is SOP. After ninety days they change things up. Usually they tell you." Sensing my tension, he assures me. "Breathe. We got this."

Hanging up, I tell Jeff before he has the chance to ask: "I have no idea what's going on. I am not an employee of Trust One. You and I are in the same boat. No idea why."

"Then it'll be easier for you to quit and keep selling drugs."

Ignoring Jeff, I check out Facebook. I have one new message from the jeweler: "My insurance money came through and I got more inventory. Beautiful SG diamonds. Set up an appointment." I respond quickly and set up a time to meet over the weekend. I might not be an employee, but I'm going to solve this murder.

Trying not to get too worked up over my non-employee status, I respond to emails from Bob. Two hours pass, and I get through only half of the messages while Jeff falls asleep. I receive another message while online. Mark sends me an email labeled "Funny." I resist temptation and decide not to view the note until I finish all my homework. I feel as if I've returned to grade school and no one's bothered to tell me. I don't want BW to suspend me or hold my mentally challenged ass back another year.

PLAYTIME

Jeff's cell phone rings and wakes him. "Hello? How are you, Natalie? I really had a great time last night."

I interrupt his conversation. "Yeah—you had a really, really good time." Jeff laughs and rushes her off the phone. He tells her he'll call her tomorrow, but right now he needs food. Before Jeff finishes his conversation, the two of us have walked to a brewery and are sitting down. I warn him that I still have another couple hours of work, and he gives me a typical Jeff answer.

"Come on, Jacky!" I know better, but I still throw down drinks like a freshman at his first frat party. After we make our meals and three pitchers disappear, we pay and walk to another bar. Jeff questions my manhood as two beautiful women stand next to us at the bar. He whispers in my ear, "Are you going to quit drinking and turn down hot women? You aren't married."

At this point, intoxication takes over and I order shots for Jeff, the girls next us, and myself. Turning to them without saying a word, I hand them their two shot glasses. The blond, directly next to me, asks, "What's this for?"

I slur my speech. "Ice breaker. You two models show my friend a good time!" The flattery works well—the girls slam the tequila and thank me with kisses on the cheek. Jeff feels left out,

so I tell them he paid for the drinks. Jeff winks at me as they both kiss him. I speed out the door in a drunk rage. I remember that I still have hundreds of pictures to review. I use the computer in the workroom at the hotel. Even though I'm a little tipsy, I remember not to use my computer.

Why was Jerry in Arizona? I just cannot figure it out. And what's the deal with this porn star? What is his connection to SG? I drink an entire pot of coffee while reviewing photo after photo. So far, two things strike me as odd: Reggie is in one picture with another guy. This guy with him has a Chase Bank hat on and a black jacket that says "Army Ranger." Great—now my mind is consumed with military militia men and dirty diamond dealers. Sounds like a Jay-Z song.

My eyes finally get fuzzy at 4 a.m. I pass out in my room and hope the wakeup call works. At some point in the early morning, I awake and become curious about whether tonight was the night Jeff has managed a threesome, so I get up to peek into his room. He is out cold on one bed and the two girls from the bar are cuddled together on the other one. They are in sorority T-shirts and short shorts. The paternal part of me pulls the bed sheet over them.

JACK WATERS, PI

Ace Investing finances the majority of the casinos around Kansas and Missouri. Trust One wants to take a bite out of the business, starting with the Grand. Jeff had agreed to email me all the information he could remember from last year. Ace wanted Trust to help, but Grand discouraged the deal from going through. Making my way up to the twenty-first floor, I try to jog my memory regarding the other details Jeff shared with me.

When the elevator opens, I am in the coolest-looking office I have ever seen. The carpet shines bright red, and pictures of dogs playing poker decorate every wall. The front desk has an ace of spades engraved into the dark wood. Jazz music softly plays in the background, and the waiting area contains a craps table with giant, fuzzy dice. I'm ready to gamble.

Before I can introduce myself, a man in a grey suit approaches me. "Hi, Jack. I'm Sam Kohl. It's a pleasure to meet the detective that brought Kevin Slim—AKA "Jason Murphy"—to justice. We've heard a lot about you. We appreciate you locating him; he defrauded us out of millions of dollars. Now, your secretary called and said we could only repay you with a favor. She said you wanted to review the casino files. Trust, I'm sure, loves to read this shit. We have nothing to hide. And you can tell Bob

West: we're the investors, and he can provide services. Sweep accounts, high rates, special coverages. That's shit we need." I'm thinking this all seems a little too easy. And Kevin is MIA. Do I tell them that?

I have no idea what to say. Suddenly, I'm a detective with a secretary. Shit—I don't even have an office. Sam continues to praise me. He offers me his firstborn; I accept a pen with an ace carved on the top instead. I'm in a mild state of shock. I feel as if my identity has been swapped and no one bothered to tell me I'm a super-agent. He thinks I run a detective agency in Chicago and that Trust One paid me to find Kevin Slim. But why should I ruin his perception of me? Honesty and morals fly out the window as I maintain the facade. I like the sound of my new title: Jack Waters, Private Detective. My tagline could be "Fighting crime, on your dime." I'll have to work on that.

My imagination momentarily gets the better of me. I imagine a small office with a hot secretary (Cholet) and my client, Dana Sugar (who is even hotter), smoking a long, thin cigarette. And everything is in black and white. Mental note: quit watching old detective movies.

I return to reality and begin to fish for information. "Last I heard, Jason Murphy was MIA."

Sam creepily places a hand on my shoulder. "He's dead. They found him in his house yesterday morning. Cops have been scoping out his property since you figured out his new name and whereabouts. Kid had a rap sheet: cheating at the casinos, assault charges, drug dealing, diamond theft. I'm sure the cops won't work too hard investigating his death." Fuck, fuck, fuck! I was just in that guy's backyard. I take a deep breath and remind myself that I was just doing my job.

The bodies are starting to pile up a little too quickly. Jerry, Thor, porn star. How does a porn star steal millions of dollars from a casino? I wish Jerry had given me a few more hints. "Hey—when you worked with Trust One for the Grand deal, other than Jeff, who was your contact?"

"Jerry 'Numbers' Walters. Relative of yours? That kid was amazing with a database. One of the reasons I'm letting you see our files. That kid could've hacked in and stolen everything."

"My cousin."

"I'm sorry about that. That kid was too nice, smart and young to die."

This feels like Beetlejuice. Maybe if I say his name three times he will appear. But there is no way he stole money. No way. Not Jerry. He had money; he wouldn't know what to do with millions of dollars. I check my phone. As I try to convince myself that Jerry is completely innocent, I find Bob's email and start answering a few questions. As much as I want to hide from all this, I need to put the pieces together and figure out what's going on. I also need to keep my nose clean; I can be linked to Thor's death—and now Jason's, too.

The meeting ends as Sam tells me, "Use the information any way you like." I wonder if that includes handing it to the competition. We shake hands and I thank him. Just as he's walking me out, Jeff saves me a phone call by pulling up in the rental car. After another handshake, I hop in the car and we drive away.

Before asking Jeff how he timed everything so well, I play the tape. He listens while speeding to the casino. Jeff tries to console me. "He said use it any way you want. Well, you want to give it to BW. Relax. Before we start gambling and drinking, we'll check out the info you stole—I mean, 'legally acquired.' Your bat phone is ringing."

I pick up my secret phone. It's always a surprise when I discover who's calling me. "What up, homey? I would like a few kilos of Chi-town's finest diggity dank!"

I'm surprised Joe would give a Trust One employee my secret number. "Syd, what's up? How did you get this number? And what phone are you using?"

"Relax, brother. I'm on your side. Don't you know I need you more than you need me? They always kill the brother in these scenarios. I need my kung fu friend. Here's what I got for you. Bob flew out to Arizona with Steve. The cats think Jerry was

somehow involved. This is getting deep. It might be time to call some cops and let the five-o figure this out."

"I wish it was that easy. There's something going on. Either Jerry was set up or he played a role in all this. It's just too coincidental."

"I knew Jerry and there is no way he was into this shit. Your cuz was framed. My advice? Buy a gun and take a vacation. This is my Jack phone. Call me later."

Before I can get too anxious, Jeff begins to describe his night with the two drunk sorority girls. Since I know nothing happened, I doze off.

"Wake up! Wake up, boy!" A large prison guard puts his cold, hard, black club against my throat. "You're in my world now. Have fun in the showers, pretty boy!"

Jeff shakes me out of my little nightmare. "Jack. Jack! Wake up! We're here. Let's get ready to lose some money." He pops the trunk and we grab our luggage. Before reaching the front doors, Jeff's phone rings. "Hello; this is Jeff. Hi, Bob. How are you?" Without waiting for a response, he continues, "We're having a blast. No, he's still at Ace. Believe me Bob—I'm not working too hard. I'll make sure Jack has a little fun. But he always has to respond to all those messages you send him; fewer notes might ease the tension. Thanks for the bonus and this trip. I have some things to do for the office on Monday, but after that I'll be in New York. Just call me Tuesday. Thanks again." Jeff shakes his head in amazement as he clicks the phone off.

"What the fuck! Are you paid to entertain me?" Jeff admits Bob gave him a bonus and asked him to show me a good time while on my first road trip. BW thinks all the emails and fun might help keep my mind off the legality of my work—or all the craziness. "So far, I haven't done anything against the law, right?"

"Sure. Whatever helps you sleep."

Jeff holds the door for me, and we walk to the front desk. My new life as Jack Waters, PI, continues as the man at the desk hands me two all access security passes. He reaches behind the table and pulls out a thousand dollars in chips, courtesy of the

casino. "These chips will be waiting for you when you're ready to gamble." While locating our room cards, he calls the director of the casino. "Sam, Mr. Waters and Mr. Riley have arrived." Putting the phone down, he looks at me. "Sam will be down in a minute. Here are the keys to your luxury suite." He hands us the cards with the holes that work like keys, but he never asks for my credit card or to sign anything. I ask if he needs us to sign anything. "Mr. Waters, it's our pleasure to serve you and to treat you and Mr. Riley. I am Walter. Anything you need, just dial zero."

I should be happy and excited, but doubt fills my mind. Jeff reads my anxiety and pulls me outside. "Excuse us, Walter. We have to run to the car." Once outside, Jeff starts laughing. "I have no idea why they're treating us like rock stars, but let's just chill out and ask questions later. Shit like this only happens once in a lifetime, so suck it up and enjoy the ride. Sam, the director, pulls no punches. He'll tell us why the royal treatment. Forget your crazy life for one night. Tomorrow we'll do some digging. Tonight, roll the dice."

Walking back thru the entrance, I think about my family. You never know when your time will run out. Unless you have a condition where the doctor says six months, you just never know. My dad is looking down on me and telling me to gamble, and my mom is telling me to remember to floss. Tonight, I'll do both. Before I can get misty-eyed, Sam introduces himself.

"Jeff, good to see you. Jack—great to meet the man that brought Kevin Slim to justice. Follow me; I'll take you two upstairs." We step into the elevator and Sam immediately starts talking loudly. "I'm not stupid. I know Bob hired you to locate Kevin, and I know that you've already been to Ace. I told your secretary this was not to be a business weekend. She wouldn't let us give you any reward money. That's why we flew you here as a guest and gave you some funny money to blow. When I heard Jeff was coming it verified my theory. Tell Bob our business requires a human touch. I hate most of the stiffs and kiss-ups like Steve Smith at Trust One. He sent Jeff here because I actually like him. Tell Bob to send me a rep or two to interview. They don't

have to live here, but I want them in KC a few days a week. If I can stand any of them, great. Now gamble, eat, drink, and get laid. Saturday, we golf at noon. Jeff, you know the course. Bring Jack and we'll talk tomorrow." Sam rides back down the elevator and we walk to our room.

Before stepping inside our suite, I turn to Jeff. "How much is this account worth?"

"About a million a year and millions more as they open up in Vegas and Dubai. The financial structure and business plan stress aggressive growth." My phone rings and cuts Jeff short.

BW's raspy voice speaks from the other end, asking me how everything is going. I give him the bottom line, "Sam wants individual attention. He needs a smart and personable manager to handle the multi-million-dollar account." While Bob responds, I tiptoe inside my huge, high-class room. The moment my feet meet the thick carpet and gaze across the plush suite, my eyes open so wide I hope they stay in their sockets. I lose track of everything Bob says as I attempt to take in the remarkable splendor that surrounds me.

A quick rundown of the place: full kitchen, wet bar, leather sectional, love seat, marble dining room table, seventy-inch television, separate bedroom, massive bathroom with a shower and Jacuzzi, water cooler, fireplace, balcony—and the list continues. Imagine the hotel room of your dreams, take away the naked partners, and there you go. As I check out the stocked liquor cabinet, the hotel phone rings.

"Bob, can you hold a minute?" I place one phone down and pick up the other. "Hello? Hi, Walter." He asks whether everything is satisfactory, and I raise my voice to answer. "No! This room sucks! I need a bigger room with more stuff! Just kidding; this place is amazing. I keep waiting for someone to tell me this is all some kind of joke and I've been 'punked.'" Before I get back to Bob, Walter offers me a bottle of champagne.

Back to Bob: "Sorry about that, sir. As you were saying?" Bob finishes up our conversation by asking me to do some recruiting for the casino. The position pays seventy thousand dollars, with

a bonus. "I'll line people up for you next week." Before he hangs up, he instructs me to have fun and not reply to any emails until Monday.

A knock on the door gets Jeff's attention. He runs out of his room and greets the clerk with our champagne. I tip the guy five dollars and grab some glasses. "Jeff, welcome to luxury."

While downing the bubbly, we flip between Spice and sports. We joke about how Jeff hasn't gotten laid in days and how we're getting paid to drink and gamble. "This is the life, Jacky." Taking a break from our normal channels, I scan the movie stations to see if a good flick is starting. When we finish the bottle, Jeff runs to his room and comes back with another one. "Surprise!" We party like old people and pass out while watching the classic film station.

"Jeff! Wake up. It's five in the morning."

"Wow, we know how to party. Shit, we only have seven hours to lose a couple thousand dollars." Sleep wins out over gambling. We make a plan to wake up at nine and then gamble till tee time. We figure it'll only take a few hours to give the money back.

"You sure we can't keep the money, Jeff?"

"Yea it's marked. They created funny money as a marketing ploy for corporations. Book some rooms for meetings, get free money …"

SWINGING IT

After a shower and a room-service breakfast, we hit the craps tables. Since we're both fuzzy on the rules, we leave the table down 500 and separate. I continue to hand my money back at blackjack, roulette, and poker. Jeff approaches me with a hundred dollars in chips as I play my last hand of poker. I borrow his money and throw it in the enormous pot. The other guys fold. I take seven hundred dollars and walk away without showing them I had nothing. I cash in my chips and give Jeff his hundred back. "Shit, you should give me another hundred for not laughing at your pair of threes."

Golf is awful. We play the back nine and it takes forever—mainly because I suck. Jeff hits most of his shots well, but short. Sam just barely beats me. After the game, we hit the nineteenth hole. The bartender at the little station looks like a porn star. She has wavy blond hair, light blue eyes, dark-red lipstick on probably fake lips, with definitely fake breasts pouring out of her shirt. I pass on the drinks. Sam sips on scotch, and Jeff has a Jack and Coke. The bartender tries to convince us to do some afternoon shots. She pours salt on her bare shoulder, puts a lime wedge in her mouth, and hands Jeff a shot of Tequila. Jeff licks her shoulder, slams the shot, and smooches her while trying to suck the

lime in her mouth. I take a picture and will later label it Jeff and the Porn Star. Sam says his ring prevents him from making out, and I tell her, "I'm not that drunk." Okay, that sounded pretty mean; but I think she understands. The germaphobe in me is wondering how many guys have licked and kissed her today.

Sam and I each buy Jeff another shot. Jeff has no problem complying, and stumbles to the car as we say goodbye to Sam. "Sam, thanks for everything. I'll send some applicants your way as soon as I find them. Jeff and I love this place! I cannot wait to visit the one in Vegas." A few handshakes later, we're on our way back to the airport. I drive while Jeff comments on Gena.

"Nice girl. I think we really bonded."

"You could call it that." The ride to the airport is a short one. When we arrive, my flight is due to take off in an hour and Jeff's in a half hour. Jeff is going to fly home for a couple days and might stop in Chicago as he heads toward the East Coast. "I'm going to miss you, drunk."

"Thanks, Jacky. Hey—if you need anything, call. I don't have one of your drug dealer phones, but I can get one." Jeff's plane is about to board. We hug. "It's the booze talking, but I'm going to miss you. Mainly because you're my good luck charm."

"Once I hit Chicago, it's back to reality. Thanks for the fun."

LOVE?

I somehow get bumped to first class again. It feels lonely without my partner. I order a cocktail in his honor, take a few sips, and sleep till we land. I feel joy and nervousness when I realize I'm home. Walking to the taxi stand feels exhilarating. Hearing the foreign accent of my driver excites me. I yell, "To Wrigleyville, my man!" Even traffic makes me happy. "Look at this traffic. God, it's good to be home!" Listening to people honking and watching crazy drivers cutting each other off is somehow comforting. "What a bunch of assholes. Right, Nibu?" Nibu and I chat about basketball and his son's soccer scholarship to Wisconsin. Traffic dies down a couple miles past the airport and we reach my apartment before six. I'm ready to figure out what's going on with Jerry, Trust One and me.

The outside of my building never looked so beautiful. Flowers bloom around the front door and a small tomato garden blossoms on the side of the building. I buzz my apartment, hoping John's home. I can't wait to see him. Hugs greet meet as I walk thru the open door. Both John and Dana put arms around me, but only Dana kisses me. "What—you can't show me any love, John?"

"Oh, what the hell!" With that, John plants one on my cheek. The two of them have been playing video games since three and

have just won the NBA championship; the Portland Trail Blazers over the Miami Heat in four straight games. Dana goes upstairs to shower and tells me to come up when I'm ready.

I jump in the shower, shave, spray on some cologne and put a little goo in my hair. Throwing on a white tee and some jeans, I'm ready. I run to the corner store and buy a tiny arrangement of deep purple and bright yellow tulips. Walking directly to Dana's, I knock on the door, turn the handle, and hear her call out, "I'm in the bathroom!"

Dana's skin glows, and she smells like vanilla sugar. Under her robe she's wearing nothing but lotion and dark red toenail polish. Even her painted toes turn me on. I start kissing the back of her neck and then make my way to her luscious full lips. Placing her on the sink, I continue to kiss the rest of her body as she leans against the mirror. I try not to miss anything—her ankle, the back of her knee, her fingers, and everything else. She takes off my shirt and slowly unzips my pants. Before we go further, I take another look at her face. "You are so beautiful and sweet. You melt my heart. Whether it's just staring into your eyes, holding your hand, or kissing you, I never want to forget this feeling. You have to move in with Alexis or stay with your parents. I'll fall apart if anything happens to you."

With that, tears begin to well in her eyes and we heat up the bathroom. The entire mirror is steamed up as we have sex. Then we walk to the bedroom and start all over.

In the morning, we decide to make challah French toast and venture downstairs. "Listen, Jack—I am going to help you. I can do research. I have a brand-new computer; never been used."

"Fine. You can research Kevin Johnson. I want his bio. His story. How did he go from Army Ranger to porn star to whatever he did? And any info on his death."

My place smells like nasty BO. Someone needs to shower ASAP. "Biked to Wisconsin while you two had your own little marathon," John tells us. "You guys had a good night. I could hear you two bouncing around all night. I almost went upstairs to make sure no one was hurt."

Dana appears shocked. "Really?"

Before John can answer, I assure her he's only kidding. He gabs on about the noise and shaking bedposts, as Dana listens with guilt written all over her pretty face. While they discuss last night's activities, I make a list of goals for the week:

- Hunt down Reggie
- Talk to Jeweler
- Beg Julie at Mind & Soul to see me
- Find some friends who could work in KC for casino
- Finish reports for Bob
- Talk to Joe about paperwork

Dana reads over my shoulder and asks, "Where's the Dana time?" John joins the conversation, too, asking why I left his name off my to-do list.

"Children, there's plenty of Jack to go around. I'll spend Monday, Wednesday and Friday with Dana, and the other days John gets my full attention. Sunday we will spend as a family." They both agree to the arrangements.

I cook up some chicken with a honey soy sauce and loads of rice noodles. I call Alexis while mixing up a tomato-cucumber salad. Now that she lives with Mark, it takes a little longer to visit.

Other than my constant paranoia, life is good. I have an amazing girlfriend, live with my best buddy, and my sister is about to get married. I will feel a million times better when I can solve Jerry's murder. While I ponder all of this, Joe calls. "Jack, I need your uncle's social security number. I called Alexis and got all her information, and I have your work papers. With your uncle's info, all the pieces might come together to solve the puzzle. Something is definitely not kosher. Act normal until we talk Thursday." Act normal? Shit, I've never been normal.

Q/JAMES

Before I can start to worry too much over Joe's call, Tyler stops by. "Hey, Jack. Come on over, buddy."

Since Tyler moved in and the dudes moved out, his apartment is OCD-clean and extremely organized. His bookshelves are alphabetized by author, and he has a magazine section dating back to 1998. "I'm not saying this to be rude, but you would think a dude with a collection of Men's Health magazines dating back to the '90s would be Abercrombie-model ripped."

"Donuts. They're holding me back. I fucking love a good donut. I don't need that fancy, infused, fashionable fare. Hook me up with good, old-fashioned fried dough."

Since Tyler is a graphic designer, his computer is huge. I didn't realize Apples came in extra-large sizes. A collection of gadgets sits next to his computer ... table? This monstrosity is way too big to be called a desk. "Jack, I set up a spy camera up front. Nothing to report except for this guy. You know him?"

Though the figure in the blurry video is wearing a black hoodie and Sox hat, it's clearly Reggie. "Yes! This guy is involved. We need to find him."

"Okay; I'll work on it. In the meantime, you're going to need my help. My dad owned a security company growing up, so I

installed cameras, alarm systems, surveillance and other shit. If I didn't love art so much, I would have totally been an engineer and built technology for spies like you. Let me see your secret phone."

"You are totally that guy from the James Bond movies—Q. The one with the gadgets."

"Thanks. Now watch." The first thing he does is add some apps to my phone. One app scrambles video signals. The other disables locks—not all locks, but most file cabinets and doors that require fobs. The next app sets off fire alarms. "Yea, I figured this one out in college with a couple IT geeks. Perfect for tough finals."

"IT geek friends? You mean your only friends."

The middle finger briefly appears, and then Tyler is back to business. "If you ever have questions, or forget how something functions, look at the notes in your phone. While you were making fun of me, I put in some info."

"Thanks, dude. I really appreciate this. To be honest, I'm scared to death. Something is going on here."

"You got some good people helping you. We're not going to let anything happen to you." I walk away after giving Tyler a hug. All I can think about is Dana. I feel this pit in my stomach. I can't let anything happen to her.

TOO DEEP

Sunday draws to an end with John and Dana falling asleep as I organize my paperwork. My mind races as I replay Joe's voice in my head: "Not kosher." I flashback to college and see good old Dr. Powers.

Wearing a short-sleeved button-down shirt—which no one should really wear—with a faded grey tie, and matching slacks, he offers a warning. Yelling like a mental patient, he tells me, "Watch your back! When the SEC grabs hold of these upper-class snobs, golfing on Sunday and talking about their company offering a three-for-one split in two months, they take them to court. Someone talks. Someone always talks. One of the guys gets jealous because he was too stupid to buy a thousand shares, and before you know it the other assholes have to shell out fifty grand to their good buddy the judge to forget the whole deal. Companies find a fall guy when they cheat. The CEO appears on the news, full of shit, lying his ass off, blaming Joe Blow new guy. Remember: if you think you're in too deep, you probably are."

I put off sleep and dig into the mass of material collected on my road trip. Companies handed me detailed information: growth plans, estimated layoffs, restructure maps, golden parachute amounts, minutes from meetings and other information

that resembles Chinese. The first projects I work on are basic; with each case the amount of material grows. BW has purposely weaned me on easy, bullshit cases like BBB and Mind and Soul. Once he's hooked me, he throws in the casino, EO and the insurance company.

By six o'clock in the morning, I am already at the office. Jeff had told me that all his files are in the cabinet behind Penny's desk, so I start digging. I start the video blocking app. I'm sure there's a camera in here somewhere. Next: the key fob app. Works like a charm. I quickly text Tyler: "I HEART U."

BBB and Muscle's are bigger investments than I imagined. Reports on land, cost and receipts fill BBB's folder. Next to the BBB file is info on Health Hutch, a rip-off of BBB set to open next year. Muscle's folder contains a letter from Jerry to BW, about selling workout data to companies in order to measure ROI on proactive health spending. Jerry suggests investing in the health industry diversely and vigorously. He advises that they start locally, with places such as Mind and Soul, BBB and Muscle's. The letter lists all the companies I report on, plus several others. I photocopy the letter and keep searching.

Each file resembles the next, and I begin to see a trend. Each case starts with an initial investment and insurance options. Trust One buys a significant share in the company to help the company through rough times, or as venture capital for startups. If the company goes public: boom—the IPO boosts Trust One's earnings. Seems like smart investing, but a little shady. Before anyone notices I'm in the office, I head home. I need to work on my reports.

I feel this pressure, despite not being an employee, to do well and figure out what happened to Jerry. Jerry would do the same for me, and I don't want to let him down. I remember how he called me at school, telling me, "I have a real job. I can actually pay my school loans—and rent! Living the dream." Memories of Jerry swirl around my brain as I reach my building and head to Dana's.

Dana is working from her kitchen table. "Jason Murphy is still a mystery to me. How was he involved in all this? Was he the

ringleader?" She answers her own question quickly. "The one job you gave me was to research him. He seems too simple. He was arrested a handful of times. Kicked out of casinos for cheating; he had a solid mind. He took the ACT in '96 and scored perfect in the math section. Made the papers in St. Louis." Dana did her research. "He was tossed out of the Rangers for drug use. Interviews from insider porn websites said he 'fucked with attitude.' Cocaine did him in—dealing it, not taking it. And the final piece: his Facebook page."

"I LOVE YOU! Now go to bed while I look at his page." A quick kiss and I'm glued to the internet. The friends of a porn star are interesting. He had a fan page, but it looks like no one's updated it in years. Under 'Jason Murphy,' he has almost one thousand friends.

At 1:30 a.m., I strike gold: Theodore R. Maxwell, aka Teddy, aka Reggie! Facebook friends with Jason Murphy.

FAST FORWARD

The week flies by as I create my reports for BW. I continue to do my own research on the files, taking pictures and notes on everything. Now I'm using my acquired skills to figure out how to screw Trust One. Their files look like FBI files. Not only is there data on company statistics, but in-depth information on each president of the company. And this isn't college transcript info:

> *Tom Keefer: Russian descent. Parent: Patty and Jon. Siblings: Sarah and Stacy. Married in 2003; divorced in 2005. No kids. Ex remarried. Tom remains single. Dating Caren Price. Lives in CA. Arrested for assault with a .22. Bar fight. Record cleared after community service. No time served. Investors are father and angel investor Spiro Granz. Spiro Granz: 34, LA resident. Worked at startup Boom. Bought by Yahoo for $8.5M. Started TechCo; sold for $12.5M to Amazon. Belongs to Bel Air Golf Club, Temple Beth El, ...*

It looks like Trust One is networked through these companies, duplicate business plans, and possibly building files for insider trading. Something is not kosher, and my new best friend,

Sydney Phelps, is somehow involved. His name and Jerry's are all over the reports.

My stomach drops. I have no idea who to trust anymore. And since Syd is my workout partner, I will have to look him in the eye four times a week and try to play it cool. Is he building a file on me?

I will need to come clean and approach him, and soon.

In the meantime, I have an appointment with Leslie of Leslie's Jewels. Her store burned down in a fire that basically closed four diamond shops. I'd asked her to meet me at a Starbucks on the south side, near her house.

"Child, why did you want to meet me here?"

"It's near your home office. And I feel comfortable around my people." She she laughs softly and puts her hand on my hand, as if we're old friends.

"Alright, Jack—what's the story? Why have so many people wanted to talk to me?" Her light-hearted tone has changed. Her posture is erect and she's gripping her purse as if I'm going to steal it. I turn on the fuzz app and come clean.

"I work for Trust One. I found out someone who worked for SG Diamond killed my cousin. Your shop burned down. You are insured with Trust One. You turned down an offer for a new store and took the cash. The other three individuals who lost their businesses in the fire are either MIA or dead. Can you help me?"

With a fake smile, Leslie leans in and whispers, "Son, you don't want to know. All I can say is Baker Boys, shop next to mine. They dropped prices so low, crackheads were buying three-karat rings. They sold low-quality shit. Stopped buying from SG. Then my shop burned the fuck down with most of the building."

She stands up, scans the place and raises her formerly hushed voice. "Come here and give me a hug the right way, boy." As we embrace, the whisper returns. "Lose my number. And watch your ass. You find the inside guy."

I scribble "BB," and walk quickly to my car. My heart racing is the only thing I hear. Is this what a heart attack feels like?

As I unlock my car, I feel something sharp against my back. Without looking behind me, I quickly jump into my car and lock the doors. I turn to face the tapping against my window, and my worst fears immediately subside. "Thanks. I appreciate that. Can I give you a reward?"

The old man standing on the other side of my car door smiles. "Just be careful with your cell phone." Without thinking, I toss the cell phone on the passenger seat and drive off. As I reach Lake Shore Drive, the phone rings. But that's not my phone.

"Cracker, you better be alone."

NEXT LEVEL

"Thanks for the phone."

"Burn it when you're done. Like those jewelry bitches burned my store. Don't dig deeper, son. I'm taking the check Dave Heeder gave me and I am done with this shit."

"Dave Heeder?"

"Yeah, he's my insurance agent. He's fake, but the man took care of me." I can tell she's about to exhale a cigarette, "I quit smoking twenty years now. Then this shit." Leslie hesitates but I can tell she wants to tell me more.

I plead for more information. "Can you tell me anything that could save my life?"

"Stay away from The Giant. He looks like one bad motherfucker. His little black friend carries a gun. They were security for the building. Never trusted them."

"Does the big guy look like Thor?"

She laughs. "He sure does. He used to meet with his partner and an older skinny white guy. Wore some Army hat."

"Where did you see them talking?"

"Right next to the building was a McDonald's. I saw them there Monday mornings, 6 a.m. Like clockwork." She hangs up, and I have one thought: three days. In three days, it will

be Monday. Is this case that simple? And how the hell is Dave Heeder involved?

Using my new cell phone, I dial Mind and Soul and disguise my voice. I did not leave there on good terms. I adopt a thick Eastern European accent, "Hello. I am customer service, Trust One. This is courtesy call. Can you tell me who your agent is? Does he do good job?"

Bob answers, which is the best situation. "Dave Heeder. He's great." Bob hangs up before I can thank him.

Coincidence or not, I will be looking into the Dave files. My private phone rings. It's becoming hard to keep track with three. I can tell from the voice: it's Joe.

"Joe, I'll be home soon."

His tone is unusually serious. "Stop by the restaurant."

Finally, Joe needs to meet with me. His concerned look wrinkles the corners of his eyes. "I've been at your bank. I've read your Uncle's FBI files. Yes—FBI. I studied Alexis's inheritance, Jerry's estate documents, and I figured it out. First, you are not an employee of Trust One." My mouth opens, my left hand lightly slaps my face, and I take a seat. Joe explains how the letters I signed ranged from a car lease to stock orders to statements of confidentiality. I signed letters specifically stating I cannot discuss any of the information I obtain through my relationship with Trust One executives. My car, company credit card, cell phone, computer, and camera are all purchases I made. My signature stamps the car lease, and my interest, consulting fees, and dividends are how I'm paid. My inheritance pays a chunk of my living expenses. I closely examine all the papers on my kitchen table, and then it hits me: JW is Jay Waters. All my uncle's signatures resemble the JW on letters to BW. My own fucking uncle. The initials ER still elude me; they appear often on the files. "Jack, they planned everything. You were hired before you even met Bob. Flashing money, arranging your cousin's and uncle's wills—it was all a setup."

Standing up, I hear Bob's voice. I replay him telling me, "You were hired before you even stepped in the door." All the

paperwork I organized from Trust One files—it might make sense to Joe. I grab the folder and ask Joe to read.

His eyes widen as he tells me, "This is not good." Joe skims through the material with a look of confusion and worry tattooed across his face. "The laws broken here range from fiduciary to anti-trust and I see a lot of misrepresentation. But I haven't finished law school yet, so I'm not sure what I just said. Let's meet next Friday and discuss the facts. I'll need a week to research."

Before Joe leaves, he offers more help: he agrees to visit The Grand Casino as an applicant. Dana and John hit the sheets—of their respective beds—as I email Bob about a prospect. Since he never sleeps, I get a reply instantly. "Thanks. Get some rest." Shit, I'll take all the time I want. It's not like I work for Trust One.

With my mind reeling and a bottle of whiskey in my system, I wake up at noon the next day. Dana is holding a tray of food in front of me. "You finally got some sleep." Disorientation slowly fades, and my nerves relax as I read the date on the newspaper next to my eggs. Today is Saturday.

Dana feeds me eggs and fruit. Before finishing breakfast, I apologize. "I'm so sorry for my behavior. Distant, cold and distracted Jack will no longer neglect you." Staring into her sparkling eyes, I speak from the heart. "Every time I look at you, it takes me back. When I saw you for the first time in years I thought, 'Wow! What a beautiful girl.' With every day I see you, your beauty multiplies. You bring me to emotions I've never felt, and take me to incredible, dreamy, happy places. Butterflies fill my stomach when you enter a room, and tears well up when you leave. I love you." Wow. Jack Waters told a girl he loves her. No one will ever believe that. I hope Dana reciprocates.

Tossing the tray to the ground, Dana wraps her arms around me and starts to cry. "I love you too, Jacky!" I forget my world of espionage and focus on Dana.

"I want you to work from home. Your parents' home."

"Jack, you are so paranoid."

"Here's the truth. I'm not an employee of Trust One. Something fishy is going on there. A guy died in Arizona. I was

fishing around his house two days before cops found his body. My cousin was murdered. The guy who hit him—dead. One of his friends is looking for me and knows about you."

"Jack, I'm already staying at Mark's or your place. I am safe."

"Here's a ticket to see your folks. I love you." Tears flow from Dana's eyes and drop from her long lashes. "Please. Tonight, we party. At the end of the night, Joe will take you to the airport."

BANANA IN THE TAILPIPE

Tyler is a full-time graphic designer, part-time security chief. When I follow him into his condo, his TV is on and displaying the view from the east side of our building. "See that car? It stops by every other night and parks there. Hangs out an hour or so, then leaves. Guy never gets out of his car. He drives around a few times."

We watch him drive down the block, following cars that resemble mine. We zoom in. It's Reggie. Thanks for the security detail, Bob. When the car parks, it sits for a few hours.

Thirty minutes into reviewing video, we pick up a pattern. "Tonight, he's coming around 2 a.m.—right when we get home."

Tyler looks at me with an inquisitive gaze. "What do we do, boss? Gotta draw this guy in."

"Can we Beverly Hills Cop him? You know—put a banana in his tailpipe?"

"I'm not sure that works, Jack. What if we pepper spray him?" Tyler pulls out two cans of pepper spray and a taser and lays out a plan. We'll walk by his car and spray into his windows. If the windows are up, I'll hop into my car and drive it into his. Simple enough. When he gets out of the car, we'll shock him, tie him up and question him.

"We're getting a little crazy here, Tyler. Let's just block him with my car and then we'll hop out and question him."

The party has already started in my unit. Old school. Beastie Boys music is playing, and guests have already arrived. S and S, Lisa and Mark stop in, and Jeff Riley surprises us before he heads to Los Angeles, asking "You got a bed for me?" Stacey plays DJ and keeps changing the music while everyone drinks like they're in college: beer in one hand, shot glass in the other. Two strong cocktails and a body shot with Dana clouds my reasoning. I call Syd and tell him he has to go out with us. Tonight, I will confront him about my suspicions. First, I must lick the salt off Dana's neck. Instead of doing the shot, I take the lime out of her mouth and kiss her. Everyone leaves the kitchen as we make out against the stove.

A few more drinks and not only do I forget work issues, but recalling my name is becoming a challenge. When we hit the club, I start pounding water. I need to be sober in a few hours. My rock star sister is dancing on the podium while some freak pretends to slap her ass. Mark stands around laughing and talking to the guys—and to the twins. Yes, we now roll with beautiful twins named Cara and Lena. They look great in their black mini-skirts and tops one size too small for their chests. Sydney has been dating Cara for a couple weeks. The twins dance near the rest of the gang. Tyler talks to the bouncer as if they are lifelong friends. I find out later that they went to high school together. I forget my world for a moment and enjoy dancing to the music with Dana.

> Dip, drop and stop
> Don't take her to the floor
> Work with me and she'll be begging for more
> I'm going to bring you real close
> Then take you apart
> Listen, now we're going to start
> Dance cheek to cheek, now glide
> Turn around and hit it from the backside

216

Take her shoulder and hold 'er
Let your hands do the walking
Yea, now we're talking
Now turn her so you're face to face,
and take a little taste
Dip, drop and stop
Yea, that's what it's all about …

The song ends, and we start kissing. Sydney breaks up the smooching and starts to dance with Dana. He's got moves like a professional hip-hop dancer. Jeff, John and I attempt a move or two and fail. Alexis steps down from the stand and joins our circle. Everyone, including the twins, is shaking it as Syd and I head to the bar. He orders us some shots. "I miss you, Jack. You don't come into the office anymore. We see each other at the gym and that's it. BW said your reports amaze him. He also told me he saw you leaving the building at 8 a.m."

My phone buzzes. "Syd, give me two minutes." I run back to Dana.

Dana's smile could brighten a blind man's day. It sparkles and shines and is magnified by her dark skin. And then there's that dimple. When I tell her she's perfect, she says, "I could never be perfect; I have an asymmetrical dimple!" But she is as close to perfect as I can comprehend. As she's sweating and kissing my cheek, I am focused on protecting her. "You have to leave now. The cab just texted me. He's out front. I love you."

"I don't have my stuff. I need to run home."

"I got you covered." I turn to Sarah. "Bag, please! I packed a bag with some necessities and had Sarah bring it here." I'm too paranoid to let Dana go to back to our place before this is over. "Here are those necessities. And thanks to my great salary at a job I don't really have, I put five hundred dollars on this card. Buy yourself some new clothes."

Per our plan, no one says goodbye to Dana—at least not with words. It's mostly winks. Tyler's connection has the back door open for her. She walks down the "employees only" hallway, and

I have this horrible feeling that it's the last time we will see each other.

I return to Sydney. "Syd, I have been checking out the files. There's a lot of stuff with your name on it. Research—like, CIA shit. It's intense. The biggest twist: I am not an employee of Trust One."

Sydney drops his shot glass before he can take a drink. The rest of the group continues to party as he and I head toward a booth to talk. He tells me BW never told him whether I was an independent contractor or worked for the company. The files with his name puzzle him.

"I do some technical assistance on our new acquisitions, and research. Nothing intense. Simple shit. Jerry did a lot of research. Was his name in there?"

"JW was on a few items, as was yours, and Bob West. I think there's some insider trading going on. And fraud. I can't figure it out yet, but the diamond people are somehow involved."

Syd appears shocked, but a smile begins to form. "Blackman and Robin, baby. Tomorrow we'll read over your files. I'll bring the info I got. I keep it all." We each down a glass of water and watch as a girl trips and nearly falls while staring at Syd. "Man, ever since I've been dating Cara, girls have been sweatin' me like I'm the finest piece of chocolate on the planet."

Cara overhears him as she approaches. "Wanna dance, chocolate truffle?" Sydney grabs Cara's hand and leads her to the dance floor. An hour of grooving leaves us sweaty and tired. We drop off the twins and begin our search for Reggie.

CPD

We corner the car outside the apartment. Immediately, I can tell it's not Reggie in the driver's seat. "Tyler, they don't all look alike. That's not our guy." A window rolls down and the driver holds out a badge.

"CPD. I'm your night watch. Keep walking."

Okay. So, the cops are watching the building. I should feel good, but I don't. With all the crime around the city, one officer assigned to my apartment means something is not kosher.

As we walk upstairs, I get a text from Dana. "Limo? Hope so. Just got in."

"If the sign said SUGAR, relax & enjoy the ride."

"Yes. And thx. XOXOX."

Surprisingly, none of the guys are making fun of me. Tyler heads to his place and Jeff follows him. Since Syd is sleeping on my couch, I don't have room. At home I start to feel a little more at ease and manage to fall asleep almost immediately.

"BANG, BANG, BANG."

It's 5 a.m. and it sounds like a cannon is going off in my apartment. After the cannon, I hear a siren. As I become fully awake, I smell smoke. I run to the front door, where the cop holding a flashlight seems to explain the loud banging. But what about the smoke?

219

"Son, the smoke is coming from your upstairs neighbor's unit." A rush of adrenaline overtakes me, and I race up the stairs like it's a competition. I kick open Dana's door, and the smoke is coming from the bathroom, where there seems to be an electrical fire. I hear the deep booming voice of the cop: "No water." He runs into the bathroom with Dana's flour canister and douses the curling iron blow dryer with flour.

Moments later, three firemen arrive, open all the windows and start to clean up the room. I take Officer Rhodes to Tyler's unit. "How did you miss that?" I ask him, my tone maybe a little too accusatory.

"Kid, the girl either left that shit on or he came in the back door. I didn't think we needed two cops out here. What are we doing in this Radio Shack of an apartment?"

Tyler appears in a blue robe and fluffy slippers to answer the question. "Surveillance cameras. One in the front and one in the back."

Tyler signs on to his computer so fast I worry there'll be another fire. He turns on his TV and pulls up the back camera. "Here we go." He rewinds a little. "And there he is. Gray hoodie, black hat, jeans, and yellow high tops."

Officer Rhodes speaks. "He knew no one was going to be in there. He also knew I was out front. By the time the smoke hit outside he was long gone. And you better watch out—that bulge in his back is a gun. This isn't an episode of Scooby-Doo."

STAKEOUT

Usually, I'm able fall right back asleep any time I wake up in the middle of the night. But when a cop bangs on your door while your girlfriend's fire alarm is going off, it tends to work like caffeine. I'm still tired, but more jittery and nervous. The best thing to do when one is up at 5:30 in the morning? A diner breakfast.

Jeff, Tyler, Sydney and I squeeze into Tyler's Suzuki Sidekick and head to the nearest IHOP, while John hops on his bike and heads toward Wisconsin. He's normally out of the house by now.

As we all spread out in our booth evidently made for giants, I look straight at Jeff. He seems to register the suddenly serious look on my face. "Here's the truth, Jeff. I am not an employee of Trust One. As you know, my job is to get ridiculous information for Bob. I took the job for one reason: to find Jerry's murderer. He's dead, but whoever put this together is still alive. And they are hunting me. When you get home, you need to find a new client. Trust One is going down."

Jeff looks stunned. Trust One has been his biggest client for years. His father had known Bob since college. A thought bursts into my achy brain, and I blurt, "Your father's initials are ER!"

"How did you know that?"

"He's the missing the link. He might not have knowledge of any master plot, but his initials are written on many reports as acting CEO."

Jeff looks confused for a moment, then says, "My father died a year ago." Before I can begin to wonder whether Trust One had anything to do with that, he adds, "Heart attack." He explains how the death was kept on the downlow. He and his brothers buried their father with a small group of family and friends. His father built Riley Consulting on a shoestring budget and, given his years of managerial experience, his death could have easily ended the business. Jeff kept the death a secret to protect the company; he knew his father would want it to prosper. Not many clients would trust a young punk to analyze and offer suggestions for thousands to millions of dollars. Jeff's eyes tear up and he goes to the restroom to compose himself.

Sydney and I console Jeff the best we can. BW pretty much keeps Riley Consulting in business. Tyler cuts in. "Hey! With Jack's help, I picked up a bunch of clients. We have a handful of clients with his sister; we can refer consulting work your way."

Jeff thanks him and changes the subject. "So then, what's next for you guys?"

"Tomorrow morning, our fire-starter is going to be meeting with his partner in the diamond district. We'll be there—see who he's with, take pictures, go to the cops and see what happens. We also have a ton of files to turn into the SEC. It's going to be a busy month."

Tyler again cuts in. "I got us a van. We're going to stake out the McDonald's and the attached building. Today we'll go out there and put cameras and mics all over the place. We want video and sound. I have a ton of surveillance equipment from when my dad quit that part of the business. He gave me all his crap."

I turn to Tyler. "Have you been taping Dana and me having sex?" A much-needed laugh comes at the same time as our pancakes.

"Yes!"

Tyler is a pro. Who knew? He outfitted the McDonald's table that would most likely be used—and a few others—with tiny

cameras and microphones, which he stuck to gum under the table. For safe measure, he put them in the bathroom, too. "But not at penis level," Tyler reassures us.

Sydney laughs. "Then why even do it?"

"You guys are some sick fucks," Tyler says. "Anybody want a burger?"

Sydney immediately becomes serious. "Talk about sick— those burgers are nasty! Let's get out of here."

We head back home, and I am quickly fast asleep. Just as quickly, I'm awakened.

"Wake up, dude." Sydney's deep whisper rouses me. "Jack, it's time for the stakeout. Tyler is in the van; we need to go."

Sydney looks intimidating standing over me in dark jeans and a black T-shirt. His muscles bulge as if there are foam abs under his shirt.

I sit up in bed. "I'm up. Coffee."

Sydney hands me a coffee and a piece of gum. "Man, are you still doing kung fu? Because your breath is kicking."

"Funny. Let's go. We aren't robbing anyone, so I think I'll be okay in this getup."

Sydney asks, "Man, you don't even want to change your drawers?"

"I'm going to pee through them, so what's the point?"

The van is a little smaller than I'd imagined. Syd drives as I take orders from Tyler. "I feel like I'm in a buddy cop movie. Syd, you better be careful."

Before Tyler can finish my thought, Syd beats him to it. "This black guy is not dying. You hear me! Keep my ass alive captain kung fu!"

As we near the restaurant, the video monitors pick up the feed from the cameras. Background noise begins popping in and out. The signals get stronger as we find a parking spot a block and a half away. Tyler barks out more orders. "Relax. We have two hours before they're supposed to get here. Let's get some shuteye. I'll set my phone. There's a microwave; we can heat up the coffee later."

Syd asks, "How many stakeouts have you been on? You're a little too calm."

"My dad mainly put in systems, serviced them—but occasionally he'd help out with a divorce spy job, help out cops with technology. Or if someone famous was in town, a security company would call him for help. Those were fun …"

I doze off as Tyler rambles on.

BOOM BOOM

The noise being picked up by the restaurant microphones gradually rises. I open my eyes and briefly struggle to remember where I am. The ninety-minute nap feels like I drank a pot of coffee—minus the jitters and potential digestive ramifications. "Tyler, that nap was a great idea. I feel awesome!"

While fiddling with the equipment's volume levels, Tyler says, "Yup—ninety minutes and twenty minutes are the perfect amount."

Sydney chimes in. "Designer, secret agent, sleep expert: Tyler B. You must have some hidden demons to be this good at this shit."

The monitors are all picking up clear signals, but nothing's going on beyond the McDonald's workers getting things ready for the day. The doors unlock with a loud "CLICK"—the only sound we hear for the next thirty minutes.

"They might not come," I say. "How long do we give it?"

Tyler flashes a knowing smile and, just like that, two guys walk in. Syd raises his voice. "That's fucking Steve Smith!" Right behind Steve, I spot the obnoxious shoes I last saw running from my house. In the shoes—Reggie, of course.

"Does anyone else find it odd that they're meeting early in the morning at McDonald's to talk about some criminal activity, and

225

they bring in their own coffee?" No one answers me as Steve and Reggie start talking.

Steve asks, "What happened with the fire? Did you not know about the rent-a-cop?"

"Listen—the girl was gone. Like some fucking magic trick. They all hit the club together. The dudes come out with no women. I go inside and walk around—nothing. I go back out and wait around until the place closes and no sign of the bitch. I rushed over to the apartment and saw the rent-a-cop, so I went in the other way. Girl wasn't there either."

"Why did you start an electrical fire?"

"The girl leaves on a curling iron, hair blow dryer, flat iron. Something shorts; doesn't look like someone started a fire. And once the fire gets going, she has all this flammable hair spray. That fucking rent-a-cop should've been gone."

As they sip their Starbucks coffees and nibble on egg sandwiches, I ask again, "Does anyone else find it odd that they brought their own coffee?"

"Shh!" is the only response I get.

"The files we planted at the office are working," Steve says. "The crap I tell Bob he needs to get for reports—the Karate Kid is doing it. They got that kid in so deep the SEC will have a field day with Bob. And once they realize Dave Heeder runs the policies for SG, they'll get him and your boss."

Reggie asks, "You think Shoman's going down? You got the account info?"

"Better him than us. Shoman's a greedy asshole. All the shit he's had you and your partner do? Jail will suit him fine."

A smirk appears on Reggie's face. "How do you like the coffee?"

A loud noise briefly scrambles the sound as we watch Reggie fall forward onto the table. Syd yells, "Fuck!"

A few seconds later, Steve's head hits the table. "It's like Romeo and Juliet. What do we do?"

Tyler dials 911. "There's a shooting at McDonald's. Diamond district." Before we can discuss our next step, sirens echo outside—and inside—the van.

A few cops and EMTs run into the restaurant, which seems to surprise the five employees. It's apparently normal for people to pass out while eating Egg McMuffins. I ask Tyler, "Do we tell the cops any of this? Should we go in there?"

Syd chimes in. "Yes, we should. Fuck this shit. We're not cops. The only guns I've got are the ones popping out of my T-shirt. If we keep pretending we're Miami Vice, someone's gonna get hurt. These diamond people do not mess around. Blood diamonds are for real!"

Tyler turns to Syd. "Look: Reggie is gutshot. Steve fired from under the table before the poison kicked in. What would we say to the cops—we were tailing these guys for fun? Why didn't we call them before? And now we have a recording of them talking about our boy and SEC violations? Fuck that."

My excitement takes over and I shout, "Let's get us Shoman!"

"Listen, Crockett and Tubbs. This shit is real. Two dudes just killed each other. Cops are scoping out the scene. It's only a matter of time before they find our cameras."

Tyler starts editing the video. Any mention of my name is deleted. "Boys, we cannot trust anyone. That is the problem. Cops see this video and they know nothing. There's no proof that Shoman—whoever that is—did anything illegal. All they know is that two people are dead."

My phone rings, and the caller ID reads "Chicago Police Dept." As my heartbeat pulses through my shirt, I answer. "Hello?"

"Jack, it's Officer Rhodes. Listen: we found Reggie—dead. We need to run the shoes to make sure it's a match with your fire starter, but it's the same crazy-ass color. Hopefully, you're out of harm's way. Do you know a Steve Smith?"

"Coworker. Met him once."

"Any reason he would he be with Reggie?"

"My only guess is that he was the inside man at Trust One. All the robberies and fires with the Jewelry stores—he could've been working with Reggie on those."

"I'm going to need you to come in for questioning. Now I'm not tossing you in jail. You aren't implicated or even suspected in shit. To be honest, we just need your help."

"I do have some info. But I have no idea who to trust anymore. You would be a safe bet, having saved me from Reggie." We set up a meeting and end the call.

Sydney gives me a thumbs up. "Listen, good cop-bad cop, let's let someone handle this."

Tyler just shakes his head. "They'll find the cameras soon. Tell them you did it yourself. We know nothing. You borrowed the shit from me, for work. I'll create an invoice."

Syd laughs. "Is it just me, or is Tyler a little too good at this shit? You move in right as Jack starts his job. You're a designer, but also James Bond. Who do you work for?"

Tyler adopts a serious tone. "I'm Special Agent Cox. I work for the FBI."

"I fucking knew it!" Syd yells.

"Syd, how gullible are you? This truck says Brody Security on all the equipment. His dad really did own a security company. Trust me—no offense, Tyler—there's no way he's FBI."

Tyler smiles. "You guys give me a little too much credit. You grow up with this shit and it's second nature. I remember my dad finding a camera in my closet and threatening to kill me, yelling, 'You sick fuck! Tape your sexcapades when you get your own place.'" We laugh and Tyler continues. "I'm going to burn a disk for you, and another few just in case. We'll all have one handy in case something happens."

INTERROGATION

Officer Rhodes meets us at DePaul's library. They have study rooms you can use when it's slow. I bring my laptop and show him the video without saying a word.

"That is fucked up. We wondered how and when the spy cameras got there. No prints."

"Now level with me, Rhodes—what the fuck is going on?" I don't know that I'll get an answer, but I ask, "Who is Shoman?"

"He works for SG. No idea about his official title, but he runs Chicago, Arizona, Las Vegas, and New York. Distributes the goods with his team. We thought he might be behind the fraud, but no proof. All his guys are ex-military and they are good. Reggie was the biggest screw-up. And you met Thor and Sammy."

"Who the hell is Sammy?"

"He was in your martial arts class. The day you broke that dude's shoulder."

My chest is thumping so loudly it sounds like I have a bass boost on it. This is probably another guy who's trying to kill me. "He's a tall guy with blond hair? Would be attractive if he didn't have huge braces?"

"That's his nickname—Brace Face. I know: real mature. I'm surprised you never beat him up."

"Tall guys scare me. He only watched the day I went crazy. So how long have you been investigating him?"

"The FBI has been investigating this case for over a year. When your cousin was killed, they brought a few of us in on it. You got to be careful, kid. This is real. It's not too often we have a poisoning and a shooting at the same time. You should disappear for a few days. Maybe a few weeks. No idea what's up Shoman's sleeve."

"Use me. Seriously—I want to help."

"Kid, these people will burn down your family's houses. They already tried to burn your house down. We got this."

"Listen, this isn't a shot at you, but my cousin died because you didn't get it. Three people are dead. They want me dead. Keep watching me. I have pictures from Arizona; I'll send them your way."

"Stay out of trouble. We'll watch you. Don't try and be a hero. I'm afraid someone else will come for you."

"You got it all wrong. They're done with me. They solved their problems. There is just one thing missing: money. Shoman, whoever he is, wants whatever cash Steve Smith siphoned off the top. Maybe I can help him get that cash. Maybe Bob West is in on it."

"Jack, it's over. Let us take it from here. There will be a new set of eyes on you. Anything happens, call me. Bob knows everything. He's been working with us for months."

"Did he know about the fake files or whatever they are outside his office?"

"Nope. We are going to run through them tomorrow. I think they were there to frame Bob. He's clean. Although he looks the part of an evil character, he's cool."

INTERVIEW TAKE II

My paranoia keeps me up for another night. I'm wide awake when Bob calls me. "Hi, Jack."

"Wow—I'm getting Bob on the phone right off the bat. I feel so important."

Bob sounds serious. "Let's have breakfast at Big Bad Burger."

"Sure. I never tested out their Big Bad Breakfast. How about eight?" The line goes dead, and I'm going to assume that's a yes. It's been a while since we met. And I'm not sure if I can trust him. Then again, Steve Smith was my HR guy.

Big Bad Burger is near the train, which seems to explain why there's a long line at this time. I order two breakfast sandwiches and sit down in a booth. I can smell the baked apple that's cooked inside the chicken sausage and devour both sandwiches before Bob arrives. Maybe there's a line because this sandwich is finger-licking good.

I stand up to greet the great Bob and get a firm handshake. He starts talking before I can get a word in. "I'm sorry, Jack. I pulled you into this horrible mess. I just found out yesterday we never even hired you. Fucking Steve Smith. He was such a kiss-ass. I never even considered that out of all my asshole employees he'd be the shithead."

"I thought that since I was getting all this crazy information for you, I was not an employee on purpose."

"The info was a stretch. We have legal. I was not going to let you break the law. Push the envelope? Yes. The law? No. You need to be careful. And now that I have access to all Steve's email accounts, I can work with the cops to get Shoman."

I pretend to know more than I do. "They want the cash he was siphoning off for himself. I know who helped him." This is a huge stretch, but here it goes. My only theory: "Cynthia Rocks. That bitch took care of everything. All my paperwork was handled by her."

Bob looks like he's about to call my bluff. "She is a bitch. And she and Steve were close. Not sure she has the balls to steal money. Forge your paperwork, sure; but steal from a diamond empire? No way."

"What if she didn't know?" I throw together a plan. "He probably said, 'These are the accounts, move this money.' It's only a matter of time before Shoman connects the dots."

An evil grin takes over Bob's face. "What if we lead them to her?"

"Fuck. You are one crazy mastermind." I'm having a tough time getting on board. Sure, I hate her, but these people will burn down her parents' house and kill her siblings.

Noticing my apprehension, Bob assures me, "Listen, the cops will have an eye on her. She'll be fine. These are the people that took out your cousin—and possibly your uncle."

My heart sinks. My uncle was like a father to me, just as Jerry was like a brother. I didn't even question his death. After my aunt died, I'd assumed living without her was too hard. "I'm all in."

Before I can ask him about my uncle, Bob is on the phone. "Dave, how the hell are you? Actually, I'm calling with some bad news. Steve is dead. I got a call from the cops. I'm putting our rock star on it. No, I have no idea what happened. I have to talk with family, cops, and Cynthia Rocks. She's always the first to reach out. Bitch wants to sell his shares, get commission and find another corpse. Yea, everyone knows her. We'll be in touch."

Bob puts away his phone with a huge grin on his face. He winks at me and smirks. "Done."

"Dave ... Shoman?"

"No, silly—Dave Heeder. That's not Shoman's name."

"I knew that slimy piece of shit was dirty. Why don't we just go after him? How have you not fired him?"

Bob shoots me a serious look. "Dave is clean as a whistle. His only mistake is that Steve set him up with this dirty diamond company. Dave tells Shoman everything. He has no idea how dangerous the man is. And because his inventory is big bucks, Dave gets rich off them and is too dumb to ask serious questions. He's going to tell Sy Shoman."

"So we follow Cynthia, Sy will come for her, we nab him? Is that the plan?"

"It's not that easy, kid. The cops will handle it from here. I have no idea what to tell you. You want a real job? See me when this blows over. In the meantime, keep consulting your clients. No sudden changes. This place is booming. Keep up the good work. I'm going far away."

Bob winks at me and walks out without a goodbye. I'm even more confused now. That was the quickest spy meeting I've had, and I have no idea if Bob is legit or full of shit. Is he leaving the country?

SITTING TIGHT

"Dana, I promise—I'm fine. How are you? What's going on in the Dirty South?"

"I miss you, Jack. I'm worried about you. Why don't you just go on a vacation? Let the cops solve it. You've done your part."

I try to assure Dana while I park outside Cynthia's house. "I'm fine, baby. Laying low. I have to run. I love you." Trying not to look too obvious, I begin my own stakeout. After a few hours of nothing going on, I look up to see someone breaking into her house. Sammy! I totally recognize that guy from the martial arts class.

It's the middle of the day, this guy is breaking in, and no one sees it but me? This is crazy. Thank God for cell phone cameras—but I should've upgraded. Across the street and a few cars behind me, I spot a cop. It's hard to miss Rhodes—he has a chest like a WWE wrestler. I wonder whether he's following me or Sammy.

Sammy pops out of the apartment like he was an invited guest, smiling and nodding as if someone is actually home. He walks slowly down the street and gets into a van. What the hell did he do up there? Plant some cameras? Steal files? Kill Cynthia?

The van doesn't move for an hour, and neither do I. Thank God for granola bars. A loud tap on my passenger window scares the crap out of me. "Rhodes! You scared the shit out of me."

235

"Kid, I told you to get out of Dodge. What the fuck are you doing here? Go home, fuck your girl, go to bed. We got illegal wiretapping, trespassing, stalking, breaking and entering; and the list goes on. Sit here for another thirty minutes after I drive away."

"You think this guy is just going to turn Shoman in?"

"Kid, this is Sammy's third strike. If he doesn't talk, it's thirty to life."

"And how did you know he did all that?"

"We have the place bugged. Cynthia is in hiding. You should do the same."

"Noted." Rhodes disappears through the rows of cars and trucks behind me. Before the thirty minutes is up, I see Sammy's van driving away. All I want to do is follow him, at least for a few miles.

As I start to drive, my secret cell phone rings. I don't recognize the number, but since only five people know mine, I pick up. Before I can say a word, Rhodes is shouting at me. "Go fucking home! Take the next right turn and go home now! I will shoot out one of your tires if you don't turn!"

I turn right. It might be time to lay low.

FAMILY TIME?

"Alexis, I'm sorry. I'll meet you for dinner tonight if you're free. I can explain everything. I'll come to you."

With a lot of attitude, she barks, "Fine. I'm going to order from Joe. What time?"

"Give me an hour." John looks at me, wondering why my conversation has been so cryptic. "Home phone, John. I got to be careful."

"I'm moving out." My elated reaction confuses my best friend. "Why are you happy about this? You have gotten so weird."

"You're not safe here. No one is. Not until it's over. And I want you to be safe."

John gives me a concerned look, which I'm sure I'll be getting from my sister. "Jack, why don't you just get out of the country? Your obsession to solve this is worse than your crush on Dana in junior high. It's not your problem to solve. You did your part. You're risking all our lives for this."

He walks out of the room, seemingly uninterested in my response: "I'm trying to save everyone! Do you think I knew it would be like this?!" All this talk of running away reminds me of something my dad used to say—if everyone is telling you that you're the asshole, maybe it's true. I would love to run away, if

I weren't certain that these people would find me. I don't think John is listening, but I continue explaining myself. "I'm paranoid. I'm afraid these guys will kill you, Alexis, Dana, and everyone else I care about. I'm going to see Alexis."

Walking to the Gold Coast takes me forty minutes. I could have taken a train, but the crisp summer night feels therapeutic. And I can see if someone is following me on the sidewalks easier than if I were on a crowded bus or train. Yes—the paranoia is real.

Approaching Mark's high-rise building gives me a false sense of security. A building with a doorman is safer than Alexis's walk-up apartment, I think to myself. The only people let up are delivery people and friends. My heart starts to pound through my hoodie as I suddenly imagine someone attacking Joe. He would have no idea, and never see it coming. My walk becomes a sprint.

As I run, I decide to test out Siri. "Hey, Siri. Call Joe."

"Sorry. There's no number for O." I repeat myself, and the call goes through.

"Hey, Jack! I'm about to bring you a pizza, salad and some pasta."

"Don't get out of your car! Double park. I'll come to you."

"Relax, brother! You're acting crazier than usual." I hear the sound of metal on metal. "Shit! Someone just hit my car!"

I start to run faster. "Do not get out of your car. Do not unlock the doors. Wait for me." My heart rate is skyrocketing. I'm two blocks away and I can see the accident. Well, it's not an accident if someone plans to do it. Joe tries to convince me it's an off-duty cop. "Shut up and listen to me. It's a tall redhead with braces," I manage to tell him while huffing and puffing. Joe confirms my description as I see Sammy walking toward his car. "Roll down your window enough that his head can get through. When I push him in, roll it up fast to choke him."

"I don't like this, Jack. But okay." In a flash, I bump Sammy from behind, and his head winds up inside the open window. Joe actually listens to me—the window quickly goes up, squeezing Sammy's neck. He tries to talk but can't; his face is turning as red as his hair.

"Listen, you son of bitch. You tell Shoman he fucks with me only, and that I don't have his money." Joe rolls down the window a drop and Sammy manages a whisper.

"If that bitch doesn't transfer the funds in twenty-four hours, someone will die. Shoman will do it himself, but of course I'll help."

Uncontrollably, I elbow him in the ribs so hard my elbow actually hurts. Sammy lets out a whispered groan.

The tough Jack rears his head again. "You tell Shoman: he comes for me. The mystery man with no face is bullshit. I have pictures of him from Arizona. Him and your pals Reggie and Thor."

Joe drops the window all the way down. Sammy stands and clutches his side as he walks to his car. Shaking, I get in Joe's car.

"Who the fuck are you?" Joe asks. "You need to get out of town."

"I can't. Not until he and his partner are behind bars."

"If you have all this evidence, why can't they arrest them both?"

"Great question, Joe. They can't find Shoman. He's hiding somewhere, and the dude is like a hide-and-go-seek champion."

"At least you still have your sense of humor. Take this food up to Alexis. She's texted me at least ten times since this shit went down here. I need a drink."

I give Joe a huge hug. I can't believe this is my life. "Text Alexis. Tell her it's all good, and that I'll be up in a second."

As I head up to Mark's unit, I have no idea what I'm going to say to Alexis. Do I tell her the truth? That I need ice for my elbow because I just broke some bad guy's ribs?

Tears begin flowing down my cheek as I walk through the door, and Alexis gives me my second vice-grip hug in less five minutes. Being in her embrace, and crying, feels like my parents' funeral all over again. "I can't handle losing any more family," I tell her. "Stay here, in this apartment, until you hear from me. Make Mark stay with you until I call. Promise me you'll do that. Please."

"Jacky, I'll do it. But you have to promise me you'll be smart. This isn't *24,* and you aren't Jack Bauer. And stop hitting people! Your elbow is starting to look like a fucking melon."

239

"How do those UFC guys do it?" I laugh, then turn serious. "This really hurts. The worst part—this food smells amazing, but I think I might have to puke."

After the ice and ibuprofen kick in, I call a cab. We take the long way home, and I'm pretty sure no one is following us. When we get there, the only light on in my buildings is Tyler's. Since I'm deathly afraid to be alone, I knock on his door. "Give me five minutes and I'll stop in," he tells me.

Five minutes feels like five weeks. In the meantime, Dana doesn't answer my call, and neither does Syd. Where is everybody? I will kill Shoman and Sammy if I anything has happened to Dana. A knock on the door interrupts my dark thoughts.

"Tyler, you will not believe what happened. Sammy tried to get to Alexis." As I tell him the story, Tyler's green eyes never fully open. I don't think it's possible for him to be a better listener. It's as if he wants them more than I do.

"I have an idea, Jack. Wait in your car all day and night. Not your actual car—a rental. Park across from the building. Once Sammy comes for you—and I believe he will—you're out of the way. You call the cops. Shoman will be close, too; they'll nab them both. And you can relax, I can go to Denver, and life can become normal-ish. You like it? Maybe Syd can join you. I'll stay at home base, and when you give me the signal, I'll smoke him out." I give him a confused look and he explains, "I have pepper spray. It's nothing hardcore."

Tyler's plan makes sense. He has not steered me wrong, and I trust him. Once you watch a double murder with someone, it's like you're BFFs. I try Syd again.

"My brother from another mother! What's up?"

"I need your help. Can you rent a car and park it outside my house?" Syd quickly agrees to the plan and a feeling of immense relief comes over me.

I get a little carried away packing up snacks. My backpack is filled with water bottles, mixed nuts, dried fruit, bananas, apples, KIND bars, granola, peanut M&M's, and pretzel rods. I really need to thank John; he's a grocery store god.

THE BUDDY SYSTEM

Syd pulls up in a white Toyota Camry with tinted windows. After no one drives by for twenty minutes, I sneak into the passenger side. A wink and a hundred-watt smile greet me. "You just can't get enough of the chocolate. It's cool. It happens to all the bitches."

"How are you so calm right now?"

Before he can respond, he checks out the goody bag. "What the fuck? Did you rob a 7-Eleven? Are we running a marathon tomorrow? I didn't need this much food after we won the Rose bowl!"

After defending my nervous packing, we start chatting about women—before Sydney takes the first of many bathroom breaks. "Dude, you have the bladder of a seven-year-old girl. Who drinks a gallon of water at each meal?"

"I like to hydrate! And I have an enlarged prostate, okay? Are you happy now? We all have shit. Just wait till you finish puberty."

We take turns sleeping until morning. I feel like a bad cop, because I want to sleep more—and get out of the car. "You couldn't have gotten us a van?"

"You ungrateful bitch. All the Escalades were gone, too."

"Escalades? We're not shooting a rap video, and we're not pro ballers. I just want to stretch my legs, and maybe kidnap someone. You can't kidnap someone in a Camry."

"I'm going to kidnap you in a minute. What type of snack do you recommend for breakfast? You think we could order pizza to the car, or would that be a giveaway?"

My secret phone goes off, and I love Tyler more now than I did yesterday. Before my door is partially open, Sydney smells the egg sandwiches and yells, "That's totally faster than Jimmy John's! I love Tyler! That dude is part ninja, part homemaker."

I flash a serious look. "Can I go back to sleep after I eat this?"

Hours pass with nothing but trains going by and a few stray cars. Lunch is a granola bar, peanuts, and a banana. It's actually filling if you're spending the day sitting. It's remarkable how often the train zips by, and how loud it is. I'm gaining a new respect for people who live out of their car. Interrupting the silence, Sydney announces, "I've got to poop. You okay?"

I hand him a Men's Health, toilet paper, and hand-sanitizer. "Take your time."

"You're like a fucking boy scout. Thanks, bro!" With no cars or trains passing, Syd runs out of the car. Two minutes later, a black car drives by and parks a few spaces behind me. The tall redhead, Sammy, gets out of the car, and I text Syd and Tyler.

Sammy walks past my car, stops, and then doubles back. I wish I had a gun—or at least a bullet-proof rental car. Sammy taps on the window with his gun and motions for me to get out.

"You cracked my fucking rib." His gun is no longer pointed at me, but at the ground. I might have a heart attack, or soil my pants, or both. "I told you: twenty-four hours. And you wanted to die first."

A train passes, as if perfectly timed to cover up the sound of gunfire. With his eyes focused on me, Sammy does not see Syd running toward him like Jesse Owens—but someone does. The black car starts to move as Sydney tackles Sammy. A gun goes off, and the car veers into a stop sign.

"Syd! Say something!"

"I'm okay! You?"

I vomit before answering. "I'm okay. PS—nice tackle."

DISAPPEARING ACT

Five cop cars, an ambulance, and two fire trucks pull up within minutes of the shooting. Sammy is laying on the ground, a little out of it, but not shot. Inside the black car is one dead man: Shoman. Shot in the head.

"Officer, I saw nothing. Sammy had a gun, and I knew there was a dude in the car. I heard the shot go off but I had no idea where it came from."

The cop points to our building and says someone inside shot him. "Who lives there?"

I give him some names but explain that two units are vacant and everyone else is out of town except for Tyler—and he doesn't have a rifle. As the ambulance drives off to bring Shoman to the morgue and the cops are arresting Sammy, we head upstairs.

I bang and bang on Tyler's door, but no one answers. Rhodes appears out of nowhere. "Gentlemen, I stop staking out your place for one morning, and what the fuck happens?" He produces a key and opens the door. The place is empty and smells like bleach. There's not even one beer in the fridge. "You have any pictures of this Tyler?"

While I tell the same story again, but this time to new cops, Rhodes calls our property management company. I eavesdrop, but all I hear is, "Mold was found. When?"

I duck into the bathroom and call Brody Home Security, "Hi. Are there still any Brodys that work here?" I finally reach Tom, the owner. "Hi, sir. Do you have a son named Tyler?"

"I have two beautiful daughters that are—thank God—out of the house, and living together in the Loop. What can I do for you?"

CONCLUSION

Okay. So now you're wondering: What happened? Well, read on.

VP BW: Bob West might not have been bad after all. He stepped down from his position at Trust One and began to help open burger joints. He fell in love with the breakfast sandwiches at Big Bad Burger and decided to invest a good amount of his cash in this new venture. I must admit, seeing him flip burgers puts a smile on my face.

Cynthia Rocks: Avoiding jail time was her main objective. She now volunteers, helping at-risk women with financial literacy. It was court appointed. Her relationship with Steve Smith was all business, and she turned over all the files and information she had. Steve had millions of dollars across numerous continents.

Brace Face: Good old Sammy is behind bars for life. His connection to Reggie and Thor was the military. He received medical attention for cracked ribs and the concussion Sydney gave him with his first tackle in over a decade. He told the court he was afraid of me, and that my hands were lethal weapons, so pulling a gun was equal force. The judge laughed, which slightly hurt my feelings.

Joe: Since quitting the pizza business, he lost twenty pounds and his fake Italian accent. He is now a lawyer at Trust One. I'm not sure why he took a job there, but they were very impressed with his research. He still loves Italian food and wine.

John: Moved back in with me. Now that our unit is no longer watched by cops or criminals, he feels much safer. He is dating Cholet and will actually sleep in on Sundays when she is next to him. We double date and hope to one day be best-friend couples, living in the suburbs, and taking our kids to little league. But that is several years away.

Mark and Alexis Ladd: The happy couple extended their honeymoon in Hawaii from two weeks to three. Alexis quit her job to work with her brother, get an MBA and one day have babies. She has no life, but I think that's how she manages marriage and our firm. Mark refuses to leave his company, insisting the work is rewarding and that his staying there has nothing to do with the year-round basketball league.

Jeff: The president of Riley Consulting started another company. Evidently, running one successful business was not enough. Since the company fell into his lap after college, he never had a chance to follow his own dream. The dream—of working in the sports arena—became a reality when Jeff started a high school athletic program. He matches young athletes with coaches, advises families on scholarships, and helps with the recruiting process. Riley Consulting helped my company, Plum Promotions (we found a new graphic designer), with many referrals.

Sydney Phelps: Sydney has become one of my closest friends and coworkers. He is our IT department and web developer. Our unstructured office allows him the hours he needs to work out and edit the book he encouraged me to write.

Tyler: Tyler Brody is a mystery. We managed to take zero photos of him, and he disappeared. The only thing I know is that he saved my life by shooting Shoman. Officer Rhodes has a theory that Tyler was hired by a rival diamond company to kill him. Either way, I owe Tyler my life. I can only hope that he's on a beach somewhere, having a drink, and not staked out in a van.

Dana: She's no longer staying at her parents' house. In fact, I stay at her house. It's nice that I still have a closet at John's because there is no room for more clothes anywhere in her two-bedroom unit. Things are going well. I want to buy her a ring, but neither of us is really into diamonds.

ABOUT THE AUTHOR

Aside from writing, Ron works in the nonprofit world,
writes about wellness, and speaks at events.

In his free time, Ron enjoys exercising, experimenting
in the kitchen, and spending time with friends and family.
Stay tuned for his second novel.

For speaking inquires, email rkrit312@gmail.com.